Evangelical Worship

Evangelical Worship

An American Mosaic

MELANIE C. ROSS

OXFORD
UNIVERSITY PRESS

Oxford University Press is a department of the University of Oxford. It furthers
the University's objective of excellence in research, scholarship, and education
by publishing worldwide. Oxford is a registered trade mark of Oxford University
Press in the UK and certain other countries.

Published in the United States of America by Oxford University Press
198 Madison Avenue, New York, NY 10016, United States of America.

Library of Congress Cataloging-in-Publication Data
Names: Ross, Melanie C., author.
Title: Evangelical worship : an American mosaic / Melanie C. Ross.
Description: New York, NY, United States of America :
Oxford University Press, [2021] |
Includes bibliographical references and index.
Identifiers: LCCN 2021015577 | ISBN 9780197530757 (hb) |
ISBN 9780197530771 (epub)
Subjects: LCSH: Public worship—United States—Case studies. |
Evangelicalism—United States—Case studies.
Classification: LCC BV15 .R67 2021 | DDC 264.00973—dc23
LC record available at https://lccn.loc.gov/2021015577

DOI: 10.1093/oso/9780197530757.001.0001

1 3 5 7 9 8 6 4 2

Printed by Sheridan Books, Inc., United States of America

To John Frye,
a musician after God's own heart

Contents

Acknowledgments

A mosaic is only as good as the glue that binds it together. The following individuals and institutions held this project (and its author) together over a long course of research and writing, and it is a joy to acknowledge my debts.

I have no idea what makes churches respond affirmatively to a cold call from an unknown researcher hoping to study their worship. The risks to participating in this kind of project are great; the rewards relatively few. There is no financial incentive, no way of censoring what interviewees disclose, no guarantee that the worship service won't go spectacularly awry in some unforeseen way. Yet the seven congregations in this study welcomed me unreservedly: an instinct rooted, no doubt, in their commitment to following Jesus's example of unconditional love and lavish hospitality. To Park Street Church, Moody Church, North Point Community Church, The Village Chapel, and the three congregations I do not directly name: I owe you more than I can repay. The evangelicalism of headline news is an unrecognizable caricature of the real thing I found when I stepped through your doors.

I am grateful to Yale Divinity School Dean Gregory Sterling and Yale Institute of Sacred Music Director Martin Jean for their many encouragements and for funding the sabbatical leave that enabled me to complete the manuscript. My travel was made possible through generous support from the Henry Luce Foundation, which granted me a year as a Henry Luce III Fellow in Theology, and from the Louisville Institute, through its Sabbatical Grant for Researchers. Michael McGregor and my colleagues at the Writing Beyond the Academy program at the Collegeville Institute restored my confidence and enthusiasm for writing at a time when both were flagging.

Paul, Sally, and John Zink provided a home away from home during the Chicago leg of my research. Marti and Bob showed me every corner of their beautiful part of the Pacific Northwest. Chris, Martha, Miriam, and Fiona were my extended family in Atlanta. Lexi and her mom kept me well fueled with pie and vanilla chai during my sojourn in the Southwest.

Halfway through this project, I was diagnosed with cancer. It is no exaggeration to say that I owe my life—and my remission—to my Smilow Cancer Center team, through whose skillful hands God worked. If you ever receive a devastating diagnosis, I pray that the person delivering it is as kind and compassionate as Liane Philpotts. Brigid Killelea and Alexander Au cut the cancer out and stitched me back together with a combination of science and artistry that, years later, still leaves me in awe. Maysa Abu-Khalaf and Suzanne Evans oversaw my chemotherapy and radiation treatments. The weekly encouragement they provided was as strong and bracing as the medicines they prescribed. An army of people carried me and my family through this time, but Nora Tubbs Tisdale, Jan Holton, Tisa Wenger, and Micah and Katharine Luce deserve special mention. Jen Anderson taught me to "Do Today Well." Appreciative head scratches go to Findus (on gracious loan from Teresa) and Marilla for their therapeutic feline companionship.

Theo Calderara and the team at Oxford University Press waited patiently for this book, graciously accommodating all the extensions I requested in the face of a personal medical crisis and a global health pandemic. Thank you, Theo, for your wise counsel, your cheerful persistence, and your confidence that this was a subject worth writing about. Rona Johnston, book whisperer extraordinaire, brought her insatiable curiosity, keen historian's eye, and impeccable editorial instincts to bear on every sentence of this project, transforming both the writer and the writing in the process. I didn't know I had this book in me until Rona helped me find it.

John Witvliet kindly allowed me to try my ideas out at the Calvin Symposium on Worship in Grand Rapids. Thanks are due to him and to the following individuals who read the manuscript in part or in its entirety: Mark Noll (my Luce Fellow respondent, and the scholarly giant upon whose shoulders all of us who study evangelicalism stand), departmental colleagues Teresa Berger and Bryan Spinks, Catherine Brekus, Jessi Hott, Todd Johnson, Tommy Kidd, Joyce Mercer, Johnny Miller, Nathan Mitchell, Mary Moschella, Lester Ruth, Don Saliers, and Carolyn Sharp. These wise conversation partners sharpened my arguments and saved me from many mistakes. The faults that remain are mine alone.

So many wonderful graduate students have improved this book through their enthusiasm, intelligent questions, and research assistance. In particular, I thank Emily Dolan Grier, John Hodges, Drew Konow, Justin Kosec, Adam Perez, Betsy Shirley, and Emily Wing for transcribing interviews, compiling annotated bibliographies, tracking down footnotes, and commenting on drafts. Special appreciation goes to EmmaRae Carroll, who went beyond the call of duty to get the manuscript across the finish line.

Other friends, colleagues, and loved ones have contributed to the project in less overt, but no less meaningful ways. Bill and Gloria Gaither gifted me their time, a beautiful Bible, and a rich conversation about worship that I will always cherish. Many of the theological seeds that came to fruition in these chapters were planted during my undergraduate years in the Music Department at Messiah College. William Higgins, Larry Landis, Ronald Miller, Richard Roberson, William Stowman, and Linda Tedford have influenced the trajectory of my life and scholarship in more ways than they will ever know. My beloved college piano professor, Carol Anderson (d. 2019) did not live to see the completion of this book, but I hope it would have made her proud. Lawrie Merz and John McGuire, Evie Telfer, and the Ostrander, Curry, Morgan, and Twigg clans all came into my life during those formative years in Grantham and have since become extended family.

I owe thanks to Siobhán Garrigan and Martha Moore-Keish, who regularly inspire me with their scholarship, their cooking, and their lives lived well. Writing buddies Tisa Wenger and Almeda Wright hold me accountable, but also help me not to take myself too seriously. Bruce Gordon, Chloe Starr, and Gabby Thomas have provided meals, consolation, and invaluable advice. Callista Isabelle and Jen Statler are the best friends a girl could ask for: time melts away every time we talk on the phone or meet up for crepes. College roomies Gretchen Bisbort, Stefanie Campbell, and Debra Close are as dear to me today as they were when we graduated; their love and text messages have been a sustaining lifeline. My sister, Heather, regularly reminds me that there is more to life than work, and that an evening spent binging cupcakes and *The Great British Baking Show* usually puts problems back into proper perspective.

I have saved my most important thanks for last. Many parents of academics give their offspring's books pride of place on the coffee table but never read a word of their contents. Bill and Janet Ross are an exception to the second half of this rule. They devoured chapter drafts as quickly as I could write them, awaiting each new installment with the eager impatience of a Harry Potter fan at a midnight bookstore launch. My constant supporters and biggest cheerleaders, their feedback has shaped this book in ways both great and small. Being their daughter is my greatest blessing.

Evangelical Worship is dedicated to John Frye, Pastor of Worship and Care at Calvary Church (Lancaster, PA) in gratitude for his thirty years of love and ministry to the congregation. As you will read in Chapter 1, John was my high school piano teacher. However, the lessons I've learned from him go far beyond how to play notes on a page. In recent years, concepts like "building a brand," "personality-driven worship," and "growing a platform" have worked their way into church lexicons. John is the antithesis of all these things. In a commercialized worship world that is fast and loud, he is gentle and quiet. In a musical culture that constantly demands new highs, he is grounded and steadfast. Every time he sits behind a keyboard or picks up a baton, John does the impossible: he makes the congregation forget they are witnessing a musician at the top of his craft by ushering them into the presence of God. John, I thought of you during every service I describe in the pages ahead. I pray this book unites you in encouragement with others who know the joys and challenges of your calling firsthand. May you and your counterparts across the country always know this: your grateful congregations appreciate you more than words can express.

Soli Deo Gloria

MCR

New Haven, CT

Introduction

The Significance of Evangelical Worship

"Next year in church," tweeted popular American evangelist, author, and Bible teacher Beth Moore on Easter Sunday 2020, expressing the hopes of Christians around the world.[1] Moore's four-word message came as America was beginning to reckon with the immensity of the Covid-19 pandemic. By the end of March, coronavirus cases had been confirmed in all fifty states. Residents in many parts of the country had been ordered to stay home; schools and businesses had closed their doors to slow the virus's spread. Churches around the world, including the Vatican, canceled all in-person services.

Impatient with the economic slowdown and stock market plunges, President Donald Trump emphasized his eagerness to see the nation return to normal. At a Fox News town hall on March 24, he broadcast his hope that the country would be "opened up, and rarin' to go by Easter"—a date that was then a little more than two weeks away. "Wouldn't it be great to have all the churches full?" he mused. "You'll have packed churches all over our country," he predicted. "I think it'll be a beautiful time."[2]

Medical experts and religious leaders alike condemned the president's aspirational timeline. Shortly after Trump's remarks, an editorial in the evangelical magazine *Christianity Today* warned that congregating during a pandemic would damage the church's witness. "Rather than looking courageous and faithful, we come off looking callous and even foolish, not unlike the snake handlers who insisted on playing with poison as a proof of true faith," the magazine cautioned.[3] Moore's Easter Sunday tweet could similarly be interpreted as a mild rebuke. Believers would not come together, even for the most joyous, significant celebration in the Christian calendar, until conditions were once again safe. "*Next year in church.*"

But we can also read Moore's tweet with a different emphasis. In Judaism, the Passover Seder ends with the invocation *L'Shana Haba'ah B'Yerushalayim*— next year in Jerusalem. Before the creation of the State of Israel in 1948, this saying expressed the desire for all Jews to be able to return to the homeland, just as they did after leaving Egypt. At Passover 2020, many Seder meals were small and subdued: grandparents, siblings, cousins, neighbors, and friends could not crowd around a shared table. Under the circumstances of

Evangelical Worship. Melanie C. Ross, Oxford University Press. © Oxford University Press 2021.
DOI: 10.1093/oso/9780197530757.003.0001

the pandemic, *Washington Post* editor Ruth Marcus observed, "Next year in Jerusalem" was still a statement about geography, but it also expressed a longing for a better world."[4] Moore's tweet can be heard as a similar expression of yearning. "Next year *in church*." Suddenly without the religious practice they had experienced as a self-evident Sunday fact, Christians were hungering for corporate worship: that is, the experience of singing, praying, reciting creeds and confessions, reading scripture, and partaking in communion while gathered in the same physical space.

As I completed the text of this book during the pandemic, I heard Christians exploring the very question that had launched me into this study: why is worship so central to Christian identity?

The Significance of Corporate Worship

Before the pandemic, evangelical pastors routinely reminded their congregations that spiritual formation involved much more than showing up at a particular building once a week. However, as houses of worship remained shuttered and Zoom fatigue set in, faith communities discovered that being in the same physical space at the same time each week mattered profoundly. Digital platforms could not reproduce the touch of a hand extended in peace, the musical vibrations of singing side by side, or the felt presence of other worshippers sharing the same creaky pew. In 1997, decades before the pandemic, professor of biblical spirituality Donald Whitney argued that something unique happens in live corporate gatherings that cannot be replicated in private devotions or by watching worship. "There are some graces and blessings that God gives only in the 'meeting together' with other believers," he insisted.[5] With the arrival of Covid-19, pastors broadcasting their sermons from living rooms and believers celebrating Eucharist in their kitchens suddenly understood this truth in a new and visceral way.

My interest in evangelical worship has also proven fortuitous for another unexpected reason. When I began my research in 2014, the chances that Donald Trump would ascend to the presidency two years later seemed more than remote. In their analysis of the election results, pollsters and pundits fixated on the overwhelming support Trump received from a constituency often called "white evangelicals." Traditionally, the term *evangelical* has referred to a group of self-identified Protestants who hold a high view of biblical authority, have a cross-centered theology that affirms the idea that Jesus suffered and died to atone for humans' sins, and stress the importance of individual conversion and evangelism—a definition this book also assumes.[6] Scrambling to understand how a people known for their public piety and strict personal morality had helped elect a philandering, church-avoiding businessman to the presidency, scholars began seeking out new methods for studying this faith tradition.[7]

For example, Molly Worthen, journalist and historian at the University of North Carolina, has posited that white evangelicals' loyalties are more deeply formed by the nightly consumption of conservative cable news than they are by the practices of Sunday morning. Specifically, she proposes, Fox News, a "repetitive, almost ritualistic thing that people do every night," shapes viewers' fears, desires, and ideals of America in a way that the church simply cannot match. Worthen wrote in a 2017 *New York Times* article of seeking answers from conservative and progressive critics of white evangelical politics for why the election had gone the way it did. Their answer: "Pay attention to worship, both inside and outside of church, because the church is not doing its job."[8]

Historian Kristin Kobes Du Mez makes a similar point about the inadequacy of corporate worship in her book *Jesus and John Wayne: How White Evangelicals Corrupted a Faith and Fractured a Nation*. Du Mez posits that the reason pastors wielded little influence over the actions of their parishioners during the Trump campaign was because books, magazines, music, films, ministry conferences, blogs, T-shirts, and home decor do more to shape the evangelical movement than any of its official theologies. "A few words preached on Sunday" could not compete against the steady diet of religious products that evangelicals consumed day in, day out.[9]

But as this book explains—and as the creative, reflective, and engaged communities I visited for its research make so evident—corporate worship cannot be summarily dismissed.

To understand why, consider theologian Kevin Irwin's illustration of Christian identity as three concentric circles, arranged from smallest to largest like an archery target. Writing from his own Roman Catholic tradition, Irwin defines the innermost circle as liturgy: the rites, prayers, and ceremonies that are held in common by all Catholics throughout the world. The second concentric circle— wider than liturgy—is prayer, which includes devotional aids such as *lectio divina*, centering prayer, and meditation. The third and largest circle is spirituality: the way one's daily life in the world is shaped by the revelation enacted in the celebration of the liturgy. The three circles of liturgy, prayer, and spirituality are interrelated. Genuine Christian spirituality requires liturgy as its anchor and mainstay, just as corporate worship returns participants back to daily living with their vision of the Christian life sharpened.[10]

These three concentric circles are equally useful in the study of American evangelicalism.

I am using the word *worship* in this book as a synonym for what Irwin describes as *liturgy*. The subject of the ensuing chapters is the the "bullseye" of the target: that which happens when evangelicals gather together in the name of Jesus Christ, by the power of the Holy Spirit, to meet God through scripture, song, prayer, proclamation, and the celebration of baptism and the Lord's Supper. This "bullseye" is no indicator of political uniformity: evangelicals who worship in the same congregation may disagree sharply over which candidate to support for public office. Furthermore, evangelical devotional practices and spirituality are mediated by a variety of factors, including geography, socioeconomic class, gender, and so on. These secondary and tertiary aspects of the tradition—the ways evangelicals vote, consume media, share their faith, raise children, and so on—are deserving of study, but without the anchor of corporate worship, the concept of evangelicalism loses much of its explanatory value and meaning. Evangelicalism may be *more* than what happens when congregations gather for corporate worship, but it is never anything *less*.

Scope and Parameters of the Study

Evangelical Worship is the first book to examine how a multiplicity of evangelical congregations use worship to unite with, and differentiate themselves from, one another. I embarked on a four-year course of fieldwork between Boston, Chicago, Atlanta, Nashville, the Pacific Northwest, and the American Southwest. Four of the churches I write about are identified by name and location: these congregations are well established within the evangelical world and are capable of bearing the burden of academic inquiry.[11] I have assigned pseudonyms to all the pastors and individuals interviewed in the remaining three congregations; in some cases, I have also tinkered with identifying details.[12] This anonymity was necessary because of the small size of the congregation and/or the sensitive nature of the topics disclosed: internal church conflicts, experiences of racial discrimination, the presence of undocumented immigrants in the assembly. In all seven fieldwork sites, church leaders gave me advanced permission to attend services and meetings, and the congregation was aware of my presence as a researcher. Without their support, generosity, and candor, this book would not have been possible.

Since no work can be comprehensive, I have chosen to limit the scope of my inquiry in four ways. First, all of the churches in my study are self-governing. They are either nondenominational or part of a network that supports and strongly encourages local autonomy (i.e., the Vineyard Association, the Conservative Congregational Christian Conference). Another fascinating book could be written about evangelical congregations that operate under different ecclesial polities—particularly within denominations like Presbyterianism or Methodism, which produce their own liturgical resources.

Second, although the churches I studied range in size (from fewer than fifty to more than thirty thousand members) and geographic region, all of them are located in cities or suburbs. The Rural Matters Institute at Wheaton College's Billy Graham Center rightly points out that "as more people and resources move to urban settings, the rural heartland has gradually become under-resourced, overlooked, and often forgotten."[13] There is a movement afoot to plant evangelical churches in rural areas, an effort that requires strategies and resources markedly different from those used in any other context. I regret that practical and professional restraints prohibited research in one such community.

Third, all congregations in this book happily, or in one instance more hesitantly, self-identify as evangelical.[14] There are other stories still waiting to be told by congregations that have a more complicated relationship to this word— theologically conservative African Americans, for example, or worshippers in Holiness, Wesleyan, Nazarene, and Anabaptist traditions. This study makes no claim of comprehensiveness. I have chosen to prioritize depth over breadth, in the hope that evangelicals of all stripes might recognize something of themselves in the chapters that follow. (For a detailed explanation of and justification for my research methodology, see Appendix A.)

An American Mosaic

The seven case studies at the heart of the book constitute what I am calling an "American mosaic." A mosaicist creates an image by juxtaposing a series of blocks of pure color next to one another, employing strategic tensions to give the composition an overarching unity. Similarly, I have chosen seven church "tiles" that each represent a key type of evangelical worship and arranged them in a deliberately ordered tension.

The story then begins at Park Street Church in Boston, where Harold John Ockenga served as pastor from 1936 to 1969. In 1947, Ockenga coined the term "neo-evangelicalism" (later shortened to "evangelicalism") to describe a new movement of conservative Protestantism that accepted the doctrinal premises of fundamentalism but rejected its cultural isolationism. The evangelicalism Ockenga imagined was a "big tent" coalition. It encompassed a wide spectrum of believers—Calvinists, Arminians, Baptists, Presbyterians, and more— who were united by their shared commitment to the centrality of scripture, an atonement-based gospel, the necessity of conversion, and the expectation that Christians would be active in their churches and communities. The members of those congregations sang music from a hymnal every Sunday, followed a few national teaching programs on Christian radio, and subscribed to one or two magazines produced by trustworthy evangelical publishers. Park Street Church

(Chapter 2) and Moody Church (Chapter 3) are historic examples of this branch of evangelicalism.

The explosive growth of megachurches in the 1980s and 1990s began to change the character of evangelicalism. Megachurches catered to the needs of religious "seekers" and bore little resemblance to traditional congregations. Pastors ran these churches like corporations, measuring success in terms of customer satisfaction. Since crosses, liturgies, offering plates, and hymns were thought to make "unchurched" people uncomfortable, megachurches replaced them with drama, video presentations, and easy-to-sing songs performed by a band. Sermons became less expositional and more topical, tending toward subjects like money management, marriage and parenting, and sexual purity. North Point Community Church (Chapter 4) is representative of this shift. The worship innovations of megachurches divided evangelicals: some supported the new experiments, hoping that they would attract more nonbelievers to the church, while others objected to what they perceived as a therapeutic gospel and "church-lite" stylings.

At the turn of the century, two new worship developments frayed the unity of the original big-tent coalition even further. A younger generation of Christians rejected not only the theological superficiality of megachurch evangelicalism, but also the epistemological certainty of classical evangelicalism. Emphasizing that God revealed a storied narrative in scripture rather than a systematic theology, these "post-evangelicals" formed a network of "emerging churches" that elevated dialogue over propositions and mystery over certainty. Many of these new ecclesial communities looked to Catholic, Orthodox, and Anglican traditions to recover liturgical practices that had long been missing from other expressions of evangelicalism. Wayfarers Collective (Chapter 6) serves as an example of a congregation that has been shaped by the emerging church movement.

Around the same time, a second group of evangelicals reacted to the megachurch movement by calling for a recovery of precisely the Reformed doctrines that emerging churches found most problematic: for example, the depravity of fallen humanity, the sovereignty of God, and the necessity of substitutionary atonement. These neo-Reformed evangelicals are responsible for the rise of a "modern hymn movement," which has produced new texts with doctrinal depth and singable melodies. The Village Chapel (Chapter 7) stands in this tradition.

As the twenty-first century continues to unfold, new emphases and movements have introduced additional complexity to the evangelical mosaic. Churches like Koinonia Vineyard (Chapter 5) have become a key point of contact between traditional evangelicalism and Pentecostalism, introducing elements like supernatural healing, extraordinary "words of prophecy," and speaking in tongues into corporate worship. Intentionally multiethnic congregations like

Holy Inheritance (Chapter 8) are raising neglected questions about how racial prejudices impact a congregation's ability to worship together in unity.

The deliberately ordered tension of tiles in *Evangelical Worship* can be understood in a second way. In each of these examples of evangelicalism—classical, megachurch, emerging, neo-Reformed, charismatic, and multiethnic—worship is the vehicle through which congregations negotiate and express their theological identities. International relations experts Bahar Rumelili and Jennifer Todd suggest that there are three key paradoxes of identity negotiation, each of which we see at work in a section of this book.[15]

The first tension is between constancy and change. The biblical storyline itself is an example of this paradox: Christians believe that the church is both a continuation of the people God called in Genesis *and* that the work of Christ and the coming of the Holy Spirit birthed a genuinely new community. Relatedly, when congregations tell the story of their identity in the twenty-first century, they must locate themselves somewhere between stagnation and chaos. Choosing a position means confronting a complicated knot of questions: How can we account for development while still claiming to be who we have always been? Conversely, how can we claim to be the same when so much has changed over time? Exactly what degree of continuity with the past is necessary to maintain a unified identity?

Part I explores the strikingly different ways three of the most storied congregations in American evangelicalism have negotiated these questions in their worship. Park Street Church and Moody Church wrestle with how to maintain a historic identity without becoming a museum, placing them closer to the "constancy" end of the continuum. North Point Community Church gravitates toward "change," emphasizing that the service patterns and musical repertoire that worked in previous decades must be replaced if a church hopes to be relevant to a new generation.

The second paradox is between consensus and contestation. On one hand, identity requires consensus: the group publicly endorses certain beliefs, practices, and norms while rejecting others. On the other hand, and at the same time, individuals in the group may feel tension between their ascribed identity (what the organizational gatekeepers expect them to be) and their assumed identity (the way they see themselves). Individuals and subgroups—in this case, congregations—sometimes subvert their ascribed identity when they feel that "consensus" is being imposed upon them from on high.

Part II examine this bottom-up/top-down tension. At Koinonia Vineyard, one African American member wrestles with the contradiction between her vision of activism (assumed) and her Caucasian pastor's desire for the congregation to remain politically neutral (ascribed) during a time of national racial unrest. The next two chapters shift to the subject of music. The Village Chapel emphasizes that the Bible commands Christians to sing and is closer to the "consensus" end of the continuum. Churchgoers at Wayfarers Collective in Portland are less likely to submit to authority by singing when directed, placing their community nearer to the pole of "contestation."

Part III highlights the final paradox of identity negotiation: sameness and difference. An identity does not change across diverse circumstances and contexts (sameness). At the same time, identity is dependent upon difference, a fact that is rooted in humanity's tendency to represent reality in binary terms. Individually and collectively, we define our "ingroup" identity in relationship to the "outgroup" of which we are not a part: Caucasians are not African Americans, Methodists are not Roman Catholics, and so on. Holy Inheritance, a multiracial congregation, works to integrate its Christian identity (which all worshippers share) with a variety of ethnic identities (which some, but perhaps not all, or even most, worshippers share). Chapter 9 concludes the book, drawing together all seven case studies and probing questions of sameness and difference from an ecumenical angle.

The chapters that follow offer a close reading of several evangelical congregations, but this book is not, in the end, about the liturgy of any particular subgroup. Instead, by focusing on a number of colorful fragments, I argue that we can conceive of an interconnected whole: that fascinating, complex, and vibrant mosaic known as American evangelical worship.

PART I
CONSTANCY VERSUS CHANGE

1

"My Worship Has Been Hijacked"

Forty Years of Worship Wars

A few months into my research, I received an email from an acquaintance with whom I had discussed this project: a man I am calling "Warren."[1]

Warren, an affable curmudgeon in his retirement years, is a committed evangelical Christian. He and his wife have attended the same local church for half a century, and many of their friends are similarly long-term members. Their children have grown up in this church, physically as well as spiritually. When the kids were very young, Warren racked up volunteer hours rocking babies in the nursery and reading Bible stories to toddlers. As they grew into teens, Warren chauffeured his brood to a cornucopia of church-sponsored events: Awana clubs, Pinewood Derby races, drama rehearsals, youth group meetings, service projects, summer campouts, and more. The church has experienced many changes over the course of Warren's tenure. Warren has watched senior pastors come and go. He has been regularly cajoled to support new expansion projects, fundraising campaigns, and church initiatives. Some generational shifts—reading scripture on personal electronic devices with enlargeable font—have met with his approval. Others—coffee in the sanctuary, blue jeans in the pulpit—decidedly have not. But for fifty years, Warren has supported the church through its ups and downs with his loyal attendance, tithing, and prayers.

When Warren learned that I was writing about worship, he decided to undertake a reflective journaling project of his own. Although he is not the type to wear his heart on his sleeve, Warren felt strongly enough about recent changes in his church's worship to write the following words:

> A musical loop is running over the sound system. It sounds "churchy" in some vague way. The music is up-tempo, familiar feeling, but not specifically identifiable. A few minutes pass and the worship team begins to gather on the stage with their travel mugs and water bottles. For the most part, they are younger, good looking. For the past half hour, they have been running a soundcheck. I am not entirely sure what that entails. I am uncertain as to exactly why we need a worship team, what their function really is, or what they contribute to the worship experience. (They do seem to know the words to all the new songs that keep coming at us.)

Evangelical Worship. Melanie C. Ross, Oxford University Press. © Oxford University Press 2021.
DOI: 10.1093/oso/9780197530757.003.0002

As they begin to set up, taking their mics and assuming their positions, it comes to me again—that annoying knot in my stomach. I am uncomfortable with what is coming. I can't help it. I don't want to feel this way. I don't want to come to church on Sunday morning dreading what's going to happen.

Our smiling worship leader makes his entrance, casually dressed, guitar hanging from his shoulder. He's flapping his arms with his palms up, motioning us all to stand, or perhaps to join him on his higher spiritual plane. I always have the same reaction: it just doesn't feel right. It almost never feels right.

"Lord Jesus, we love you so much this morning. We need you. We want you. We are here to worship you." We, we, we. What they sing are largely praises—songs praising God, songs praising us for gathering to praise God, songs praising us for wanting to praise God, songs praising the depth of our desire to praise God. I wonder what happened to the respectful, prayerful, reverent entrance to God's holy presence; quieting our hearts, asking Him to meet with and speak to us? Familiar resentment builds in me. I shouldn't have to come to church afraid of what the worship team is going to come up with next. I shouldn't have to feel each Sunday that my worship has been hijacked.

I feel tears start to well up in my eyes. I can't sing. I don't care about the music or the antics. I would really like to sit down but that would call attention. Does my disappointment matter? Does God feel my pain, or does worship "of the people, by the people, for the people" trump my spiritual needs?

This is my dilemma.

"Timothy," a proud grandfather of two and a classically trained musician, works at a place I am calling Hillcrest Community Church. ("Hillcrest" is a midsize evangelical church located in the same town as—but not directly connected to—one of the congregations featured in this book.) Timothy, who spoke on the condition of anonymity, has outlasted five senior pastors. "There's been a lot to figure out," Timothy admits. "How do you work with this person? What's their personality and style? How am I going to adapt what I'm doing?"

For Timothy, the most recent leadership transition has been the most challenging. The church's new leader, Pastor Matthew, a freshly minted seminary graduate, models his vision for corporate worship after the practices of megachurches like North Point (see Chapter 4). Timothy makes it clear that he harbors no ill will toward his new boss: "It's not a hostile environment. Pastor Matthew is truly appreciative of my ministry here." But one of Timothy's new challenges has been learning to share his kitchen with many untrained cooks.

Whereas Timothy used to plan weekly worship alone, in conversation with the senior pastor and with input from the church organist, there are now at least three non-musicians who, as Timothy puts it, "speak into" the process: "We have Pastor Matthew, who is the main teaching pastor. Then there's Mark, who is head of the tech department, and Luke, who is responsible for the creative elements of the service. Mark now leads the worship-planning meetings, and for a while, I really struggled with that," Timothy reveals. "Everybody in that room speaks into song choice, into transitions, into the ambiance in the sanctuary. We would have fifteen-minute discussions on microphone glitches. Every week I would go in and feel like, 'Well, I used to do that [part of worship] and now I don't. And I used to do *that*, and now I don't. Every week I was in there, my responsibilities were kind of being stripped from me. I've been in church work my entire adult life, and now all of a sudden, there's not really a role of minister of music."

The more I talked with Timothy, the more it became clear that the issue at stake was not simply the question of authority: who gets to have the final say over what happens any given Sunday. Timothy's pain was theological, not managerial. The model of corporate worship that he had spent a lifetime building and nurturing at Hillcrest was rapidly shifting in ways he could neither understand nor control. "I've always thought of myself first as a minister and then as a musician," Timothy reflects. "When I think about the music ministry team at Hillcrest, I see us first as a family of believers. When there are joys or challenges—someone has a baby, or someone has surgery, or someone's kid has just turned away from the Lord—whatever happens, we're praying for one another and trying to support one another." Timothy's affection for the vocalists and instrumentalists under his leadership is evident. "We sing together, we make music together, and we have a role in the church, which is to lead others into a worship experience with the Lord." However, current trends in church music worry him. "It seems like it's more about video and lighting and projection and transitions," he muses. "It's so much more about getting a polished end product and about the experience while you're doing it."

Timothy thinks for a long minute, choosing his next words carefully. "We're still in the middle of all this. I don't know if I can say that it's wrong, but it's certainly *different*, and my role is different. I've had to do some soul searching. I've said to God, 'If you have work for me to do, I'm willing to do it—even if it's outside my comfort zone or it means I have to learn new skills.'" He pauses. "I just wasn't expecting that the obstacle may be the very thing that I'm trying to serve: namely, the church."

Corporate worship includes many elements: prayers, preaching, responsive readings, and more. However, evangelical arguments over the most appropriate songs to sing in church have been so intense in recent history that the subject of music warrants its own chapter. A reductionistic treatment of the topic might proceed something like this: Explain that some evangelicals like "traditional" music, others like "contemporary" music, and still others have forged a middle path with a "blended" approach. Insert technical definitions for each of the adjectives in quotes. Conclude that none of the approaches is inherently right or wrong; point out that musical taste is highly subjective. Suggest the time has come for all the evangelical "worship tribes" to dwell together in unity.

However, it is not possible for me to write about evangelical worship music with this kind of detached objectivity. I have a bachelor's degree in music education, advanced degrees in liturgical studies, and a lifetime of musical experiences in the evangelical church. Because of my expertise and biases, this chapter is a momentary methodological departure from the congregational studies that follow it. Instead, I turn to a mode of study called *autoethnography*: "an approach to research and writing that seeks to describe and systematically analyze (*graphy*) personal experience (*auto*) in order to understand cultural experience (*ethno*)."[2]

The concept of autoethnography emerged out of anthropology in the mid-1970s in response to a "crisis of representation," as scholars became increasingly troubled by social science's supposedly objectivist limitations. In particular, they began to notice how frequently the "facts" and "truths" that scientists "found" were "inextricably tied to the vocabularies and paradigms the scientists used to represent them."[3] A previous generation of anthropologists believed that through discipline and the practice of detached observation, they could keep their findings free of bias. By the end of the twentieth century, however, these scholars began to doubt their capacity (and their right) to represent the lives of others in research and writing.[4]

The example of Martin Stringer, professor of liturgical and congregational studies at the University of Birmingham, UK, is illustrative. In the 1990s, there was little scholarship situated at the intersection of theology, worship, and ethnography. Stringer's 1999 book, *On the Perception of Worship*, was a notable exception. In one chapter, Stringer describes a methodological dilemma. After conducting interviews and attending services in a Baptist church community for several months, Stringer was invited to present his findings to the congregation. The conversation did not unfold as Stringer had anticipated:

> "This," I told them, "is what worship means to you." The only problem was, it wasn't! In the discussion that followed, individual members of the congregation rejected most of what I had just been saying. [My academic formulations] were not wrong, but they were not right either, and between "not wrong" and "not right" there lies a gaping chasm.[5]

Autoethnography tries to bridge the gaping chasm between "not wrong" and "not right," recognizing that research is never done from a neutral or objectivist stance. Ellis and Bochner explain,

> Autoethnography is an autobiographical genre of writing and research that displays multiple layers of consciousness, connecting the personal to the

cultural. Back and forth autoethnographers gaze, first through an ethnographic wide-angle lens, focusing outward on social and cultural aspects of their personal experience; then, they look inward, exposing a vulnerable self that is moved by and may move through, refract, and resist cultural interpretations.[6]

This back-and-forth process results in a particular kind of narrative: one that prioritizes evocative over analytical writing, refuses the impulse to abstract and explain, and stresses the journey over the destination.[7] The following autoethnography—one part historical analysis, one part autobiography—brings the seismic shifts in church music that Warren, Pastor Timothy, and I have experienced into better view.

Beginnings

My parents both grew up in Christian churches. My father, a self-described "Methodical Baptistic Presbyterian," attended all three of the Protestant churches in his small town at various points during his childhood: a rotation determined by how well my grandmother liked the preacher and the content of his messages on any given week. In the mid-1950s, his family put down more settled roots in the Christian and Missionary Alliance Church. My mother remained in the same small, loving congregation—a nondenominational church founded by her Swedish immigrant ancestors—from birth through her high school graduation. Shortly after their marriage in 1973, my parents moved to Lancaster County, Pennsylvania, and made Calvary Church—a large, conservative, nondenominational congregation—their new spiritual home.

My parents were starting their lives together at a time of exciting new developments in Christian music. During the 1970s, Calvary Chapel in Costa Mesa, California, had become the epicenter of the Southern California Jesus movement.[8] Chuck Smith became the pastor of Calvary Chapel in 1965, when the church had only twenty-five members. Smith grew the church to a few hundred members by the late 1960s and was eventually convinced by his wife and teenage children to open the church to members of the hippie counterculture. Some of these young people began writing songs to and about Jesus in their own rock musical style. Four recently converted young men created a band called Love Song and approached Smith about playing their music in church. The group sang a song for him in the church parking lot, and Smith, excited by what he had heard, invited them to sing it at a Bible study that evening. A new musical movement was born. By 1971, Calvary Chapel had a cadre of musicians who played at worship services, Bible studies, and Jesus music concerts on Saturday nights.[9]

Calvary Chapel decided to start Maranatha! Music to support all the new artists the church was turning out. Maranatha! Music began in a Sunday school classroom at Calvary Chapel, and its first release, *The Everlastin' Living Jesus Music Concert* (1971), was recorded with a loan from Smith. The album was an immediate sellout among the Jesus People in California, and it quickly drifted eastward as friends mailed copies to other friends. The label's second album, *Come to the Waters*, featured the group Children of the Day, who had been singing at Calvary Chapel since 1969. Although Maranatha! Music had no formal distribution or marketing, its first two releases sold a combined total of more than twenty-five thousand copies.[10] Musical historian Paul Baker suggests that one reason for the label's success was its zeitgeist:

> Everything in the Jesus-movement years crackled with joy and exclamation; the true Spirit of the Lord was manifest in the young people. For the first time in that generation of wars, riots, and tumultuous unrest, the young people were being offered the love and peace of Jesus on recordings which could be played over and over, ministering in their own special language.[11]

Numerous artists recorded and released albums in the 1970s, including Country Faith, The Way, Blessed Hope, Good News, Mustard Seed Faith, Karen Lafferty, Ernie Rettino & Debbie Kerner, Kenn Gulliksen, Daniel Amos, Kelly Willard, and the Sweet Comfort Band. Their songs came to be known as "message music" because they were intended for testimony and evangelism.

Maranatha!'s eighth release in 1974, *The Praise Album* (later known as *Praise 1*), was particularly significant in the history of Christian music. *The Praise Album* featured scripture-based choruses like "Seek Ye First," "Father, I Adore You," and "Open Our Eyes." It was the first collection of songs intended to be used in church services as a supplement, or even replacement, for traditional hymns. *The Praise Album* marked the moment when worship music and evangelistic music began to split into two separate branches with distinct markets. Although Maranatha! Music had released both "message music" and "praise music" throughout the 1970s, the leadership decided drop the former and focus exclusively on the latter.

An important reason for the shift from "message music" to "praise music" was the change in audience. Whereas the early Maranatha! catalog focused on evangelistic songs written for non-Christians, by the late 1970s, the main consumers of Maranatha's catalog were middle-class Christian youth and their youth pastors looking for contemporary music they could use in church settings.[12] The *Praise Album* was a major success, in part because its music was able to draw together two sides of the generation gap. As Paul Baker observes, adults might not have liked new message music and Jesus rock, but they could "tolerate and even enjoy the Scripture choruses." Conversely, "Young people had little trouble with the age-old 'antique' Scriptures when they were put to pleasant music that was easy to learn."[13] Over the course of the decade, Maranatha! went on to release seven additional albums for congregational worship: *Praise II* (1976), *Praise Strings* (1976), *Praise Strings II* (1978), *The Gift of Praise* (1978), *Praise III* (1979), *Hymns of Praise* (1979), and *Praise Strings III* (1979).

1977–1995: An Autobiographical Overview

I was born in the late 1970s, at the end of a decade the press would characterize as the "third great awakening" of American evangelicalism.[14] A series of Gallup polls in the second half of the decade found that half of all Protestants—a third of all Americans—claimed to be "born again," prompting *Time* and *Newsweek* to declare 1976 the Year of the Evangelical. The devout Southern Baptist Democratic presidential candidate, Jimmy Carter, introduced the word *evangelical* into the national vernacular, and former Nixon aide Charles Colson's autobiography, *Born Again*, shot to the top of the book charts. James Dobson's Focus on the Family was founded in 1977, the year of my birth. Three years later, my sister was born (Figure 1.1).

Figure 1.1 The Ross family sits ready for church (from left to right: William, Melanie, Heather, Janet)

Lititz, Pennsylvania: circa 1983. Photo credit: Paul Zink.

My sister and I occupy a unique place in modern American history. Writer Anna Garvey calls us "the Oregon Trail Generation," a reference to a popular 1980s video game that many of us played while growing up. The Oregon Trail Generation was born at the tail end of the 1970s and the start of the 1980s. We are something of an enigma: a micro-generation that is one part Gen X and one part millennial. Garvey, a fellow member of the Oregon Trail Generation, explains:

> A big part of what makes us the square peg in the round hole of named genera-
> tions is our strange relationship with technology and the internet. We came of
> age just as the very essence of communication was experiencing a seismic shift,
> and it's given us a unique perspective that's half analog old school and half dig-
> ital new school.[15]

Unlike the millennial generation that followed us—the "digital natives" who can never remember a time before computers—the Oregon Trail Generation grew up on the cusp of changes that transformed modern life. We were the first group of high school students to do research for papers in both card catalogs and cyberspace. We grew up learning how to navigate then-new technologies (i.e., the internet, email) that most Americans now take for granted. Garvey's impressions resonate with my own: "Because we had one foot in the traditional ways of yore and one foot in the digital information age, we appreciate both in a way that other generations don't. We can quickly turn curmudgeonly in the face of teens who've never written a letter, but we're glued to our smartphones just like they are."[16]

I see a parallel generational dynamic at play in the world of church music. I grew up with one foot in traditional hymnody and one foot in the modern wor-ship age, which helps me appreciate both kinds of music in a way that other gen-erations might not. I turn curmudgeonly in the face of teens who've never sung from a hymnal, but I lift my eyes to the screen and raise my hands in worship as naturally as they do.

I inhabited three distinct sonic worlds growing up. The first was that of Christian Contemporary Music (CCM). I discovered CCM in my tween years, at a moment when I was at a musical crossroads. A few years before our family had to navigate the turbulent waters of junior high, one of the cassettes that played regularly from our tape deck was a children's ditty called "The Computer Song":

> Input, output: What goes in is what comes out.
> Input, output: That is what it's all about.
> Input, output: Your mind is a computer whose
> Input, output daily you must choose.[17]

The lyrics reflect the technological language that was beginning to make its way into the Oregon Trail Generation's lexicon. (Subsequent verses enjoin the listener to "debug your mind of sinful bytes" and to "let the Bible be your primary feed.") But more importantly, the song mirrored my family's approach to 1980s secular music culture. The sexual innuendos of mainstream pop artists and the crotch-grabbing antics MTV stars were out. But finding musical "input" appropriate for an eleven-year-old on the cusp of adolescence proved challenging. (My parents' preferred radio station played innocuous elevator music twenty-four hours a day, but the mere mention of its call letters earned me ridicule from my classmates.) The solution came in the form of WJTL, a Lancaster County radio station that broadcast CCM twenty-four hours a day.

When my parents were growing up, Christian radio stations had devoted most of their programming to preaching, with occasional musical acts and hymns interspersed between messages. However, Christian radio experienced a boom in the mid-1970s. Federal communications laws changed, allowing churches and religious organizations to qualify for more airtime. Christian radio stations changed their format, replacing preaching with Contemporary Christian Music in a style that mimicked that of top 40 secular music stations. In 1988, music minister and business entrepreneur Howard Rachinski established Christian Copyright Licensing International (CCLI), a system that tracked the copyrights of Christian worship songs sung in churches around the world. Within ten years, CCLI would become the equivalent of a *New York Times* bestseller list for Christian worship songs. In 1995, SoundScan—an information system that tracked the sales of music through barcodes—began monitoring the sales of Christian music. In April of that same year, *Billboard* magazine began ranking the top Christian Contemporary albums.

My second sonic world was praise and worship music. My peers and I sang praise and worship songs with gusto at Wednesday night meetings, weekend retreats, and summer church camps. A number of factors contributed to their popularity. Praise and worship choruses like "We Bring the Sacrifice of Praise," "Cry of My Heart," and "Lord I Lift Your Name on High," were more syncopated than hymns and were fun to sing. "As the Deer," "Humble Thyself," and "Hiding Place" were appropriate for quieter, more reflective contemplation. Some of the CCM artists featured on WJTL radio were also penning new praise choruses: for example, Michael W. Smith's "How Majestic Is Your Name" and Twila Paris's "We Will Glorify" and "He Is Exalted." The lyrics to all of these choruses were simple, often scripturally based, and could be easily memorized. Best of all, these songs did not require a piano or an organ for accompaniment: they could be easily played on a portable guitar. When my high school prayer group, which met early in the morning before the first homeroom bell, decided we wanted to start our time together with singing, I taught myself a smattering of basic guitar chords, enough to play most of the songs in my well-thumbed *Maranatha! Music Praise Chorus Book*. Praise and worship music was not high art, but it did not need to be. My peers and I sang it sincerely, in informal and intimate settings, and it met a spiritual need.

My final and most important sonic world—traditional hymnody—I learned from my parents and from Calvary Church. Hymnody was, and remains, my native musical tongue: it is so deeply embedded within me that I have no memory of learning how to sing it. From the first Sunday I was old enough to sit quietly through the worship service, through the Sunday I left my home congregation to go to college, I sang all the stanzas of at least three hymns every week. As a young child, I was mesmerized by my mother's strong alto voice; I learned to sing in harmony by osmosis, through years of singing next to her.

My three sonic worlds of CCM, praise and worship choruses, and traditional hymnody began to overlap, albeit very slightly, my sophomore year of high school. In 1992, Calvary Church called John Frye, a talented church musician from the Southeast, to be its new minister of music (Figure 1.2). With new leadership came a new hymnal: our congregation switched from *Worship and Service Hymnal* (published by Hope Publishing Company in 1966) to *The Hymnal for Worship and Celebration* (published in 1986 by Word Music). Although the difference in titles seems negligible, the contrast between the hymnals' contents is significant.

Figure 1.2 John Frye (center), with Heather Ross (left) and Melanie Ross (right)
Lancaster, Pennsylvania: December 2012. Photo credit unknown.

Like its predecessor, our new hymnal was primarily composed of "great hymns of the faith." However, as senior editor Tom Fettke noted in its preface, the goal of the new hymnal was to "combin[e] the dignity of our musical heritage with the need for a worship resource book that speaks to the hearts of the 'people.'"[18] The latter half of this goal meant that our new hymnal contained songs written within the last thirty years: Bill Gaither's "He Touched Me," Ralph Carmichael's "He's Everything to Me," Jack Hayford's "Majesty," and Michael W. and Deborah D. Smith's "Great Is the Lord" (to cite just a few examples). As one reviewer noted, the hymnal made "no attempt . . . to replace hymns with choruses."[19] Nevertheless, the contemporary additions meant that a small subsection of the songs heard on Christian radio were making their way into congregational song.

Another striking feature of our new hymnal was that it included twenty-three brief services, each based on a specific theme. Each service was preceded by a short scripture narration and included three or four hymns joined together by piano/organ interludes. They often concluded with a climatic choral ending. The choir played a significant role in the *Hymnal for Worship and Celebration*: twenty-one hymns had optional descants, and forty hymns had special choral endings. "These features," a reviewer pointed, "are especially useful for integrating the choir with the congregation and for supplying the musical variation for a church that sings vibrantly."[20] The hymnal even included several choral works: six pages of Handel's "Hallelujah" chorus, an excerpt from "For unto Us a Child Is Born," Stainer's "God So Loved the World," and the Lord's Prayer solo by Malotte. These additions were not as well received: a second reviewer worried that their inclusion "may only lead to congregational coveting of the choir's role in Christian worship."[21] Be that as it may, the important thing to note is that in the mid-1980s and early 1990s, the publishers of the *Hymnal for Worship and Celebration* could safely assume that their constituency maintained a strong, active choral tradition.

Pastor Frye changed my musical life in every way for the better. He started a youth choir to supplement the adult choir and the children's choirs already in place, taught me how to accompany congregational hymn singing during our weekly piano lessons, and invited me to play Sunday morning preludes and offertories. In fall of 1995, I left home to start a degree in music education at Messiah College (now Messiah University), in Grantham, Pennsylvania.

1995–2000: The Corporate Buyout and Modern Worship

While I was in college, the Christian music industry would undergo a series of transformative changes. In the mid-1990s, Word, Benson, and Sparrow (the three major CCM recording labels) were in the process of being bought out by the secular record companies EMI Christian, Provident, and Gaylord.[22] The secular labels had distribution systems that the Christian labels could not match. As Sparrow president Bill Hearn explained, EMI (the company that bought out Sparrow) would inform Walmart that if the store wanted to see a thousand copies of a recording by EMI artist Garth Brooks, "then you have to take [Christian recording artist] Steven Curtis Chapman. . . . And man, we saw Steven go from thousand [units] a release to one million a release like that."[23] The new secular owners provided the Christian labels the funding and networks necessary to grow their artists' careers.

Although some observers worried that CCM had sold out to "the world," Christian label heads stressed that their secular owners never pressured them to water down their gospel message. As Don Cason, then an executive at Word, recalls,

> They were saying to us, "We don't want to change what it is that you do. We don't want you to create another Madonna, or Britney Spears, or 'N Sync, or whatever. We've got those. We want you to still do what you do. Continue to create the product with the same authenticity, but just do it better, and make it more economical, and get more sales results by our ability to go into venues [like Walmart, Kmart, and Target]."[24]

In other words, the secular companies were less concerned about lyrical content than with how to drive the Christian labels toward increased profitability.

The new owners of CCM had two strategies for increasing sales. The first, already described, was to help Christian artists cross over to the secular marketplace. Insofar as this goal furthered evangelistic efforts, many Christians found it unproblematic. For example, Hearn stressed, "As long as the music is still quality and carries a message of integrity that is consistent with Scripture, then I want to put it everywhere I can . . . [EMI has] provided us with a system that I am more than happy to use."[25] The well-respected church consultant Lyle Schaller compared the corporate buyout of Christian music to Macmillan and HarperCollins publishing religious books. Schaller suggested that the situation was analogous to a preacher who drives a car made by a profit-making corporation to get to church or make hospital calls: no one complains that the minister has compromised his or her faith by getting behind the wheel. "[Christians] have a long tradition of profit-making organizations and corporations servicing the churches to help them proclaim the gospel," Schaller pointed out. "I don't see any problem."[26]

The secular labels' second strategy for profitability was to find new inroads into Sunday morning worship—a task that would prove more problematic. John Styll, editor of *CCM Magazine*, accurately summarized the dilemma facing the Christian music industry: "Virtually all of its consumers gather together on Sunday morning—a perfect 'marketing opportunity'—but . . . the church as an institution has little use for much of its product."[27] Statistical analyses show that in 1995, approximately 35 percent of the US adult population attended church weekly. However, less than 4 percent of the public purchased Christian music. "Somewhere in that gap lies opportunity for both the church and the Christian music industry," Styll mused.[28]

The elephant in the room was the financial bottom line. Christian label heads were now serving two masters, oscillating between the spiritual needs of their listeners and the performance expectations of their new owners. In 1995, Integrity president Mike Coleman spoke the language of both worlds deftly:

> I have sensed among consumers of many denominations, a very real and growing hunger for something that's genuinely spiritual and life-changing. God is causing people who really are turned toward Him to be hungry in a way that I haven't seen in years. . . . The greatest challenge is reaching the millions of people in the target audience. There are literally millions of consumers we're not reaching.[29]

It is clear that Coleman is speaking to two different audiences simultaneously. The idea that "God is causing" people to be newly "hungry for Him" provides spiritual rationale for selling more Christian music. The phrases "target audience" and "millions of consumers we're not reaching" suggest a more secular logic at work.

Introducing Modern Worship

Marketing music to the church may have helped meet a spiritual hunger, but it also presented significant new financial possibilities for the record labels. Warner Alliance president Neal Joseph commented, "We still have not addressed the continuing dilemma of how to impact the church. We as a company and as an industry really need to make it a priority."[30] Benson president Jerry Park was similarly direct: "The challenge is to achieve real growth to the extent that our [new] owners expect of us. We have got to do a better job of attracting new buyers. To do that, we've got to use some new methods."[31]

Four years later, two linchpins of the new marketing strategy were becoming clear: a younger demographic and an edgier sound. In 1999, Deborah Evans Price, a journalist for *Billboard Magazine*, ran a story with the title "Worship Music Targets Youth."[32] Several new labels had been launched with this goal in mind, including Integrity's Vertical Records and EMI Christian Music's Worship Together. Joey Elwood, president of the new Gotee Records label, suggested,

While [Christian Contemporary Music] is a wonderful vehicle, and [youth] love it, it's only half of what they really want. It's the entertainment side of what they want. . . . I don't think the younger generation has had songs from contemporary artists that they could actually participate in [in] concert, and I think kids are hungry for that.[33]

Danny McGuffey, senior VP/GM of Integrity, also emphasized consumer demand: "Most people have a real desire to worship . . . and none of the companies have really provided that component for kids. Now that it is being served up in their language, it's like a light bulb has gone off."[34] Both McGuffey and Elwood downplayed the fact that the Christian music industry had aggressively targeted the church as a key growth market. Instead, Elwood framed the exploding popularity of worship music as a case of the tail wagging the dog: "I wouldn't really credit the record companies as much as I would the kids out there in the churches. Kids are demanding it, and we're just reacting to that demand."[35]

The "modern worship"—the industry's new name for the genre—that I listened to in college differed from the Maranatha!-style praise and worship I played on guitar for my high school prayer group in at least three significant ways. First, much of the new music was imported from England and Australia. At the end of the 1990s, Nashville EMI executives discovered a new style of music made popular by young worship leaders and bands in the UK, including artist Matt Redman and the group Delirious?. Nashville executives seized on the British music: they described the style as "anointed" and said it had a special quality that was "hard to put your finger on."[36] Many executives resonated with the music personally. Steve Rice, who was at the time the vice president of EMI CMG's music-publishing department recalls, "I was blown away—not by the production quality, but by the songs. They really spoke to my heart, and I thought 'this is exactly why I got into Christian music.'"[37] American worshippers were similarly enchanted. UK artists, and their songs skyrocketed to popularity in the United States so quickly that ethnomusicologist Monique Ingalls compared their impact to that of the Beatles and the Rolling Stones and dubbed the new movement the "British Invasion" of American evangelical worship.[38]

The second factor that distinguished modern worship music from 1980s praise and worship music was its sound. Along with the Australian worship band Hillsong, UK artists introduced new musical stylings to American worship. Whereas Hillsong worship featured a "slick, radio-ready pop style" that mirrored the style of pop ballads heard on secular radio in the 1990s, UK worship featured "heartfelt guitar-driven rock."[39] Many of the new worship songs featured a "bridge," a musical transition that takes the singer back and forth between the refrain and the verses. (Although musical bridges had long been common in pop music, they had rarely been used in congregational song prior to the

1990s because of their complexity for communal singing.)[40] Generally speaking, modern worship songs had a much wider musical range and were more oriented toward a performer's voice than a group voice.

Finally, the late 1990s ushered in an era of congregational song that placed greater focus on the worship leader. The new "personality-driven praise and worship" was a marked departure from the 1980s.[41] In the 1980s, the album artwork for the bestselling early Maranatha! *Praise* series was "faceless": it featured scenes from nature—a road in the woods, a castle surrounded by rolling fields, a sunrise over the ocean, a snow-covered mountain—scenes that drew the listener's attention away from musical celebrities and toward the beauty of God's creation.[42] Furthermore, early Maranatha! albums did not disclose the names of performers. Instead, they were organized under the in-house generic choir name "The Maranatha! Singers." This intentional anonymity was similarly intended to keep the listener's focus on the praise of God rather than on a particular singer's voice or personality.

Ron Kenoly, one of the first personalities to emerge in the genre, reflected, "When I began leading praise & worship [in the 1980s], worship leaders were just kind of an anonymous bunch of people. The church leaders didn't really want to attach a personality to that particular role."[43] Kenoly recalled submitting demo tapes to one of Maranatha!'s producers in 1984 and being told his voice couldn't be used because it "had too much personality." Five or six years later, the industry shifted completely. Kenoly went to work for Integrity Music, where he reports that the company that "was excited for me to lead the praise & worship that emerged out of my own personality. [Integrity] didn't do a generic presentation. It was personality-driven, and since then it has caught on."[44] The new "stars" of modern worship would reject that designation, insisting that they were merely worship leaders who facilitated others' encounter with God. Be that as it may, the days of "faceless worship" were over. Kenoly was one of the first people whose picture was featured on the artwork of a praise-and-worship album.

I was nearing the end of my college years when modern worship took off in evangelical churches. I participated in a musical internship in a local church as part of my senior-year coursework, and the notes from my 1999 portfolio offer some insight into that period. The first is that worship in the churches that I was attending was planned thematically: congregational singing, choir anthems, and musical specials reinforced the subject of the sermon. My journal records the advice of Geoff Twigg (1954–2018), the worship pastor who served as my internship mentor:

> Geoff once explained his philosophy of planning worship by using the medium of art. He explained that Rembrandt's students painted the folds of cloth, the reflection of the light, and all the minor intricacies of a work, and then the master himself

would put the crowning touch—the face—into the work. In order for the painting to be complete and to appear holistic, the students had to learn the styles and peculiarities of their teacher. The background was not complete without the face, and the face was not complete without the background. In the same way, worship leaders give color and coherence to the focal point of Sunday morning—the sermon.[45]

As a college student, I had questions about how exactly the worship leader / senior pastor relationship was to work. My portfolio included a reflection about my own experiences of planning worship during high school in the mid-1990s:

> On the occasions when our Music Minister was out of town or on vacation, it became the responsibility of the teaching pastor to plan worship as well as the sermon. When I accompanied congregational singing on these particular Sundays, I almost invariably knew which hymns I would be playing without any advanced notice. The process was simple: I flipped to the Topical Index at the very back of the hymnal where there was a listing of hymn medleys. I then practiced the one that was most closely related to the sermon topic. I guessed correctly almost every time.

By 1999, however, choosing repertoire had become more complicated and controversial, and the question of what to sing on Sunday morning frequently divided evangelical congregations. At least three factors fueled the evangelical worship music wars.

First, the new "modern worship" songs sounded strikingly different from their "praise and worship chorus" predecessors. In my early teenage years, publishers like Maranatha!, Hosanna, and Integrity had produced pleasant-sounding, scripturally based worship songs that brought both sides of the generation gap together. By contrast, "modern worship" had a younger and edgier sound and was more difficult to sing corporately. Monique Ingalls defines the genre of modern worship as "rock band instrumentation, standard pop-rock song forms, harmonies built upon cyclical chord riffs, and rhythmically complex tunes."[46]

Second, modern worship songs were proliferating with astonishing rapidity. In his book *Music through the Eyes of Faith* (required reading for my senior-year college capstone course), Harold Best reported: "Presently the church is caught somewhere between its enormously rich musical heritage and an unprecedented rush of musical options and technologies." Best worried that evangelicals' obsession with relevance and contemporaneity and their "general antipathy toward anything old" were combining to make "hymnbooks, hymn singing, and pipe organs the chief symbols of archaism."[47]

Finally, several influential thought leaders of the time—particularly those who defended traditional worship practices—added more fuel to the fire with arguments from the field of aesthetics.[48] Ken Myers' *All God's Children and Blue*

Suede Shoes is a good example. My senior-year book club had heated debates over Myers work, particularly his claim that aesthetic judgment is not subjective. "Is something 'beautiful' just because I like it," he asked rhetorically, "or does it have some objective quality rooted in creation that allows me to *recognize* that it is beautiful?"[49] Myers affirms the latter, noting that in Philippians 4:8, the apostle Paul "does not say that we should reflect on what we *think* is lovely, or whatever we *feel* is admirable. We are to give sustained attention to whatever is *objectively* true and noble and right."[50] In short, Myers argues that it is not a matter of "I like Bach, you like Bon Jovi, praise the Lord anyhow."[51] Some forms of music are qualitatively better than others. This line of reasoning exacerbated tensions in the musical worship wars, evidenced in Myers own telling observation: "Try telling someone from the Barry Manilow School of Liturgy that something is schlock and they will regard you as an arrogant elitist."[52]

All three of these tensions—generational conflicts over style, the fast pace of change, questions about aesthetic values—show up in my portfolio. For example, in 1999 my twenty-two-year-old-self wrote, "I know there are many individuals in my generation who cherish hymns, and there are many older adults who are excited to see some new changes in worship trends. But the task of choosing music for both groups seems daunting at best. What are the criteria for differentiating between 'good' and 'bad' worship songs?" I was searching for an elusive golden ratio—one new song per every two familiar songs in a set, perhaps—that would keep everyone in the congregation happy.

The portfolio offers no definitive answers to the questions I was raising. However, when I read between its lines today, an important sign of the time come into focus. Whereas the hymnal functioned as an external authority in the early to mid-1990s—theoretically, both the preacher and the lead musician could consult it and come to similar, even identical, conclusions about song selection for a given Sunday—by 1999, that authority was swiftly eroding. The evangelical musical canon was expanding so rapidly that print mediums like hymnals could not keep up. Congregations began abandoning them entirely. Implicit in my question about adjudicating the difference between "good" and "bad" worship songs is a question of authority. Without a hymnal to adjudicate, who gets to pronounce the definitive aesthetic word? In 2001, I set off to graduate school to explore these and other questions in an explicitly theological context.

2000–2010: Convergence, Commercialization, and Homogenization

Shortly after I began graduate school, *Worship Leader* magazine ran a cover story in 2002 entitled, "Boundary Crossing: How CCM Is Seeking to Find the Heart of Worship."[53] The story captures the spirit of the time—an era in which worship was becoming an increasingly hot commodity:

> It might be a slight exaggeration to say that anybody with an iota of musical gifting—from the singer-songwriters to the person who shakes the tambourine in your church's worship band—has a worship CD that they're either promoting on their Web site or selling out of the trunk of their car. But the exaggeration would only be slight, for sure. Over the last decade, worship music has become the fastest-growing category of music within the world of contemporary Christian music (or "CCM") effectively displacing all other musical subgenres.[54]

The blurring of the lines between worship and CCM started with the radio success of groups like Delirious?, Sonicflood, and MercyMe: bands who all began their musical careers as worship leaders. Then Michael W. Smith, a bestselling CCM artist who had helped define the "message music" genre in the 1980s, released his platinum-selling album *Worship* in 2011. Industry observers called Smith the progenitor of a seismic cultural shift toward worship.

Many other CCM artists with no previous background in worship music quickly followed Smith's lead, releasing worship albums that covered popular "modern worship" songs already being sung in many US churches.[55] By 2003, almost half of the top 20 albums in Billboard's Christian music charts were worship albums, and several had sold enough to break into the Billboard 200.[56] As *Worship Leader* editor Davin Seay put it, consumers were eager to buy "anything and everything emblazoned with the magic word: worship."[57]

A combination of factors contributed to the commercial success of worship music. Smith's *Worship* album was released on September 11, 2001. Former GMA president Frank Breeden was one of many who suggested a link between the country's mood and the sales of worship: "Since September 11, people I talk with in all sectors of society want to hear the unique message of the gospel, loudly and clearly. They don't want ambiguity or polite conversation. They want something they can count on."[58]

The shift to worship music also came at a crisis moment for many Nashville artists. The mainstream success that the CCM industry had achieved in the 1980s and 1990s had come at a price. By the late 1990s, several high-profile CCM artists had succumbed to personal problems and public scandals. Scotty Smith, founding pastor of Christ Community Church in Nashville and mentor to many Christian recording artists, saw the industry's newfound interest in worship songs as a way of pushing the "reset" button. He reflected, "There is an incredible longing and credible evidence of this community of artists saying that we need to regain our center." Pastor Smith praised the "movement toward worship orientation," suggesting that CCM artists were beginning to realize that they needed to be more focused on "the doxological nature of the kingdom of God."[59] Finally, artists and executives were quick to credit the Holy Spirit for the commercial success of worship music. INO Records president Jeff Moseley deflected any human praise: "It's a common misconception that a record company can actually sell records. All we can do is point people in our direction."[60]

While it may be true that record companies cannot lead horses to water, they can—and often do—take measures to salt the oats. Christian labels are no exception: many required their new CCM artists to sign contracts with clauses that obligated them to release a worship album if called upon by the label.[61] Russ Breimeier, and editor and music critic for *Christianity Today*, recounted a recurring conversation he had with new and independent Christian artists who solicited his honest feedback about their recent releases:

> Here's where things got dicey. No, [the artists] didn't get defensive; most are quite gracious. Instead, when discussing their "weaker" tracks, some of these artists surprised me with their replies. Basically, they said something along the lines of, "Oh, that song was added to the album at the last minute. The record label wanted a certain number of worship songs for potential radio play."[62]

Letters to the editor of *Christianity Today* confirmed Breimeier's fears about the marketing of worship music. One parent wrote in, "My teenage son and I are tired of this worship music craze . . . it seems like it's become a fad and a marketing ploy." She continued, "I get excited when I learn that one of my favorite artists is putting out a new album, only to groan when I find out it's another worship album. I personally can't wait until the whole phase is over."[63] Another reader concurred: "Honestly, I stopped buying worship albums a while ago when I noticed that they were becoming like Christmas albums—everyone has to do [at least] one and they all rehash the same music."[64]

The oversaturated market eventually bottomed out. In 2003, Dean Diehl, vice president and general manager at Reunion Records, opined, "We're at a high water mark in terms of the flood of worship-related product. But we're rapidly approaching a trend fatigue. I think once the tide recedes, a few real worship artists will be left behind, and will continue to create the genuine article."[65] Diehl's words proved prescient. CCM artists stopped producing albums that covered modern worship songs. However, a few new celebrity worship leaders (including Chris Tomlin, David Crowder, and Matt Redman) and a few CCM artists who successfully rebranded themselves as "worship artists" (including Michael W. Smith and Third Day) continued to sell strongly.

A final shift was afoot in worship music at the turn of the new century: individuals were spending considerably more time listening to it in their cars and homes. In 2003, Twila Paris, a veteran CCM artist and songwriter whose songs "He Is Exalted," "We Bow Down," and "Lamb of God" are included in many modern hymnals, observed: "My definition of worship is that which is useful in a corporate setting. But even that isn't a hard and fast rule. What I've seen lately is an explosion of what I'd call 'personal worship,' where people are worshipping in everyday settings, listening to CDs in their home or car." Paris continued, "[In the late 1990s], worship was something that happened in church on Sundays. The pastor, the worship leader and a few of the faithful in the congregation might have a passion for it, but that was about it. Now people are bringing it into every aspect of their lives, literally."[66] Paris's instincts were accurate: worship music was migrating from the public church sanctuary to personal spaces like the home or the car via radio, CDs, and personal listening devices.

This shift had been long in the making. Ever since the mid-1990s, Christian labels had been marketing their worship products for devotional use outside the four walls of the church. For example, in 1995 and 1996, Maranatha! Music published an advertisement in *Worship Leader* magazine that featured the interior of a luxury sedan with the large-letter caption, "Welcome to the new sanctuary." Smaller type invited readers to "make your car a place of worship with Maranatha! Music." An even smaller grouping of words promised: "Praise. Worship. Peace. Refuge. Safety. Encouragement. Anywhere."[67] As ethnomusicologist Anna Nekola points out, "The message here is anything but subtle. Listeners should load worship music CDs into their stereos to transform their mundane automobiles into sacred sanctuaries, and their ordinary commutes into spirit-filled worship experiences."[68] By the early 2000s, Christian magazines were flooded with print advertisements for worship products that depicted what readers desired to escape from or to: "from traffic jams to mountains, from laundry to a serene meadow."[69] And by 2005, many Christian album reviews, especially those in the "modern worship" subgenre, no longer mentioned corporate, Sunday-morning church worship at all. American evangelicals were coming to understand worship music as something to be listened to, not something to be reproduced in a group setting.

By 2010, modern worship had come full circle. CCM artists were no longer covering modern worship songs; instead, new worship music began to take on the characteristics and values of Christian radio. The most notable new development was the worship industry's obsession with a woman known simply by the name of Becky. Becky is the personification of Christian radio's target demographic: its quintessential listener.[70] Becky is somewhere between the ages of thirty-five and forty-two. She's been married twice and has three kids. She's a middle-of-the-road evangelical Christian, neither radically liberal or radically conservative in her political or spiritual beliefs, and she attends church about twice a month. Becky spends a lot of time in the minivan, schlepping her offspring to and from soccer practice. The music in the car is always Christian radio, which Becky trusts because of its safe, positive message.

Christian radio programmers know that Becky likely grew up listening to the hits of pop radio and that she has expectations about what "sounds good." According to Nashville musician and scholar Dave Perkins, "Becky makes consumer decisions through an inherited set of quality control filters." She "expects her Christian songs to sound as pleasing as pop songs," which means that contemporary worship music "must please Becky musically—in songwriting, performance, and production—or she will lose interest, despite the Christian lyrics."[71] In short, "New worship music coming across the desks of music directors at adult contemporary Christian stations meets a litmus test: Will Becky like it?"[72]

Proponents of Christian radio are quick to point out there's nothing wrong with stations knowing who their listeners are and programming accordingly. It makes good business sense. Furthermore, as syndicated Christian radio personality Brant Hansen argued in a *Washington Post* op-ed, this type of music meets a particular need:

> Christian radio has managed to capitalize well on something you might notice if you use Spotify: Radio executives have figured out that people want to access music for specific needs and for specific moods. That's why Spotify now offers "Morning Acoustic Chill" and "After Work Run." It's not always about high art. Christian radio is adjusting to this particularly well and embracing the fact that people see Christian music as encouraging and uplifting. Listeners know they live in a judgmental world and they want a reminder, particularly in traffic after a long day, that God still loves them, and still wants them, even in spite of themselves.[73]

But other artists and thinkers have expressed doubts about this philosophy. As early as 1995, church music scholar Don Hustad had called for a clear separation between the music sung in church and the music played on Christian radio. His recommendation was for churches to declare themselves "independent of contemporary music styles" and encourage "all to separate their music for entertainment (whether rock or Bach) from their music for worship."[74] Some fifteen years later, industry insider Michael Gungor would advocate for the adoption of new categorical labels like "Positive Alternative," "Family," or "Religious." Whatever the language, Gungor was adamant that Becky's music "should not be included in the same category with liturgical music, and it should not be called 'Christian.' It is a categorically different thing. . . . Since when was Christianity a safe, positive alternative for the family anyway?" Gungor queried with a note of irony.[75]

2010–Present: The New Worship Leader

In 1977, a church music veteran noted that keeping the Jesus Generation in the church meant being willing to put up with "guitar-plucking kids who play three bad chords but smile a lot."[76] Forty years later, the next generation of guitar-plucking kids—whose technical proficiency has moved well beyond three chords—is frequently and derisively compared to rock stars. Given the rapid musical and cultural changes within evangelical worship—including bright stage lights, dimly lit sanctuaries, multiple screens, moving graphics, and loud volumes—this comparison felt inevitable.

But in the second decade of the twenty-first century, many worship scholars and practitioners began to actively resist such caricatures. The title of the 2013 book *Worship Leaders: We Are Not Rock Stars* is perhaps the most on-the-nose example.[77] Other authors proposed alternative, more constructive metaphors. Instead of "rock stars," Constance Cherry compared worship leaders to engineers and designers. Her 2010 book *The Worship Architect* makes the case that gathering, Word, Table/response, and sending constitute the four "load-bearing walls" of the worship structure. Zac Hicks's 2016 book *The Worship Pastor* was written in response to a felt need.[78] As Hicks explained in an interview: "I can't tell you how many young worship leaders I've talked to over the last 5–10 years who are sick of the rock star model."[79] Each chapter of Hicks's book proposes a different vocational metaphor: the worship leader as "Theological Dietician," "War General," "Corporate Mystic," and "Mortician," to name a few.

I too bristle at facile worship leader / rock star comparisons, largely because such caricatures are not in keeping with the integrity of the young worship leaders I have come to know and help train. In 2010, I completed my PhD and accepted a job as a professor of worship leadership at a small, Christian liberal arts college. My expertise in worship was more scholarly than practical (I had never been on staff at a church), and the evangelical churches I had attended as a graduate student drew primarily from denominational musical resources. I was unprepared for how much the nondenominational evangelical world had changed during my graduate school hiatus. The first cohort of undergraduate students I taught helped me to view the new musical landscape through their eyes.

One of the first lessons I learned was that the thematic approach to worship planning I had found so invigorating during my own college years—one in which congregational music was chosen to support and reiterate the subject of the sermon—had grown stale for many congregations. In 1999, my college mentor Geoff had compared thematic worship to a Rembrandt painting. By 2012, author and blogger Sheila Wray Gregoire dismissively referred to this way of thinking as "the 'eye shadow should match your purse' philosophy of worship." Gregoire, to put it mildly, was not a fan: "If the pastor is preaching about the inerrancy of

Scripture, not every song you sing needs to be about the inerrancy of Scripture. Worship isn't about teaching people the sermon," she stressed. "Worship is about giving God His due. . . . It's much more important for people to encounter God during worship . . . than it is to use those songs to preach a specific message."[80]

I suspected that the songs that enabled evangelical congregations to encounter God in worship were less and less likely to be traditional hymns. In a class on John and Charles Wesley, I referenced "O for a Thousand Tongues to Sing," "Love Divine, All Loves Excelling," and "Christ the Lord Is Risen Today." The same students who sang modern worship choruses full-throatedly multiple times a week in chapel gazed back at me blankly during the historical lecture, with no spark of musical recognition. Later that semester, an eight-year-old friend from church and I were reading aloud together when she stumbled across an unfamiliar word. "What's a hymnal?" she asked me in puzzlement. Although the evidence was only anecdotal, the times certainly seemed to be changing.

My students in the worship leadership major were required to take a course called Multimedia, Technology and Worship, but classes in choral arranging and conducting were only elective. (Few if any of the students expected that conducting a church choir or orchestra would be part of their future ministry responsibilities.) Furthermore, these students were facing stresses I could never have imagined twenty years earlier, including the pressure to make Sunday morning music sound as polished and produced as it did on Christian radio.

I worried especially about the young women in my courses, who would soon be navigating uncharted, and very gendered, waters. Some evangelical churches would rejoice in their training and accept their gifts without question, citing the example of Miriam leading the Israelites in worship in Exodus 15 as biblical precedent. Many other evangelical congregations, however, subscribe to a complementarian theology that holds that men and women are equal in personhood but distinct in their roles in the home and church. For example, influential author and worship leader Bob Kauflin writes that in his church, the role of worship leader "includes elements that involve a degree of teaching, leading, and pastoring, which we believe the Bible says are male roles in the church. For that reason, all our worship leaders are men."[81] In Kauflin's church, and in thousands of evangelical churches like it, women are invited to sing, read scripture, write songs and "[model] expressive engagement"[82]—valuable contributions, to be sure, but presumably non-salaried ones. Would the women in my classes be able to find employment that compensated them fairly for the time, work, and student loan debt they had taken on to earn their worship leadership degrees?

In fact, I worried about career longevity for all of my students. Numerous internet discussion boards are dedicated to the topic of age discrimination in modern worship. One thirtyish-year-old worship leader writes about a candid conversation with a friend: "We [both] wondered whether in ten to fifteen years, we would be viewed as out-of-date, irrelevant, washed up, and cheesy—one of those old guys trying to look and act young. Ultimately, we questioned whether we would be as effective in doing our task once we started 'looking old.' "[83] Another recounts a conversation with a guitarist from a neighboring church: " 'It's an issue of *branding*,' [the young guitarist] declared matter-of-factly. 'We're trying to reach twenty-somethings, so it's really important to sound just like what people hear on the radio.' His implication is clear: You can't do that with old people."[84] My young students would graduate with an age-based competitive edge in the job market. But what would happen in two decades' time, in a church culture that has come to believe that "if we want to 'reach young people,' a forty-something at the helm is no good"?[85]

My students were passionate and opinionated but quick to laugh at their mistakes. They indulged my nostalgia for hymns they considered "old fashioned" and introduced me to new worship artists and repertoire that had been significant in their own spiritual development. I watched them gain confidence in their burgeoning musical leadership skills, and when they graduated, I wondered—with equal parts optimism and apprehension—what the future of church music held for us all.

Concluding Reflections

If you, like me, have had the privilege of being loved by a cat, you might recognize the following scenario. You are sitting quietly in your favorite chair, absentmindedly stroking the cat's soft fur while she purrs contentedly. Suddenly, from out of the blue, her head swivels around and she gives your hand a good, hard chomp.[86] Your instincts are defensive: "I didn't do to deserve that!" But animal experts agree that the fault is yours, not the cat's. In the feline world, there is a fine line between what is pleasurable and what is annoying, and cats react swiftly when the sensitive areas of their bodies are overstimulated. Your furry companion has tried to tell you this with her body language—flattened ears, dilated pupils, a swishing tail—but you have ignored her signals and pressed on to your own detriment. In frustration, the cat sends you the only message she knows you will understand. Her intent is not to hurt you, but simply to say, "Stop! I've had enough."

When it comes to discussions of worship, I deeply empathize with the cat's plight. My reaction to worship pastor and author Stephen Miller's 2013 piece, "The Modern Worship Music Wars," is a case in point.[87] Miller suggests that old debates about hymns and choruses have taken on a new, more subtle tone. He writes:

At first glance, the worship wars that once plagued the church seem to have died down . . . until we walk out of a church service that didn't meet our own standards. We have become professional critics of corporate worship. We complain about everything . . . from key signatures to instrumentation; from the worship leader's fashion sense to vocal tone—it's all fair game for our consumer-driven critique.[88]

I read these words, feel the Spirit's conviction, and recognize that discomfort I am experiencing might be medicinal for my soul. So far, so good. I am still purring, content to keep reading.

"Worship is war. But it is not to be fought over our own preferences. We must turn our energy towards killing the selective, prideful nature within us."[89] My eyes narrow. The tip of my tail flicks. Long pent-up frustrations begin to rise. "The next time you go to church and the music is too loud or the leader is singing that song you don't like, go to war. Fight against the sin at work within yourself. Fight against consumerism and disunity. Fight for a grateful heart. . . . Fight the true war of worship."[90] And there it is: the suggestion that any problems in modern worship lie not with the songs, but with the internal disposition of the singer. The author has unwittingly stroked a patch of highly sensitive fur, and the paragraphs that follow produce in me the equivalent of a forceful feline *chomp*.

Quantitative studies indicate that musical worship wars are beginning to wane. In 2015 the National Congregations Study, one of the most rigorous surveys of local religious congregations in the United States, reported that over the last seventeen years, organs, choirs, and church bulletins have decreased significantly within evangelical congregations.[91] Applause, raising hands, and drums are all on the rise. Although some evangelical congregations held both "traditional" and "contemporary" services at the turn of the twentieth century, even that practice is far less common today.[92] The authors of the study suggest this may be a sign that "the 'worship wars' are less of an issue for congregations than they once were."[93]

But numbers alone cannot provide a vocabulary for describing the wars' aftermath. In 2011, *Christianity Today* senior managing editor Mark Galli suggested that we are "living through a tense truce, if my local congregation is any example." My own experiences, however, suggest that Galli understated the issue and chose to err on the side of generosity. The metaphor of "truce" implies that two sides temporarily agree to stop attacking each other in order to discuss peace terms. But many hymn-lovers cry foul: there was never a negotiating table to begin with. If worship wars are no longer being fought today, it is only because, after two decades of intense conflict, the "Davids" on the side of tradition have been soundly trounced by the "Goliath" that is the multimillion-dollar commercial worship industry. Demands like the one set forth by Miller—that the vanquished check their grief (and their beloved repertoire) at the door and en-thusiastically belt the new melodies of the victors—coupled with the insinua-tion that anyone unwilling or unable to do so is spiritually deficient ("fight for a grateful heart" . . . "kill the selective, prideful nature" . . . "fight the true war of worship")—only rub salt into an open wound.

Every Sunday, I experience cognitive dissonance: the uncomfortable tension of holding two conflicting thoughts at the same time. The first thought is im-mense gratitude for the individuals who are leading us in song. None of the ones whom I have known personally seek fame or recognition. All of the ones whom I have known personally place more emphasis on scripture than on Top 20 wor-ship hit charts. Every person in the church has an opinion about the music; these opinions are often in direct opposition, and worship leaders strive valiantly to satisfy all parties. Many of these leaders are bivocational: they write chord charts, rehearse teams, and plan repertoire in the midst of full-time family and work responsibilities. When I look at the worship pastor standing on the platform, I do not see an aspiring rock star. I see a leader trying hard to do the right thing by their congregation and their God, week in and week out, without fanfare or public thanks. I see a person who is beloved by their elderly grandfather, their infant daughter, or their undergraduate worship professor. I see an individual following the biblical injunction to lead the congregation in singing a new song unto the Lord. I am wholeheartedly rooting for their success.

And yet. Every Sunday morning, I inevitably feel . . . heartbroken? fu-rious? . . . about the traditional evangelical hymnody that is weekly being lost. Those are strong adjectives—not quite the right ones, but the closest I can find to get at my sense of powerlessness. To suggest that the worship wars of the late twentieth century were waged over musical "preferences" is to fundamentally misunderstand the complexity of the controversies. Ice cream flavor is a pref-erence. One person likes vanilla, another strawberry, and a third butter pecan. A significant percentage of the population would be upset if Breyers decided to discontinue mint chocolate chip, but they would eventually swallow their disap-pointment and move on to another palatable flavor. They would not go to war. People will, however, take up arms if their homes are being threatened. *Home—* a concept laden with deep memories and complex feelings—gets closer to the emotional core of my disquietude than does the anemic language of "preference."

Historian Josh Kun coined the word *audiotopia* to describe the way music can function as a dwelling place. Kun spent hours in the local record store as an adolescent, listening to anything and everything he could get his hands on. He recalls, "Building my record collection was my way of building my own world, creating an alternate set of cultural spaces that, through the private act of lis-tening, could deliver me to different places and different times and allow me to try out a different version of myself."[94] Audiotopia is what happens when music is experienced "not only as a sound that goes into our ears and vibrates through our bones but as a space that we can enter into, encounter, move around in, inhabit, be safe in, learn from."[95] Every song, Kun suggests, is an "almost-place," existing in its own "auditory somewhere" that is neither entirely material nor entirely ephemeral:

> I can put on a song and live in it, hear it, get inside its notes and chords, get inside its narratives and follow its journeys and paths. Dropping the needle or pressing the play button [is] the equivalent of walking into a building, entering into an architecture of sound, a space that can be seen and experienced only if it is heard.[96]

This is a feeling that anyone who has ever listened to a favorite mixtape from days of yore knows well. An entire world can live inside a song. As Kun puts it, "A song is never just a song, but a connection, a ticket, a pass, an invitation, a node in a complex network."[97]

The process works in both directions: not only do we inhabit songs, but songs also inhabit us. When you hear music, "Something outside of you is entering your body—alien sounds emitted from strangers you sometimes cannot see that enter, via vibration and frequency, the very bones and tissues of your being."[98] It is, in some ways, like the experience of consuming the bread and wine of communion. Indeed, historian Mark Noll points out that for early generations of evangelicals, "hymn singing became almost sacramental. It was the one physical activity that all evangelicals shared, and it was the one experience that bound them most closely together."[99]

I will not presume to speak for Warren or Pastor Timothy, whose stories I recounted in the introduction to this chapter, or for any other member of the Oregon Trail Generation. But here is what my experience of evangelical worship has felt like as of late: a musical home being dismantled, plank by plank, against my will, by an industry that knows there is more financial profit in new construction than in historical preservation. I miss hymns with visceral grief: the way I lifted my voice with a congregation and inhabited their four-part harmonies, the way they connected me to saints who had sung them before my birth. In Vinita Hampton Wright's novel *Velma Still Cooks in Leeway*, the titular character reflects on life in an old family home: "Now that I'm staring back on more than half of my life, I can see that you never live your life alone, anyway. You *are* your family and all their experiences. They *are* with you, no matter how many coats of paint you slap on the woodwork. . . . Their conversations still wander the rooms and hang near the ceilings, some days more than others."[100] To inhabit a familiar hymn is to live in a family home where the ancestors remain quietly present.

Many would argue that hymnody has not been lost in the twenty-first century but has simply changed and evolved to keep up with the times. For example, some worship artists have "retuned" hymns by taking texts that are in the public domain (i.e., "On Jordan's Stormy Banks," "O Love That Will Not Let Me Go") and setting them to fresh, rhythmically driven melodies. Others writers leave the text and tune of a hymn unchanged, but add their own musical "stamp" to the piece by adding new material. For example, in "The Wonderful Cross," Chris Tomlin retains the hymn tune melody HAMBURG and Isaac Watts's text, "When I Survey the Wondrous Cross," but inserts an original rock chorus after the verses. Still other composers like Graham Kendrick, Stuart Townend, and Keith and Kristyn Getty are writing new "modern hymns" with weighty theological lyrics set to modern soft-rock-style tunes.[101]

Simply put, ever since the binary language of "traditional" versus "contemporary" entered the American church vernacular in the mid-1990s, the dichotomy has proven problematic. Neither category is monolithic, and the line between them is often porous.[102] The churches we will meet in the next two chapters—Park Street Church in Boston and Moody Church in Chicago—recognize this reality and have cultivated unique approaches to transcending differences over worship within their respective congregations.

2

"Stately and Set Apart"

Upholding Tradition in Boston

Every year, some four million visitors to Boston walk the Freedom Trail, a 2.5-mile path—marked by red paint and bricks—that snakes through downtown Boston and commemorates sixteen sites related to the American Revolution. Some will hire guides in eighteenth-century colonial costumes to escort them along the trail. Others will download smartphone apps with historical tidbits and opt for a self-guided approach. Along the way, they will pass museums, meetinghouses, burial grounds, and other historical markers that tell the story of the nation's beginnings.

The third stop on the tour is Park Street Church, which novelist Henry James described as "the most interesting mass of bricks and mortar in America."[1] Park Street Church, with its red brick exterior and towering white steeple, exudes New England confidence and prestige. The earliest inhabitants of Boston dubbed its location at the intersection of Tremont and Park Streets "Brimstone Corner": a recognition of both the church's fiery preaching and the fact that brimstone (the sulfur used to make gunpowder) was stored in its basement during the War of 1812 (Figure 2.1).[2]

Visitors learn that the building, completed in 1809, is the site of many historic firsts. Park Street Church was the site of one the first Sunday schools in the US Sunday School Movement (1818). It sent the first Christian missionaries to Hawaii (1819). The famous abolitionist William Lloyd Garrison gave his first major speech against slavery at the church, in 1829. The patriotic hymn "America" (also known as "My Country 'Tis of Thee")—composed by Park Street's music director, Samuel Francis Smith—premiered at the church on July 4, 1831.[3] The Prison Discipline Society (America's first prison ministry), the American Temperance Society, the Animal Rescue League (America's first animal humane society), and the Boston Chapter of the National Association for the Advancement of Colored People (NAACP) all had their beginnings at Park Street Church.[4] What Freedom Trail visitors may not be told is that Park Street Church has also played a significant role in the creation of American evangelicalism as we know it today.

This chapter begins with an overview of Park Street Church's history and an explanation of how its most famous leaders launched a new theological movement in the mid-twentieth century that would steer a middle course between the extremes of fundamentalism and modernism. However, influential leaders and institutional

Evangelical Worship. Melanie C. Ross, Oxford University Press. © Oxford University Press 2021.
DOI: 10.1093/oso/9780197530757.003.0003

Figure 2.1 Park Street Church on "Brimstone Corner"
Boston, Massachusetts: November 2016. Photo by author.

histories can only take us so far: as I argue throughout the book, American evangelicalism as it exists "on the ground" is best understood through an analysis of corporate worship. In particular, the members of Park Street Church struggle with how to maintain their church's historic identity without becoming a museum. The solution is an organic interpretation of progress. Just as a seed contains all the genetic information necessary to become a mature plant, so too Park Street Church leaders believe that healthy change unfolds slowly and logically, according to a predictable trajectory, from a single point of origin. This understanding of progress is reflected in its preaching and musical repertoire. While God's covenant with Abraham unites Israel and the New Testament church into a single people of God, a musical "covenant" penned in 1810 by the church's first musicians unites nineteenth- and twenty-first-century congregations into a single Park Street Church. The concluding section discusses the concerns of some Park Street members who wonder whether the church's long-standing emphasis on continuity unnecessarily hinders fresh, new, or surprising developments in worship.

Church History and Cultural Context

Park Street Church came into being on February 27, 1809, in response to a rapid wave of Unitarian theology that was sweeping across New England. "There is one, and but one living and true God, subsisting in three persons, The Father, The Son, and The Holy Ghost," the church founders declared. "These three are the one God, the same in substance, equal in power and in glory."[5] In early nineteenth-century New England, these were fighting words. Unitarian defenders of "rational religion" were rapidly gaining ground, and by 1803, eight of the nine Congregational churches in Boston were served by ministers who no longer held the historic Trinitarian view of mainstream Christianity. In fact, at the time of Park Street's founding, there was only one other church out of seventeen in Boston that still rigorously adhered to belief in the tri-personal nature of God.[6] For Congregationalists, the last straw was the installation of Henry Ware, a convinced Unitarian, as the prestigious Hollis Chair of Theology at Harvard University: the nation's chief training ground for Congregational ministers was now being led by those who rejected historic Trinitarian Christianity. Congregationalists established an alternative school, Andover Seminary, in 1808, and Park Street Church was formed one year later.

"We laid our plan on a very grand scale," one charter member recalled. "Our meetinghouse must be larger and higher than any other in the city."[7] The small congregation raised $70,000 to build what was plausibly the grandest church in the city at the time.[8] The impressive church building could seat eight hundred congregants and was designed by English architect Peter Banner in a style similar to that of Christopher Wren. Solomon Willard, architect, designed the wooden spire—which, at 217 feet, would rise just visibly higher than the golden dome of the Massachusetts State House, which sat one block away. The steeple made Park Street the tallest building in the United States for thirty-six years: it was, in the words of one Park Street pastor, "a Puritan finger pointing to God."[9] The building was completed in less than eight months.

Despite these auspicious beginnings, Park Street fell on hard times in the last decades of the nineteenth century. Attendance plummeted from 1,100 in 1886 to 336 in 1901. The church was obscured for several years behind an ugly network of scaffold while construction crews dug subway tunnels into the Common—a project that was not completed until 1897. Furthermore, the church had employed a series of pastors whose leadership divided the congregation. Finally, increasing numbers of Park Street congregants were abandoning the city for what they hoped would be a better life in the new suburbs. This urban flight ate away at the congregation's finances. Like many churches of the day, Park Street employed a pew-rental system: every member who left Park Street for a suburban church took substantial revenue away from the annual budget. In 1894, the congregation was forced to remodel its basement so it could rent the space to a commercial florist and fruit grocer. By the turn of the century, many members were convinced that the only solution to the church's fiscal difficulties would be to sell the property and relocate to the suburbs.[10]

In the end, the church building was spared by a Preservation Committee composed of architects and lawyers—a group that, ironically, included many prominent Unitarians. The committee noted that the Park Street Church building was "a beautiful and time-honored feature of Boston, bound up with the very thought of Boston in every mind." Theological differences aside, no one wished to see the church's famous steeple replaced by a "dry-goods emporium" that would "dominate the view of the State House" and "be a blot forever on the landscape of the city."[11] In 1905, Arcturus Zodiac Conrad, known by his contemporaries as A. Z. Conrad, assumed leadership of the church and helped turn its fortunes around. Conrad's life was as colorful as his name: he survived an Indian uprising in his boyhood, married into the family of John Adams (wedding Harriet Narcissa Adams in 1885), and earned a PhD from the City College of New York (now New York University) in 1891. At the age of seventy-six, Conrad created a stir in the congregation when he married the twenty-seven-year-old church organist less than a year after the death of his first wife.

During his long pastorate, which lasted until his death in 1937, Conrad brought Park Street Church back to life. Under his leadership, the congregation financed a new organ, paid off the building's mortgage, and refreshed the church's exterior, stripping off several layers of old paint to restore the original brick and white clapboard. The changes at Park Street were visible inside the building as well. At the church's centennial anniversary in 1909, Conrad noted that in the three years since he had assumed leadership, "Morning congregations have more than doubled. Evening audiences have quadrupled. *The tide has turned.* A hundred encouraging features attend our work."[12] From 348 members in 1905, the church nearly doubled its membership by 1910, and by 1916 had passed 1,000 members. By the 1930s, Park Street numbered over 1,800 members.[13]

Park Street and the New Evangelicalism: Conrad, Ockenga, and Wright

The 1930s was a significant decade in the life of Park Street Church. The stories of A. Z. Conrad, Harold John Ockenga, and J. Elwin Wright—three important leaders in the church—illustrate the zeitgeist of the era.

A. Z. Conrad

Park Street pastor A. Z. Conrad was the first leader to articulate Park Street's theological position in the early twentieth century. One hundred years after its resistance to progressive Unitarianism, Park Street faced a new challenge in the fundamentalist-modernist controversies sweeping through American churches. Prior to the Civil War, evangelicalism was the dominant expression of Christianity in the overwhelmingly Protestant United States. However, after the Civil War, powerful new forces like urbanization and industrialization and important new intellectual developments like Darwin's evolutionary theory and higher criticism, which emphasized the human aspects of biblical origins, began to weaken the power of evangelicalism in American culture. Between 1910 and 1915, the Bible Institute of Los Angeles published *The Fundamentals*, a series of pamphlets that defended the central tenets of orthodox Protestant theology, particularly the inerrancy of scripture, against the rising tide of theological modernism that was influencing Protestant denominations. In 1920, Curtis Lee Laws, editor of the Baptist newspaper *Watchman Examiner*, coined the term *fundamentalist* to describe "a person willing to do battle royal for the fundamentals of the faith."[14]

Conrad emphatically rejected all attempts to label him a fundamentalist. However, historian Margaret Bendroth points out that this point was probably lost on most of his contemporaries.[15] Conrad was never reluctant to make his opinions known on matters theological or cultural. He assailed modernism from the Park Street pulpit: "The adulterated, eviscerated, emasculated gospel of modernism blasts everything it touches. Avoid it as you would a pestilence."[16] Conrad also introduced a popular question-and-answer period on Sunday night, in which he fielded inquiries from the general public: "Are not the lipstick inebriates a serious menace today? What proportion of leisure should be spent for pleasure? Should not bank deposits be guaranteed? Is not the present cost of coal unreasonable?"[17] Bendroth wryly observes that after his death, the local press remembered Conrad—somewhat fondly—as "a man of few doubts" whose "natural inclinations were to attack" if controversy promised a larger audience.[18]

Conrad was well aware of how his colleagues perceived him: "Many of my brother ministers class me with the Fundamentalists, and to be sure I am a thousand times nearer to them than the modernists." However, he adamantly insisted on more theological nuance: "I am not a Fundamentalist. I refuse to thus be labeled because I cannot accept their extreme positions. . . . Let me tell you what I am; I am an evangelical Christian."[19] Conrad embraced fundamentalism's insistence on the inerrancy of scripture, the literal virgin birth, and the bodily resurrection of Jesus Christ, but rejected fundamentalism's tendency toward anti-intellectualism. Conrad was aware of European theological developments in biblical scholarship and early in his career even offered his cautious support. In 1926, he argued, "It is perfectly proper that the severest test should be applied to what is claimed to be the Word of God. Evangelicals find no fault with Biblical criticism if it is honest and consistent."[20] Two years later, he similarly stressed that "no disciple of Jesus shrinks for one moment from the application of all scientific knowledge to Biblical criticism."[21]

However, historian George Harper has shown that as the fundamentalist-modernist controversy dragged on, Conrad found it increasingly difficult to be charitable toward modernists. In 1931, after battles that split conservatives and liberals in Baptist and Presbyterian denominations, Conrad warned of dire consequences for Christian higher education: "These institutions have many of them fallen into the hands of apostates. . . . Theological seminaries . . . are suffering from serious blight from the destructive influences of supervisors whose eyes have never been opened."[22]

Harold John Ockenga

Harold John Ockenga, the pastor who would replace Conrad at Park Street, had firsthand experience with the seminary controversies Conrad was referencing. At the start of the 1929 academic year, twenty-four-year-old Ockenga had a difficult decision to make: one that would shape not only the trajectory of his life, but also that of the evangelical movement. Ockenga was just about to finish his graduate studies at Princeton Theological Seminary, a school that he loved. Princeton "is a most beautiful, cultured and scholastical place,"[23] Ockenga wrote in his journals. He was dazzled by the school's gothic architecture, magnificent libraries, and intellectual prestige. A gifted student and a recognized campus leader, Ockenga thrived at the seminary.

But at the seemingly idyllic campus, students and faculty alike were deeply divided by the fundamentalist-modernist controversies ravaging the Presbyterian Church. In the summer of 1929, just as Ockenga was posed to start his final year of study, the conservative faculty of Princeton (including Ockenga's beloved mentor, J. Gresham Machen) withdrew from the seminary to establish their own institution, Westminster Theological Seminary, in Philadelphia. Machen was a well-known figure at Park Street Church: A. Z. Conrad admired his conservative stance in the theological controversies of the day and often made the church's pulpit available to him as a sounding board for his anti-modernist messages.[24]

Machen and the colleagues who founded Westminster saw themselves as carrying on a distinctive brand of "Old Princeton Theology" that had developed during the middle to late nineteenth century under conservative Presbyterian leaders like Archibald Hodge and Benjamin Breckinridge Warfield. Hodge and Warfield concluded that nothing in the new historical-critical methods justified any serious modification of the church's traditional views on the authorship, composition, or origin of the biblical books. Apparent discrepancies in the Bible did not qualify as errors.

As a student, Ockenga agonized over the decision he had to make. "I did so want to graduate from Princeton," Ockenga confided in a letter to a friend, "but if it is modern, I'm afraid my principles will turn me elsewhere. Most of my friends are going to the new seminary. What do you think I should do?"[25] In the end, the choice was clear. "When I came back [to Princeton], I found all these internationally known professors and all my friends going to the new seminary," he reported in 1929. "It was a matter of taking a stand for Christ against the modernist encroaches."[26] Ockenga graduated from Westminster, not Princeton, in May 1930. Six years after graduation, Ockenga assumed the senior pastorate of Park Street Church.

J. Elwin Wright

Like Conrad and Ockenga, many Protestant laypersons in the 1930s found themselves at a crossroads. One on hand, they were losing influence in mainline denominations. On the other hand, they did not fully identify with the reactionary, belligerent fundamentalist movement. Moderate conservatives sought a third way between defensive fundamentalism and mainline theological liberalism, and the person most responsible for building a consensus among them was J. Elwin Wright.

Wright had inherited leadership of a Pentecostal parachurch ministry, the First Fruits Harvesters Association, from his father. Harvesters were devoted to winning souls and teaching radical holiness in New England, a region often written off as lost to the evangelical cause. Harvesters went out from their base in the village of Rumney, New Hampshire, to hold revival meetings and organize new churches, and then invited constituents back to Rumney every summer for camp meetings and Bible conferences. When the younger Wright assumed leadership of the organization, he broadened the theological stance of the Harvesters, advocating that Christians from all denominations across New England should be invited to attend conferences, that a variety of evangelical speakers should participate, and that the Harvesters should help existing congregations rather than forming new ones. Eventually, the association would change its name from the very Pentecostal-sounding First Fruit Harvesters to the more inclusive New England Fellowship.[27]

A turning point for the organization came during a five-day summer conference at Rumney in 1929, the same summer when Ockenga was agonizing over whether to leave Princeton for Westminster. Eyewitnesses report that at Rumney, several hundred pastors "put their arms around each other, tears coursing down their faces, as they realized that not too far from them was the pastor of another denomination who really loved the Lord and His Word."[28] The event was so successful that talk began of a New England–wide revival. Park Street pastor A. Z. Conrad recognized the potential of the network of pastors, and the next year, in 1930, he invited Wright to Boston to conduct youth services at Park Street on Sunday afternoons for several months each winter.[29]

In 1932, the New England Fellowship moved its headquarters to 5 Park Street, an office building adjacent to the church. It soon opened a bookstore, which was dedicated in a service led by Conrad. Park Street Church and the New England Fellowship became the center of a growing conservative Protestant network that spanned across Boston and much of New England.[30] In 1934, Wright joined Park Street Church, and two years later Ockenga became senior pastor. Wright and Ockenga had met at Rumney in the summer of 1936, and their friendship was renewed when Ockenga took up his new responsibilities at Park Street. The idea of duplicating the New England Fellowship on a national scale emerged, and Ockenga and Wright crisscrossed the country, drumming up support for what would eventually become the National Association of Evangelicals. Ockenga served as the organization's founding president from 1942 to 1944. Once again, Park Street Church was at the center of the new movement: in 1943, the NAE settled into office space at the church, and in 1944, Ockenga became its executive secretary.[31]

Park Street Themes

The stories of Conrad, Ockenga, and Wright illustrate three themes that regularly recur throughout Park Street's history. First is the difficulty of evangelical ministry in New England. In his 1942 opening address to the body that would eventually become the National Association of Evangelicals, Ockenga lamented that the cause of evangelical Christianity in America had been reduced to individuals and individual congregations: "New England is an example of this sad situation. Evangelicals, one after another, have been so frozen out that the territory is almost a mission field . . . evangelically an arid waste."[32] As we will see, many evangelical Christians believe that not much has changed in the last seventy-five years: New England still appears to them a spiritual "wasteland" where theological liberals and Unitarians seem to have won the day.

The second theme is Park Street's role in the formation of a new, self-conscious evangelical identity. From Conrad's insistence that he was an *evangelical* rather than a fundamentalist to Wright's and Ockenga's tireless work in establishing the National Association of Evangelicals (and later, in 1950, the World Evangelical Fellowship), Park Street Church played a critical role in establishing a new theological movement. Ockenga spelled out the goals of the "new evangelicalism" in a speech printed in the church's newsletter, *The Spire*: "to develop an intellectually respectable apologetic for orthodox Christianity, to move beyond the separatism of fundamentalism . . . and to recover an 'evangelical social conscience.' "[33]

Ockenga's phrase, "an intellectually respectable apologetic" signals a third Park Street Church theme: a commitment to what I will call "academic evangelism." The founders of Park Street Church were deeply committed to the life of the mind: every one of Park Street's first four ministers became a college president when his tenure at Boston had been completed.[34] Furthermore, in every era of its history Park Street Church has attracted literally thousands of faculty members and students from the city's elementary, secondary, undergraduate, and graduate-level educational institutions. In a sermon from 1950 entitled "Boston at the Crossroads," Ockenga reflected on the wealth of educational offerings in the area:

> We have more degree-granting colleges and universities in Massachusetts than we have in any other State of the Union and sixty per cent of them are concentrated right here in Boston. Go down the Charles River. You will see also the greatest technical Institution of learning in the whole world. You will see the greatest private university in America. You will see likewise one of the greatest City universities that we have in America.[35]

Ockenga himself had a formidable intellect, and he accumulated four advanced degrees, including master of arts and doctor of philosophy degrees from the University of Pittsburgh.[36] This achievement particularly stood out in the early decades of the twentieth century. Historian Brooks Holifield points out that in 1926, no more than 27 percent of clergy in the largest Protestant denominations had a college and seminary education. Fully 50 percent had only a high school education or less.[37] By contrast, Ockenga famously prepared his sermons from the Greek text of the New Testament, wrote them out in advance, and delivered them flawlessly from memory—an exegetical feat that earned him the respect of the leading academic lights of Boston. Ockenga was invigorated to be working in the "Athens of America," an environment that required deep theological and ideological engagement with leading secular and religious minds of the day.

During his time at Park Street, Ockenga also was influential in establishing new centers of evangelical higher education. In 1947, he teamed up with popular Californian Charles Fuller to found Fuller Theological Seminary in Pasadena, California, which was intended to be the "Princeton of the West."[38] After his retirement from Park Street, Ockenga was appointed president of Gordon College and Divinity School (later Gordon-Conwell Theological Seminary) in Hamilton, Massachusetts, an institution with a similarly Reformed theological ethos. The theological trajectory from Ockenga's graduate school years to his role in the formation of evangelical seminaries is clear: as historian Donald Dayton has noted,

"Today one cannot teach at Gordon-Conwell without standing in the line of Warfield, the old Princeton theology, and the Protestant orthodox doctrine of Scripture.[39] Ockenga's role in the creation of new institutions of higher learning that were neither "fundamentalist" nor "liberal" raised the church's profile—already high in the evangelical world—to even greater heights.

In summary, Park Street Church is a foundational "tile" in the American evangelical mosaic. This important church came into being the year that Thomas Jefferson was completing his last term in office, and at a time when other heroes of the American Revolution, including Paul Revere and John and Abigail Adams, were still alive. It was at the forefront of the nascent movement in the 1940s that birthed the National Association of Evangelicals, Gordon-Conwell Theological Seminary, Fuller Seminary, and *Christianity Today*. Today, the church enjoys a national reputation for conservative Reformed orthodoxy and for a commitment to the life of the mind: specifically, for presenting intellectually viable alternatives to the perceived extremes of historical criticism. In the service description that follows, we will see what Park Street's academic evangelism looks like in practice.

Service Description

On a chilly Sunday morning in late November, sunlight spills through the large, clear windows that line the walls of Park Street's sanctuary. In keeping with the church's Puritan heritage, the room is simple and austere: the pulpit at the front of the room is the main point of visual interest. A second-floor balcony wraps around three walls of the room and provides additional seating.

Congregants seated on the left side of the room can hear the sounds of street traffic and watch the bustle of life on the Boston Common. Congregants on the right side have a view of the Granary Burial Ground, final resting place of Revolutionary War heroes Samuel Adams, John Hancock, and Paul Revere. This juxtaposition—life on one side, death on the other—was striking to the first Park Street congregation. "What better position could be had for the new meeting-house?" one church historian asked rhetorically in 1861. "On one side there would be a view of the most agreeable character; on the other, monitors of the short duration of earthly life, and the surety of an eternal departure from the endearments of this world."[40] Present-day church facility manager Richard Elliott offers a more succinct summary: on Sunday morning, "You're sitting in a place between the life you're living now and the eternal life."[41]

In a document that details the church's philosophy of corporate worship, Park Street leaders describe the "flavor" of Sunday morning services as "generally middle-of-the-road": neither freeform ("We fully embrace a traditionally ordered service that allows us to join with so many generations who have come before us") nor fussily ritualistic ("We refrain from ascribing inappropriate significance to extra-biblical liturgical practices, and favor directness and simplicity").[42] But despite its claims, Park Street's worship would likely feel somewhat surprisingly formal to many twenty-first-century evangelicals. Organ preludes and postludes provide musical bookends to congregation worship. A robed choir sings anthems and service music in a choir loft behind the congregation (Figure 2.2).

The Park Street Church bulletin is peppered with terms not commonly used in evangelical churches. For example, this morning after the prelude, Park Street's children's choir sings an introit. The bulletin lists not only the title of the piece, *Laudamus Te*, but also information about the words ("adapted from the Gloria in Excelsis, ancient Christian hymn") and the music ("written in 1980 by Natalie Sleeth, 1930–1992"). Two additional footnotes explain that the phrase *Laudamus te* means "We praise you," and that the anthem "uses a macaronic text, which most commonly connotes poetry that mixes Latin with the vernacular language." Music minister Nathan Skinner, who holds a bachelor of music degree from Gordon College and a masters in sacred music from Boston University, argues that this level of contextual detail is important. The congregation should know whether a piece of music is forty or four hundred years old. Furthermore, Skinner stresses that a hymn's text and tune are seldom written by the same person. By listing both the lyricist and the musical composer, Skinner explains,

Figure 2.2 Park Street Church sanctuary, choir loft in center balcony
Boston, Massachusetts: November 2016. Photo by author.

he is helping the congregation understand that music does not operate "on some sort of a prophetic singer-songwriter [all-in-one] model, where things just sort of come into being in a mysterious way."[43] Writing music for corporate worship is, in Skinner's words, "both a craft and a discipline."

After an organ prelude, an introit by the children's choir, and a call to worship from Psalm 18, the congregation sings the first hymn of the morning: "Now Thank We All Our God." Following a prayer of confession, the congregational recitation of the Lord's Prayer, and the passing of the peace, the adult choir sings the anthem "Summer Ended," music by Charles Wood (1866–1926) and words by Greville Phillimore (1821–1884). The words of the anthem are printed in the bulletin, and reflect the service's Thanksgiving theme with references to God's faithfulness during "seedtime, harvest, cold and heat."

A leader from the Young Adults Ministry comes to the platform and reads the morning scripture, Genesis 12:1–4, aloud to the congregation. "Hear now the word of the Lord," she announces:

> The Lord had said to Abram, "Leave your country, your people and your father's household and go to the land I will show you. I will make you into a great nation and I will bless you. I will make your name great and you will be a blessing. I will bless those who bless you and whoever curses you I will curse. And all peoples on earth will be blessed through you." So Abram left as the Lord had told him and Lot went with him. Abram was seventy-five years old when he set out from Haran. He took his wife Sarai, his nephew Lot, all the possessions they had accumulated and the people they had acquired in Haran. And they set out for the land of Canaan and they arrived there.

The reader concludes with the pronouncement, "This is the word of the Lord." The congregation responds in unison, "Thanks be to God."

Senior pastor Gordon Hugenberger takes the podium and starts his sermon. "Our text this morning in Genesis 12 is arguably one of the most important passages in all of scripture when it comes to the unfolding plan of God's work of redemption," he informs the congregation. Hugenberger explains that Genesis 12 is one of four "mountaintop promises on which one sees the whole vita of God's work." (The other three are Genesis 3:15, where God imbeds the promise of the gospel in his word of curse to the serpent after the fall; 2 Samuel 7, where God makes a covenant with David that is ultimately fulfilled in Jesus; and Jeremiah 31, where God promises a new covenant.) "You and I are heirs," Hugenberger reminds the congregation. "We are the seed of Abraham—the one through whom God's promises would ultimately be fulfilled corporately." In the words of the sermon title, the church has been "blessed to be a blessing."

Hugenberger asks members of the congregation to raise their hand if they have left a community at least five hundred miles away to come to the greater Boston area. Hugenberger notes that the politics, landscape, and weather patterns of New England are vastly different from those in the Midwest. "Everything about where your home was only seems to be highlighted by how different it is here," he suggests. Hugenberger asks for another show of hands: "How many of you set off for Boston when you were seventy-five or above?" Hugenberger points out that at this age, "no one is looking to get uprooted," as Abraham was.

The point Hugenberger is seeking to drive home is that discipleship always has a cost. It may not entail a geographic move, like Abraham's. "The path you're going on isn't a path from Boston to Boise," he stresses, "but a path from this world to the next." The "leaving" that counts is "leaving the old life, allowing Christ to be Lord, and living out the rest of your life here as a pilgrim—a sojourner whose citizenship is in heaven." As the sermon draws to a close, Hugenberger invites the congregation to consider the shape of verses 2 and 3. "There's a concentric outline of seven clauses in verses 2 and 3. The first three and the last three all have verbs in the indicative. The fourth clause—the punchline—is imperative," he stresses. Consider the following:

I will make you into a great nation (12:2a).
I will bless you (12:2b).
I will make your name great (12:2c).
You will be a blessing (12:2d).
I will bless those who bless you (12:3a).
The one who curses you I will curse (12:3b).
Through you, all the peoples of the earth shall be blessed (12:3c).

Hugenberger points out that "the first three [clauses] are about what God is going to do *for* you," while "the last three are about what God is going to do *through* you." The pivotal middle clause emphasizes the reader's responsibility: "You will be a blessing." "Underline the word *will* in your head," Hugenberger advises. "It's like when your mother said, 'You *will* eat your vegetables.' It's not a prophecy. It's not a suggestion. It's a command."

Hugenberger reminds the congregation that the offering that is about to be collected presents the church with the opportunity "to be a blessing, collectively, to the world." He then closes the sermon with a brief prayer, asking God to use the members of the congregation in their workplaces as a blessing to their coworkers, in their homes as a blessing to their neighborhoods, and in the country as a blessing to the nation. The congregation stands to sing the hymn "Lord, Whose Love through Humble Service." The final stanza of the hymn reminds participants they are "called from worship into service" by sharing God's abundant life with the world.

After the hymn has concluded, the Park Street Orchestra plays Mozart's *Church Sonata in D Major* while offering plates are passed down the rows of pews. When all the contributions have been collected, the congregation thanks God by singing the doxology, followed by the hymn "Come, Ye Thankful People, Come." The congregational singing is robust and well supported by the pipe organ, church orchestra, and swelling trumpet descants. After the triumphal climax of the hymn, a member of the pastoral staff dismisses the congregation with a benediction from Numbers 6:24–26: "The Lord bless you and keep you; the Lord make his face to shine on you and be gracious to you; the Lord turn his face toward you and give you peace."

Homiletical Analysis

A close reading of Pastor Hugenberger's sermon underscores several ways that Park Street Church remains in continuity with its theological and academic history. As a college student, Gordon Hugenberger sat under the teaching of Harold John Ockenga, who attended Westminster Theological Seminary (which, as we have seen, had broken away from Princeton Theological Seminary). Relatedly during his seminary years at Gordon-Conwell, Hugenberger was mentored by Old Testament scholar Meredith Kline, who taught for many years at Westminster. Clearly, Hugenberger stands in the theological tradition of Westminster, which carries on the theology of "Old Princeton." This training is evident in at least two ways in the sermon I have described.

First, like his theological mentors, Hugenberger is committed to Reformed covenantal theology. At the beginning of the sermon, Hugenberger stresses that God's relationship with Abraham is the key to understanding how the Old and New Testaments relate. He also notes that this is a point on which evangelical Christians often disagree. Congregations that espouse a dispensational theology (including Moody Church, which we will meet in the next chapter) emphasize the discontinuities between the two testaments. Classical dispensationalists posit a clear distinction between Israel and the church: they are *two* distinct peoples of God. God's promises to Israel are "earthly" (i.e., prosperity in the land of Palestine), while the church's inheritance is "heavenly." By contrast, Park Street's covenantal theology stresses the unity between Old and New Testaments, and the idea that there is only *one* people of God. In the words of Reformed theologian R. Scott Clark, "The church has always been the Israel of God and the Israel of God has always been the church."[44] In the same spirit, Hugenberger reminds the congregation that this covenantal "one people of God" perspective isn't simply a case of "modern theologians trying to put unity where there was none." Instead, it is a reflection of Galatians 3:8, where Paul writes, "Scripture foresaw that God would justify the Gentiles by faith, and announced the gospel in advance to Abraham saying, 'All nations will be blessed through you.'"

The second place Hugenberger's educational training is evident is in the way he approaches the biblical text. The conservative scholars who broke off from Princeton to form Westminster believed that the Bible was inerrant and could stand up to any charge the skeptical higher critics might try to lobby against it. God had so inspired the biblical authors that everything they recorded in the pages of scripture—including history, geography, biology, and theology—was entirely without error. Champions of conservative orthodoxy argued that the Bible made such claims for itself and that an unbiased investigation of internal evidence would prove it.

Robert Dick Wilson (1856–1930), one of the faculty members who left Princeton to assist in the founding of Westminster, is an excellent exemplar. In the preface to his *Scientific Investigation of the Old Testament* (1926), Wilson professed reliance upon "the evidential method," that is, "the Laws of Evidence as applied to documents admitted in our courts of law," to settle the most important interpretive questions.[45] The goal for conservatives was to beat higher critics at their own game, amassing evidence from paleography, Semitic cognates, and archaeological inscriptions, and matching liberal scholars footnote for footnote to prove that the Bible's historicity was completely trustworthy.[46]

The challenge for proving the historicity of Abraham and the book of Genesis is that very few significant archaeological remains from that period have survived. Two academic perspectives have emerged in response to this difficulty. "Minimalists" believe the Bible is a religious document that should not be read as an objective account. They assume the Old Testament is not historical unless proven otherwise. Historical critical scholars J. Maxwell Miller and John H. Hayes are representative of this minimalist view:

> We hold that the main story line of Genesis-Joshua-creation, pre-Flood patriarchs, great Flood, second patriarchal age, entrance into Egypt, twelve tribes descended from the twelve brothers, escape from Egypt, complete collections of laws and religious instructions handed down at Mt. Sinai, forty years of wandering in the wilderness, miraculous conquests of Canaan . . . is an artificial and theologically influenced literary construct.[47]

Conversely, "maximalist" scholars believe that until there is concrete evidence to the contrary, readers should assume that the events of the Old Testament happened as described. At stake for evangelicals is the Bible as God's inerrant (or infallible) word: the veracity of the history recounted in its pages is significant, and it cannot be regarded as fiction without significant theological loss. Therefore, maximalist biblical scholars Iain Provan, V. Philips Long, and Tremper Longman III argue that "theology is inextricably intertwined with *actual events*."[48] In direct opposition to the minimalist perspective, Provan, Long, and Longman insist:

> One cannot conceive of the original audience as thinking of Abraham as other than a real person, or of his movement from Ur to Haran to Canaan as other than a real journey. It is inconceivable that the author(s) of Genesis intended the audience to think these persons and events were other than "real." Scholars who use terms like "saga," "fiction," or "folklore" to describe the genre of the patriarchal narratives are therefore not so much telling us about the actual genre of the text as they are expressing their own lack of confidence (for whatever reasons) in the historical reliability of the materials.[49]

Provan, Philips, and Long follow the Old Princeton approach of taking the words of biblical writers at face value. They propose that by studying the grammar of the passage and working to understand the biblical statement in light of its historical background, a scholar can come to understand the intentions of the original author, which communicate God's own ideas. Next, the scholar can seek out convergences from archaeology, ancient records of the same event, and credible witnesses from the time in which the text was written. When these two lines of evidence are pursued independently and point in the same direction, the evangelical exegete can feel reasonably sure that the historical event in question actually took place.

Pastor Hugenberger follows this approach as well. In December 2001, Hugenberger offered an adult education class entitled "Evidences for the Historicity of the Bible." The first PowerPoint slide of his presentation read, "The following is a comprehensive list of every archaeological discovery that conclusively disproves the accuracy of the Bible." The second slide is blank. Hugenberger reminded the class that "there have been *no* such archaeological discoveries." Hugenberger went on to suggest that a number of biblical details have archaeological confirmation, including evidence that supports the historicity of the Bible's account of Abraham and the other patriarchs.

In the sermon I have sketched, Hugenberger is aware that critical biblical scholars assume that the story of Abraham was invented about 1000 BC. However, he rejects this historical-critical interpretation, instructing the Park Street Church congregation to "think of Abraham as having lived about as many years before Christ as we are now living after Christ. The date is about 2000 BC." Hugenberger draws on archaeology to paint a picture for the congregation: "With all the discoveries that have been made in the late twentieth century, we now have a pretty good idea of what life looked like during [the time of Abraham]. It wasn't just living in caves or huts." Pyramids had been standing for five hundred years, the great civilizations were a thousand years old, and literacy was reasonably widespread.

Other parts of the sermon nod to Hugenberger's maximalist understanding of scripture.

For example, Hugenberger suggests one of the challenges Abraham would have faced was that of learning a new language: "He would probably have been speaking an old Akkadian language where he was living, and would have needed to learn the Amorite language." Hugenberger explains that the two are sister languages with lots of shared vocabulary, but it would still have been a difficult transition, "like moving from German-speaking Europe to Dutch-speaking Europe."

In addition to language barriers, Hugenberger points out the challenge of Abraham's new living conditions. Ur of Haran—the city that Abraham left—had a thousand years of established civilization with an extensive library. Furthermore, it was a center of commerce. "We have evidence of imports coming from Afghanistan across Haran, then Ebla, then Ugarit, and ultimately to Cypress." The distance is approximately two thousand miles—the equivalent of going from Boston to Salt Lake City, Utah. Hugenberger cites archaeological evidence from the nearby city of Ebla, where over two thousand clay tablets were discovered in 1974 and 1975. "In these tablets, you have administrative text, and we learn that textiles, foods of various kinds, and wine were all being passed through Haran." By contrast, Canaan—the land to which Abraham was called—was a backwater, with no comparable libraries or architecture. In his exegesis, Hugenberger clearly assumes that Abraham was a historical person and that the historicity of his journey in Genesis can be corroborated by archaeological evidence.

Musical Analysis

Park Street's biblical and musical hermeneutics are strikingly congruent. In his sermon preparation, Pastor Hugenberger first determined the genre and context of the Genesis passage, then confirmed the veracity of its truth claims by showing how they coalesced with both extra-biblical evidence and other passages of scripture. When music minister Nathan Skinner first came to Park Street, many congregants told him that their church "has always held a high view of worship." Skinner approached this claim like a maximalist biblical scholar: he sought out secondary archaeological—or in this case, archival—evidence to substantiate it. (In his own telling of the story, Skinner emphasizes that he was not satisfied by mere congregational hearsay: "My thought was, 'Show me.'")

The Congregational Library and Archives is located about a block away from Park Street Church. The library, a national repository for papers and artifacts related to eighteenth- to twenty-first-century American Congregational history, houses all of Park Street Church's most important historical documents. While browsing the collection, Skinner was delighted to discover a ledger from the Park Street Singing Society, a church-associated group founded in 1810. The ledger records that soon after the organization of Park Street Church, and several months before construction of the building was complete, several individuals met to discuss how worship should be conducted in the new facility. According to the document, worship in the newly erected church should "increase devotional feelings," "elevate the affections," and "cultivate a taste for scientific music." The society's aim was to "introduce into the sanctuary . . . tunes of a character more strictly *sacred* than were in use of the churches of that day"; specifically, "the plain and solid music of the old masters" was to be used, rather than the "light and fuging music" commonly employed by other churches of the day.[50]

Some historical parsing can help us understand why members of the Park Street Singing Society championed "scientific music" over the "light and fuging music" common in the mid-1800s. In the decades preceding the American Revolution, a new style of sacred music had developed in the American colonies. Protestant churches across New England began singing from books of hymn tunes published by local musicians like William Billings—a talented, self-taught musician who worked as a tanner by trade. Billings invented a lively new way of setting hymns and anthems, which came to be known as the fuging style. Composers of this music used unconventional methods. Their melodies have been aptly described as "a commingling of fiddle tunes, psalms, ballads, camp-meeting tunes, and anthems."[51] They wrote each line of their three- or four-part hymns separately, emphasizing polyphony rather than vertical harmonic lines. The music was full of dance-like syncopation, unresolved dissonances, and parallel and open fifths: crude harmonic "mistakes" according to the rigid European conservatory rules of the time.[52] Further flouting convention, songs were often written in "shape note": a system of triangles, rectangles, and diamonds that helped musically uneducated persons learn the tunes.

The power of fuguing music came from hearing it performed. An 1882 article in *The Atlantic* described the sound as vivacious, with "voice parts moving in a sort of mutual imitation in quick time, chasing one another around."[53] The tradition, now called "Sacred Harp singing," lives on today in the Deep South. In a 2003 news story profiling the musical genre, NPR reporter Melissa Block observed that Sacred Harp singing "isn't at all like the soaring tones of traditional gospel music. . . . This is full-body, shout-it-out singing. The harmonies are stark and haunting—raw, even. In Sacred Harp, you don't want a sweet sound."[54]

The "scientific music" that early Park Street Church members championed was a genre that developed in reaction to the popular fuging style of singing. Thomas Hastings (1784–1872), who wrote the first important philosophical treatise on music by an American-born author, and Lowell Mason (1792–1872), the famous composer and music educator, were two of the earliest and strongest advocates of the scientific approach.[55] Scientific music focused on "regular harmonies, stately melodies, and on tunes and arrangements that members of the congregation could sing well if they were given a little bit of choir practice."[56]

Hastings, Mason, and their like-minded colleagues sought to write music that adhered to the musical rules laid out by Handel and Hayden. They spurned melodies that had secular associations. Most importantly, scientific musicians believed the texts of sacred music should be elevated above all musical embellishments. In his description of fuging music, Billings rejoiced that

> while each [voice] part is thus striving for mastery, and sweetly contending for victory, the audience are most luxuriously entertained, and exceedingly delighted in the meantime, their minds are surprisingly agitated, and extremely fluctuated; sometimes declaring in favour of one part, and sometimes another. Now the solemn bass demands the attention, now the manly tenor, now the lofty counter, now the volatile treble, now here, now there, now here again—O inchanting! [sic] O ecstatic! Push on, push on ye sons of harmony. [57]

This description neatly summed up one of the critics' strongest objections to fuguing tunes: because the four voice parts staggered and overlapped their musical entries, the words of the song were greatly obscured. (Think of the song "Row, Row, Row Your Boat." When sung as a round, the intelligibility of the words is less important than the integrity of the harmonies.)

As a corrective, Mason argued that church music be "simple, chaste, correct, and free of ostentation."[58] Music in the scientific style would rely on homophonic block harmony rather than counterpoint. Relatedly, Mason insisted that texts "be handled with as much care as the music" so that the two might work together "to convey a single feeling, mood, or idea."[59] Two famous examples of scientific music include Mason's "Nearer My God to Thee" and Hasting's melody TOPLADY, which undergirds the hymn text "Rock of Ages."

The Park Street Singing Society embraced Mason's strictures. The ledger reports that the group met every week and spent a great portion of the time "drilling upon what would be considered by singers of the present day as *dull music*."[60] Undaunted by the naysayers, the Society pressed on: "It was then deemed important that the *words* and the *music* should be properly combined, and that the former should be so distinctly enunciated that the singing should be with *understanding*."[61]

Fast-forward to the twenty-first century, where Skinner carries forward the same ethos at Park Street. He becomes animated when discussing the hymn "And Can It Be," a favorite of Gordon Hugenberger. Skinner acknowledges that the melodic line can be difficult to sing: "It has a really wide range, it has lots of notes, and they go by very quickly. In some ways, it's like 'The Star-Spangled Banner'— it goes very high and very low—and yet we keep singing it." Skinner continues in the vein of his nineteenth-century colleagues: "The energy and exuberance of a person saved by the blood of Jesus Christ finds an outlet in a melody like this. There's really no other option: any tune that were less would not really fit the text that we're singing."

Skinner is equally passionate about the hymn "When I Survey the Wondrous Cross," which is sung to different tunes in the United States and Great Britain. The melody most familiar to American congregations is named HAMBURG. Skinner observes that HAMBURG "has a very limited range: every note is next to every other note. It's very constricted—sort of the opposite of 'And Can It Be.' That's a natural reaction to surveying our Lord on the cross," he continues. "When you're hit with tragedy, you're not going to use big, flowery words and wide ranges. You think of the blues: very short phrases, limited in range in certain contexts. In a sense, that would seem to reflect the text pretty well." The Park Street Church congregation, however, sings this hymn to the tune of ROCKINGHAM, the melody more widely used in Canada and Great Britain (Figure 2.3). Skinner explains the

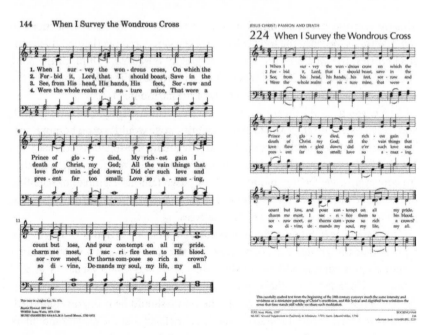

Figure 2.3 HAMBURG tune on left; ROCKINGHAM tune on right

rationale for this decision: "[ROCKINGHAM] has a much wider range. It's also in triple meter: it has multiple notes per syllable, so it feels much more expansive and free." Skinner sees an important theological correlation between text and tune: "I think that for the Christian, when we survey the wondrous cross, what we should be surveying is not principally the sadness of Christ dying, but the beauty and joy and goodness of our salvation accomplished through it."

Skinner's description of his interview for the position at Park Street Church underscores his musical priorities. "I said, 'Look, if you want someone who's going to come in and tell you that the music in the morning and evening services are like two different flavors of ice cream—different but equally good—you can find that person. If you want someone to tell you that we just haven't had a chance to sift through all the new songs, and that them some of them will have the longevity of Charles Wesley's hymns, there are certainly many people who are willing to say that. But that's not me, and I don't think that's Park Street.' "

Skinner knows that Park Street Church is an outlier. Most twenty-first-century evangelical churches have chosen commercialized, rock-infused worship music over organs, robed choirs, and traditional hymns. Skinner himself feels more affinity with historical, traditional practices of worship but stresses that he has never sought to impose his preferences on the congregation: "I certainly don't have it in me to sell the argument to a church like this that we need to do something just because it's what *I* think we need to do, or because *I* think it's good." This is precisely what Skinner appreciates about the historical ledger: "It tells me that Park Street's musical philosophy is not just *my* narrative. We are continuing on exactly what the church was doing in its founding." He reads aloud one of his favorite lines: "To introduce into the sanctuary . . . tunes of a character more strictly *sacred* than were in use of the churches of that day." "This document affirms that Park Street's worship sounds stately and set apart—some might even say 'dull'—and that decision is intentional," he notes approvingly.

Continuing Challenges

Park Street Church's commitment to worship music that sounds "stately and set apart" has not gone unquestioned. In 1992, Associate Minister Daniel Harrell was charged with bringing "contemporary worship" to Park Street's then-dying evening service. Instead of mixing old and new music within a single service, the church decided to offer "traditional" music in the morning service and "contemporary" music in the evening service. Walter Kim, associate minister at the time of my study, attended Park Street Church as a graduate student during these years. "The rest of the country had already introduced contemporary worship in the 1990s," Kim explains, "but New England didn't really catch on to the trend. When Park Street Church introduced contemporary worship to the metro Boston area, no other downtown churches had anything like it. College students were like, 'Wow! This is something we can't get anywhere else.'" Subsequently, the new Sunday night service attracted students from Harvard, MIT, and Boston University, as well as young adults who rented apartments downtown or drove in from the suburbs.

By 1995, the evening service was drawing six hundred young adults; three years later, in 1998, attendance jumped to over eight hundred. By 2003, even the *Boston Globe* had taken notice. In a lengthy article, the *Globe* reported that Park Street Church had become "the flagship church for college evangelicals from about 20 campuses in the Boston area. . . . These days more than 1,000 students show up at Park Street Church most Sunday evenings."[62] The church added a second evening service to accommodate the large student crowds. At one point, these two Sunday evening services represented 40 percent of Park Street's weekly attendance.[63]

However, shortly after the *Boston Globe* article was published, Park Street's evening service numbers began to decline sharply: from 816 attendees in 2004 to 263 attendees in 2015.[64] At least three grounds can be cited for this shift:

1. In the early 2000s, the church made a strategic decision to shift more attention and resources to family ministries. In short order, the congregation hired its first full-time family minister, a full-time youth pastor, and several part-time directors for children's ministry programs. Consequentially, the number of three- to twelve-year-olds at the church grew steadily: from 200 in 2005 to 294 in 2015—a net gain of 47 percent.[65]

2. The number of immigrant churches in Boston doubled between the 1960s and 2000—a phenomenon scholars have dubbed Boston's "quiet revival." Much of the increase is due to the growth of immigrant-focused evangelical and Pentecostal churches. Boston College historian Marilynn Johnson explains that "during the 1950s and 1960s, Christian student groups at local universities were the seedbed for new churches serving more educated Asian immigrants."[66] In the South End of the city, Puerto Rican Pentecostals organized several new churches that became the foundations of a dynamic Latino Pentecostal movement in Boston.[67] Haitians, Brazilians, and Africans also proved to be avid Protestant church builders. Gordon-Conwell Theological Seminary became a training ground for immigrant ministries, working with Park Street Church and other established evangelical churches to spread the gospel among the city's newcomers.[68]

3. Missionary activity increased among non-immigrants. With its reputation for progressive thought and distinctly secular intellectual culture, Boston has long presented a special challenge for missionaries. Recall Ockenga's

1942 characterization of New England as an "arid waste" and "mission field" from which evangelicals had been "frozen out."[69] Just over seventy years later, in 2014, Boston-based Pastor Joe Souza estimated that "only 3% of the population in the greater Boston area knows Jesus as their personal savior."[70] Christians from other parts of the country began relocating to New England, motivated by the concerns voiced by Southern Baptist theologian Albert Mohler: "New England, like Europe, is fast becoming a post-Christian culture. And, as the late Lesslie Newbigin reminded us, evangelizing a post-Christian culture will be far more difficult than evangelizing a culture that never knew Christian commitments. As New England has followed Europe, will the rest of the nation follow New England?"[71]

Between 1980 and 2000, the number of Protestant churches in Boston more than doubled.[72] This rapid influx of new churches meant that for the first time in its history Park Street needed to "compete" with other churches for young adults and college students.

Compete is in many ways an inaccurate descriptor of the historic church's relationship to the newcomers. When its evening services were nearing capacity in the early 2000s, Park Street Church advertised new church plants and churches in the suburbs on its own website. Today, Park Street Church senior leaders are deliberately generous with their time and advice, fielding calls for advice from the younger, less-experienced leaders of the new churches. The spirit of friendship and cooperation they cultivate harkens back to the ethos of the New England Fellowship and, later, the National Association of Evangelicals. In his 1942 address to the assembly that would later become the National Association of Evangelicals, Ockenga noted that there were "many lone wolves in ministry today" who had been blessed by God in their individual endeavors. Ockenga warned that unless evangelicals were "willing to run in a pack," they faced annihilation.[73]

However, Park Street Church's spirit of cooperation has also had unintended consequences. "It used to be the case that Park Street was the only game in town if you were a student looking for an evangelical church," Skinner reflects. Pastors from out-of-state would counsel their Massachusetts-bound college freshmen, "Go to Park Street. It's [theologically] solid, and you're in Boston, the bastion of liberalism." Today, college students can pick from among a wider array of offerings in the city. "You find solid people who say, 'We all go to Aletheia' or 'We all go to Reality Boston' [two of the newer church plants]. Now that's there's more than one option, it takes a little more to convince students that they should choose Park Street," Skinner observes. The church's concern about the decline in college-age attendees is not simply about raw numbers. Another staffer explained to me, "Park Street's imperative is to be making disciples. If the college-age demographic isn't in the church, it means that nobody's bringing their unsaved friends. When you're in a dorm setting, it's easy to ask 'Hey, want to check out my church?' That doesn't happen when you're in your forties."

Walter Kim explains that the questions with which Park Street Church is currently grappling are those of identity and balance. "Historically, we've had this great ministry to college students who, in turn, go out all over the country and the world. We don't want to lose the ability to influence the next generation of Christians, but we also want to maintain the recent gains we've had in the area of family ministries." As Park Street's annual report stated in 2015, "Boston has been called 'the Athens of America' because of the defining presence of more than 100 colleges and universities in the metropolitan area with more than a quarter of a million students. How can we step out in faith and obedience, as we did in the past, to reach a much greater proportion of this spiritually needy population?"

Practical musical considerations are inherent in this question. College students and young adults—the population most likely to attend the evening service—are transient, arriving and leaving on a regular four-year cycle. However, individuals with long-term investment in Park Street Church—both monetary and temporal—have told the leadership that contemporary worship music makes no sense to them. Kim describes this as a "mushroom" situation: "We have a huge [evening] gathering of a diverse student population that's being financially supported by a narrow stem of older, long-term folks. The power structures are such that there's a reason why contemporary music is only kept in the evening and never introduced in the morning." Kim notes that ideally the distribution of resources across morning and evening services would be more equitable.

Nathan Skinner sees the situation very differently. Whereas Kim was happy to use the terms "traditional" and "contemporary" as a shorthand for describing Park Street's morning and evening services, Skinner is not. "We intentionally do not use those words on our website or any public-facing materials," he clarifies. "The 4:00 p.m. service just says, 'Sunday night band' and the morning services say, 'choir and organ.'" The terms "traditional" and "contemporary" are not nuanced enough for Skinner, who stresses that all of Park Street's services are both.

Skinner explains the difference between morning and evening services this way. "Morning services are self-consciously in full continuity with an unfolding two-thousand-year tradition and the western Church's musical development." Skinner has occasionally used Gregorian chant in the morning services. ("I put a little contextual note in the bulletin saying something like 'Wouldn't it be great if we knew what music the earliest Christians used? Listen to some Coptic chant and compare it to this . . . there are similarities.'") Skinner will also occasionally program "modern hymns" by composers like Townend and Getty in the morning services. However, the pieces the morning congregation most enjoys singing tend to fall between these two historical extremes. Skinner cites "O God beyond All Praising" and "O Love, How Deep, How Broad, How High" as hymns that are sung with particular gusto.

By contrast, the evening service is less interested in covering two thousand years of musical history. Instead, it focuses on developments of the last two hundred years, taking its cues from the music that came out of American revivalism. Skinner explains:

> I would say that in the 4:00 p.m. service, it's considered more desirable for the music to have an immediate emotional impact. Now, if something doesn't have an immediate emotional impact in the morning services, I don't consider that a problem: I know what the music is going to do over time, and I've selected the repertoire for its staying power.

For example, Skinner recalls introducing the hymn "This Is the Night" (sung to the tune INTERCESSOR) to the congregation during a Maundy Thursday service:

> I got an email after a guy who, after four years of singing ["This Is the Night"] said, "I have trouble with hymns, but this hymn, somehow the shape of the melody . . ." Basically, he suddenly got it and everything snapped into focus. He loves the hymn now, but it took him four years to get there.

Skinner notes that if a song doesn't grab the people in the evening service the first time it is sung, "That's a strike against it. The emotional appeal of a song is a factor in both services, but especially in the evening, where the desired emotional trajectory is shorter."

Skinner compares the musical differences between morning and evening services to the gender debates between egalitarians and complementarians that have raged within evangelicalism since at least the 1970s. Egalitarians believe that the rulership of Adam over Eve was a result of the fall, not part of the original created order. Accordingly, in a marriage relationship, husbands and wives are bound together by mutual submission and responsibility. In the same way, Walter Kim sees morning and evening services as nonhierarchical partners: different in musical style, but equal in function. A person could attend either service and receive comparable benefit. Conversely, Skinner would characterize the relationship between morning and evening services as complementarian. Gender complementarians believe that while men and women are equal "in dignity, value, essence and human nature," they occupy two distinctive roles: namely, "The female [is] to offer willing, glad-hearted and submissive assistance to the man."[74] In the same way, morning and evening services have distinct, complementary roles.

As Skinner explained it to me, in morning worship, Park Street is committed to using "the sacred music that the church tradition has to offer." Music in the evening service plays a different role. As the church's document on its philosophy of worship states,

> The evening service was originally conceived as an outreach to new Christians and those considering the Faith. The music is meant to be immediately accessible, with culturally familiar musical and lyrical forms. While the music in continuity with past centuries of worship has many benefits, those benefits may not be realized by a worshipper for whom the music and poetry are as unfamiliar and inaccessible as a foreign language. The evening music is an additional opportunity to approach that most basic shared goal: singing praise to God.[75]

"It's not a devaluing of the evening service to say that it's trying to accomplish something different than the morning service," Skinner stresses. "To say that both are 'created equal' does a disservice to the evening service by trying to shoehorn it into something that it's not."

Furthermore, Skinner strongly critiques the "mushroom" perspective in which a narrow stem of older congregants financially support ministries for younger generations: "Having a truly intergenerational congregation means valuing older folks for their wisdom, not their money." Skinner notes that many young people eventually leave the evening service in favor of the morning service. Sometimes they do so because they have married and started families: morning services have comprehensive children's programs. But Skinner—who is in his early thirties, married, and the father of young children—believes that his peers are also beginning to develop a greater appreciation for worship music that can stand the test of time. "When's the last time you heard someone sing, 'Lord, I Lift Your Name on High?'" he asks pointedly.[76] "My generation is starting to realize that all the songs we once thought were so meaningful can't be passed down to our children."

In the end, these conversations are about much more than finances and musical repertoire. At stake is the question of how God works in history. One significant critique of Reformed covenantal theology is that it does not adequately account for the fact that God can move in surprising and unexpected ways. As biblical scholar Ben Witherington writes, "Sometimes this way of interpreting the New Testament so heavily in light of the Old Testament has led to the elimination of the whole notion that much new is even going on in the New Testament."[77] Instead, the New Testament is seen as the fulfillment, completion, or perfect expression of the Old Testament. Some members of Park Street Church might ask a related question: has the church focused too much on fulfilling the founders' original vision, without allowing for the possibility of genuinely new twenty-first-century developments?

Walter Kim affirms the importance of having worship that "connects us with the history of the church." At the same time, he points out that "the drawback is maybe an inability to ask the question, 'What does it look like to be missional now, in our context, in the way that Park Street Church conducts worship?'" Kim believes this question needs to be asked of homiletics as well as music. While Park Street Church has long been committed to academic evangelism, Kim worries that the pendulum has swung too far:

> There are a lot of bright people in the Boston area, but given the low level of biblical literacy in the culture right now, you can have a Nobel Laureate come to our church and actually be befuddled by our sermon. You can no longer assume a base level of common religious language and knowledge. Gordon [Hugenberger] has talked about how even some professors have come up to him and said, "You know, you lost me on some of this." The congregation doesn't have the kind of general background that, twenty years ago, we could have banked on.

Kim respects churches that are able to worship God, edify believers, and provide an entry point for those with no prior biblical background or church experience. "That's a conversation Park Street needs to continue to have," he concludes. "Honestly, I don't think we've resolved it."

3

"Suddenly We're in a Different Era"

Navigating Transition in Chicago

Early in my visit to Chicago, Moody Church senior pastor Erwin Lutzer was eager to help me pinpoint his congregation's location on a theoretical map of American Protestantism. "Harold John Ockenga was one of the people who began what became known as evangelicalism," Lutzer explained, "and the difference between it and fundamentalism was that evangelicalism was going to engage culture and the world, rather than the isolation [of the fundamentalists] that took place after the Scopes trial." Lutzer offered his paraphrase of the events of the 1940s: "Ockenga said, 'We need a new evangelicalism with a better face that engages culture.' And that's who we [at Moody Church] are."

Given the subject of the previous chapter, it is particularly interesting that Pastor Lutzer drew an immediate connection between Park Street's most famous pastor, Ockenga, and the Chicago evangelist for whom his church is named: Dwight L. Moody (1837–1899). The two congregations intersected at several historical moments. Park Street pastor A. Z. Conrad was born on November 26, 1855, only seven months after the eighteen-year-old Moody converted to evangelical Christianity, and always considered Moody to be a role model.[1]

Moody, who was born in Northfield, Massachusetts, established a vital summer conference series in his hometown that did much to keep revival fires burning across New England. Moody's three-month evangelistic campaign in Boston (1877) had its origins in a meeting held in the Park Street Church vestry.[2] And at one point in Ockenga's Park Street pastorate, Moody Church tried (unsuccessfully) to lure the Bostonian pastor into a position of leadership in the Chicago congregation.[3] Moody Church is only fifty years younger than Park Street Church, and like its New England counterpart, the Chicago congregation regularly faces questions about how best to continue the church's storied legacy and historical identity in the face of twenty-first-century challenges. It has brokered a solution in keeping with the dispensational theology of its heritage.

This chapter begins with a brief history of Dwight L. Moody and the church that bears his name. In the next section, I discuss why Moody Church is a tile that requires special handling in the evangelical mosaic: critics, sympathizers, and academic historians regularly debate about whether to classify its unique

Evangelical Worship. Melanie C. Ross, Oxford University Press. © Oxford University Press 2021.
DOI: 10.1093/oso/9780197530757.003.0004

theological hue as "fundamentalist," "moderate," or "liberal." After a description of a Sunday worship service, I show how the dispensationalism popularized by founding father Dwight L. Moody continues to influence the congregation's theology of worship today. Dispensationalists believe that while many of God's commands apply at all times to all people, others are more directly applied to specific dispensations of time or only to the nation of Israel. Dispensationalists believe that some of God's commands carry through from one dispensation to the next, while others can be modified, added to, or discontinued. Relatedly, Moody adheres to a philosophy of music that draws on a variety of eras: some songs stand the generational test of time, others from a previous era have been phased out, and new repertoire is regularly introduced.

Church History

Dwight L. Moody was born on February 5, 1837, on a remote farm in rural Massachusetts. He was the sixth of nine children, and his alcoholic father died unexpectedly when Moody was four years old. Moody dropped out of school in fifth grade to help support the family's needs, but when he turned seventeen, he went to Boston in search of opportunity. Moody sold shoes in his uncle's shop in Boston, working toward a personal goal of amassing a fortune of $100,000. One of his uncle's conditions was that Moody attend the Congregational Church of Mount Vernon. In 1855 Moody, who had been raised in a Unitarian church, converted to Christianity and began his career as an evangelist.

Two years later, on impulse, Moody relocated to the city of Chicago. Horrified by the plight of the homeless children who wandered the city's dangerous streets, he gave up his business ventures and turned to full-time ministry. In 1858, he started a Sunday school for impoverished children in a red-light district to the north of the Chicago River. His class met first in an abandoned freight car, then in a vacant saloon on Michigan Street. Moody enticed underclass immigrant children to his mission with free candy and pony rides and drew in adults through his evening prayer meetings and English classes. Moody, by all accounts a spellbinding teacher, was soon reaching some fifteen hundred children and their parents each week. The Sunday school became so large that the former mayor of Chicago gave Moody rent-free space over the city's North Market for his meetings. On November 25, 1860, President-elect Abraham Lincoln visited Moody's Sunday school, which further bolstered the evangelist's reputation in the city.

In 1864, twenty-seven-year-old Moody opened the Illinois Independent Church, the seed from which Moody Church grew. Seven years later, this building was destroyed in the Great Chicago Fire. Moody quickly rebuilt a makeshift structure, the Northside Tabernacle, which served both as a church and as a relief center for those who had lost everything in the conflagration. Soon after, in 1873, Moody accepted an invitation to conduct a series of evangelistic missions in England, Scotland, and Ireland. Together with song leader Ira D. Sankey, he preached gospel messages to crowds of thousands. Moody and Sankey developed a hymnbook, *Sacred Songs and Solos* (later called *Gospel Hymns and Songs*), which grew out of the music performed prior to each of Moody's messages. The book sold more than eight million copies and raised $35,000—money that Moody and Sankey donated to rebuilding the church back in Chicago. Many of the songs Moody and Sankey popularized in their book, including "Rock of Ages," "Onward Christian Soldiers," "It Is Well with My Soul," "Jesus Loves Me," and "Blessed Assurance," are still sung in churches today.

When Moody and Sankey returned home from their two-year tour, they were hailed as celebrities. Moody received invitations to hold crusades in Brooklyn, Philadelphia, New York, and other main North American population centers. For the remainder of his life, the evangelist traveled extensively—some estimate a million miles—and preached revival sermons to overflow crowds. In 1886, Moody established a Bible Institute that would eventually bear his name.[4] If Fuller was the academic "Princeton of the West," Moody Bible Institute was conservative Protestantism's "West Point." Moody wanted his institution to produce "gap-men"—people who could "stand between the laity and the ministers" by going into the city to do mission work among the factory and shop workers who remained largely outside the church.[5] Students were not required to learn Hebrew or Greek. For Moody, time was of the essence, and evangelism was imperative.

As Moody's reputation grew, so too did attendance at the church he had founded, causing the congregation to relocate as it outgrew a succession of buildings. In 1925, the congregation settled into its permanent (and present-day) home at the corners of North Avenue, Clark Street, and LaSalle Street. Although D. L. Moody died in 1899 without having pastored, or even attended, the building that bears his name today, he remains the church's guiding spirit.

A Contested Legacy

Over the course of his lifetime, Moody created a network with three institutional legs: large, autonomous urban churches; Bible institutes; and independent missionary organizations. However, Michael Hamilton notes that despite this large theological footprint, "the movement centered on Moody never gave itself a name, and historians have yet to figure out what to call it."[6] The difficulty in classifying the "Moody movement" is that Moody was a peacemaker during his life, not a fighter. He frequently invited liberal Christians like Josiah Strong (a proponent of the social gospel), Henry Drummond (one of the earliest and most popular exponents of evolutionary theology), and William Rainey Harper (New Testament scholar and later president of the University of Chicago) to speak at his summer conferences alongside his network of conservative friends.[7] Biographer James F. Findlay rightly observes that behind a "facade of apparent unbending conservatism" lurked a "refreshing common sense" that allowed Moody to consider and learn from a variety of perspectives.[8] When Moody liked someone as a person, he was willing to overlook the fact that he disliked their theological opinions.

Moreover, Moody stayed out of major controversies of his day, including political campaigns to outlaw the teaching of evolution in schools. Because the survival of his network depended upon appealing to a broad spectrum of conservative Christians, Moody spent his time promoting noncontroversial subjects like evangelism, missions, Bible teaching, and prayer—topics that would not divide his constituents or shrink his support base. As a result, the Moody network attracted individuals whose primary commitment was not to a denomination, but to Moody's unique interdenominational vision of Christianity. This ecumenical ethos rankled liberals and conservatives within the denominations: both groups complained that the Moody network people were "disloyal."[9]

Moody died more than two decades before Henry Emerson Fosdick preached his famous 1922 sermon, "Shall the Fundamentalists Win?" Fosdick proclaimed that there was a great battle in the church between "fundamentalists" and "modernists" or liberals. Fosdick did not accuse those who simply held conservative theological opinions of being the problem: he granted that there was room for debate. The problem, he argued, was that self-described fundamentalists were "driving in their stakes to mark out the deadline of doctrine around the church, across which no one is to pass except on terms of agreement."[10] Fosdick argued that the virgin birth had not been mentioned by either Paul or John, and doctrines like biblical inerrancy, premillennial belief, and opposition to evolution could not be found in any of the historic creeds: there was little warrant to claim that they were "essential." How would Dwight L. Moody have responded?

Protestants of all stripes were quick to claim Moody's legacy for their side. Conservatives at Moody Bible Institute championed the evangelist as their own, rightly stressing the importance Moody had placed on the doctrine of premillennialism and his concerns about higher criticism. (During his life, Moody claimed that higher criticism was "ruining revival work and emptying the churches" because it robbed believers of the religious confidence necessary for evangelism.)[11]

However, Dwight Moody's two sons, Will and Paul, had a different vision for their father's legacy. In 1920, Will Moody wrote to Moody Bible Institute, stating that he could no longer "recommend any young person . . . attend the Institute" or take "its correspondence courses." The reason, Will explained, was that he had heard of "an organization" that refused "to employ any further graduates of the Institute in their work" because they were schismatic and "pharisaical," making premillennialism "the touchstone of orthodoxy" and thus a "point of 'cleavage'" rather than "of union between Christian people." Will concluded that Moody Bible Institute had "departed from the spirit and attitude of my father." Shortly after Fosdick's 1922 sermon, Will asked the president to cease using the name "Moody" in connection with the institute.[12] In 1923, Will's more liberal younger brother, Paul, even wrote a public letter to the *Christian Century*, suggesting that "were he living today," Dwight L. Moody would be "more in sympathy" with men "like Fosdick," who preached "the love of God and the power of Christ," than with the fundamentalists persecuting them because "they will not subscribe to certain shibboleths." By 1920s standards, Paul admitted that his father was "a conservative," but pointed out that Moody "was, *for those days*, a liberal."[13]

Warren Wiersbe, pastor of Moody Church from 1971 to 1978, describes a similar experience of feeling caught between "conservative" and "liberal" labels. In his book *Be Myself: The Autobiography of a Bridge Builder*, Wiersbe stresses that he is, "without apology," a "doctrinal fundamentalist" who affirms the inerrancy of scripture, the deity of Christ, and his virgin birth, and the atoning death, bodily resurrection, and second coming of Christ.[14] Yet Wiersbe notes that during his years of ministry, the ecclesiastical situation in which he operated was both difficult and slippery: "The test of your Christianity depended on the people you fellowshipped with and the leaders who influenced you."[15] Fundamentalist Christianity was highly fractious. Colleagues in ministry quickly turned on one another over slight disagreements, branding their former friends as "apostates, liberals, compromisers, [and] neo-evangelicals."[16]

Wiersbe experienced this discrimination firsthand. For ten years, Wiersbe had run a ministry in Kentucky of which fundamentalists approved. However, upon relocating to Chicago and assuming leadership of Moody Church, "I became suspect. Within a few years, my attackers were calling me a compromiser and a neo-evangelical."[17] Any time Wiersbe mentioned a "disapproved" writer or preacher in a *Moody Monthly* column, he received mail from readers who accused him of being a liberal. When Billy Graham's associate evangelist spoke at Moody Church in 1976, Wiersbe reports that he "got blamed for causing both [Moody Church] and [Moody Bible Institute] to apostatize!"[18]

Left of Fundamentalist, Right of Evangelical

Today, the most useful description of Moody Church's theological position comes from an interviewee who described the congregation as "left of fundamentalist, but right of evangelical." Senior Pastor Erwin Lutzer was quick to affirm his predecessor's analysis: "All evangelicals were fundamentalists at one time," Lutzer stressed, "and it's the fundamentalist faith that we [at Moody Church] hold to." But although the church today aligns itself with the conservative theology of *The Fundamentals*, it has also taken steps to distance itself from the brand of fundamentalism that developed in the 1970s and 1980s, when conservative Protestants became active in American politics. The key figure during this time was Jerry Falwell, televangelist, Independent Baptist pastor, and founder of Liberty University. Falwell and other religious conservatives were alarmed by a number of national developments, including the civil rights movement, the women's movement, the gay rights movement, and US Supreme Court rulings that banned institutionally initiated group prayer and Bible reading in public schools and that affirmed the legal right to abortion. In 1979, Falwell founded the Moral Majority—a political lobbying group that advanced conservative social values. Falwell's strategy for uniting strategy cultural conservatives was enormously effective: the Moral Majority quickly grew to several million members and is credited with helping Republican Ronald Reagan win the 1980 presidential election. It remained a strong force for the next decade, but dissolved in 1989 after several prominent evangelists, including Jim Bakker and Jimmy Swaggart, became embroiled in scandal.

While Lutzer is eager to embrace the *fundamentalist* label on questions of doctrine, he has long worried about entanglement of church and politics. Lutzer takes a pessimistic view of human efforts to usher in the Kingdom of God. There is no theological reason to hope for the betterment of the world until the return of Christ. In Lutzer's words, "Laws are limited in their power; they cannot make people good, nor can they make godly families. Our [Christian] message must be more radical than any governmental policy could possibly be."[19] Furthermore, favoring one political party risks alienating individuals who align with the other. Lutzer fears that "the unwise intertwining of evangelicalism and right-wing politics" creates "a stumbling block to many who might otherwise be open to the message of Christianity."[20]

If fundamentalists have hidden the cross under the American flag, Lutzer worries that "seeker-sensitive" evangelical churches (like the one we will meet in the next chapter) have obscured the cross in a different but equally egregious way. He reflects, "When England was going from being a theistic country to becoming the largely post-Christian country it is today, an author remarked that during the transition period the cross was preached, but it was so bedecked with flowers that nobody could see it."[21] For Lutzer, the phrase "the cross bedecked with flowers" concisely describes the problem with seeker-sensitive evangelicalism. He explains,

In many evangelical churches, the Word of God is not faithfully taught. Even among those who believe its message, there are many who choose to focus on some of the more positive aspects of Scripture, without declaring "The whole counsel of God" as the saying goes. As a result, the Gospel itself lies buried amid a host of other priorities and so-called "practical" matters.[22]

Lutzer offers the example of "a Muslim family" that "recently converted to Christianity at great personal cost." In Lutzer's recounting, the family visited a large, well-known evangelical church "with the hope they would hear instruction from God's word. Instead, the pastor preached a sermon on the benefits of good nutrition."[23] For Lutzer, this kind of preaching is the equivalent of spiritual malpractice. Time is fleeting; the day of the Lord is coming like a thief in the night (2 Peter 3:10). Subsequently, Christians "should not invest our time and dollars in dispensing good advice, but rather Good News."[24]

In short, Moody Church is trying to chart a middle course between the cultural denial of fundamentalism and the cultural accommodation of evangelicalism. Lutzer further stresses that Moody must be a church that is both "repulsive to the world because of our authentic holiness and yet very attractive to the world because of our love and care."[25] An inside look at a Sunday morning service shows how the congregation walks this tightrope.

Service Description

If a visitor to Boston set out in search of Park Street Church, they would easily locate the building by its quintessential red brick facade and tall white steeple. By contrast, a visitor to Chicago would have a difficult time identifying Moody Church without the benefit of signage.

John Fugard, whose architectural firm Fugard and Knapp designed the church building, reported in 1925 that Moody Church "presented an opportunity unique in ecclesiastical architecture."[26] The building needed to be able to accommodate a large congregation and give everyone a clear view of the pulpit. A theater- or cathedral-style building could have accomplished this purpose, but Fugard felt that the symbolism of these models contradicted Moody Church's theological identity. A theater, Fugard explained, would not have been a "harmonious and fitting setting for the life which it shelters." Although a cathedral could provide "a fitting setting for the ritual of a Catholic service," Fugard and the leaders of Moody Church believed that it was the wrong architectural model for worship that privileged the preached word.

Fugard's ingenious design for Moody Church was taken in part from Hagia Sophia, the cathedral built in Constantinople, Turkey, in the sixth century. The building is famous for its massive dome, which curves 110 feet from east to west and soars 180 feet above the floor. Taking that as their inspiration, architects designed the Moody Church sanctuary with a 68-foot vaulted ceiling—as high as a six-story building. However, the architects felt that the rich, lavish character of Hagia Sophia did not express "the economy and simplicity which the life and service of The Moody Church demand."[27] As a way around this problem, they turned to the massive, thousand-year old Romanesque churches in the Lombard region of Italy. These churches made good use of brick and terra cotta—a more cost-effective option than cut stone—which inspired the architects to enclose Moody's vast auditorium in brick (Figure 3.1).

Today, the Moody Church sanctuary is the largest non-pillared auditorium in the Chicago area and features a cantilevered balcony on three sides. The auditorium originally had seats for about 4,000 people; today it holds about 3,750. (Chairs have been removed to add a cross aisle on the floor, enlarge the front platform, and install technical equipment. The church is likely to remove more seats for similar adaptations in the future.) Each seat has an unobstructed view of the pulpit (Figure 3.2).

On most Sundays, the generous choir loft behind the pulpit is filled with robed choristers. Written above them in gold letters is the verse Hebrews 13:8: "Jesus Christ is the same yesterday, today and forever" (Figure 3.3). A stately display of organ pipes runs across the loft. Directly below the choir is a two-tiered platform.

Figure 3.1 Exterior view of the Moody Church sanctuary
Chicago, Illinois: September 2014. Photo by author.

Figure 3.2 Sunday worship at Moody Church

Chicago, Illinois: September 2014. Photo by author.

Figure 3.3 Moody Church choir loft

Chicago, Illinois: September 2014. Photo by author.

A solid wood pulpit is built into the upper level; the lower level seats the small orchestra that is a regular part of worship. A four-manual Reuter organ console sits to the right of the orchestra platform; a concert grand piano and caged drum sit on the left.

The symbols of the pulpit and the organ are integral to Moody's theological identity. On January 15, 1985, an arsonist broke into the church and set fire to the front of the sanctuary. The church sustained around $750,000 in damages. The pulpit, grand piano, and organ console were completely destroyed; every one of the surviving four thousand organ pipes—some of which were enormous, others the size of a little finger—had to be taken out of state for cleaning and repairs. The Sunday immediately after the fire, Lutzer preached a sermon entitled "Beauty from Ashes." Lutzer told the congregation that while there was no way of knowing the arsonist's motives, it was clear that the individual wanted to strike at the heart of Moody Church's ministry. "What could be more central to our purpose than a pulpit, from which the good news of the Gospel is preached?" Lutzer asked rhetorically. "What could be more basic to our worship than the musical instruments by which we give praise to God?"[28]

Erwin Lutzer (b. 1941) grew up on a farm in Saskatchewan, Canada, the youngest of five children. He graduated from Winnipeg Bible College, then earned a master of theology degree from Dallas Theological Seminary in 1967. While serving as senior pastor at Edgewater Baptist Church in Chicago, he also completed an MA in philosophy from Loyola University. In 1977, Lutzer and his family visited Moody Church for the first time. Warren Wiersbe, then senior pastor, had fallen ill the morning of their visit. The two preachers crossed paths in the lobby—Wiersbe on the way out, Lutzer on the way in—ten minutes before the start of the service. Wiersbe hastily asked Lutzer if he would fill the pulpit that morning. Lutzer agreed, and immediately began scribbling the outline of one of his recent sermons on the back of an envelope. Looking back, Lutzer recalls, "As I stood on the platform that morning and looked out over the large congregation, I said in my heart, 'Lord, if they ever call me to be the pastor [at Moody], I'll say *yes!*'" Wiersbe resigned from Moody Church in 1978, and in November of 1979, thirty-eight-year-old Lutzer was called by a unanimous vote to be the church's next senior pastor. He began his official pastorate on January 1, 1980.[29]

On this morning in 2014, Lutzer steps to the pulpit and opens the service with a short prayer. Specifically, he asks "Jesus, our High Priest" to "unite our hearts to fear your name" and to grant the congregation "all that we need to worship [God] acceptably . . . in spirit and in truth, and with freedom." The themes that Lutzer has introduced in his prayer—the holiness of God, the "high priesthood" of Jesus—will recur many times during the service.

As Lutzer sits down, Tim Stafford, pastor of music ministries, stands up to take his place. Like Lutzer, Stafford is wearing a coat and tie. He has a friendly, open face, an earnest way of speaking, and a self-deprecating sense of humor: in short, he fits the profile of a native mid-Westerner. Stafford, however, grew up in the Pacific Northwest, where his father worked as a pastor of music. Stafford joined the music staff of Moody Church in 2001, immediately after graduating from Moody Bible Institute with a music degree in vocal performance. He continued his musical studies while working at the church, completing a master's degree in choral conducting from Northwestern University in 2008. That same year, when Stafford was barely thirty years old, the church promoted him to pastor of music ministries.

Stafford stands in a long line of Moody Church leaders who strive to be peacemakers. He recounts how as a young man contemplating his future in church music, he decided that he wanted to be a bridge-builder: to lead a ministry that could last beyond five or ten years. "I didn't want to be on some island with twenty young kids, trying to make up our own thing," he reflects. "If I'm going to figure out church music for my generation, I want to know who I am and what I'm inheriting." Before Stafford assumed leadership, Moody Church worship used the organ, piano, brass, and choir every Sunday. Today, Sundays have a slightly more contemporary feel. While the organ, choir, and orchestra are still regular features in the service, congregational singing is now led by a band. Stafford is the first pastor in the history of Moody Church to preside over worship while playing a guitar. Stafford conducts Moody's sixty-voice choir in a musical call to worship, then leads the congregation in singing four songs that emphasize God's sovereignty and transcendence: "Holy God," "Agnus Dei," "Fairest Lord Jesus," and "In Christ Alone."

Between the second and third musical pieces, the congregation reads a passage of scripture aloud responsively. The first verses set the tone for the sermon that will soon follow:

> And every priest stands daily at his service, offering repeatedly the same sacrifices, which can never take away sins. But when Christ had offered for all time a single sacrifice for sins, he sat down at the right hand of God, waiting from that time until his enemies should be made a footstool for his feet. For by a single offering he has perfected for all time those who are being sanctified. (Hebrews 10:11–14, ESV)

Lutzer returns to the podium to offer a pastoral prayer. He begins with intercessions for the global church: "for [God's] people in Iraq, Iran, and the Middle East . . . and for the church—however small—in North Korea. Make your people strong in the face of opposition, persecution, unanswered questions, and disease." He then prays for Moody Church: "Grant us the grace to be loving, courageous, upfront, not ashamed of the gospel of Jesus Christ." Lutzer asks for God to be near "to those who are ill, or going through times of financial need, relational issues, and disappointing news," and intercedes for "all those who have never personally trusted Christ as Savior." After the pastoral prayer, the choir sings an anthem while the offering plates are passed. The congregation sings the doxology, then settles in to hear the morning's sermon.

Lutzer has honed a specific homiletical template. He begins by choosing a keyword in his study, then structures the sermon around it. When Lutzer teaches seminary preaching courses, he encourages his students to "begin with an intro, lead [the congregation] to where you want them to go, then you tie the ribbon at the end by referring to the introduction."[30] The keyword acts as a needle, sewing the sermon into a coherent piece of cloth. Although it is never explicitly stated, this morning's keyword appears to be *blood*. The bulletin includes an outline, with space underneath each point for the listener to make notes. The three questions for the morning are: (1) What does the blood of Christ mean to God? (2) What does the blood of Christ mean to us? and (3) How does the blood of Christ cleanse our consciences?

As an introduction, Lutzer begins with a reading from one of the most famous scenes in English literature: Lady Macbeth washing invisible blood from her hands. "Out damn spot, out I say. . . Here's the smell of blood still. All the perfumes of Arabia will not sweeten this little hand. . . . All the oceans of the world would not wash the blood from my hand. Rather, my hands would make the seas red."[31] Lutzer reminds the congregation of the episode's tragic ending: "With no relief from her plagued conscience, Lady Macbeth committed suicide." "Wouldn't it be wonderful," Pastor Lutzer suggests to the congregation, "to know that when we really mess up, as Lady Macbeth did, that there is a place where we can park our guilt. That's the purpose of this message today. But in order for us to get there, we're going to have to plow through some very basic ground." Pastor Lutzer promises his audience that the effort will prove worthwhile: "When we get to the end of the message, I'm going to be giving you very important, transforming truths that I believe are going to be a means of deliverance for hundreds of people who are here today, and even more who are listening by other means. I have that much confidence in the blood of Jesus Christ," he stresses.

Initially, there was nothing striking to me about Pastor Lutzer's phrase— "confidence in the blood of Jesus Christ." If anything, the language registered as slightly archaic: "confidence in the blood" sounded like a turn of phrase Dwight L. Moody might have used when addressing his nineteenth-century audiences. But as I talked to Moody staff members later in the week, the declaration took on an additional layer of meaning: it was a subtle signal that the sermon the congregation was about to hear would be markedly different from one that might be preached in a megachurch like North Point (next chapter).

Consider my conversation with Moody Church executive pastor Bill Bertsche. Before coming to Moody, Bertsche and his family attended services at a contemporary-styled evangelical megachurch. Looking back on the experience, Bertsche reflected, "I think my biggest concern was the way sermons were packaged when I was there. It left me feeling like, '[This church] doesn't have confidence in the Word of God to actually change lives, even if what is proclaimed is not palatable on the surface.'" The problem, Bertsche quickly clarified, was not doctrinal: "To whatever extent the gospel was preached, it was clear." Rather, Bertsche was concerned with "the overall approach—that maybe [the megachurch] is diminishing some of the power and impact of the Word by packaging it the way they do."

In a later conversation, Lutzer agreed, adding that too many evangelical pastors "cherry-pick verses of scripture about how Jesus helps you to become a better this and a better that." In Lutzer's words, too many pastors "preach that you should believe the gospel because of the ways in which it will benefit you." Missing from their sermons are "an emphasis on the depravity of man, the holiness of God, and the urgent need to humble ourselves and approach God through Christ's sacrifice alone." Lutzer's commitment to "plowing through" difficult biblical terrain and his "confidence in the blood of Jesus Christ" signal his distance from those preachers who would stress that "man is essentially good, God wants you happy and personally fulfilled, [and] the key to real change is positive thinking."

Lutzer starts with the first question of his three-point outline: "What does the blood of Christ mean to God?" He notes that "there's blood everywhere in the Old Testament" and recounts the Passover story from the book of Exodus, in which God spares the lives of all Jews who have marked their doors with the blood of a sacrificial lamb. Lutzer explains that these animal sacrifices are a temporary solution to the problem of sin—a placeholder until Jesus's death on the cross in the New Testament resolves the problem of sin for all time.

As Lutzer warms to his subject, he invites the congregation to turn to Hebrews 10:19–22 (RSV), which he reads aloud:

> Therefore, brothers and sisters, since we have confidence to enter the Most Holy Place by the blood of Jesus, by a new and living way opened for us through the curtain, that is, his body, and since we have a great priest over the house of God, let us draw near to God with a sincere heart and with the full assurance that faith brings, having our hearts sprinkled to cleanse us from a guilty conscience and having our bodies washed with pure water.

Lutzer proceeds to unpack the imagery, which helps the congregation answer question 2: "What does the blood of Christ mean to us?" Lutzer explains that in the Old Testament, the priest was the only person permitted to go into "the

Holy of Holies"—the inner sanctuary where God dwelt. Today, however, the restrictions have changed:

> Rather than many priests (who worked in eight-hour shifts), Jesus is now the one and only Priest.
> Rather than many sacrifices, Jesus offered Himself, the One and only Sacrifice.
> Rather than standing as the priests did (indicating that their work was never done), Jesus sat down because His work was completely finished.
> Rather than the worshipper bringing an offering, Jesus Himself is the offering that can "perfect us forever."[32]

Lutzer begins to wrap up by asking a rhetorical question. "You might be saying, 'How does it relate to my depression? What does it say about my guilt or the sense that I am constantly held back because of my past?'" The pastor responds with three "transforming truths." First, he emphasizes that "the blood of Jesus gives us full, unfettered access to God," regardless of any serious issues with which an individual may be struggling. Second, human beings must give up trying to save themselves. Here, Lutzer offers an example. "It's like a guy on a plane once said to me. 'You know what my biggest fear is when I stand before God? That I'll be standing behind Mother Theresa on the Day of Judgment and will overhear God say, 'Now lady, I think you could have done more.'" Lutzer assures the congregation that this imaginary scenario will never happen: "God says, 'When I see the blood, I'll accept you: when you trust the blood of Christ, that is the basis of my acceptance.'"

The final application is that the consequences to human sin need not debilitate a believer's joy in God. "Retrain your conscience to accept God's word as truth, not your feelings," Lutzer urges the congregation. "Feelings will lie to you. They'll tell you that there is no hope. But that's a lie," Lutzer stresses. Ultimately, God alone has the power to make life-and-death decisions: "When this world is going to be better off without you, *God* will call for you and he will take you home. Let him make that decision."

Lutzer's sermon neglects nuances from academic psychology that other pastors might choose to stress. Ed Setzer, who took interim leadership of Moody's pulpit after Lutzer's retirement in 2016, drew attention to several of them in a *Christianity Today* editorial entitled "The Christian Struggle with Mental Illness." Setzer points out that mental illness is not simply a spiritual issue: a chemical imbalance "doesn't go away by prayer or by reading your Bible alone." Stetzer reminds readers that "on top of spiritual measures, there are beneficial and helpful medications and treatments available to fight this illness," and that people should feel no shame in taking advantage of them. Scripture and medication or counseling are "neither enemies nor mutually-exclusive," and the church needs to become a safer place for those who struggle with depression and mental illness.[33]

Lutzer would undoubtedly agree with Setzer's caveats. But this morning, his focus is on salvation. "It's too late for Lady Macbeth, you know," Lutzer concludes. "She went her way in Shakespeare's play." But Lutzer promises the congregation that they can have the assurance of heaven. "You can receive Christ as Savior right now. You can say, 'Today I believe that Jesus died, and that he finished it, and that I bring nothing to the table except my sin. It all has to do with him and his matchless grace.'" Lutzer invites anyone who is interested to meet with the prayer team at the front of the sanctuary after the service. "If you receive Christ as Savior, tell one of us. We're always delighted to hear what God does through the preaching of his Word." The congregation responds by singing the contemporary hymn "Before the Throne of God Above." The lyrics of this piece mirror the theme of the sermon. In fact, the first four lines are a direct paraphrase of Hebrews:

> Before the throne of God above
> I have a strong and perfect plea [Hebrews 4:15–16]
> A great high Priest whose name is love
> Who ever lives and pleads for me. [Hebrews 4:14][34]

The final stanza of the hymn reiterates other sermon highlights, emphasizing that Jesus is humanity's "perfect spotless righteousness," that sinners' souls have been "purchased by His blood," and that as a result of this sacrifice, their lives are "hid with Christ on high." The hymn is rich with theology and imagery about Christ as the ultimate intercessor and advocate before the throne of God. "No sin too great, no despair too deep that Jesus can't come and rescue us. What a great God we serve!" Lutzer declares as the final notes of the song fade. After a few short announcements, he dismisses the congregation with a benediction: "And now Lord, through the blood of the everlasting covenant, make us perfect in every good work to do his will, working in you that which is well-pleasing in your sight. To you be glory, dominion, and power forever and ever. Amen."

Homiletical Analysis

There are clear differences between Pastor Hugenberger's sermon on the story of Abraham in Genesis (Park Street) and the message that Pastor Lutzer preached. Park Street sermons focus on a single passage of scripture, which the preacher works through verse by verse, offering historical and contextual information to aid listeners in understanding the passage's meaning.

At Moody Church, Lutzer describes his preaching style as "topical exposition." Instead of commenting on all the verses of a given passage, Lutzer decides on the main topic of the passage and winnows out or briefly summarizes any extraneous material that does not directly contribute to the sermon's one big idea.[35] (Lutzer also plans his sermons knowing that each one will be broadcast over the *Moody Church Hour* radio program. Occasionally he refers to a previous message when there is a connection or a context, but each talk must be able to stand alone as an independent unit.) Sometimes this radio-conscious structure also anticipates a reading audience. The sermon I have described was later published, as were all other sermons in the series, in the book *The Power of a Clear Conscience: Let God Free You from Your Past*. The sermons are edited as chapters and do not necessarily feel like sermons in their new form.[36]

Lutzer's homiletical approach of choosing topics and keywords has a long and storied history. In the 1870s and 1880s, the Plymouth Brethren—a group that strongly influenced D. L. Moody—instituted the practice of "conversational Bible readings." Conversational Bible readings, also simply called "Bible readings," were a substitute for the sermon: a leader read a string of Bible passages on a common theme, image, or symbol, and then explained each passage in light of the others, showing a gradual development of a theological idea throughout the literary whole of Scripture.[37] In 1879, an expert of the time explained that to do a Bible reading, one must "select some word . . . and with the aid of a good Concordance, mark down . . . the references to the subject under discussion . . . thus presenting all the Holy Ghost has been pleased to reveal on the topic."[38]

Leading intellectual lights at Princeton were unimpressed with this approach. Francis Patton, the conservative president of Princeton University, took aim at the new method in an 1890 article on preaching:

> Then there is what is called a Bible-reading; very good too in its way, but a very poor substitute for a sermon. I supposed that the Bible-reading is a feature of the school of thought of which Mr. Moody is such a distinguished leader. With some of the theology of some members of this school I have no sympathy; and I particularly object to their arbitrary and unhistorical system of interpretation. . . . But few, I fear, know the English Bible as they do. I advise you to learn their secret in this regard, but do not adopt their shibboleths; and I warn you against supposing that you have given an adequate substitute for a sermon when, with the help of Cruden's Concordance, you have chased a word through the Bible, making a comment or two on the passages as you go along.[39]

Conservative Princetonians theologians objected to "Bible reading" because it was superficial and unscientific. They believed that in order to understand the Bible, one must first determine the original meaning of what the biblical authors wrote, a task that required philology and historical context. Bible reading was nothing more than stringing together prooftexts.

However, James M. Gray (1851–1935), president of Moody Bible Institute, pushed back, insisting that the Bible was written for ordinary people, and one need not be an elite scholar to understand and interpret it. Gray knew both Greek and Hebrew but downplayed their importance. (Studying the original biblical languages is not a high priority for Lutzer either, who admits, "I have forgotten virtually all of the Hebrew and Greek I knew in seminary, but thank God there are many excellent tools that do our exegesis for us.")[40]

While teaching at Moody Bible Institute in the 1890s, Gray developed a popular and highly influential way of studying scripture that came to be known as the "synthetic method." D. L. Moody saw how much the method helped students and encouraged Gray to perfect it and make it available to more people. Gray took Moody's advice and published a series of synthetic Bible studies in the *Union Gospel News* in 1900. In 1904, he explained the method in more detail in his book *How to Master the English Bible*.[41] Gray emphasized that unless students first grasped the panorama of scripture, they would easily get lost by more detailed study. He recommended reading through the entire Bible, from Genesis to Revelation, each book in a single sitting. After completing this enormous assignment, students could narrow their focus to an individual book and the development of its themes. Finally, after studying numerous biblical books this way, the student was ready to consider common doctrines and overlapping ideas across the entirety of scripture.[42]

The difference between an "Old Princeton" approach to exegesis (exemplified by Gordon Hugenberger at Park Street) and a topical or "synthetic" approach to preaching (demonstrated by Erwin Lutzer at Moody) lies in their contrasting interpretive logics. Both Park Street and Moody Church pastors agree that the Word of God is inspired and without error. However, Park Street emphasizes the historical and scientific nature of scripture. The job of a scholarly pastor like Gordon Hugenberger is to use all the analytical and academic tools at his disposal—history, archaeology, linguistics, and extra-biblical sources—to establish the original meaning of what the biblical authors wrote. Once this original meaning is determined, common sense dictates that all readers or listeners will come to the same interpretive conclusions.[43] Conversely, dispensationalists like Erwin Lutzer stress that divine truths cannot be discovered simply on the basis of common sense or academic study. Rather, they are available to anyone who, under the guidance of the Holy Spirit, is willing to spend time "decoding" the elaborate theological themes, types and antitypes, and intertextual references that make up the unity of scripture. One of the primary theological frameworks linked to this homiletical approach is premillennial dispensationalism.

Understanding Premillennial Dispensationalism

In the previous chapter, Park Street senior pastor Gordon Hugenberger began his sermon with the observation that the patriarch Abraham was the key to understanding how the Old and New Testaments relate. Hugenberger also noted that this is a point on which "evangelical Christians are often at some division with each other: the dispensational view interprets these connections one way and the more Reformed view sees them [another]."[44] The sermon by Pastor Lutzer that I have described is an excellent example of dispensational theology: as such, it provides several important points of contrast from Park Street's Reformed covenantal hermeneutic. In this section, I offer a brief explanation of dispensational theology before demonstrating how the two congregations' biblical hermeneutics correspond to their differing musical philosophies.

But first, two important caveats. First, although I will be contrasting the theologies of Park Street and Moody, it is important to emphasize the two churches share the same basic understanding of the gospel. The churches agree that the sacrificial system was provisional and temporary in the Old Testament era and that it received its fulfillment and terminus in the light of Christ's coming. Furthermore, their areas of theological agreement—on the Trinity, on Chalcedonian Christology, on salvation by grace alone through faith in Christ— far outweigh their areas of disagreement.

Second, Erwin Lutzer (in his late seventies at the time of this writing) is from a generation of pastors whose classic dispensational views are becoming increasingly rare. Graduates from traditional bastions of dispensational theology like Moody Bible Institute are less likely to share the strength of Lutzer's convictions on eschatological matters like the rapture or God's future land promises to the nation of Israel. Though Lutzer's theological position is reflected in Moody Church's official doctrinal statements, church membership is not dependent on stated agreement with dispensational theology. With these cautions in mind, we turn to an analysis of dispensational thought.

Dispensationalists divide history into ages of divine history known as epochs, or dispensations. Dispensationalists disagree about the exact number—some say as few as three, others as many as twelve—but many follow the teachings of John Nelson Darby (1800–1882), who delineated seven:

1. The Dispensation of Innocence (from innocence to the Fall)
2. The Dispensation of Conscience (from Adam to Noah)
3. The Dispensation of Human Government (from Noah to Abraham)
4. The Dispensation of Promise (from Abraham to Moses)
5. The Dispensation of Law (from Moses to Christ)
6. The Dispensation of Grace (from Christ to today)

7. The Dispensation of the Kingdom (a thousand-year rule ushered in at the end of time)[45]

What makes dispensationalism unique as a theological system is not the fact that its adherents divide history into distinctive time periods, but rather that they draw a fundamental distinction between Israel and the church.

To understand the difference between dispensational and covenantal theological perspectives, consider a basic question of biblical interpretation: how do the Hebrew scriptures relate to the New Testament? Evangelical answers to this query can be plotted on a continuum that runs from the belief in absolute continuity to the belief in absolute discontinuity. Park Street Church, which espouses a covenantal theology, is close to the "continuity" end; Moody Church, which champions dispensational theology, is closer to the "discontinuity" end.

Covenant theologians believe that the relationship between Old and New Testament is porous. The Old Testament sacrificial system foreshadowed the new covenant, and the new covenant proclaimed the accomplishment of what the law anticipated. Thus Calvinist philosopher Greg Bahnsen argues that ancient Israelites were expressing faith in the New Testament Christ by participating in the sacrificial system:

In the greatest Bible lesson of all time, Christ expounded, "beginning with Moses and all the Prophets . . . what was said in all the Scriptures concerning himself" (Luke 24:27). . . . The Mosaic law does not stand in antithesis to the Gospel of Christ that was afterward proclaimed. . . . Christ was the focus and aim of the Mosaic law or old covenant (Rom. 10:4), just as he was of the Abrahamic covenant and promises of old.[46]

The substance of God's saving relationship remains the same under both testaments.

Conversely, dispensationalist theologian John Walvoord argues that there is simply "no teaching [in the New Testament] that the nation of Israel as such becomes the church as such," nor are Gentile Christians ever designated as "Israelites" in the Bible.[47] In this understanding, "Specific kinds types of revelation are assigned to specific types of people for specific times"—creating "a veritable watertight compartment that sees revelation as being a sort of mail that pertains only for the people it was addressed to in those times."[48] In the sermon I have described, Pastor Lutzer instructs the congregation that "the Old Testament era is gone and the New has come,"[49] and that "when we get to Jesus, the Lamb of God who takes away the sin of the world, *suddenly we're in a different era*."[50] A recurring theme in Lutzer's sermon is that Jesus has definitively ended the dispensation of the Mosaic Law and opened a new dispensational era through his atoning sacrifice. "Now notice here," Lutzer exhorts the congregation when he reaches Hebrews 10:20: "The author is saying that come to God by 'a new and living way': *new because it was not in the Old Testament.*"[51]

The broad counters for a dispensationalist understanding of salvation history are as follows. During the first five dispensations, God dealt exclusively with his chosen people, Israel. When Israel rejected Jesus as the Messiah at the end of the fifth dispensation—as prophecy said they would—God "unexpectedly postponed Jesus' return, started putting together a new people, the church, and unplugged the prophetic clock."[52] The church today lives at the close of the sixth dispensation: a period of time spanning from Pentecost to the eve of the great tribulation (Matthew 24:21; Revelation 6–19), which dispensationalists call the "Great Parenthesis."

Theologians had two different views about how the period between Christ's ascension and return would look. Prior to the American Civil War, revivalists such as Jonathan Edwards and Charles Finney believed that life on earth would grow better and better until the millennium arrived, and that, consequentially, it was important to improve the world in order to hasten the coming of Christ. For example, Finney declared in 1835 that if Christians had gone to work ten years earlier, "the millennium would have fully come into the United States before this day."[53] But Dwight L. Moody, the first significant premillennial evangelist in North American history, sounded a more pessimistic note. Moody believed that the world would get worse and worse until Christ returned to set up a visible, thousand-year reign of peace. Moody's view comes through clearly in his 1877 sermon, "The Return of Our Lord":

> Some people say, "I believe Christ will come on the other side of the millennium." Where do you get it? I can't find it. The Word of God nowhere tells me to watch and wait for the coming of the millennium, but for the coming of the Lord. I don't find any place where God says the world is to grow better and better.... I find that the earth is to grow worse and worse.[54]

Moody put the doctrine of Christ's premillennial return to pragmatic use, urging believers to witness more boldly and entreating unbelievers to go through the door while there was still time. Indeed, Moody's premillennial eschatology and his philosophy of evangelism come together in his most often-quoted statement from the same sermon: "I look upon this world as a wrecked vessel.... God has given me a lifeboat and said to me, 'Moody, save all you can.'"[55]

What happens after the Great Parenthesis? Recall that God is now working with two distinct people—Israel and the church—and that he chooses to work with only one of them at a time. Therefore, the seventh dispensation will proceed in two phases. In the first phase, God deals with the church by "rapturing" all living and dead Christians to their inheritance in heaven (1 Thessalonians 4:13–17). After the rapture, those left behind undergo a period of tribulation. After this tribulation, God would fulfill the promises made to Abraham, Isaac, Jacob, and ethnic Israel. Jesus will return to earth for a second time, and the Jewish people will be restored to Palestine.

Tim Stafford suggested that the majority of evangelicals tend to believe in dispensationalism: "If you ask an evangelical, 'Do you believe that you'll be raptured before the return of Christ?', by and large, I'd expect that person to say yes." Statistical evidence offers support for this hypothesis. The *Left Behind* book series by Tim LaHaye and Jerry B. Jenkins, which explains American premillennial eschatology through fiction, sold over sixty-three million copies and was a major cultural phenomenon. Scholar Timothy Weber called it "the most effective disseminator of dispensationalist ideas ever."[56] They eclipsed even Hal Lindsey's 1970s bestseller, *The Late Great Planet Earth*, which itself was translated into fifty languages and sold over thirty-five million copies.[57] Stafford is right: premillennial dispensationalism is indeed alive and well among evangelicals.

Dispensationalism has always had critics. For example, in 1958, Louisville Presbyterian Seminary faculty member W. D. Chamberlain complained that dispensationalism treated the Bible like a mosaic:

> I have a pin, about the size of a quarter, which contains a bunch of white lilies, with green stems and yellow stamens, on a black background. Twenty-seven pieces of stone were used in making it. It is truly a work of art, but if one should conclude that this mosaic supplies the key to the understanding of the geological formation of the environs of Florence, he would be sadly wrong. So it is with "Dispensational Truth"; it is a mosaic made up of verses taken at random from the Bible. Since it is biblical material there is good in it, but it is not a key to what the Bible means.[58]

Recently, however, scholar B. M. Pietsch has offered a more generous interpretation, suggesting that dispensationalism provides an alternative evangelical response to the challenges of higher criticism. In his book, *Dispensational Modernism*, Pietsch argues that dispensationalism and higher criticism "represented mirrored opposite images of each other, twinned outgrowths of shared modernist thinking."[59] Higher critics interpreted discrepancies as evidence of multiple origins, authors, and editorial hands at work: in short, as proof of the composite nature of the biblical text. Old Princeton biblical scholars tried to beat historical critics at their own game, refuting their objections footnote by footnote. Dispensationalists brokered their own solution, distinct from that of the conservative Princeton theologians. In contrast to evangelicals who sought to prove the harmonization of scripture, dispensationalists acknowledged the same alleged contradictions as the higher critics but performed an act of "interpretive jujitsu" by arguing that differences in dispensations were intentional—distinct parts of a working engine—and should be taken as evidence of God's masterful, overarching design.[60] This concept of variegated unity helps explains not only Moody Church's systematic theology, but also its philosophy of musical worship.

Musical Hermeneutics

Stafford's philosophy of church music involves three continuums: ancient and modern, simple and eloquent, familiar and new. He elaborates: "We value rich history and inherit the church's song, but we don't isolate ourselves from the revitalizing forms of the young." In the same way, the church finds immeasurable value in "simple songs that bring forth a childlike heart of faith," while deeply appreciating "demonstrations of God's creative nature in masterful works of all kinds." Finally, "What is familiar to some may be new to others, and everyone needs both in their routine for healthy growth."

Stafford's three worship continuums borrow from the work of Harold Best, emeritus professor of music and dean emeritus of the Wheaton College Conservatory of Music. Best stresses that all points along the continuum of church music are neutral: new, for instance, is not "good," nor is familiar "bad." At the same time, he insists that there is "progression, or increasing value" along the spectrum. Best supports his logic with a scriptural model of milk and meat: both are wholesome and life-giving, but as individuals grow in maturity, they are expected to progress from the former to the latter. So too with church music: "In this way we can insist that depth is eventually preferred over shallowness, strangeness over familiarity, complexity over simplicity and the like."[61] Best explains that when this progression is followed, the two ends of the continuum will enhance one other, rather than compete:

> Just because I am eventually urged and able to engage with depth does not mean that I must avoid or should no longer enjoy shallowness. On the contrary, each remains a part of my "diet" in the same sense that I can drink milk even as I chew meat. Paradoxically, I will then be able to drink my milk and chew it too, because my eating meat brings new depth to drinking milk. That is, if I delve into the complex meat of Romans 7 and 8 or Hebrews 11 and 12, I will find that the simple milk of "Jesus Loves Me" will begin to taste like meat.[62]

Stafford furthers the food analogy by comparing the task of planning worship to that of preparing a meal. Although some might describe Stafford's approach as "blended," he emphatically prefers the descriptor of "bundled":

Imagine your favorite meal: maybe Thanksgiving or a grand restaurant. Now take everything on the table and blend it. Still appetizing? I like the word *bundled* better. Every [musical] genre I include gets its full flavor, and I don't try to do everything in one service every week. We move through a variety of approaches to music over a six- to eight-week period.

Stafford points out that it is difficult to get a good feel for Moody's music program without attending for an extended period of time—perhaps even a year. "A first-time visitor with certain expectations might be disappointed, but that is the risk I have to take for the good of the congregation over the longer haul." He continues,

Sometimes it bothers people because I'm more open-ended. I won't condemn things. I'm more like, "Well, could it stick here?" It's like gardening: let's wait and see what grows. I don't know if everything [I plant] is going to "take" or not. You have to wait a season or two before you really see the fruit. If I drive too hard on an outcome, I miss the process and the network of people we have. If I push the gas pedal too hard, it will flood the engine.

Continuing Challenges

Early dispensationalist teacher A. T. Peirson (1837–1911) compared the structure of scripture to that of the human body: Old and New Testaments are like "two eyes and ears, hands and feet" that "correspond to and complement one another," and need to be studied side by side.[63] Continuing the analogy, he stressed that the human body is "bound together by joints and bands and ligaments, with one brain and heart, one pair of lungs, one system of respiration, circulation, digestion, sensor and motor nerves." In scripture, as in anatomy, "Division is destruction."[64]

In the same way, Stafford believes that the dualities of "ancient and modern," "simple and eloquent," and "familiar and new" correspond to and complement one another. Stafford and his team of musicians are the ligaments that hold each pairing together. "I need that one congregation feel," he stresses. "I want the possibility of an eighty-year-old woman and a twenty-two-year-old kid sharing something . . . [I want] someone who loves hymns, someone who loves revival music, and someone who loves new music to all know and appreciate each other." In short, Stafford is passionate about variegated unity:

Every model has disadvantages, but I can say that if Moody was equivalent to what people call a contemporary church, it would have lost a part of its soul. If it didn't have its backbone in hymnody with the effective use of a trained choir, we will have lost something immeasurable. If it was taboo for us to sing new songs with guitars or a gospel beat and a horn section every now and then, we would have an irrational view of the gospel. I am motivated by the thought of inclusion in worship and discouraged by isolation or division.

Stafford is able to bring together musical styles that have caused "worship wars" in other evangelical churches. Nevertheless, he realizes that there will always be underlying tensions that need to be managed. In particular, Stafford believes that many young adults have stunted musical tastes. Stafford notes that "a four-year-old may have fits about eating vegetables. But it's a skill they learn, and vegetables eventually become a natural part of their palette so that as adults, they can then move more easily to a variety of foods." However, he worries about the child who has never been taught to eat vegetables and later refuses to try them as an adolescent: "What happens when that teenager becomes an adult and raises children of their own?"

As we saw in the previous chapter, Park Street's music minister Nathan Skinner believes that today's young adults are becoming increasingly appreciative of traditional church music. He observes that many Park Street twenty-somethings have moved away from the contemporary evening worship service and have joined the morning worship service because the musical tone of the morning "feels more worshipful." For Skinner, the process of worship music appreciation moves in one direction. "A young person might suddenly discover, 'What's this treasure in mom's attic?' The reverse probably isn't true. Someone who's grown up with treasures is not going to say, 'Oh look! Tupperware!'"

At Moody Church, Stafford is less convinced. Stafford worries that because so many twenty-first-century churches cater exclusively to teenagers' musical tastes and preferences, many of the young adults who come to Moody have never learned that "it's healthy, from an aesthetic point of view, to sometimes *not* like something" and still remain open to trying it. "I know that people who hate contemporary music and love hymns can be very closed-minded," Stafford admits. "But a lot of those older adults have been more open-minded to younger generations than the youth have been to them."

4

"Something Better Has Come Along"

Championing Innovation in Atlanta

"Dwight L. Moody was part of the founding of evangelicalism," one of my interviewees from the previous chapter mused, "but I don't know that we [at Moody Church] are at the center of it anymore. We were at the beginning. I don't know that we are now." The oldest extant megachurch in the United States, Moody Church broke through the two-thousand-person attendance mark when Moody was alive and continues to maintain similar figures in the twenty-first century.[1] Yet my interviewee had a point. The image of American evangelicalism that most readily springs to mind is unlikely to be of a church like Moody Church and very probably of something like North Point Community Church, near Atlanta, Georgia.

In the 1940s, around the same time that Ockenga and colleagues were inventing the National Association of Evangelicals, Christian leaders began creating "youth-friendly" versions of the faith. Given that Hitler's power base included a fanatical youth movement, American adults in the 1940s feared that their unemployed, idealistic youth could be just as easily manipulated by communists or fascists. Evangelicals began calling for the mass evangelization of young people as a means of saving the world. A new generation of evangelicals rose to meet the challenge with an organization called Youth for Christ, which reached national prominence with wildly popular Saturday night youth rallies.

The peak years of the Youth for Christ rallies came at the end of World War II, between 1944 and 1950, and continued strongly in many places through the 1950s. Youth for Christ rallies across the country followed a similar pattern of youth-tailored revivalism: "Saturday night in a big auditorium, lively gospel music, personal testimonies from athletes, civic leaders or military heroes, and a brief sermon, climaxing with a gospel invitation to receive Jesus Christ as personal Savoir."[2] Opponents criticized the movement for selling out to worldliness and cheapening the faith through gimmicks. Youth for Christ leaders responded that in light of the world crisis, youth needed to be reached by any means necessary. Furthermore, since Youth for Christ rallies were not church services, it was fine for them to be entertaining.

The 1950s marked the beginning of a process that Thomas Bergler dubs the "juvenilization" of American Christianity: "The religious beliefs, practices,

Evangelical Worship. Melanie C. Ross, Oxford University Press. © Oxford University Press 2021.
DOI: 10.1093/oso/9780197530757.003.0005

and developmental characteristics of adolescents [were becoming] accepted as appropriate for adults."[3] This process was accelerated in the 1970s, as youth ministry became increasingly isolated from the life of the rest of the church. Churches began to hire youth pastors—many of whom were former staff members at organizations like Youth for Christ—to offer specialized ministries targeted to teens. While the senior pastor focused on adult-oriented worship planning, the youth pastor took on similar responsibilities for the younger members of the flock. Parents were happy that "the 'kids' were busy inside the walls of the [church], rather than hanging around out in the parking lot."[4] Congregations repurposed existing rooms and suites or built new facilities to support youth activities.

In 1972, twenty-year-old Bill Hybels and his friend Dave Holmbo were leading an unconventional youth group at South Park Church in Park Ridge, Illinois. Hybels and Holmbo came to the conclusion—novel at the time—that Christian and non-Christian teens had different spiritual needs that required different spiritual programs. For high school students who were already Christians, Hybels and Holmbo developed a discipleship meeting called "Son Village," which met on Monday nights. Son Village gatherings included a time of fellowship, forty-five to sixty minutes of expository biblical teaching, musical worship, and a time of prayer. By contrast, "Son City" met on Wednesday nights, targeted non-Christian teens, and followed a much less traditional format. Wednesday nights were designed to make non-Christians as comfortable as possible in a church environment: they included team competitions, contemporary music, dramatic performances, and a nonthreatening, nonjudgmental evangelistic message.

In Son City, Hybels had found a formula that worked. Hundreds of students were coming to Christ. By 1975, there were over twice as many students in Hybels's youth group as there were adults in the church. The youth ministry budget, which had started at $300 in 1972, exploded to $80,000 by 1975.[5] Hybels decided to leave youth ministry and start Willow Creek Community Church— "an adult Son City" that would implement the evangelistic methods of the youth group at an adult level. Volunteers from the newly minted Willow Creek Community Church went door-to-door asking community residents if they regularly attended a local church. If the answer was no, they were asked why. Four primary reasons emerged: (1) the church was irrelevant to daily life, (2) church services were lifeless, boring, and predictable, (3) pastors "preached down" at parishioners and made them feel harshly judged, and (4) the churches were always asking for money.[6] Hybels and his team proposed that their new church would faithfully preach the gospel while addressing these four objections.

Thus began a new way of doing church: one that avoided distinctive Christian terminology and symbols in order to make services more accessible to the unchurched. Willow Creek offered weekend "seeker services" to individuals who were exploring Christianity and midweek "believer services" for core members who wanted deeper Bible teaching and worship. By the late 1980s, weekend attendance reached approximately nine thousand. Profiles of Willow Creek began appearing in secular media outlets, including the *New York Times, Time* magazine, *Fortune*, the *Wall Street Journal*, the NBC *Today Show*, and an ABC documentary reported by Peter Jennings.

Evangelical leaders around the country were watching the experiment with interest. In 1991, Andy Stanley, a dedicated student ministries worker, traveled from Atlanta to South Barrington to attend a leadership conference at Willow Creek and stayed for the weekend service. Stanley recalls, "Those few days at Willow—listening to Bill Hybels talk about leadership in the church, looking at their structure, the fact that they were really organized around reaching people who are far from God, the fact that [Hybels] had also started in student ministry—it was a defining moment."[7] Stanley was considering a total departure from the style and philosophy of ministry he had grown up with, but several respected mentors had told him his new ideas wouldn't work. Looking back, Stanley recalls, "Bill Hybels and his incredible staff . . . gave me the courage to attempt something new. They gave me permission. I just needed to see someone else go first."[8] Four years later, North Point Community Church was created.

Church History

In November 1995, Andy Stanley, the thirty-eight-year-old founding pastor of North Point Community Church, stood in front of a crowd of believers gathered at a North Atlanta convention center and announced, "Atlanta does not need another church. What Atlanta does need is a safe environment where the unchurched can come and hear the life-changing truth that Jesus Christ cares for them and died for their sins."[9]

Andy Stanley, son of Charles Stanley (pastor of First Baptist Church in Atlanta, founder of the global evangelistic organization In Touch, and two-time president of the Southern Baptist Convention), knew the challenges of church ministry firsthand. Prior to starting North Point Community Church, Andy Stanley had worked for his father at the downtown location of First Baptist—a four-hundred-thousand-square-foot warehouse complex that could comfortably accommodate about eight hundred people. Since the warehouse had no hallways or lobbies—nor a choir, orchestra, or any of the trappings of a traditional worship environment—Stanley and his team had a creative freedom. As Stanley recounts, "While we didn't know exactly what we were doing, we knew what we didn't want to do. We didn't want to re-create environments designed for church people."[10] The community was curious about First Baptist's new experiment: by the end of the second month, the warehouse church had added a second service and was closing in on two thousand adults in worship.

When Stanley eventually left First Baptist Church to start North Point Community Church, he carried the vision of the warehouse experience with him. North Point Community Church started with a staff of six and held services every other Sunday night. For its first year, the fledgling church rented space from the Galleria Convention Center in Atlanta. Original members laugh at the memory of seeing "No Point Church" advertised in large letters on the convention center's state-of-the-art electronic marquee. Clearly, the sign engineer had taken some creative liberties upon discovering that "North Point Community Church" had too many letters to fit onto one screen.[11]

But the new congregation did have a point: "to create a church that unchurched people would love to attend."[12] (North Point defines "unchurched" as not having attended a church for five years or longer.) In the mid-1990s, the idea that there were individuals who were either unfamiliar with or antagonistic toward traditional forms of Christian worship was a significant paradigm shift, particularly in the Southeast, the buckle of the Bible Belt. Reflecting on this history, Stanley laid out his interpretation of the divide he hoped his new church would bridge. Simply put: "Church was church. Either you went or you didn't. [If] you wanted to go, it was easy to find one. And for those who didn't attend, they knew what to expect on those rare occasions when it was unavoidable."[13] However, Stanley and his team were troubled by the fact that most pastors seemed to operate under the assumption that all the people in their congregations were already believers. They were similarly worried about the multitudes of young adults who left church when the childhood answers they were given about God and life no longer worked. North Point Community Church would be different from other Atlanta churches in being designed from the ground up as a place where seekers, starters, and people who had drifted away from faith could ask honest questions with no fear of judgment.

By December 1996, the young church was stable enough to purchase an eighty-three-acre site in the middle of Alpharetta, a small town fifteen miles north of Atlanta. Two years later, the congregation moved into its new twenty-seven-hundred-seat auditorium. By the end of its first year, North Point was conducting two services and averaging over four thousand each week in worship. No one had anticipated such rapid growth, and the leadership struggled over how to proceed.[14] The church had only been in existence for a year and a half, and without knowing how far the growth curve would extend, it didn't seem prudent to spend millions of dollars to tear down the original sanctuary and construct a new six-thousand-plus seat worship center. In the end, North Point opted for a faster, less costly solution: constructing a second "overflow" auditorium directly behind the original. Together, the two auditoriums could accommodate five thousand worshippers at a time, which allowed the church to grow quickly without taking on the stresses of a building campaign. The back-to-back worship centers—often dubbed the "Siamese sanctuaries"—each had their own music, sound, and lighting teams, meaning North Point could run two separate services simultaneously.

One vexing piece of the puzzle remained: how could Stanley be in both locations at the same time? The solution—novel at the time—was a live video feed from one sanctuary to the other. Music and announcements were live in both places. When it was time for the morning message, Stanley preached live in the east (main) auditorium, while the congregation in the west (overflow) auditorium listened to and viewed a high definition, crystal clear projection of larger-than-life-sized Stanley giving the same message. The first Sunday the second auditorium opened, the leadership wondered whether people would "check out," knowing they were watching a projection. One attendee recalls the relief he felt that first Sunday when Stanley asked a polling question—"How many of you in this room have ever . . ."—and hands shot up all over the second auditorium. "This *worked*," he recounted. "People connected with Andy—even on video."[15]

What started as a solution to a problem eventually became pivotal to North Point's growth strategy. As attendance continued to swell in Alpharetta, church leaders looked into the possibility of opening a second campus to reach regular attenders who drove more than 20 miles to attend services. In 2001, Buckhead Church, located in an affluent uptown district of Atlanta, became North Point's first satellite church. Buckhead Church followed a format similar to the west auditorium at the Alpharetta campus: music, announcements, and special segments were presented live, and then a prerecorded message was delivered by video. A third location, Browns Bridge Church, opened in 2006, using the same combination of live music and prerecorded messages. Fourth and fifth locations (Woodstock City Church and Gwinnett Church) were added in 2011. The most recent addition to the North Point family is Decatur City Church, which was added as a sixth location in 2014.

Today, messages are no longer prerecorded, but are simulcast live so that all locations experience the same sermon at the same time. Nor is Stanley's physical presence limited to the Alpharetta campus. Because all six churches have identical cameras, switchers, projectors, and screens, Stanley can give his message in person at any North Point auditorium, from where it is streamed to all the others. To make everything coordinate, the originating location starts five minutes before the other campuses. Receiving churches record the content as it happens in real time and play it back after their own announcements and music have concluded.

North Point is keenly aware that all new and innovative ideas, including video church, become institutionalized and over time may no longer be the best way of doing ministry. When David McDaniel, North Point Community Church's multi-site video venue expert, was once asked, "How long can a church survive on video preaching?" his response was straightforward: "When we sense that video teaching is no longer an effective means of leading people into a growing relationship with Jesus Christ in that particular church, we will transition to a live communicator."[16] Andy Stanley affirms this prioritization of mission over method, adding, "When video preaching no longer serves the mission of our church, it's got to go. It'll just be another ugly old couch that somebody will have to carry out to the street."[17]

But no one predicts the rumbling of trash trucks in the near in future. In 2014, North Point Ministries (the umbrella name for all campuses) was named the largest church in America.[18] More than twenty-three thousand adults participate in worship at one of the six metro Atlanta locations, and thousands of others attend North Point Community Church's "strategic partner" churches: autonomous congregations across the United States and Canada that are officially aligned with North Point's vision, mission, and strategy. North Point's influence extends beyond brick and mortar: sermons and leadership messages are accessed over one million times each month via North Point's websites.[19]

The North Point Template

One the most significant changes North Point has introduced to American evangelical worship is that of structure. This point is usefully illuminated by a three-minute video that North Point posted to its blog in May 2010. The short clip, entitled "Sunday Morning," was produced for the church's annual leadership conference and was intended to be a humorous set up for a keynote talk by senior pastor Andy Stanley. The little video ended up doing much more. Within a week, it had gone viral in the evangelical blogosphere. Some viewers were delighted by the parody; others were deeply offended. Either way, "Sunday Morning" set off a wave of social media–fueled discussions about the state of contemporary evangelical worship. If one is looking to understand the controversial role of megachurches in shaping North American worship life, this video clip is a good place to begin.

A young technician slides a thick pair of headphones over his ears and takes his place behind a state-of-the-art soundboard. "You can't stop it," an unseen narrator cautions. "It's coming to a town near you." The scene shifts to a slow-motion shot of a performer applying powder to his face with a makeup brush. Musical tension builds as the voice-over continues: "It used to be called 'Contemporary.' Some call it 'Relevant.' We're so cool, we call it . . . (*dramatic pause*) . . . 'Contemporvant.'" The worship auditorium explodes with sound and color. Lights flash and a bearded hipster fiercely strums an electric guitar. He bounces on his toes in time to the music and confidently intones, "Opening song; lights and big drums. You know it's cool because you heard it on the radio." "He's right. That *was* cool," the voice-over affirms approvingly.

Next, Welcome Guy—a young staffer sporting a graphic tee, faded jeans, and cool glasses—springs lightly across the stage and takes command. After welcoming everyone "with arms wide open, revealing my tattoo so you know I have a past," he makes a transition to the band and invites the congregation to stand. The camera shifts to a burly, flannel-clad worship leader who opens his set with "the song everyone knows." This nondescript tune is immediately followed by a musical number recently written and recorded by the worship leader: the "new song that nobody knows." Burly Worship Leader closes his eyes, furrows his brow, and intently crones, "I want you to learn this song / and buy my record in the bookstore / after the service."

A familiar string of evangelical tropes follows: the collection of the morning offering ("It's between you and God, but we're tracking it!"), a video clip introducing the topic of the day (the "title package"), and the senior pastor's drama-infused message ("speaking softly to draw you in," before "emphatically driving home my point"). After a long prayer ("so that the worship leader can get back on stage"), the service culminates in a closing song ("with strings that will make you cry"). The voice-over announces that this "new kind of church" will be "coming soon to your town." The worship auditorium fades to black, reiterating the trailer's titular message: "Sunday Morning . . . coming this weekend."

Shortly after the video was released, Twitter exploded with viewer responses.[20] The video struck a chord because many viewers recognized or identified with the subculture it parodied. As *USA Today* commentator Cathy Lynn Grossman observed, "I once went to a conference of young evangelical pastors and every one of them looked like a character on this video."[21] Many evangelicals took the satire in good humor, echoing the assessment of popular songwriter and worship leader Bob Kauflin: "It's a good practice, and even humble, to poke fun at ourselves. If we think that everything we do in our meetings is as sacred an [*sic*] inviolable as Scripture, we're living in unreality." Specifically, Kauflin appreciated the fact that "folks at North Point are exposing temptations common to many churches today, probably including their own."[22]

However, when others analyzed the video, they saw their deepest fears about twenty-first-century evangelicalism writ large. "Did you notice how everything was centered on the stage?" one blogger queried. "What does that make people the people in the seats . . . the audience? If the medium is the message, what message is sent, week after week, by having the majority of time, energy and money devoted to a stage production?"[23] Others were even more scathing in their critiques: "Now onwards and upwards with more and better video, graphics, cameras, lighting, presenters, music and preachertainers—until Christotainment Excellence™ is achieved and the appropriate rewards handed out."[24]

Not surprisingly, words like "stage production," "preachertainers," and "Christotainment" make North Point insiders bristle. As one leader confided to me, "I think the biggest misconception is that we are an entertainment industry; that we are just about entertainment—all smoke and mirrors and a light show. That's hard to hear. I look at my own faith journey, and I just think, 'You [critics] don't know. People just don't know.'"

One point North Point insiders believe their critics don't understand is that their church has developed a specific template. To understand this concept of a template, it will be helpful to make an initial distinction between what liturgical historian Robert Taft calls a "surface structure" and a "deep structure."[25] A church's surface structures include observable phenomena that are subject to frequent change: things like styles of dress, sermon topics, musical genre, and song selections. Underneath this surface, however, lies a deep structure. A deep structure comprises a congregation's conscious and unconscious assumptions about how the church works: it explains the "how" and "why" of a church's actions. Stanley's synonym for deep structure is "template," and he notes that every church has one. Even if the pastor cannot articulate it, "Anybody who has attended your church for six months or more has a pretty good idea of what it is."[26] The challenge is to make the template align with the church's stated purpose. Among North Point leaders, this process of alignment is known as "clarifying the win": having a specific goal to reach and a clear map of how to get there.

The notion of template is not unique to North Point. For many Christians, the deep structure of Sunday worship is a fourfold journey of *gathering, Word, Eucharist,* and *sending.* Each movement leads logically to the next: the congregation is gathered together, addressed by the Word, fed at the table, and sent back into the world changed by their encounter with God. Indeed, Lutheran and Reformed traditions define the church as "the community of believers created by Jesus Christ through the gospel rightly preached and the sacraments rightly administered."[27] If these two criteria—Word rightly preached, sacraments rightly administered—are met, then one can objectively speak of a Christian church. Furthermore, many Christians might argue that overlaying the celebration of Word and sacrament with an overtly pragmatic goal ("clarifying the win") is a crass misrepresentation of the true nature of worship. Ultimately, Christian worship is, in Marva Dawn's provocative phrase, "a royal 'waste' of time"—not the means to a greater end, but an end in and of itself.[28]

However, Stanley proposes that this line of thinking can easily lead to a "designed by Christians for Christians only" church mentality, a point I will explore in more depth later. Stanley's insight is representative of the significant divide in ecclesiology today. Simply put, the central question is this: is the Sunday morning gathering meant primarily for the spiritual formation of "insiders" (discipleship) or for the conversion of "outsiders" (evangelism)? For all the churches I visited, including North Point, this is a false dichotomy: the most robust answer must be "both/and," not "either/or." Stanley often stresses that his homiletical goal is not only for "skeptics to doubt their disbelief," but also for "believers to believe deeper."[29]

But even allowing for this caveat, North Point believes that most traditional churches have swung too far to the "discipleship" side of the pendulum on Sunday mornings. Stanley laments, "It's a shame that so many churches are married to . . . a culture in which they talk about the Great Commission, sing songs about the Great Commission, but refuse to reorganize their churches around the Great Commission."[30] Stanley has done precisely this kind of reorganizational work at North Point.

If a critic visits North Point and sees only lights and big drums, Welcome Guy's tattoos, and Burly Worship Leader's new song, she is not looking deeply enough. Undergirding all of North Point's technological bells and whistles is a carefully crafted template. It is not the classic fourfold structure of gathering, Word, sacraments, and sending, but rather a threefold pattern of *engage, involve,* and *challenge.* North Point's goal on Sunday morning is for an unchurched attendee to enjoy the service so much—to find the setting so appealing, the presentation so engaging, and the content so helpful—that he or she is comfortable inviting another unchurched friend the next Sunday. The *engage, involve,* and *challenge* template was created to support this goal.

The *engage* portion of the service includes the pre-service experience (i.e., the parking lot and hallway procedure, check-in for children, and the process of finding seats in the auditorium), an opener, and the welcome. Openers are usually a song (often secular) or interactive game designed to engage the audience. The point is to get everyone in the audience to smile or laugh so that visitors discover what it feels like to have fun inside a church. There is also a word of welcome that, because it is aimed at guests, never includes "insider" announcements geared toward the regular attendees. The welcome signals the end of the *engage* period.

The service trajectory then moves to *involve.* Once the audience has been emotionally engaged, it is possible to involve them physically. The *involve* segment usually includes a short time of singing, since truth put to melody has the power to emotionally engage a listener like no other medium. It also includes the act of baptism. Any person seeking baptism in a North Point church is required to video-record a three-minute testimony that will be shown on the Sunday morning of their baptism. This rule is ironclad: "No video, no baptism. We don't have any verses to support that. It keeps the baptism numbers low. But baptism is central to our worship and arguably our most powerful evangelism tool."[31] Like music, baptism videos also engage the audience emotionally, since it is very hard to argue with someone else's story of life change. Those being baptized invite not only family members, but also unchurched friends.

The final portion of the service, *challenge*, is the place in the service where the preacher presents the gospel in uncompromising terms, preaches against sin, and tackles emotionally charged topics in culture. The message is the place where North Point runs the greatest risk of offending the audience—a fact that does not bother Stanley:

> One of the myths about large churches is that they are large because they com-
> promise the gospel, water down the demands of discipleship, and skip the tough
> issues, all for the sake of building crowds. While that might be true in a handful
> of cases, that is certainly not the norm. We don't mind offending people with
> the gospel. We assume we will offend people with the gospel. As a preacher, it's
> my responsibility to offend people with the gospel.[32]

The *challenge* portion of the sermon taps into a common emotion that everyone in the audience, whether believer or skeptic, can share. There are no uniquely "Christian" problems, Stanley stresses: "None of us feels like we have enough money. Every married couple faces similar challenges. We all wonder what happens when we die." If churches want to engage non-Christians, they should "begin at the place where all of us shrug our shoulders and say, 'I don't know, but I wish someone would tell me.'"[33]

Stanley explains that this is the method by which Jesus, the master preacher, engaged his diverse audiences. Jesus started his most famous parables by tapping into common experiences that evoked a common emotion: a lost sheep, a lost coin, a lost son. Similarly, North Point works hard "to create a moment early on when everybody in the room is in agreement, shaking their heads in the same direction." Stanley recognizes that some will object to this approach as emotional manipulation. He offers this rationale in response:

> If you started an imaginary conversation with me about how cheap and unbib-
> lical that approach is, you are experiencing just how powerful this approach
> is. You are emotionally engaged. You are interested. You are interested because
> you disagree. Some of my favorite messages are the ones where I open up with
> a statement that makes everybody uncomfortable. Create tension and you've
> created interest.[34]

In order to create tension and interest, Stanley is selective about the scriptural texts he addresses on Sunday morning. Instead of preaching through books of the Bible, he preaches topically, choosing scriptural themes and applications that address specific issues that people in the community are wrestling with. The parts of scripture that address sexual purity, money, and family life receive the most frequent and repeated attention. On the Sunday morning of my first visit to North Point, the subject of giving was front and center.

Service Description: "Be Rich"

"A new day is dawning and love is on the move." A catchy, upbeat melody plays in the background as the congregation assembled at Alpharetta turns their attention to two large screens at either side of a professionally lit stage. The video features individuals from across the country holding placards that announce the location of their churches: Pittsburgh, Pennsylvania, Jacksonville, Florida, Chattanooga, Tennessee, Clarkston, Washington, and Colorado Springs, Colorado, to cite just a few. The farthest location is Cape Town, South Africa. These congregations will be partnering with North Point in an enormous project called "Be Rich," which will be the focus of this morning's service. The video alternates between shots of individuals holding location placards and clips of volunteers raking leaves, loading trucks with Christmas presents, serving food, and sorting clothes donations. The song is based on themes found in Philippians 2:15 (NIV), which entreats Christians to be "blameless and pure, 'children of God without fault in a warped and crooked generation.' Then you will shine among them like stars in the sky."

Engage

As the video concludes, Joel, an early-middle-aged pastor with an athletic build, takes the stage and smiles warmly. "Good morning and welcome to North Point. My name is Joel, and I'm one of the pastors on staff. You've come on a great Sunday!" Joel tells the congregation that the song they have just heard was written by several North Point musicians specifically for this day, and that it will be made available as a free download on the church's website. "It's called 'Shine Like Stars,' and that's what we hope to do through this, our eighth annual 'Be Rich' initiative." Joel goes on to explain that "Be Rich" is North Point's annual giving and serving campaign—a time when the six North Point churches in Metro Atlanta and twenty-four partner churches domestically and internationally unleash a wave of generosity in their local communities and around the world through nonprofit partnerships.

"Let me tell you what you're going to experience today if you're new to our church," Joel continues. "We're going to sing a little bit today, and we have some great folks leading you in both of our auditoriums. Then you're going to hear from John Doe, who will tell his story through video. That will be a special celebration. Then our senior pastor, Andy Stanley, is back here live at North Point." The week before, Stanley had preached from the Buckhead campus, and friendly applause in the auditorium signals that the Alpharetta crowd is pleased to have him home. Joel invites the congregation to rise: "Why don't you stand up, say hello to somebody next to you, and then we're going to get started."

Involve

After a short pause, Brian, the morning music leader, greets the assembly. He introduces himself and the two vocalists, one male and one female, who have joined him on stage, and then announces, "We're glad that you're here, and we're excited to lead you! The first song that we're going to sing together celebrates the greatness of God and how he saved each and every one of us. As you learn it, sing it out." The music swells, and Brian cheerfully exhorts the crowd: "Come on!" (Figure 4.1)

If you reread the introductory service dialogue, you'll notice that neither Joel nor Brian has used the word *worship*. This omission is intentional. North Point

Figure 4.1 Congregational singing at North Point Community Church
Alpharetta, Georgia: October 2014. Photo by author.

leadership continually stresses, "If you want to create a church that unchurched people love to attend, you've got to think like an outsider."[35] Since this musical portion of the service looks and sounds like *singing* to an unchurched person, it makes sense for the person up front to simply call it that. "If you think there might be unbelievers in your weekend gathering, drop the term *worship* from your weekend vocabulary," Stanley suggests.

The first song praises God who "has shattered our night with the light of a million mornings." The lyrics of this tune reference "the Holy One," "the Lord," "God," and "the mighty king," but do not mention Jesus or the Holy Spirit explicitly. This is a strategic choice. North Point musicians typically open with songs that highlight God's glory revealed in nature, or God's love, power, mercy, and forgiveness—theological concepts that will probably not be offensive to a first-time visitor.

The second song is more Jesus-centric, and Brian introduces it with a transition. "The song that we're about to sing is full of promises—for me, for you, and for everyone in this room and everyone watching. These are words that we can claim and find a foundation for our lives. It goes like this." He begins to sing the first verse of "In Christ Alone," a modern hymn that clearly outlines the gospel message. The congregation sings the tag of the song—"I find my strength, I find my hope; I find my help, in Christ alone"—repeatedly. "That hope is the reason for everything we do," explains Brian as the song winds down. "It's the reason we gather; it's the reason we celebrate; it's the reason we sing. Thank you for celebrating and singing with us today. You guys can have a seat, and we're going to continue the celebration. John is here to tell his story of how he found hope in Jesus Christ. Let's watch."

In the video, John recounts a story full of personal and family challenges. At a point when he was especially lonely and depressed, he met a stranger who invited him to North Point. John became regularly involved in a variety of North Point activities, and recounts finally having the courage to let God take control of his life. After thanking his family, small group, and various members of the church, John concludes, "I live life now with total trust in Jesus, and hope in his promise of redemption. Today I am so happy to profess Jesus Christ as my Lord and Savior." After the video has concluded, the baptism is performed live. The leader announces, "Because of your public profession of faith in Jesus Christ, it is my privilege to baptize you in the name of the Father, the Son, and the Holy Spirit." As John goes under the water in the large baptismal tank, the congregation erupts in applause.

Offering plates are passed down the rows, and a message scrolls down the video screens while "Shine Like Stars" plays in the background: "You may think that all we are doing is clearing the stage. But we are doing more than that. We are setting the stage for something *big*. Bigger than anything we've ever done.

Five weeks. Thirty churches. 150 nonprofits. Are you ready? Be Rich officially starts... *now.*"

Challenge

Andy Stanley, dressed in business casual, takes the stage and settles in on a stool. "It's good to see everybody as we kick off an extravaganza of generosity," he announces. Stanley explains that "Be Rich" is a monthlong campaign designed to help Christians view the concept of generosity differently and, in turn, to help the wider community look at Christians differently. Stanley's strategy for communicating the relevance of scripture is straightforward: emphasize *emotion* over *information.* Stanley observes that people come to church more in search of happiness than in search of truth: "As long as [pastors] are dishing out truth with no 'Here's the difference it will make' tacked on to the end, [they] will be perceived as irrelevant" by most of the people in the congregation.[36] This is the reason why North Point is adamant that preaching be helpful and not simply true.

As noted, Stanley does not preach verse by verse through books of the Bible. Instead, he privileges the parts of scripture that address practical contemporary topics. "While I'm a firm believer that all Scripture is equally inspired, observation tells me that all Scripture is not equally applicable," Stanley explains. "Consequently, preaching for life change requires that we emphasize some texts over others."[37] Stanley's goal is to "entice the audience to follow me into one passage of Scripture with the promise that the text is either going to answer a question they've been asking, solve a mystery they've been puzzled over, or resolve a tension they've been carrying."[38] The key is to create tension that the scripture will subsequently resolve.

This morning, Stanley creates tension by playing with the message title, "Be Rich." "For many of you, you're thinking, 'Be Rich'? I'm at a megachurch and you're talking about 'be rich'? I knew it! I can't wait to go home and tell my friends!" He then pulls a bait-and-switch: "'Be Rich' comes straight out of something the apostle Paul said in the New Testament, when he was writing a letter to his protégé Timothy, a younger guy he was mentoring. Here's what Paul says to Timothy."

First Timothy 6:17–18 (NIV) appears onscreen: "Command those who are rich in this present world . . . to do good, to be rich in deeds, and to be generous and willing to share." The words *rich* and *be rich* are highlighted in yellow. Stanley acknowledges that very few in the congregation probably *feel* rich. "I'm not going to spend a lot of time on this, but if you live in the United States of America, and if you're attending any of our churches in the Atlanta area, you are probably in the top 4 to 5 percent of wage earners in the world." The point of

"Be Rich" is stewardship: "As Christians, we believe that everything belongs to God, which means we're managers. And anyone that's managing someone else's money doesn't feel guilty, they just feel responsible."

Stanley moves from First Timothy to a discussion of the main text for the day, Philippians 2. The sermon begins to crescendo in verse 5: "On your relationships with one another, have the same mindset as Christ Jesus." Stanley explains, "The apostle Paul catapults us out of the golden rule (Do unto others as you would have them do unto you). We're going to call Paul's words in Philippians the 'platinum rule': Do unto others as *Christ* has done unto you." Verse 13—"For it is God who works in you to will and to act in order to fulfill his good purpose"—is the climax of the message. Stanley stresses that God acts through the congregation's presence, behavior, and generosity in the community. If the congregation would "respond to the people around you with compassion and generosity and character that reflects your Heavenly Father's love for you, then you, as a group, will shine like stars—just like our [opening] theme song says."

Stanley then explains the logistics of the "Be Rich" campaign. Every adult at North Point is challenged to give to "Be Rich" in three ways. First, there is a service component: find a charity in the area and sign up for one hour of volunteer work. Second, there is a food-donation component: donate at least three pounds of food to help stock area food pantries. Finally, there is a giving goal—the emphasis of this particular Sunday—where each person is challenged to donate a one-time gift of $39.95. Throughout this explanation, Stanley reiterates that 100 percent of the money will be given away to the organizations: "No shipping and handling costs. No overhead or operating expenses. No expensive vacations for the pastor and his family. We give it all away." (Figure 4.2)

North Point does not have a food bank, soup kitchen, or any of the other services one might expect to find at a church. From its very beginning, North Point instead set out to find "intersect partners": charities in the area that were already doing excellent work. To date, the church has over twenty intersect partners in the Atlanta area. Some are faith-based; others are not. North Point regularly asks its intersect partners, "Instead of competing with you, how can we help you? How can we resource you with money and volunteers? How can we elevate your status in the community so that more people will appreciate what you're doing and get involved?"

The goal for this morning is to raise $2.2 million in one day to give away. That money is earmarked to fund fifty different projects. Some of the money will help fund staff positions at nonprofits. Some will be used in programs for at-risk children in four local schools. Some contributions will be earmarked to support foster children and families. Other donations will provide job-readiness training,

Figure 4.2 Pastor Andy Stanley encourages his congregation to donate $39.95 during "Be Rich" Sunday.
Alpharetta, Georgia: October 2014. Photo by author.

or fund an employee program for veterans. There are global projects, including sending medical supplies to a West African organization that treats victims of the Ebola crisis. The list goes on.

"Everybody in the USA thinks something when they hear the word *church*," Stanley observes. "Do you know what they should think?" He answers his own question:

> They should think, "I don't believe any of that stuff Christians believe, but I've got to tell you, those are the most compassionate, generous, for-me people in our community. I don't want to go to one, but I am so glad there are churches in our community." When people hear the word *church* they should think, "Church. Christians. . . . They've got some beliefs and stuff I'm not sure about, but I'm telling you, those people make our community better."

Stanley ends by exhorting the congregation, "This year, let's 'Be Richer.' Let's do more and give more than ever before. Here's what we're going to do." As people leave, they are invited to deposit cash or check donations in buckets near the exit. There are also multiple stations in the lobby where people could donate via credit card. Those watching online are encouraged to click a 'Be Rich' button to make their contribution from home. "If everybody will participate at this minimum level, we will do some extraordinary good in the world," Stanley concludes. "So here we go. . . . On your mark. Get set. Be Rich!"

Several weeks later, the results are tallied. In the course of the 2014 "Be Rich" campaign, North Point donated 53,254 hours of service, one hundred tons of food, and $4.3 million to their local and global partners.[39]

Homiletical Analysis

In contrast to Park Street and Moody, whose services are not tailored to a specific demographic, North Point targets two distinct groups: mature believers who are concerned about evangelism, and people who grew up in the church but drifted away after high school and during college.[40] Barry Kosmin, the founding director of the Institute for the Study of Secularism in Society and a professor at Trinity College in Hartford, Connecticut, created a new category to describe many of the Americans in the second group: the "nones."[41] Kosmin and his colleagues define "nones" as "a diverse group of people who do not identify with any of the myriad of religious options in the American religious marketplace—the irreligious, the unreligious, the anti-religious, and the anti-clerical."[42] Evangelical pastors like Stanley have long been concerned by research findings about the "nones," including a 2009 report that suggested 73 percent of them came from religious homes.[43] David Kinnaman, president of the polling firm Barna Group and author of the 2007 book *unChristian*, explained the reality to pastors in stark terms:

> Imagine a group photo of all the students who come to your church (or live within your community of believers) in a typical year. Take a big fat marker and cross out three out of every four faces. That's the probable toll of spiritual disengagement as students navigate through their faith during the next two decades.[44]

In 2010, the evangelical publication *Christianity Today* offered concerned Christians a succinct summation of the current reality: "Most unbelieving outsiders are old friends, yesterday's worshipers, children who once prayed to Jesus."[45] Stanley explains it this way: the educated, dechurched millennials in his North Point congregation "are not non-Christian in the way we're accustomed to thinking about non-Christians. They're *post-Christian*, something dramatically different. This group has been there, done that, and has a closetful of camp T-shirts to show for it."[46] They know the biblical stories but no longer believe them.

Stanley is particularly interested in post-Christian attitudes toward scripture. Research by the Barna Group in collaboration with the American Bible Society from 2011 to 2016 showed that skeptical Americans are "becoming unfriendly—sometimes even hostile—to claims of faith."[47] Stanley observes that the majority of the people he has talked to who have abandoned their faith have done so because they lost confidence in the Old Testament. "People don't generally leave the church or faith because of Jesus . . . [the Old Testament is] at the top of the list."[48] Stanley offers several examples of how the Old Testament has been used in damaging ways throughout American history. Slave owners quoted it to justify their practices. White Christians have twisted its injunctions in order to condemn interracial marriage. Christian parents cite Leviticus in support of their decision to kick a child out of the house for being pregnant or gay.

Stanley is not interested in defending the morality of every event chronicled in the Old Testament. Furthermore, he is insistent that "anyone who lost faith in Jesus because they lost faith in the historical and archaeological credibility of the Old Testament lost faith unnecessarily." In marked contrast to Gordon Hugenberger, who used prehistorical resources like ancient clay tablets to establish the historicity of Abraham's journey in Genesis for the Park Street congregation, Stanley reminds the North Point congregation that "our faith doesn't teeter on the brink of extinction based on the archeology or the history of the Old Testament."[49]

Stanley's apologetic strategy is not to beat higher critics or New Atheists at their own game with point-by-point rebuttals. Stanley points out that every high school senior and college freshman is only "a click away from a podcast, YouTube video, or blog that undermines faith—Christianity and the Bible in particular."[50] Today agnostic scholars like Bart Ehrman regularly appear on television and media platforms to cast doubt on the historical veracity of the gospel accounts. New Atheists like Richard Dawkins and Sam Harris publicly argue that the Bible is harmful and that people who live by its principles are religious extremists. Even if Christian leaders are convinced that the worldwide flood and exodus from Egypt are historically and archaeologically verifiable, Stanley reminds them, "You won't be sitting beside the college freshmen from your church when a professor with more education than you shows them evidence to the contrary."[51]

Stanley affirms that the Bible is inerrant; however, he argues that defending the historicity of scripture is the wrong place for Christians to dig their trenches and mount their defenses.[52] Instead, Christians should emphasize the event-based foundation of their faith. Stanley advises, "If anybody ever starts taking a shot at your faith, especially the Old Testament, you just say, 'I know that's weird. But Jesus believed that. And if somebody can predict their own death and resurrection and pull it off, I just go with whatever they say."[53]

This point is controversial for many evangelicals, so Stanley draws on the analogy of scripture as Jesus's "birth certificate" to explain his point. A birth certificate documents an individual, but it doesn't *create* him or her. If a person's birth certificate were to be destroyed in a fire, the loss of that piece of paper would not mean the individual ceased to exist. Stanley asks evangelicals, "How would you respond to someone who refused to believe you existed until you produced a birth certificate? Crazy, I know, but this convoluted thinking mirrors the way most people think about our faith."[54] A robust apologetic for the twenty-first century will "start showing off the baby from Nazareth instead of trying to convince folks his birth certificate is accurate."[55] The Bible did not create Christianity or birth the church: instead, the resurrection sparked the movement that brought the Church the Bible.

Indeed, the "newness" of the New Testament in contrast to the Hebrew scriptures was an important focus of the "Be Rich" sermon. Stanley, as we saw, stressed that the apostle Paul catapults Christians beyond the golden rule of the Old Testament to an improved "platinum rule": do unto others as *Christ* has done unto you. In a commentary on this idea, Stanley explains that "doing for others what one hoped others would do in return was so . . . *old covenant*. Jesus . . . *raised the bar.* This was a whole 'nother kind of love."[56] Early Christians stayed behind to nurse the sick during times of plague. They visited sites where unwanted newborns—typically, baby girls and infants born with physical abnormalities—were left to die of exposure and took them home to raise as their own. Against this cultural backdrop, Christianity caught the attention and admiration of pagans. The generosity of Jesus and his followers "was so unusual, it was such a head-turner, it's amazing that it even made it out of the first century."[57] Stanley argues that if the generosity and compassion of the church changed the world once before, it can do so again.

Herein lies an important point of contrast. At Moody Church, Pastor Lutzer was bothered that so many evangelical pastors "cherry-pick verses of scripture about how Jesus helps you to become a better this or a better that. They preach about why you should believe the gospel because of the way in which it will benefit you." Lutzer believes more evangelicals should be preaching about the judgment of God. Stanley, however, unapologetically preaches that "following Jesus has made my life better and made me better fix life." He reminds the congregation that "if everyone in the U.S. decided to put others ahead of themselves . . . our culture would change. Following Jesus makes lives, nations, the world better. That in itself can't convince someone that Jesus is the Son of God, but it does get their attention."[58] The early Christian church did not get traction primarily because of its theology, which was, in Stanley's description, "weird. We believe a man came back from the dead."[59] Instead, pagans paid attention to first-century Christians because of their unusual compassion and generosity.

Despite their stylistic and homiletical contrasts, North Point and Moody Church share a basic underlying theology. Andy Stanley is a graduate of Dallas Theological Seminary, which, like Moody Bible Institute, is a flagship institution for dispensationalism. A 1981 article in *Eternity* magazine suggested that Moody

Bible Institute and Dallas Theological Seminary were "joined at the hip," as "the most 'trusted' institutions the cautious Christian public supports."[60] The issue of dispensational theology is what distinguishes both Moody Bible Institute and Dallas Theological Seminary from other brands of evangelicalism and what, according to the author, brings criticism from fellow evangelicals.[61] Indeed, in a recent talk at his alma mater, Stanley explained to Dallas Theological Seminary students that he actively avoids using the word *dispensational* to describe his theology because so many people find it problematic:

> When I'm talking to people and I know they're trying to put me in a [theological] box, and they ask, "What are you?" I don't use the word *dispensational* because they would just put an X over me. I say that I'm a sequentialist—[a word that] I made up and they can't define. . . . Now [they] have to listen instead of just writing me off.[62]

Semantic nuances notwithstanding, Stanley's sequentialism is undeniably a variation of dispensationalism. Stanley emphasizes the discontinuity between ancient Israel and the Christian church. Stanley reminds his congregation that the Bible "was organized around two covenants. One between God and ancient Israel, and one between God and everybody who wants to participate. . . . Focus on the second one. The covenant between God and Israel is obsolete."[63] In Stanley's analysis, the problem with modern evangelicalism is that it has adopted a "mix and match" approach to the Old and New Testaments, improperly blending both together to create a religion full of rules and regulations that God never intended for Christians to follow. Mixing and matching has led to a variety of theological vices: Stanley names "the prosperity gospel, the crusades, anti-Semitism, legalism, exclusivism, [and] judgmentalism" as a few possible examples.[64] Stanley believes that the act of "unhitching" Christian faith from God's covenant with Israel will eliminate churches' tendencies toward many of these problems.

Musical Analysis

The differences between North Point and Moody Church are most obvious in the two churches' contrasting philosophies of worship music. Stanley illustrates sequentialism with a musical example:

> Back in the day, cassette tapes were cutting-edge technology. Cassette tapes were the first technology to create the possibility for portable personalized music, until CDs came along, and now CDs are fast becoming obsolete. Not

because they're bad. Because something better has come along. Each of those technologies played a critical role in the evolution of music storage and portability. They were necessary steps to get where we are today. The same is true of God's covenant with the nation of Israel. Sequential.[65]

The parallels with worship music are clear. Stanley suggests that people can "appreciate [cassette tapes] without playing them"—presumably for their sentimental value.[66] In the same way, Christians can appreciate traditional hymns without singing them regularly in Sunday morning services.[67] There is no going back once culture has moved on.

But for Moody Church, Stanley's logic of replacing that which is "obsolete" with newer and better developments is inherently faulty. For example, Moody Church music minister Tim Stafford strongly believes that "the church needs to be very connected to its own story and its own history." Stafford is speaking not only of Moody Church in particular, but of the Christian church writ large. "I never want to lose the sphere of richness," he stresses, particularly "the depth of understanding that can be represented in music." Stafford wants the Moody Church congregation to experience music beyond that which "comes naturally to people and is readily available," for example, to hear excerpts from choral works like Bach's Mass in B Minor during the offertory in worship. This is one reason why Stafford is a passionate advocate for Moody Church's volunteer choir: "The oldest pieces of church music are written for choir. There's no way to replace it." While Stafford doesn't aim to perform entire classical masterworks on Sunday morning, he does want the choir to be equipped, for example, to sing selections from Handel's *Messiah* at the church's Christmas festival. "I want us to be able to experience it all, instead of binding our reputation too closely into one [musical style]," he explains. Returning to Stanley's analogy, Moody Church sees itself as an all-in-one stereo system, capable of supporting LP, cassette, CD, and digital technologies equally well.

Furthermore, Stafford believes that change at Moody Church must develop slowly and organically. "'First the blade, then the ear, then the full corn in the ear,' is ever the divine method," noted dispensationalist teacher Cyrus Ingerson Scofield. "There is a beautiful system in the gradualness of unfolding."[68] The pace of this unfolding cannot be rushed, nor can its internal logic be violated. Similarly, Moody music minister Tim Stafford compared the task of worship to that of gardening: "You wait a season or two before you really see the fruit of something. . . . I don't know if everything [I plant musically] is going to take or not, so I can't be too specific about what this place [Moody] must be."

In contrast, compare Stafford's gardening analogy with a story from Stanley's years in young adult ministry. When Stanley was twenty-six years old, he convinced the deacons of his former church to host a citywide evangelistic event for teenagers. In Stanley's sardonic recounting of the event, two thousand rowdy teenagers crowded into the very traditional Baptist church and were "entertained by *not the choir and orchestra.*" By the end of the evening, some two hundred students had come forward to pray with a counselor and give their lives to Christ. Stanley saw the event as an unequivocal success and argued that, moving forward, the church needed to rethink its outdated evangelistic strategy. The elders, however, interpreted the evening very differently, describing the event as "irreverent and unruly." Stanley recounts, "They were disturbed by what they saw taking place 'on the very spot where God's Word is preached each Sunday.' As one [elder] put it, '*That's not who we are.*'"[69] For leaders of the traditional church, growth must follow an internal logic: fruit is the expression of the original genetic information of the DNA in the seed. Continuing with the botanical metaphor, one might that Stanley's "end" (a rowdy evangelistic event) was not consistent with the church's beginning. The church had been planted as an acorn; the young Stanley was envisioning a palm tree ("That's not who we are").

A final significant difference between Moody's and North Point's musical cultures has to do with the physical act of singing. The Moody Church congregation clearly loves to sing, and Stafford encourages them in every way possible. When Stafford meets with new Moody members to talk about the music program, he always begins by asking the group to join him in singing a simple, familiar praise song. "That's your audition," Stafford announces at the end of the song. "Congratulations: you're all in! Welcome to Choir 1." Stafford goes on to explain that Choir 1 includes every person in the church: "all of us have a vocation to praise God with singing." "Choir 2"—which rehearses for two hours on Wednesday nights and performs anthems on Sunday mornings—is secondary to Choir 1. If senior pastor Erwin Lutzer is in the room, Stafford makes a winking reference to a quote attributed to D. L. Moody: "Singing *does at least as much as preaching* to impress the Word of God upon people's minds." These educational efforts have paid off. The Moody Church congregation sings with both enthusiasm and skill (often in four-part harmony), and the sound is exhilarating.

Moody Church has created what author and composer Dan Wilt describes as a "worship accompaniment culture." The ideal musical scenario for these worshippers is "hearing the voices of others around them, mingled in harmony or shared enthusiasm," much like a family around a piano. The worship accompaniment culture is "all about us, *singing together,*" supported by the band.[70] Robust congregational singing can even be evangelistic. One Moody Church member recounted bringing an unchurched friend to a Sunday morning service, praying that the visitor could sense that "we [the congregation] are singing with *everything we have*. We are worshipping God."[71]

North Point takes a very different approach to congregational song. In his book *Deep and Wide*, Andy Stanley explains, "We give [the people of North Point] permission to sing poorly. We give people permission not to sing at all if they prefer."[72] The rationale behind this decision is partly theological and partly pragmatic. Theologically, Stanley points out that "putting unbelievers or different kinds of believers in situations where they feel forced to worship is incredibly unfair." All their available options—remaining seated, leaving, or pretending to go along with something that they do not understand or believe—are uncomfortable. On a more pragmatic level, Stanley observes, "There is a segment of our population that doesn't like to sing. Ever. They don't sing in their cars or in their showers. And they aren't going to sing at church. . . . And that's ok."[73] Song leaders ought not "guilt" people into participating.

Finally, there are many individuals who are not opposed to the idea of singing but are embarrassed about the quality of their voice. One of the things Executive Creative Director Evan McLaughlin appreciated about the Sunday music at North Point was its volume: "You can't hear yourself sing, which is great," he laughed. "Well, for me it's great anyway—nobody wants to hear me sing!" McLaughlin's self-deprecating joke is emblematic of the times. John Bell, a leading expert on congregational song, notes that today one in four people has had a formational experience in which a teacher, family member, or close friend told them that their singing voice was not good enough to be heard in public. (This, despite the fact that the actual number of people who cannot replicate a melody in the right key is statistically very small.)[74] We have become disenfranchised from our own voices.

At North Point, the solution to this trifecta of difficulties—people who don't like to sing, people who are self-conscious about their singing, and people who have theological objections to singing—has been the creation of what Wilt calls a "worship immersion culture." Advocates of worship immersion were raised to listen to their music through headphones and want to feel surrounded by music in large-scale environments. They don't feel as if they need to sing in order engage. Instead, "They want to *feel* the music and lyrics in their bones. They feel close to others in the room when we are all *sharing* in the same experience . . . surrounded by, and participating in/with, the music filling our shared space."[75]

Wilt's comments were born out by my experience. At home, when I reviewed my audio recording of the service, I discovered that the musical portion was badly clipped. "Clipping" is the technical term for waveform distortion that occurs when an amplifier is overdriven and tries to deliver an output voltage beyond its maximum capacity. In plain English: the volume in the room was far too loud for my small recorder to handle. In the room, the music reverberated off the walls, pulsing in my ears and thumping in my chest. The sound was all-encompassing.

McLaughlin offered his own perspective on "worship immersion culture" with a personal story.

> Several months ago, I decided I needed to experience something different for one Sunday, so I went to a Catholic church downtown. It was amazing. There was just something very comforting about the order of the liturgy. There was a great deal of reverence and sanctity. There were parts of the service that I loved, like when the whole congregation stands and prays, "Lord, hear our prayer." I know that can become rote, but when you sit there and think, "Here is a collection of two or three hundred people calling out to God to hear our prayer," there's something so inspiring about it.

He paused before continuing.

> The reverence, the awe: where are the moments like that in North Point's service? I think about the second song we sang, "In Christ Alone." Even though we are playing it through a gigantic PA system with lots of bass, and lots of lights, the words tell the story of Christ's death, burial, resurrection, and ascension, and what will eventually be heaven's choir singing to Christ alone. There's a moment in that song where I'm like, "Wow! We are a part of this enormous Kingdom of God, both living and in the past." There's a moment in that for me.

For McLaughlin, the sound of one's own (imperfect) singing voice was less important than the congregation's collective experience of being swept up by amplified sound, synchronized lights, and theologically robust lyrics.

Todd Fields, director of worship leader development at North Point, finds its worship immersion culture troubling. "I see more people standing in the auditorium with a cup of Starbucks looking up at the screen like this (*mimics a blank facial expression*)." While Fields praised North Point's template for giving church leadership a common language and road map, he also suggested that the template unintentionally hamstrings worship leaders. Indeed, it is especially easy to feel constrained at North Point's main campus, where the timing of the live broadcast is crucial. Since Stanley's sermon is frequently broadcast live from the Alpharetta campus to all other North Point satellite campuses, the timing of worship at Alpharetta is particularly important. Fields explained, "From a timing standpoint, we can only do two songs. Welcome, two songs, and by 9:12 or 9:14

a.m., Andy's up and we're moving into offertory or baptism." This tight schedule sets an expectation in the congregation: "We train people that they're only going to get six to eight minutes of music, and then we move on to the next thing. That's hard. It's especially hard for someone to engage if they don't have that gear yet: either God hasn't developed it in you, or you don't have an affinity to worship yet. . . . I'm the guy going, 'Worship is a big deal. Music is a big deal.' I always want to be fighting for the song of the church."

North Point's approach to Sunday morning is not for everyone. However, this is a fact that Fields celebrates: "It blows my mind that God loves people and is so involved in how they can be reached with so many different expressions of church." Fields thinks of a close friend who left North Point to work at an Episcopal church: "As long as the orthodoxy of Christ, the sufficiency of the cross and resurrection, and discipleship are the main thing, then go with my blessing, dude. Jesus be glorified! There are a lot of people that are going to connect to God through [liturgical traditions]." At the same time, Fields stresses, "There are also a lot of people that would never come in a church, who don't want [liturgy]. They come here and go, 'Man, you won't believe what they did at North Point. They did this Lynyrd Skynyrd song last week!'" In response, Fields exclaims, "Well, praise God! Those people came to church. They heard Andy talk about how they can be forgiven. There are different flavors [of people and churches] and God knows them all. [North Point] is trying to think with open hands, to follow God with what has given us for this brief moment in history."

Just as the Old Testament was made obsolete by the New, Stanley believed that for a church to be faithful to its mission, it must be willing to adjust or abandon ministry models that are no longer the best means to an end. Everyone I talked to at North Point seemed keenly aware that their church's time in the spotlight would one day come to an end. "The day will come when our season of ministry will take a backseat to the next movement in the church," McLaughlin told me, "and that's OK. It *has* to happen that way. That's the way it has happened throughout the history of the church." McLaughlin maintains his sense of perspective by keeping this idea at the forefront of his mind:

> Everything in the heavens and earth is yours, O Lord. This is your kingdom. You put people in places of honor. And for whatever reason, you've chosen to put Andy and thusly the rest of us in a seat—and I don't mean this pridefully— of power, honor, and influence. We have a season when we'll be there, and then our season will come to an end. That could be one hundred years from now. It could be next week. We just don't know. We need to remain openhanded, focused, and intentional, not buckling under the weight of either external influences or internal garbage.

McLaughlin neatly summarized the underlying tension at North Point: "We don't want to become yesterday's model. We also don't want to be changing from week to week. So how do you sustain that without becoming what you don't want to become, which is either entertainment or business?" McLaughlin and his colleagues have no simplistic answers, but strive to be faithful to God's calling as they live in the center of that tension.

PART II
CONSENSUS VERSUS CONTESTATION

5

"How Can We Catch Fire?"

Prophecy and Activism in the Vineyard

Andy Stanley admits that when he suggests to pastors from other churches that they should create a template for their weekend services, he often gets the same pushback: "Theological types immediately raise their hands and ask about the Role of the Holy Spirit in worship. . . . Doesn't a template put everybody in a box?"[1] Casey—the forty-something pastor of "Koinonia Vineyard" (pseudonym)—is an excellent example of the "theological type" who would flag this as an issue.

Stanley's sermons follow a template in which the preacher first makes an emotional connection with the congregation, then introduces God's view on the morning topic as an answer to their felt need, and ultimately challenges the congregation to take action.[2] Casey finds the idea of a one-size-fits-all application anathema. "What the sermon says is going to be different for every person!" he objects. Casey compares the role of the preacher to that of a prophet: "The apostle Paul talks about the effectiveness of prophecy in a corporate setting. It has to function in such a way that people basically think, 'I have been read. I have been seen. I am exposed. God has spoken to me in such a way that my response is worshipful.'" In the same way, Casey emphasizes that scripture is a living Word that speaks directly to the heart. "I read until I find my voice—the prayer that I need to pray, or the thing where I say, 'Aha! This is my situation before God or before the world.'" Casey acknowledges that when people listen to his sermons, they might not leave with a sense of "Here's what you should do when you get home." But he is adamant that God speaks to every person who is willing to listen until they hear a living word.

Casey's point that the Bible speaks in different ways to different people at different times is noncontroversial in principle. (Evangelicals are fond of quoting 1 Timothy 3:16–17: "All Scripture is God-breathed and is useful for teaching, rebuking, correcting and training in righteousness, so that the servant of God may be thoroughly equipped for every good work.") But things quickly become complicated when two people listen to the same sermon and hear different—even conflicting—messages. What happens when Christians who are equally committed to the authority of the Bible disagree about the nature of the "good works" for which scripture is equipping them? The following story is illustrative.

Evangelical Worship. Melanie C. Ross, Oxford University Press. © Oxford University Press 2021.
DOI: 10.1093/oso/9780197530757.003.0006

I visited Koinonia Vineyard, a small West Coast congregation, on Sunday, July 10, 2016—a time when the national mood was marked by fear and mourning. A few days earlier, on Tuesday, July 5, Alton Sterling, a thirty-seven-year-old black man, had been shot dead at close range outside a convenience store by two white Louisiana police officers. The incident, which was recorded by multiple bystanders and circulated widely online, sparked demonstrations across Baton Rouge and an investigation by the US Justice Department. The following day (Wednesday, July 6), Philando Castile, a thirty-two-year-old black American, was killed by a Latino police officer who fired seven shots at him during a traffic stop in Falcon Heights, Minnesota. Later reports would show the encounter between Castile and the officer took less than sixty seconds.[3] On Thursday, July 7, the Black Lives Matter movement held a peaceful demonstration in Dallas, Texas, to protest the shootings of Sterling and Castile. A heavily armed sniper fired upon a group of Dallas police officers at the scene, killing five and injuring nine others. Upon capture, the gunman—a military veteran—stated that his agenda was "to kill white people, especially white officers" in retaliation for fatal police shootings of black men.[4]

These events were clearly on the congregation's mind the morning of my visit. Two conversations—one with "Machelle" (a volunteer musician), the other with "Gabriel" (the staff member responsible for weekly worship)—stand out. Machelle is one of very few African American members in the church. The lyrics of one worship song felt poignant to her that morning:

> Open our eyes
> to see the things that make Your heart cry
> To be the church that You would desire . . .
> Break down our pride
> And all the walls we've built up inside.[5]

As she sang these words, particularly the lines about breaking down walls and pride, Machelle thought about racial divisions in American society. The song felt like a prophetic call to action in the context of current events.

I anticipated that Gabriel, the staff member in charge of leading worship that Sunday, would similarly intuit this connection. Gabriel, a Caucasian who grew up in South Africa during the era of apartheid, has spent much of his life thinking about racial conflict. During Gabriel's formative years, his family was part of the Dutch Reformed Church in South Africa, a denomination whose teachings helped form the ideological basis for the nation's system of racial separation. "We all voted for the National Party," Gabriel remembers. "We all believed in apartheid. I have a major problem with that now."

Gabriel delights in finding unplanned, unforeseen connections between various parts of the worship service. In our interview, he remembered that the first pastor of Koinonia Vineyard never told the musicians the subject of his sermon in advance, because he wanted worship leaders to cultivate the skill of listening to God to choose the right music. Every week, Gabriel discovered serendipitous links between songs and sermon: a phenomenon that continues to this day. "It's amazing," he mused. "Sometimes we'll pick the *one* song that is the exact same theme that [the pastor] going to be preaching on—like, *exactly.* This happens more than most of the time. It happens a lot." As an experienced worship leader, Gabriel now feels, in his words, "pretty prophetic in knowing what God is doing" in worship. He explains his role with an analogy: as a worship leader, he points a magnifying glass (corporate worship) toward the sun (God). "I can't make the sun any bigger or bring it any closer," Gabriel acknowledges, "but I can change the angle of the magnifying glass. My question is always, 'How can we [the congregation] catch fire?'"

Given his experience with apartheid and his sensitivity to the Spirit's leading in worship, I was surprised that Gabriel saw no prophetic connection between his song selection and the news of the week. Gabriel is adamant, however, about separating worship and politics. Ironically perhaps, this conviction stems from his years in South Africa. Gabriel remembers that in the church of his youth, which was on the wrong side of the apartheid issue, "we got told who to vote for, what to believe, and which church to go to." Subsequently, today Gabriel has a visceral reaction to any combination of worship and politics. "Recently I went to a worship concert where [the band leader] said, 'If you're a Christian, you need to vote Republican,'" he reflects. "I just lost it. Believe whatever you want to believe politically, but don't tell [other Christians] that they have to believe that way too."

Although Machelle and Gabriel attended the same worship service, each took away a different message. The former heard a call to political activism; the latter to political neutrality. The "living word" each received depended, in large part, on their racial and cultural contexts. Theological ethicist Margaret Farley anticipated this scenario in a 1979 article that outlines two sides of a divide that has only grown starker over the past four decades. Farley observed that as current events become increasingly central to the liturgy, the Christian community becomes increasingly divided about the meaning and form of its service to the world. "*Diakonia* [service] is today not a simple matter of distributing food and clothing to the poor in the community," Farley writes. "Changes in population, in political and economic structures, and in understandings of justice have all demanded changes in Christian concepts and modes of service." While some Christians retain a traditional understanding of service as "works of charity," others call for "systemic change which will alleviate the unjust causes of human need."[6]

This divide between service as "charity" and service as "political ministry" is exacerbated by Christians' lack of a unified vision on controversial issues. Forty years ago, Farley named welfare reform, women's rights, affirmative action, abortion, and capital punishment as examples. Today, the list would also include the Black Lives Matter movement. "Can black Christians bring both their race and their religion with them into white evangelical spaces," queries Jemar Tisby, author of *The Color of Compromise: The Truth about the American Church's Complicity in Racism*.[7] This chapter addresses precisely that dilemma.

The Jesus People Movement

Koinonia Vineyard has roots in the Jesus People movement, which emerged out of the social turmoil and counterculture of the late 1960s and early 1970s. Although the origins of the movement are difficult to place, historians generally agree that the first "Jesus freaks" appeared in the midst of the 1967 Summer of Love in San Francisco's Haight-Ashbury district, urging people to follow Jesus Christ and to forsake drugs and promiscuous sex. Sympathetic individuals and church leaders opened makeshift coffeehouses where nomadic young people could access free drinks and sandwiches and, if needed, a place to stay. They also witnessed to the young people about Jesus Christ.[8] The Jesus People movement soon spread to Southern California, and by the end of the decade reached urban countercultural centers as far away as Seattle, Spokane, Detroit, Milwaukee, Atlanta, and Cincinnati.[9] Eventually, the movement spread beyond ex-drug users and hippies and came to include teenagers from mainline and evangelical church backgrounds who adopted a middle ground between the counterculture and the cautiousness of their parents' spiritual traditionalism.

Race was a problem then as now. According to historian Gretchen Lemke-Santaggelo, "Well more than half [of hippies] came from middleclass families, and fewer than 3% were nonwhite."[10] Indeed, Peter Braunstein and Michael Doyle note that the privileged status of white hippies often placed them at odds with their inner-city neighbors in the two largest hippie urban meccas, San Francisco's Haight-Ashbury and New York City's East Village. Many of the hippies who could afford to "drop out" and experiment with utopian ideals came from families that enjoyed post–World War II economic prosperity. However, the establishment they rejected was the very one that held the key to prosperity and social justice for Asians, Hispanics, and African Americans.[11] As one black resident of New York's East Village complained in 1967: "The hippies really bug us, because we know they can come down here and play their games for a while and then escape. And we can't, man."[12] A predominantly white American youth movement, hippies were generally indifferent to the causes of other racial communities. Relatedly, the Jesus People were not terribly interested in political activism, preferring to spend their energies on the work of evangelism.

In his book *God's Forever Family: The Jesus People Movement in America*, Larry Eskridge, preeminent historian of the movement, suggests that the Jesus People ethos was marked by three characteristics: (1) a literalistic interpretation of scripture that stressed Pentecostal and charismatic phenomena such as glossolalia, prophecy, and "words of knowledge," (2) a sense that the world was supernaturally charged with signs, wonders, and regular outpourings of divine intervention, and (3) an emphasis on evangelism motivated by the belief that humanity was living in the biblical Last Days.[13] Eskridge acknowledges that these three characteristics could easily apply to a broad swath of American evangelicals and Pentecostals during the 1960s and 1970s. However, what set the Jesus People apart from other evangelicals and Pentecostals of the time was their incorporation of these characteristics into "a distinctly nonbourgeois unchurchy atmosphere that was far removed from respectable America's way of doing church."[14]

The Jesus People promoted a casual, "come as you are" mood and blended elements of the counterculture into their worship. These "evangelical hippies" foreswore suits, ties, pipe organs, and hymns. They penned and recorded countless simple, biblically based "praise choruses" that could be accompanied by guitar, and distributed these songs through publishing houses that focused primarily on disseminating new worship music. The Jesus People were to a large extent responsible for the beginnings of what would eventually become the contemporary Christian music industry.

In 1971, America's leading periodicals and broadcast networks caught wind of the movement. Full feature articles on the Jesus People movement ran in American national news magazines *Life* and *Newsweek*. On June 21, 1971, the cover of *Time* magazine featured a psychedelic image of Christ with text that read "The Jesus Revolution." References to "Jesus freaks" appeared in the most unlikely of places, including the 1971 Elton John song "Tiny Dancer."[15] This publicity was triggered by a variety of factors, including the 1970 release of the British rock opera *Jesus Christ Superstar* and the cultural dissonance of hippies who embraced "old-time religion." Furthermore, as Eskridge points out, from the press's perspective, "The Jesus People made for an upbeat, reassuring 'youth angle' after several years of stories about rioting youth, draft dodgers, drug use, and the sexual revolution."[16]

As a result of this intense media publicity, the themes, music, and vocabulary of the Jesus People made their way into mainstream churches. Indeed, high school students and their adult ministry leaders used the Jesus People to create a parallel evangelical version of broader secular youth culture. The high-water mark of the Jesus People movement came in June 1972, when Campus Crusade for Christ's "EXPLO '72" conference in Dallas attracted eighty-five thousand young people for a week of seminars, rallies, and evangelism. Media buzz over the Jesus People dried up during late 1972 and early 1973; by the end of the decade, many of the movement's older, longtime members had moved on to school, marriage, jobs, families, and local church life.[17]

The Jesus People movement intersects with several of the congregations we have examined in previous chapters. Megachurches like North Point can trace their theological roots back to the movement and its emphasis on youth culture. The churches of the 1970s who accepted the hippie fashions, guitars, and vocabulary of the Jesus People reinforced the message that evangelical youth could occupy their own cultural space, distinct from that of the older generation. By teaching establishment churches that popular culture could be utilized to evangelize young people, the Jesus People paved the way for "seeker-sensitive" churches in later decades.

Furthermore, like the leaders of Moody Church, the Jesus People were dispensational in their theology. The 1960s were defined by the Vietnam War, the assassination of a president and of a civil rights leader, the sexual revolution, and the free speech, Black Power, and feminist movements. To many Americans, this turmoil made the world feel out of control. Dispensationalism's pessimistic emphasis on the world's slide into the End Times offered an explanatory framework for the cultural chaos. In the nineteenth century, Dwight L. Moody compared the world to a "wrecked vessel" and the gospel message to a lifeboat.[18] Over a hundred years later, the idea of the End Times similarly fueled the Jesus People's enthusiasm for evangelism in the twentieth century: they handed out tracts that declared "Get Ready!" and adorned their vehicles with bumper stickers that warned, "Be Prepared: Jesus Is Coming at Any Moment . . . Driver Will Disappear!"[19] In the summer of 1971, *Time* magazine reported, "Fresh-faced, wide-eyed young girls and earnest young men badger businessmen and shoppers on Hollywood Boulevard, near the Lincoln Memorial, in Dallas, in Detroit, and in Wichita, 'witnessing' for Christ with breathless exhortations."[20]

While North Point and Moody Church both owe a debt to the Jesus People movement, the church in this book that has been most significantly influenced by the evangelical hippies of the 1970s is the one we will meet in this chapter: Koinonia Vineyard. Koinonia belongs to the Vineyard Association, an evangelical religious movement that originated in Southern California and now has more than twenty-four hundred churches across the globe. Vineyard churches are typically known for their worship music and for Pentecostal-style activities that may take place during the service, including speaking in tongues, prophecy, and healing. These practices vary from church to church. In some Vineyard communities, the supernatural is front and center in the service; in others, Pentecostal-style supernatural practices are not foregrounded at all.

John Wimber and the Vineyard Movement

John Wimber (1934–1997), pastor and founder of the Vineyard Christian Fellowship, was a talented singer and keyboard player. Early in his career, he worked as a full-time musician, most famously as pianist and manager for the Righteous Brothers duo. Wimber converted to Christianity at a time when his life was spiraling into destruction. (*Christianity Today* described him as "a beer-guzzling, drug-abusing pop musician who was converted at the age of 29 while chain-smoking his way through a Quaker-led Bible study.")[21] John's wife, Carol, also converted, and the couple enthusiastically told anyone who would listen about their newfound freedom from guilt and fear of death. Eager to train for some sort of religious vocation, Wimber enrolled at Azusa Pacific College—a school associated with the Evangelical Friends (Quakers)—and studied sociology and theology. Upon graduation, he was "recorded" (ordained) within the California Yearly Meeting of Friends and took up a position as co-pastor of a Quaker church in Yorba Linda, California. Under Wimber's tenure, the church grew from two hundred to eight hundred, becoming the largest church in its denomination. Impressed with Wimber's church growth acumen, Fuller Seminary missiologist C. Peter Wagner invited him to co-lead the Charles E. Fuller Institute of Evangelism. Wimber consulted with hundreds of churches from twenty-seven denominations and met over forty thousand pastors.[22]

During his time at Fuller, Wimber's theology shifted significantly as a result of his interactions with George Eldon Ladd (1911–1982), a biblical scholar who sought to provide an academically respectable alternative to popular dispensationalism—the theology Wimber had learned at Yorba Linda Friends Community, and which continues to be taught at Moody Church. Due in part to its intense focus on the End Times, dispensationalism had become extremely popular among the Jesus People in the early 1970s. Eskridge explains:

> In some ways, the hippie Christians merely shifted cultural gears. Before, many of them pored over the *I Ching*, *The Tibetan Book of the Dead*, *The Urantia Book*, and the works of Carlos Castaneda for clues to meaning and spiritual enlightenment; now they could indulge their mystical bent by studying the symbolism and hidden prophetic clues in the writings of the Old Testament prophets and John the Revelator.[23]

Perhaps the most important catalyst for the spread of dispensational theology was *The Late Great Planet Earth* (1970), written by Hal Lindsey, a campus minister who worked in Southern California. Lindsey's book linked events of the time—the Cold War, the threat of imminent nuclear annihilation, Middle East crises, and the restoration of Israel—with biblical prophecy to suggest that the end of the world was near and Jesus's return was imminent. The *New York Times* identified the book as the "no. 1 non-fiction bestseller of the decade." In his history of the Jesus People movement, Richard Bustraan suggests that Lindsey's book is largely responsible for the popularity of similarly themed books and films, beginning with *A Thief in the Night* (1972) and running through Tim LaHaye and Jerry Jenkins's *Left Behind* book series (1995–2007).

But not all 1970s evangelicals were enamored with Lindsey's brand of dispensationalism. The most important academic interlocuter was Ladd, a professor at Fuller. Ladd, who was educated at Harvard, was part of the first wave of hires at Fuller and came with the goal of helping conservative evangelical thinkers become respected interlocutors in the liberal academic world. Dispensational theology was a stumbling block to this effort: as Vineyard scholar Jon Bialecki wryly notes, the liberal historical-critical scholars Ladd hoped to engage had little patience for anachronisms where "stinging insects [were] imagined as heralding contemporary technological innovations, such as military aircraft."[24] Ladd's solution was to shift the eschatological emphasis away from the book of Revelation and to focus instead on the Gospels—particularly the paradoxical places where the Kingdom of God was described as a future reality that had already broken into the present. Ladd's eschatology profoundly influenced Wimber and later the Vineyard movement.

Wimber left Yorba Linda a cessationist, a person who rules out the possibility of charismatic gifts in the present age. While at Fuller, however, he became fascinated by reports from seasoned missionaries and international students who gave credible accounts of combining evangelism with healing and prophecy. In this area, too, Ladd's influence on Wimber was significant. Ladd believed that many New Testament miracles were intimately connected to the concept of the Kingdom of God: in his words, they served as "pledges of the life of the eschatological Kingdom which will finally mean immortality for the body."[25] Miracles were biblical gifts of the Spirit and a foreshadowing of the kingdom; as such, they should continue to be active in the church. Vineyard leader and pastor Bill Jackson reflects on the importance of Ladd's teachings for what would later be revealed in Wimber's mature thought:

Ladd's understanding of the kingdom of God gave Wimber the theological ground he needed to explain the combination of evangelism and the miraculous that he was hearing from the missionaries at Fuller. Knowing that the kingdom was "already" gave him a basis for the inbreak of the miraculous in the present. Knowing that the kingdom was "not yet" gave him a basis for explaining why not all people were healed and why there was still suffering in the world.[26]

As Wimber's conservative evangelical paradigm expanded, he began to question his dispensational and cessationist positions. While John was teaching at Fuller, Carol had an experience of speaking in tongues. She also began to participate in a small home group at the Yorba Linda Friends Church that became increasingly dominated by charismatic worship. In a few months, the group grew to more than one hundred people, which eventually drew them into conflict with church leadership. (The Quaker leadership, which was cessationist, feared a "tongues outbreak.")[27] In April 1977, both parties agreed that the Wimbers' home group should leave Yorba Linda Friends Church.

The Wimbers formally joined their new congregation to Chuck Smith's Calvary Chapel network. For nine months, John Wimber preached from the healing-packed Gospel of Luke. His messages emphasized that Jesus preached the Kingdom of God and demonstrated it by healings. After months of praying for the sick with nothing to show in the way of healings, Wimber's biographer recounts, the leader was discouraged:

> It was a humiliating, gut-wrenching time when many people left the church in disgust. Yet Wimber would not give up. He believed that God would not let him. He was determined to see God heal people, and eventually—after ten months—he did. One young woman was healed in her home of a fever, and Wimber's exultation knew no bounds. "We got one!" he yelled at the top of his lungs on the way to his car.[28]

Soon after, the church exploded with more healings and charismatic manifestations, and attendance swelled to over fifteen hundred.

Tensions between Wimber's congregation and Calvary Chapel leadership began to mount. Chuck Smith, head pastor of Calvary Chapel, was worried that Wimber's emphasis on the Holy Spirit let too much room for error and chaos. In 1982, Wimber split from Calvary Chapel and joined a small group of Vineyard churches. ("Vineyard" was a name chosen by Kenn Gulliksen, a prolific church planter affiliated with Calvary Chapel, for a church he planted in Los Angeles in 1974.)[29] In 1983, Wimber's congregation moved into a sixty-five-thousand-square-foot warehouse in Anaheim, California, and changed its name to Anaheim Vineyard. Gulliksen, who preferred church planting to the day-to-day tasks of running a movement, turned over to Wimber the eight or so Vineyard churches that had grown out of his leadership. Shortly thereafter, some thirty other Calvary Chapel congregations pastored by leaders wanting more emphasis on the Holy Spirit left Calvary Chapel to join the association of Vineyard churches.[30] By early 1983, Wimber was the leader of a thriving group of forty churches, and the Vineyard movement was born.

Koinonia Vineyard

"Koinonia Vineyard" was founded in the late 1980s by Isaac, then in his thirties, who was trained by John Wimber in the original Vineyard Fellowship. Isaac and his wife traveled down the West Coast before eventually deciding to plant a church fifteen miles north of an urban center. In its earliest years, the young church met in a YMCA building four blocks away from the city's large college. Fourteen people attended the first meeting, the only advertising for which was a bright yellow "WANTED" poster. One congregant who has been with the church since its earliest days remembered the poster saying "something like, 'If you're a liar, a thief, a sinner, etc., we've got a church for you.'"

By the end of the first year, the church had grown to forty attendees each Sunday evening. By the second year, attendance had grown to eighty-five people: eighty-four adults and one child. Koinonia Vineyard was a church of singles: of all the adults, only six were married. The congregation eventually outgrew the YMCA and relocated a mile west to a VFW hall, a location affectionately dubbed "Vineyard for Weirdos" by congregants. For the first time, the church could meet on Sunday mornings, a shift that attracted many more families.

Kevin, an older member of the congregation, remembers the VFW hall as a "run-down kind of place. The building must have been sixty or seventy years old, and it hadn't been painted in forty years. It had dirty, mustard yellow walls all around, except for the stage, which was orange. It was the most surreal, bizarre place." Kevin informed me that "Vineyard for Weirdos" was an accurate moniker. "I think many people were drawn to the strangeness of that place—a lot of really broken people. Just about everybody had real severe issues or at least issues of one kind or another." Kevin himself is an example. When I asked my standard opening interview question—"Can tell me how you came to be a part of this congregation?"—Kevin responded:

> I can't really. I was in a very bad mental state. I actually don't have memory of about two and a half years of my life. It's spotty. I have some memories, but I actually have no idea how I found this particular church. My first memories of it were of being in a service and I'd been through some Christian-based therapy, and they seemed to be talking the same language: that being with God is healing and all this stuff. I knew the language and I appreciated that. The Spirit of God was here in a powerful way. So I stayed.

In the early 1990s, Koinonia Vineyard began renting a building that would become its permanent home. The mission-style complex had a long and eventful history. Originally constructed as an Episcopal church in the early 1900s, the building was home to a string of congregations until it was abandoned in the

1950s. After being boarded up for decades, the complex was purchased by developers in the early 1980s and turned into a restaurant and retail complex. Thai, Korean, and Vietnamese eateries took over the lower-level area where Sunday school classes used to meet. The main sanctuary space upstairs proved more difficult to rent. A nightclub failed, as did the microbrewery that installed fermentation tanks in the bell tower and beer storage vats in former classrooms. At the end of the decade, a member of Koinonia Vineyard purchased the complex and gave the church a low-cost lease for the sanctuary and upstairs offices. Today, the tangy scent of ginger and peppers wafts through the sanctuary from the restaurants downstairs. Fermentation tanks remain in the bell tower. Church members joke about the irony of a "Vineyard" replacing a brewery.

Church attendance peaked at around five hundred in the late 1990s. One church member described the time as "awesome!" and commented, "It was a packed house, filled with people who were just excited about being together and living together. Worship was powerful. People spoke the truth—and not just the pastors. Amazing prayer times." When the building was nearly at its seating capacity, Isaac made a controversial decision to break up the congregation and plant new churches in the city. One-third of the people were asked to continue worshipping in the building on Sunday mornings. One-third were asked to create a new community that would meet on Saturday nights. The final third of the group was tasked with starting a weeknight satellite church on the opposite side of the city. Each community would have its own leadership, teaching, and worship style.

The experiment failed. After two-thirds of the congregation was "reassigned," many slipped away for good, preferring to leave the church rather than participate in the new plants. The two satellite congregations struggled for a few years and eventually died out. One church member who left to help start a new plant remembered how strange it felt to return to the original worship space: "I figured that while we were across town struggling to make the new community work, Sunday mornings [at the original site] were rocking like usual." When she and her family returned a few years later, they were amazed: "Where is everybody?! People came to Koinonia for the community. Splitting up the congregation was really hard, and we never really recovered from it, numbers-wise." Casey, a seminary graduate in his early thirties, became senior pastor in the early 2000s. There were approximately fifty people in attendance at the service I observed.

Service Description

The sanctuary of Koinonia Vineyard is a jumble of juxtapositions. Upon entering, one is immediately struck by the beautiful stained-glass windows that cover the entire wall on the righthand side of the room. The rest of the sanctuary, however, looks nothing like a traditional church. There are no thick carpets or mahogany pews with comfortable cushions. Instead, the church walls are painted light salmon, and the scuffed floor is a checkerboard of pink and green linoleum tiles. Because outside community groups rent out the room for dance rehearsals and other weekday events, the congregation has opted for flexible seating. Each week, volunteers unstack chairs from rolling dollies and arrange them in forward-facing rows. The focal point of the room is a miniature stage with green theater drapes, which old-timers explain was built for comedy acts during the years when the building served as a nightclub.

On the left wall hangs a tall cross surrounded by homemade artwork. The church's creative arts team gathered a stack of blank canvases and traced a pattern across them all with a thin line of black paint (Figure 5.1). They then handed out the panels to any interested member of the congregation to take home and decorate. "It's amazing!" one interviewee enthused. "Some of the pictures meld into each other. Like, one has a red corner, and it goes into the red corner of this other one. Nobody planned that. It was just people going to God and saying, 'What should I make?' and that's what they came up with." There are no coincidences at Koinonia Vineyard. Members see God's hand at work in even the smallest of details.

Figure 5.1 Artwork at Koinonia Vineyard
July 2016. Photo by author.

The service begins with approximately half an hour of music, including the song referenced at the beginning of this chapter, which asked God to open worshippers' eyes and break down pride and walls of division. As the song ends, Pastor Casey steps forward to speak. "One of our leaders challenged me before worship began this morning," he begins. "'Are you going to say something in light of the past week? Are we [as a congregation] going to do something?' I've been reflecting a lot on that during worship." Casey has no notes. He speaks slowly, seeming to weigh each word before speaking it aloud. "I don't tend to say things the week after something happens, partly because if I did, I would say something every week." Someone in the back chuckles quietly in response, breaking the nervous tension has started to build in the congregation. Casey remains somber. "I'm not saying that as a joke," he lightly scolds. "Hundreds of people were killed in Baghdad this week. There's Brexit. And Dallas. And Turkey. These are deeply complex things that don't have quick remedies."[31]

Casey pauses, then recounts a story from his college years, a time when he worked closely with "an African American minister of significant stature, both physically and spiritually." This work involved crossing the tracks—literally and metaphorically—between one of the wealthiest communities in the United States and one of the poorest. This was the first time Casey was "awakened to awareness about racial reconciliations in the country." During this same period, he tells us, he began to read through the Old Testament. "One of the things that stood out to me is that there is a cry that runs through the entirety of scripture, which is 'Seek justice and do what is right,'" he reports, citing Isaiah 56:1. "Time and time again, the message is sent to kings and leaders: 'Your duty and responsibility is to speak for those who do not have a voice and to foster communities where righteousness and justice is done.'"

Troubled by both the economic injustices he was witnessing and the scriptures he was reading, Casey recounts, he went to his mentor for advice. Casey admits that he was expecting to hear an admonition: "Go somewhere and do ministry exclusively with the 'other'—whether 'other' meant racially, economically, etc." Instead, the African American minister counseled Casey, "Go to your own people and help them understand it"—a charge that felt "like a mandate or a commission" to the young white college student.

Looking back on this exchange, Casey reflects, "[My mentor] was someone who saw me and took me seriously in the greater context that I was a part of historically, racially, etc. But he also saw *me*, in the context of my particularity." He continues,

One of the things I've become aware of is that it's very hard to see people who one is afraid of. To really *see* another requires open-heartedness: the willingness to be influenced affected, touched, changed by someone else. It's really hard to be open-hearted under conditions of fear, and I can't think of a better word to describe the circumstances of the past week and their deeper roots than *fear*. I John 4:18 tells us that there is no fear in love, and perhaps there is also no love in fear.

Casey waits a moment before offering a final thought. "Responding to the challenge I got this morning to say something"—he stops abruptly. The silence lasts a full thirty seconds while Casey gathers his thoughts. He starts again, offering a reflection marked by long pauses:

> Part of the profound power of Jesus's ministry is that he *saw* people. We are people who bear his name. We must go forward in a way that remains willing to love, open to difference, to conflict, and to hurt. The Lord's Table [Eucharist] is a profound expression of that. All the people who were against God—who deny and betray him—he gave himself to us. . . . This is the beautiful call of God: to be a people who bring "for-ness" in circumstances and situations where there is significant "against-ness." . . . Is that enough? No. But it's a baseline. . . . Whatever else we may do, if there's not a "for-ness" in love, then I don't think we've made a lot of progress.

Casey shifts his weight self-consciously. "So. That's me. Responding 'in the moment' to a challenge to say *something*. It's not possible to say everything." He returns to his seat.

During the summer months, Koinonia invites lay congregational leaders of the congregation to take turns preaching. Although most have not been to seminary or studied systematic theology formally, the congregation is profoundly egalitarian. Echoing the Quaker tradition out of which John Wimber came, members of Koinonia Vineyard believe that the Spirit has the potential to speak through anyone who is known to the community, regardless of their title or ordination status.

This morning's reflection is led by Janine, an energetic woman in her sixties. Janine reminds the congregation the thematic focus of the summer is on dreams and visions: "our sleeping dreams, our waking dreams, and God's dreams." The national events of the week are on Janine's mind as well: she has been thinking about Martin Luther King Jr.'s "I Have a Dream" speech, delivered on August 28, 1963, in which the African American activist called for civil and economic rights and an end to racism in the United States. In revisiting the speech in preparation for her sermon, Janine was struck by King's faith and perseverance. "He had some very, very strong, beautiful dreams. He knew what was right and he did not waver in the face of great opposition. It didn't stop him from dreaming. He did not give up." Janine cites from King's famous speech: " 'Now is the time to make justice a reality for all God's children. It would be fatal for a nation to overlook the urgency of the moment." Janine suggests to the congregation that "we are having one of those moments again. [King] gave that speech in the 1960s, and here we are in 2016. So much has changed since that time, but it's not enough. More change is needed for his dreams to become reality."

Although King did not see his dream fulfilled, Janine thanks God that "he took action toward his dream and left a legacy that continues to be worked out to this day. There are dreams, and then we move with our dreams. We take action. There something for us to do. Let's not overlook the urgency of the moment," she challenges the assembly. "What is our part today in helping make justice a reality for all God's children?" These introductory remarks are clearly Janine's attempt, like Casey's, to respond "in the moment" to the challenge to "say *something*." Her message contains no more references to American racial tensions in either the past or the present.

Janine's tone lightens as she announces that her topic for the day is "about awakening to our dreams." She quotes Proverbs 29:18 in both the King James translation ("Where there's no vision, the people perish") and Eugene Peterson's paraphrase in *The Message* ("If people can't see what God is doing, they stumble all over themselves. But when they attend to what he reveals, they are most blessed").[32] Janine's own interpretation of the proverb is that "people don't do well without dreams for their lives."

Janine emphasizes that following a dream can entail risk. For Janine and her husband, it meant relocating to China for several years during the 1980s. "We had this dream to go live among other people and be a light that pointed to Jesus. As we journeyed we were like pilgrims—dependent on our host country's neighbors for community. We had no idea how to be there. We were very young Californians, moving to a very large continent!" Janine and her husband quickly came to rely on local people, who showed them how to shop and manage their food rations. New Chinese friends included the couple in community and family events. "We had to let go of our families, our culture, our fears, our unhelpful beliefs," Janine reflects, "but when we did, we learned so much."

Janine concludes with advice for the congregation. "Keep dreaming the big dreams that God gives you, and encourage one another to stay on course, working hard to bring God's kingdom in through us. Your kingdom come, your will be done on earth as it is in heaven. We wait for the final fulfillment, but we also work to see God's kingdom come on earth." She invites anyone who desires prayer to come forward, particularly those who "need encouragement, have found their dreams roadblocked, or need the Lord to awaken a new dream."

"Real Talk"

A few days after the service, Machelle, the worship leader encountered earlier, and I sit down for coffee. "Real talk," she announces. "You asked how many people of color in our congregation? It's just me."

Machelle loves the people of Koinonia Vineyard and regularly encounters God during the church's musical worship. However, other elements of the service make her uncomfortable. "I think our church has a very vague and unclear stance in terms of what's going on in the world right now, and that makes worship really difficult. I felt nothing but dread leading up to Sunday." Machelle feels that race is rarely discussed at Koinonia: "People have tried to broach it in years past. Like, 'Can we talk about what's going on in our nation right now with all these black bodies dying? Where's the church in all that? How should we posture ourselves?'" But those discussions never seemed to gain traction, and Machelle does not want to bear the burden of being the only one pushing them. When I ask Machelle if she was the leader who challenged Casey to "say something" about the events of the previous week, she shakes her head in emphatic denial. "One of my friends said, 'I feel like somebody should say something this morning.' I said, 'No. It already feels hard for me to be in the room right now, and that conversation can't be forced.'" The friend confronted Casey nevertheless, a move that Machelle believes was a mistake.

For Machelle, Casey's comments on Sunday missed the mark. "He said 'Brexit.' He said 'Dallas.' But for whatever reason, he couldn't say 'Black Lives Matter.'" Machelle appreciates that Casey, who is "very conciliatory" and "scholarly minded," tries to see multiple sides of complex situations. But on some Sundays, she is keenly aware of Casey's blind spots. "He once preached a whole sermon about diversity within the church, about how we have beautiful variety in the Body of Christ. But it was right after Charleston, and I don't think he ever said the word *race*. I'm thinking, 'A church just got shot up, and you didn't even mention it.'"[33]

After talking with Machelle, I reviewed my service transcript. Sure enough, the word *race* was never mentioned. Janine, the volunteer lay preacher, praises Martin Luther King Jr. with generic phrases: King's dreams were "very strong" and "beautiful"; he "knew what was right" and "did not waver in the face of great opposition." Listening to Janine's gloss, a listener unfamiliar with American history would not know that King's iconic speech took place only four months after African American adults and youth had been confronted by police dogs and fire hoses in Birmingham, Alabama, an event well covered in the media. Janine also omits the lines of the speech in which King expresses his fervent hope that "little children will one day live in a nation where they will not be judged by the color of their skin but by the content of their character" and that "little black boys and black girls will be able to join hands with little white boys and white girls as sisters and brothers."

Machelle's earliest remembered encounter with racism happened when she was very young. Musically precocious, Machelle was part of a performing arts troupe during her elementary school years. One season, she was selected to sing a vocally demanding Disney princess solo. Machelle was thrilled. She still remembers the elaborately detailed costume handcrafted by a family friend and the soft feel of the red-and-yellow satin against her skin. On the day of the performance, Machelle went to the microphone, took a steadying breath, and sang her piece flawlessly. After finishing, she looked out into the audience. "I could tell they were sort of laughing to each other and whispering, but I couldn't figure out what was going on." A message was slowly spread through the group. The murmurs eventually became intelligible to Machelle: "Snow Black! Ha ha! That doesn't make any sense! Snow Black . . . Snow Black . . . Snow Black!" Looking back on the experience as an adult, Machelle reflects,

> I think that was one of my first aha! moments . . . in understanding the difference between how I viewed myself and how I came to learn that the world would view me. I remember thinking, "It doesn't matter to this group that I feel beautiful in this dress. It doesn't matter that I'm singing really well, that I've worked really hard, that I'm proud of what I'm doing." What mattered to them was what they could see and that it didn't make sense. So, they felt like it was OK to laugh, and to point, and to rule out those other things. That was pretty crushing for a seven-year-old.

Twenty-first-century African American parents routinely prepare their children for the aha! moment Machelle experienced at the age of seven. Children do not understand a reality proven by research: in Tomeka Davis's words, "Young Black boys are only perceived as 'cute' for a short time before they are seen as 'adult' and therefore dangerous."[34] Consequently, one rite of passage for black youth is hearing "the talk" from their parents, families, and trusted adult figures, intended to help youth understand the harsh reality that "inhabiting a body of color can have violent or lethal consequences."[35] Supreme Court justice Sonia Sotomayor explained in 2016, "For generations, black and brown parents have given their children 'the talk'—instructing them never to run down the street; always keep your hands where they can be seen; do not even thinking of talking back to a stranger—all out of fear of how an officer with a gun will react to them."[36] Bennett Capers, Stanley A. August Professor of Law at Brooklyn Law School, recalls the version of the talk he received from his parents, including instructions for what to do if accosted by the police: "Just keep your head down and be deferential. Don't ask how come or why. Don't run. If they let you go, say 'Thank you.' Don't show your color. Don't act black."[37]

Michelle works hard to "build up my black and brown students," whom she teaches each day. She finds the prospect of parenting "terrifying." Michelle confides that she and her husband already feel "so overprotective" of the children they hope to have one day. While Janine's Sunday message made strong connections between dreams and hope, Michelle is haunted by a more troubling dream. The details are fleeting, but the dream inevitably follows the same pattern, starting with the joyful announcement that Michelle is pregnant and ending in the child's violent death. "I always wake up in tears and have to pray because it feels so real," she confides. Michelle wishes that she could envision bringing black children into a better world. But she is a pragmatist: "The question is what to do with the [world] we've got." For parents and teachers who, like Michelle, understand racial discrimination firsthand, partial solutions to that question lie in socializing children of color to understand how they may be perceived by others, and in teaching them adaptive responses to social, economic, and political barriers they might face as a result of race.

Why is this background important for understanding Sunday morning worship at Koinonia Vineyard? When a black parent has to teach their child "Ten Rules of Survival if Stopped by the Police"—a list that includes the admonitions "Always remember that anything you say or do can be used against you in court" (number 4) and "Do not resist arrest, even if you believe that you are innocent" (number 9)—generalized, well-intentioned advice from a Caucasian pastor like Casey to remain "open-hearted" and vulnerable in the face of the unknown "other" can sound irresponsible and dangerously naive.[38] To Michelle, who considers Casey a close friend, it even smacks of betrayal. "When Casey asked the congregation, 'Why are you so scared . . . ?'" Michelle's voice trails off. "The fact that you [Casey] even asked that . . . how can you, you know, be my friend and my brother and not see me, not see that this is who I am?" When she contemplates the future, Michelle is ambivalent about raising a child in the congregation. Koinonia Vineyard would "no longer be a holy place if you [white church members] touch my child's hair inappropriately."[39] In the same breath, Michelle stresses, "But I love my church. It's confusing."

As a pastor, Casey is also torn. "I talked to Michelle this week," he confided, "and I heard her concern that saying nothing isn't helpful. But I'm still wondering what to say, particularly to this congregation." Casey noted that most individuals in Koinonia Vineyard do not hold positions of influence:

It's not a congregation that's in power for the most part. We're not in political office, or law enforcement, or the military. We're a young chef starting out, a barista, a retired engineer. What is going to fix this right now? What can I say? Tell people not to shoot each other? Walk into Starbucks and look at the newspaper—these things are already being said.

Another one of Casey's pastoral challenges is that Koinonia has people on both ends of the political spectrum. He handles this diversity by "trying to keep Jesus at the center, not focusing on political issues that are polarizing—in other words, making 'every effort to maintain the unity of the Spirit through the bond of peace.'" At the same time, Casey approvingly cites "that great Desmond Tutu line: 'I don't know what Bible people are reading if they think that religion and politics don't mix.'" Casey acknowledges that there are times when "you have to come down and say, 'That is wrong. This is unjust.'" But on this particular Sunday—a few days after black men were subjected to violent deaths at the hands of white police officers, and white police officers were targeted and killed by the hand of a black sniper—Casey simply didn't feel comfortable taking a side. "You've got an outraged black community and a terrified white community. I'm aware of the complexity of the dynamics involved."

Conclusion

Liturgical scholars address concerns like the ones Casey raises by emphasizing the intrinsic link between liturgy and ethics.[40] Theologian William T. Cavanaugh points out that too often Christians settle for a simplistic, direct correspondence between what happens in worship and what happens beyond the walls of the church: "We try to 'read' the liturgy for symbols and meanings that we take out and apply in the 'real world'—the offering means we should give of our wealth, the kiss of peace means we should seek peace in international relations, and so on."[41] While there is nothing wrong with this sort of one-to-one correlation, ultimately it does not go far enough. For theologian Don Saliers, the connection between liturgy and ethics is more *affective*—having to do with internal dispositions, motivations, and emotions—than it is rule based. Furthermore, Saliers cautions against thinking that there is only a single link between liturgy and ethics, suggesting instead that the interconnections between liturgy and action are as complex and varied as the Christian communities in which they are practiced.[42] We can identify this unique relationship in two examples of how the liturgy of Koinonia Vineyard informs its participants.

Eschatology

During the civil rights era, evangelical leader Billy Graham struggled with questions of racial justice. In many ways, Graham was ahead of his time. In 1952—over a decade before the Civil Rights Act of 1964 officially outlawed discrimination on the basis of race—Graham preached against segregation in the church. He demanded integrated seating at a 1953 crusade and integrated his own ministry staff in 1957. However, historians have pointed to a weak spot in Graham's record on civil rights: namely, his instinct to uphold law and order by calling for an end to political agitation. Graham supported landmark civil rights legislation after it was passed into law, but he was a critic of the marches, demonstrations, and acts of civil disobedience that helped make reform possible.[43] When pressed by critics who wanted him to take a more activist stance, Graham was often tentative, stressing that he was a preacher rather than a prophet. "We follow the existing social customs in whatever part of the country in which we minister," he said. "I came to Jackson to preach only the Bible and not to enter into local issues."[44]

Sociologists Michael Emerson and Christian Smith suggest that Graham's premillennialism—the view that the present world is evil and will inevitably suffer moral decline until Christ comes again—influenced Graham's early understanding of the civil rights movement. In response to King's famous "I Have a Dream" speech, Graham, who had been invited to but did not attend the 1963 March on Washington, is said to have responded, "Only when Christ comes again will little white children of Alabama walk hand in hand with little black children."[45] Unlike Martin Luther King, who used eschatological language to spur political change, Graham used eschatology to emphasize the limits of politics.

The eschatology of the Vineyard Association falls somewhere between Graham's conservativism and King's activism. Following the work of George Eldon Ladd, Vineyard churches teach that the Kingdom of God is both "already" and "not yet": Jesus introduced the perfections of heaven on earth, but that reality cannot be fully realized until the Second Coming. For example, miraculous healings are possible, but because we still live in a sinful world, they cannot always happen. In the same way, Jesus revealed what is morally just, but because Christians still live in a sinful world, this justice can only be "glimpsed and glanced," as anthropologist James Bielo puts it.[46] The Bible calls the church to transform the world, but full transformation cannot happen on this side of heaven. A member of Koinonia Vineyard articulated this perspective during a time of open sharing in a later service:

I think people who don't have faith in God are really unnerved by those tragedies because they feel powerless, and so it's like a kneejerk reaction: "What can I do to make this not ever happen again?" You know, I think people of faith feel that, too, and, you know, the politicians are saying we need to vet immigrants, or we need to make it harder to buy guns, or retrain the police, all this stuff. Some of those things can make a little bit of difference, but I think our response—and this is just me—is that we have to accept that we have *limited* power to affect things, not total power. Our response is to know we're vulnerable in this world and can only do so much, but we can choose to keep trust in God and lean on him like we've never done before. We can have peace that God is in control.

This response typifies the Vineyard mindset. Vineyard churches typically refrain from political activism because they believe that real change can only come through an unexpected inbreaking of God's transcendent power.

Consider the subject of prayer. In her groundbreaking study of Vineyard spirituality, *When God Talks Back*, anthropologist Tanya Luhrmann explains what it means to a Vineyard Christian to "hear God's voice" in prayer:

> God will answer back, through thoughts and mental images he places in your mind, and through sensations he causes in your body. You still experience those thoughts and images and sensations, for the most part, as if they were your own, generated from within your own mind and body. You have to learn to experience those you have identified as God's as different.

This last point—identifying God's voice as *different* from one's own—is especially important. Luhrmann explains that in the Vineyard church, one "test" for discerning whether God has, in fact, spoken is to ask whether the thought that came to mind during prayer was "the kind of thing you would say or imagine anyway: if it was, the thought was probably yours. If not, it could be God."[47] The thoughts that are most spontaneous and unexpected—something that a person would never conceive of on their own—are mostly likely to be of an external, supernatural origin.

Building on Luhrmann's work, anthropologist Jon Bialecki suggests that a similar dynamic is operative in Vineyard political thought. In politics, as in prayer, Vineyard Christians look for a divine inbreaking that is so sharp, so shockingly unexpected that it could only have been occasioned by a divine hand.[48] It is what Bialecki calls a "radical" justice that marks its alterity by rejecting quotidian forms of practice: a vision of a world "that is always waiting for redemption but that will not find that redemption in any form reminiscent of any prior institution."[49] For instance, it may be salutary to screen immigrants, reform gun laws, and retrain law enforcement, but humanly initiated movements like Black Lives Matter or Blue Lives Matter are not the fully realized, radical inbreaking of God for which Vineyard churches pray. Ultimately, Vineyard Christians crave more than mere policy prescriptions or political change. They want a miracle.[50]

Quaker Discernment

In much writing about the Vineyard tradition, there has been a strong focus on the influence of Pentecostalism and the writings of George Eldon Ladd. Indeed, Casey reflects that when he first started his tenure as pastor at Koinonia Vineyard, the congregation had a stronger Pentecostal theological bent. However, the Quaker tradition has also made a significant contribution to Vineyard spirituality. Recall that founder John Wimber was converted at a Quaker Bible study, was ordained as a Quaker, and co-pastored one of the largest Quaker churches in the denomination. The issue of speaking in tongues ultimately led to a split between Wimber and the Quaker elders. Casey knows this historical background well, and a few months before my visit, he had preached a sermon series about Quaker spirituality. He explains,

> One of the things I think was helpful for the congregation was that I framed [the series] as a way of reconnecting with the Vineyard's Quaker roots. The first Vineyard Fellowship was a group of people who were sort of "disfellowshipped" from an evangelical Quaker church. What we do [at Koinonia] fits evangelical Quakerism in a lot of ways. We're not gathering for an hour in what Quakers would call an "unprogrammed meeting." We do have an order of service, someone who plans to speak, music. But the best Sundays are the ones where we're kind of just listening and waiting on the Lord. A lot of times, the person leading the service will say something like, "Why don't we linger here a for little bit? If you're known among us and have something that would be encouraging for the folks here, feel free to share that." Sometimes three or four people will share, and there's this really lovely coherence. Everyone in the room has the sense of, "Well, the message already got spoken." The sermon just kind of puts a bow on it. It's beautiful because it can just come from whoever, organically and genuinely. That feels very Quaker to me.

Casey also confided,

> I read a book of Quaker theology a few years ago by a woman named Margery Post Abbott called *To Be Broken and Tender*.[51] She's part of the unprogrammed/ more liberal side of Quakerism, and this book was kind of her dialogue with

conservative or even evangelical Quakerism. As I was reading it, I was like, "Wow! This is all Vineyard!"

In light of Casey's explicit references to Quakerism, I suggest that in addition to looking for a dramatic, miraculous inbreaking of the Kingdom of God (à la Ladd), there is a less dramatic but equally important formative influence at work in Koinonia's worship: the Quaker notion of "gospel order" and its accompanying understanding of ethics.

The term "gospel order" seems to have originated with George Fox.[52] Quaker scholar Lloyd Lee Wilson explains the concept:

> The Quaker gestalt enables one to perceive that God has an intent or purpose for creation—a Gospel Order—and that the entire cosmos moves in harmony with that purpose. The individual can perceive small pieces of the divine intent, which hint at larger patterns, and can live and act in ways that further (or hinder) that Intent.[53]

Wilson writes of the gospel order as "the right relationship of every part of creation, however small, to every other part and to the Creator" and notes that it is understood to prevail when every part of creation "is functioning according to the divine will—the shining of stars as well as the making of bread."[54] Wilson stresses that it is the responsibility of Christians to live in this gospel order: not only "out of the desire to do God's will, from the joy that being in that right relationship brings," but also "as a testimony to the rest of the world about the gospel."[55] As Katherine Murray writes in her study of Quaker social justice work, that the notion of "right relationship" is what drives the movement:

> Among Friends, action on behalf of social justice arises not from outward pressure for societal change but from an inward leading, a pressure within, that calls Friends into "right relationship" with the issue needing more Light, whether that is racism, oppression, abuse of power, food inequity, the need for restorative justice, exploitation of the planet, or other pressing and worthy contemporary concerns.[56]

In her study of Quaker decision-making, Jackie Leach Scully elaborates on the inward-focused nature of Quaker social ethics. Scully observes that religious groups often emphasize one of two moral frameworks: a deontological model ("Do this because God says so") or a utilitarian model ("Do this because it contributes to the greatest good for the greatest numbers").[57] Both of these frameworks operate on "an assumption of epistemological closure – the right answer can be known by following a commandment."[58] The emphasis is on the outcome: an act that can be objectively perceived and evaluated by others. By contrast, Quaker virtue ethics are *agent-centered* rather than action-centered: "They make the statement 'I am this kind of person' rather than 'I think this is the kind of principle to follow.'"[59] Continuity between one's inner and outer life is one of the cornerstones of living as a Quaker, a religious identity that is more often defined by behavior than by statements of belief.

This ethos is helpful for understanding Koinonia Vineyard, a church that self-consciously claims its Quaker heritage. "It took me quite a while to learn that the message was supposed to have an application at the end," Casey notes. As noted earlier, the notion of a "one size fits all" takeaway is problematic for Casey because he believes "the message is going to be different for each person." This is why demands to "say something" in light of political events leave Casey at a loss. Implicit in the demand is an assumption of epistemological closure ("What is going to fix this right now? What can I say? Tell people not to shoot each other?") Casey operates from within a virtue ethic where the inner life of the agent is privileged over any objective outcomes. For example, Casey explains that he approaches the task of preaching by telling the congregation, "This is how [scripture] spoke to me. Here's what I bring to this conversation. It may speak to you very differently." In his assessment, "The most important sermons are the ones that the people listening preach to themselves." Ultimately then, social change must arise from within the assembly and cannot be imposed by any single leader.

In her book *Ambivalent Miracles: Evangelicals and the Politics of Racial Healing*, political scientist Nancy Wadsworth asks pointed questions that challenge Casey's apolitical approach to societal change:

> Do [evangelicals] really want to claim that religiously driven "heart change" will somehow magically transform broad-scale racial injustice person by person, without Christians having to take public stances in the world consistent with their stated values, and to do that in the name of protecting the gospel? Can evangelicals possibly remain so stubborn, or is political ambivalence a way to keep certain people among them, like white conservatives unwilling to alter their political ideologies or party alliances, comfortable? At any rate, are they willing to allow that to appear to be the case?[60]

My study of Koinonia Vineyard took place before the tragic killings of George Floyd, Breonna Taylor, and Ahmaud Arbery. Their names are part of a longer list that includes Trayvon Martin, Michael Brown, Sandra Bland, Eric Garner, Rekia Boyd, Emmett Till, and thousands of anonymous victims of lynching, genocide, and violence perpetuated against Native Americans, African Americans, Latinx, Asian Americans, Middle Eastern Americans, and other people of color, each made in God's image. As congregations like Koinonia Vineyard debate where the line between racial reconciliation and political activism lies (and whether or not it runs through worship), they dare not forget that their answers have real-life consequences for individuals like Machelle, the students she teaches, and the children she one day hopes to bring into a better world.

6

"You Can't *Make* Me Sing"

Resisting Authority in Portland

Brett, lead pastor Wayfarers Collective, an ecclesial community in the greater Portland area, recounts an eye-opening conversation he once had with Astrid, a barista who worked at his neighborhood coffeehouse. Brett was a regular customer, and over time had developed a casual friendship with the dreadlocked young woman behind the counter. Brett learned that Astrid loved vintage clothing and gluten-free pastries, that her spiritual beliefs were more nebulous than codified ("I believe in goodness"), and that she was a proud supporter of "Earth First!," a radical environmental advocacy group. One afternoon, Astrid asked Brett what he did for a living. Brett told her that he was a pastor and braced himself for one of two reactions: awkward silence or a theological debate. Neither ensued. Instead, it quickly became clear that Astrid had no idea what the words *pastor* or *church* meant. Looking back on the experience, Brett was struck by his uninterrogated assumptions. "Before I knew anything about Astrid's background, I just assumed that she had had a negative experience with church. Not only did she not have a negative experience with Christianity, she had *no* experience at all!" he marveled. In the part of the country where Brett grew up, Astrid's experience "wouldn't even be a possibility. You either went to church or had a good reason as to why not."

In many ways, this exchange between Brett and Astrid succinctly captures the challenges of planting a church in the Pacific Northwest. Astrid is typical of the 25 percent of people in the state of Oregon who don't identify with a specific religion. This statistic motivated Monica Miller, associate professor of religion and Africana studies at Lehigh University, to interview three hundred people in Portland under the age of thirty to see how they experience religion and spirituality. Just as Astrid believes in "goodness," so too did Miller find that young people in Portland find meaning at the intersection of social, cultural, and political issues: "Art. Music. People saying, 'I believe in feeding the hungry, I believe in sharing.' That takes the place of what we would consider religion,'" Miller reports.[1]

Astrid's commitment to protecting the environment (Earth First!) is another significant cultural identifier. The Pacific Northwest is beautiful, with a landscape dominated by trees, mountains, and ocean swells. Many people who live in

Evangelical Worship. Melanie C. Ross, Oxford University Press. © Oxford University Press 2021.
DOI: 10.1093/oso/9780197530757.003.0007

the region have made a trade-off: they accept lower-paying or lower-status jobs to remain in closer proximity to these natural wonders and the hiking, climbing, hunting, kayaking, and cycling opportunities they afford. University of Oregon professor Ed Whitelaw has dubbed this the "second paycheck" phenomenon, since many residents consider their quality of life as a kind of "salary bonus."[2]

Mark Shibley, a sociologist at Southern Oregon State University, goes further, arguing that a significant number of Cascadians participate in what he calls "nature religion": an earth-based spirituality that is influenced by the indigenous tradition, the secular environmental movement, and Pacific Northwest literature.[3] Shibley believes that many, if not most, people in the region are "secular but spiritual," and that they experience the sacred in nature rather than in the confines of a building.[4]

In a sense, Wayfarers Collective and North Point Community Church are mirror images of one another. As we saw in Chapter 4, North Point was created to be a church that unchurched people love to attend. The American South—a geographical area one pastor characterizes as "the land of the over-churched and under-reached"—presented a unique set of challenges.[5] "There are more churches than Waffle Houses in Atlanta," North Point's founding pastor, Andy Stanley, once quipped.[6] Stanley's goal was to create a new, more appealing way of "doing church" in a culture that had been oversaturated by traditional forms of Southern Baptist Christianity. Conversely, the leaders of Wayfarers Collective hope to appeal to potential churchgoers in the Pacific Northwest: a culture that either rejects entirely or knows little about the claims of Christianity. Brett and his colleagues turned to the emerging church movement for help in this task.

Evangelicalism and the Emerging Church Movement

The emerging church movement is notoriously difficult to pin down. Fuller Theological Seminary professor Ryan Bolger's description offers a helpful starting point:

> Emerging Churches are communities who practice the way of Jesus within post-modern cultures. A more extended definition identifies Emerging Churches as those that take the life of Jesus as a model way to live, who transform the secular realm, as they live highly communal lives. Because of these three activities, they welcome those who are outside, they share generously, they participate, they create, they lead without control, and they function together in spiritual activities. Rather than the large church "spectator" service, these small, organic, spiritual, and often "leaderless" communities create life together as they worship over a meal in their homes and serve the poor in their neighborhoods.[7]

Most scholars and commentators date the beginning of the emerging church movement to the early 1990s, a time when pastors first began to notice that Generation X was missing from church. A decade later, Lutheran pastor Karen Ward of Church of the Apostles (Seattle) coined the term "emerging church." Ward's epiphany was that "Gen-Xers are the first marines on the beach. Every generation hereafter will be postmodern."[8] Ward and others had an urgent sense that an American church tied to the epistemology and culture of the 1950s was incapable of speaking to a wired, global, and postmodern world. More than cosmetic surgery was needed to reimagine what it would mean to be a follower of Jesus in the twenty-first century.

In the United States, the emerging church movement was born out of a Leadership Network initiative that brought together a small group of leaders who were successfully engaging Gen-X and postmodern culture with the gospel. This group included leaders such as Brian McLaren, Tony Jones, Doug Pagitt, Dan Kimball, and Mark Driscoll, who worked with evangelical publishing giants like Zondervan to disseminate books and sponsor conferences.[9] Numerous evangelical Bible colleges and theological seminaries began offering courses and lecture series on the subject of the emerging church.[10]

The seeds of what would become Wayfarers Collective were planted during this period of excitement and momentum. In the early 2000s, a small group of seminary friends began meeting informally to discuss their disillusionment with evangelical megachurches. Chief among their complaints was a sense that evangelical church services had become branded, slickly packaged events: worshippers become spectators, and musicians and pastors become celebrities. They found "gimmicks" like video clips and comic sketches distasteful, and distrusted appeals from the pulpit that smacked of emotional manipulation. Brett, the informal leader of the group and a megachurch escapee, explained his frustration this way: "I know how to have sex and balance my checkbook. I don't need more 'relevant' teaching. I want a faith that rattles me and transcends my regular life."

The friends decided to read a book called *A New Kind of Christian* (2001), by theological provocateur Brian McLaren. McClaren's bestseller reconsidered the relationship between religion and science, the meaning of salvation, scriptural authority, and literal interpretations of hell. Missiologist Ed Stetzer called it an "experiment in 'fiction/non-fiction'" that gave voice to the questions and concerns of a generation of young people who had grown up in conservative evangelical churches.[11] Indeed, many of the people I spoke to at the Collective cited *A New Kind of Christian* as a turning point in their spiritual journey.

The group also began to study the work of systematic theologian Stanley Grenz, particularly his book *Created for Community* (1998).[12] In this volume, Grenz stressed that because human beings are created in the image of a God whose triune inner life is a fellowship of Father, Son, and Spirit, we are designed for community. Grenz sought to counteract the individualism of the late twentieth century by stressing that the church is meant to model the kind of reconciled fellowship that God ultimately intends for all of creation. Grenz's work challenged the group to think beyond the evangelical idea of having a "personal relationship with Jesus." While no one disputed the doctrine of salvation by grace through faith in the person and work of Jesus Christ, all worried that evangelicalism fostered a privatized faith that downplayed the importance of community.

Although the Portland friends were disillusioned by their own church experiences, they did not want to abandon the idea of evangelism: particularly because so many people in their city had no understanding of Christianity. After much discussion and prayer, they decided to start a different kind of ecclesial community, one that would minister specifically to "unchurched" people like Astrid and "ex-churched" young adults like themselves, who had rejected "seeker-sensitive" evangelicalism. They called themselves Wayfarers Collective: a moniker that conveyed spirituality and inclusiveness but avoided the trigger word *church*.[13] In its early years, members of the Wayfarers Collective were happy to identify themselves with the burgeoning emerging church movement. But that would change later in the decade, when the emerging church coalition began to fracture under the weight of its internal differences.

At its inception, the emerging church movement was held together by its opposition to "modernist" expressions of evangelicalism. Problematically, however, it was never unified on how to address those deficits. Most leaders in the movement embraced a postmodern approach to scripture, which argued that there are multiple hermeneutical possibilities for interpreting the biblical text and not simply one "grand narrative" that defined orthodoxy for all Christians. New Testament scholar and one-time emerging church spokesperson Scot KcKnight's comments are illustrative:

The emerging movement tends to be suspicious of systematic theology. Why? Not because we don't read systematics, but because the diversity of theologies alarms us, no genuine consensus has been achieved, God didn't reveal a systematic theology but a storied narrative, and no language is capable of capturing the Absolute Truth who alone is God. Frankly, the emerging movement loves ideas and theology. It just doesn't have an airtight system or statement of faith. We believe the Great Tradition offers various ways for telling the truth about God's redemption in Christ, but we don't believe any one theology gets it absolutely right. Hence, a trademark feature of the emerging movement is that we believe all theology will remain a conversation about the Truth who is God in Christ through the Spirit, and about God's story of redemption at work in the church. No systematic theology can be final.[14]

Outspoken leaders like Brian McLaren, Tony Jones, Doug Pagitt, and Rob Bell began challenging key evangelical doctrines such as God's sovereignty, the nature of substitutionary atonement, the reality of hell, and the extent of salvation. Another leader, Mark Driscoll, became more influenced by traditionally conservative Reformed theology and removed himself from the emerging church movement to focus on developing a reformed missional network called Acts 29.[15] Several other evangelical leaders joined Driscoll in condemning the "revisionist" perspective in popular books such as *Why We're Not Emergent: By Two Guys Who Should Be* and *Becoming Conversant with the Emerging Church: Understanding a Movement and Its Implications.*[16] The two sides lobbed complaints and accusations at one another for the next several years.

Reflecting on the mood at Wayfarers Collective during this tumultuous time, Brett admitted,

> It felt hard to really nail down the ever-changing cast of characters in the emerging church. You had Dan Kimball, who was very close to what I would consider a typical conservative evangelical, except he had a pompadour. You had Reformed guys like Mark Driscoll. Then there were guys like Tony Jones and Doug Pagitt, who were all over the place [doctrinally]. I had some deep concerns about some of the things I was seeing and reading. In the end, I decided I wanted to focus my time on proclaiming the gospel, not defending the [emerging church] label.

Brett was not alone in his confusion and definitional fatigue. By 2008, the writing was on the wall. Url Scaramanga (pseudonym), a provocative writer for *Christianity Today*, posted a web article entitled "R.I.P. Emerging Church: An Overused and Corrupted Term Now Sleeps with the Fishes." Scaramanga noted that as early as 2006, evangelical publishing houses had been making plans to drop their emerging church book series and that recognized leaders and voices within the emerging church movement believed the term had become so polluted that it needed to be dropped.[17] In his "Obituary: The Emerging Church (1994–2009)," C. Michael Patton offered a similar assessment, quipping, "Stop the 'What is the Emerging Church?' seminars. Edit the 'Beware of Brian McLaren Sermons.' And don't even entertain starting an Emerging blog. As far as I can see, the Emerging Church is dead at 15."[18] By mid-2009, the consensus seemed to be that the movement had collapsed.[19]

After the demise of the emerging church movement, missiologist Ed Stetzer named one of its enduring legacies. Stetzer pointed out to the readers of *Christianity Today* that the emerging church movement "tested the boundaries of evangelicalism, forcing us to settle what theological matters we are comfortable questioning and those that are beyond the pale."[20] This sifting was certainly true for Wayfarers Collective, which now describes itself as a "missional" church that has "'emerged' from the Emerging Church movement." The word *missional* is important to Brett: it signals the Collective's agreement with the traditional evangelical doctrines like substitutionary atonement and the authority of scripture. One piece of literature I picked up at the Collective explained that the community is "theologically centrist and evangelistically oriented. We exist for the sake of the Gospel, but share the same kind of creative methodologies and concern for social justice that once characterized the emerging church movement."

After reading an early draft of this chapter, an anonymous reviewer asked if this community was, in fact, "evangelical." It is an insightful question, and leaders in the Collective like Brett (teaching pastor) and Logan (worship director)—both graduates of a well-known evangelical seminary I have chosen not to name—would respond in the affirmative. However, as the analysis ahead will show, Wayfarers Collective tends to attract individuals who have been hurt by the church and/or harbor significant doubts about traditional evangelical doctrines. "I'm starting to realize that the Collective is a lot more theologically conservative than I once thought," one interviewee confided to me (with dismay). Members on the more "liberal" side of the theological continuum are not shy about voicing their dissent, which makes this community an especially intriguing case study.

Defining Tensions

The Collective started with ten individuals; today, attendance is well over two hundred. Since its inception, the Collective has wrestled productively with two defining tensions: open membership and physical location.

Instead of appealing to logical arguments, universal reason, or objective truths, the leaders of the Collective believe the best apologetics strategy is to immerse unchurched individuals in the experience of genuine Christian community. Because Wayfarers Collective strives to be a place where people can "belong before they believe," it eschews categories of formal membership. The Collective reserves significant leadership (eldership, teaching responsibilities) for committed Christians; however, non-Christians are free to lead social justice ministries, serve in children's areas, play in the worship band, and fully participate in the life of the community without making a public profession of faith.

One advantage of the Collective's inclusive membership policy is that it allows enthusiastic new attendees to jump into community life right away. "The Collective won me over on my first visit when they asked if I could help them move chairs after the service was over," a man in his twenties recounted. Another young woman expressed appreciation for her similar experience: "When you're a guest, things are always being given to you. But I always feel better when I go to someone's house and they let me help with the dishes afterward. It means that I'm part of the family." Conversely, open membership gives other individuals the necessary time and space for spiritual healing. "I went through some really difficult experiences trying to get my faith sorted out," a former seminarian reflected. "I appreciate that this is a community where it's OK to hang back for a while." Another individual confided, "I came here at the end of a difficult transition in my life. It takes a lot for me to open myself up to people and make a commitment, and I feel like that's OK here: that I can just sort of be who I am and work through that."

The Collective's open membership policy also creates challenges. For example, while the Collective wants to allow people time and space to process their negative experiences with Christianity, Brett stresses that it would be "spiritual malpractice" to allow people to become complacent with their struggles. "Don't make a virtue out of doubt," he urges the congregation. "Wrestle with your questions. If the story of Jesus is true, it's worth the effort of trying to understand and embrace. Some of your questions may never be answered, but don't let that be for lack of trying." In other words, the Collective must manage the tension of making room for skeptics without normalizing a posture of doubt and confusion within the community. It also strives to hold the church doors open for people who are new to faith, while preventing them from closing behind people who are on their way out.

A second challenge is the group's meeting place. Wayfarers Collective, which is now eleven years old, has never owned its own facility. In its formative years, it held Theology Nights at a local pub. This location choice was intentional: it signaled that the group wasn't made up of "anal-retentive sorts of Christians" (Brett's phrase) and provided a neutral space for those who might refuse to walk through church doors. Over the course of its lifespan, the Collective has met in several other locations, including a bicycle repair shop and the back room of a pizza parlor. The choice to meet in public, nontraditional spaces embodied one of the Collective's core values: Christians are meant to engage the world, not cloister themselves away from it in a private sanctuary.

Currently, the Collective meets in a warehouse next to train tracks. There are mixed feelings about the church's current location. One member told me that he found it "refreshing" to meet in the warehouse—an admittedly "scuzzy place where they were probably doing things [our church] wouldn't necessarily approve of just twelve hours before." The less-than-ideal setting reinforced to this individual that church is about community, not a building. Others stressed the financial benefits of not owning property. Laura acknowledged that one of the things that she appreciated about the Collective was the fact that the church "doesn't put all its money inward." Laura has a problem with "fancy, gorgeous megachurch buildings" because she believes that "the equipment they require to produce Sunday morning costs more than what the Collective raises in a full year." The issue for Laura is one of stewardship: "I would have a hard time being in a church that chooses to use its resources that way."

Finally, Sawyer and Emerson, a middle-aged couple, appreciate the fact that the warehouse forces the Collective to confront difficult downtown problems, including homelessness. On their way to worship in the warehouse, members of the Collective regularly encounter homeless individuals—a reality that was not the case when the church met in the suburban pizza parlor and bike shop. "Five years ago, very few of us were truly aware that there are people who sleep under bridges," Sawyer muses. Meeting in the warehouse means "we have to see homelessness now: it makes the problem visible to people who easily looked past it before." Trains regularly speed by during services, rattling the windows and drowning out all other sounds. Many Collective members find this a major annoyance and distraction in worship, but Emerson has learned to see the situation differently: "There are people who live under those bridges: when the train goes by, they're trying to sleep. I understand how we want to create a worship situation that focuses us on God," she continues, "but the reality is, God created all these [homeless] people. If you let yourself get insulated and isolated from that world, it builds a certain lack of compassion."

But not everyone embraces the church's nomadic philosophy. Volunteers grow weary of the constant setting up and tearing down of equipment for services. Others in the congregation report feeling rootless, including this interviewee, who wished the Collective had a focused geographical mission:

> If you [own] a building, the downside of that is the upkeep and the money. But the upside is that you have a neighborhood presence. Anyone who drives down the street sees the church, and the church can help their immediate community. Right now, [our mission and justice efforts] are widely dispersed across a big city.

Sara, the mother of a six-month-old baby, was completely fed up with the Collective's current location, declaring unambiguously, "I hate the warehouse!" Sara's concerns are understandable. Volunteers who set up the room Sunday morning must clear the restrooms of used condoms from the previous night. Cars have been stolen during services. Recreational marijuana is legal in the state of Oregon and is regularly consumed by other groups who rent the space. Walking up to the warehouse front doors my first Sunday, I was startled by the management's stern warning sign taped to the glass: "NO SMOKING OR CONSUMING CANNABIS INSIDE!" (Figure 6.1)

For Sara, marijuana was the final straw. She recounted, "One weekend, the warehouse hosted a cannabis convention, and when we came in on Sunday, there

Figure 6.1 Sign posted inside the warehouse
Greater Portland area, Oregon: August 2016. Photo by author.

was still a booth in the back where live plants were growing. [Church volunteers] put a curtain over it so you couldn't see what it was, but I was really . . . ," Sara sputtered, struggling for words to express the depth of her indignation. "I did not appreciate that."

Sara articulates a growing pain in the community. Wayfarers Collective was founded as an outreach for people who had been hurt by traditional churches, or who were exploring Christianity for the first time. Pubs, pizza parlors, and bike shops felt more neutral than traditional church buildings. But many of these individuals have matured, both in their faith journey and their stage of life. The young singles the Collective originally attracted have remained in the church, gotten married, and started families. Those babies are now growing up, and the Collective has no dedicated spaces for youngsters: no nursery on Sunday morning; no place for youth group in the middle of the week. "I think we need to decide what our identity looks like now," Sara reflects. "Is it what we were when we started twelve years ago? Or is it what we are now?" The question bubbling under the surface at the time of my visit was whether the church should move to a permanent location. A traditional church building might alienate singles (the group the Collective originally targeted). But if the church continues to rent places like the warehouse—which are not conducive for children and teens—its long-term members might decide to leave.

Service Description

It is a Sunday morning in late July, one hour before the worship service is scheduled to begin. An SUV with a small cargo trailer pulls up to the garage door at the front of the warehouse, and a group of volunteers begins to unpack an assortment of cables, microphones, and electronic equipment. Someone places a small, A-frame folding sign on the sidewalk in front of the building. The sign features a picture of a Byzantine icon of Jesus, his right hand slightly raised in the traditional gesture of blessing, and the words, "Wayfarers Collective—a missional, holistic, christian community meets here, Sunday 10 am." A large train lumbers by with deafening sound, rattling the warehouse windows and temporarily silencing all conversations.

Inside, a hospitality team is hard at work transforming the large, impersonal meeting room into a cozier, more inviting space. Eight rows of sixteen folding metal chairs are placed at the front of the room, all facing a large projection screen. A small, square table is placed at the front of the room. Volunteers adorn it with a simple blue cloth, a tabletop cross, two candles, and three tealights. Two large cups—one with wine, the other with juice—appear, and someone sets out a large, round loaf of bread and a small bowl of gluten-free wafers (Figure 6.2). At the back of the room, a different kind of "communion" is being readied: volunteers brew large urns of coffee and boil water for tea and hot chocolate.

Figure 6.2 Eucharist in the warehouse
Greater Portland area, Oregon: August 2016. Photo by author.

Long tables running down the side of the room are stacked with paperback Bibles, literature about the church, and a small wooden box with a slot for financial contributions. (A framed five-by-seven sign reminds viewers of the box's purpose: "because church is free . . . but it ain't cheap.") The table also features several clipboards with sign-up sheets for service opportunities. Along the back of the table are several homemade pieces of art. The most immediately visually arresting piece is a simply painted, bearded face—presumably Jesus. Instead of eyes, the artist has covered the upper quadrant of the visage with a scripture verse typed in capital letters: "The eyes of the Lord are on the righteous and his ears are attentive to their cry. Ps. 54:15" (Figure 6.3). Justice will be a major theme in the service.

A few minutes before the service is scheduled to begin, people wander into the warehouse, pour themselves coffee, and chat with one another. One of the things Brett most appreciates about Wayfarers Collective is its relaxed approach to Sunday mornings. "I've gone to some bigger churches, and now I almost can't worship in them anymore," he explains. "There's something about all the preparation and production that seems . . ." His voice trails off. "I guess I just like the non-showiness of our Sunday times together. It's a little bit looser. A little bit more relaxed." This laid-back vibe is evident from the first moments of worship. Nearly ten minutes after the service's official start time, Brett moves to the front of the room and tries to get the group's attention. Raising his voice over the

Figure 6.3 Artwork at Wayfarers Collective
Greater Portland area, Oregon: August 2016. Photo by author.

din of conversational preliminaries, Brett announces, "Welcome to Wayfarers Collective!" Few people stop talking, but Brett presses on. "Today we are going to be reading Psalm 145 responsively. The lines marked 'Leader' will obviously be me and the lines marked 'People' will be you." The group finally settles down and people focus their attention on the portable projection screen set up at the front of the room. They recite the psalm's twenty-one verses, trading lines back and forth between leader and congregation.

A small ensemble at the front of the room—a guitar, a bass, and a handheld drum—begin to play the melody of the opening song. The piece, "Rising Sun," has lyrics that echo familiar psalm themes, including the idea that God is the light of the morning and that God's holy name is higher than the rising sun. The song was written by an American worship group called All Sons & Daughters. The group, which has now disbanded, was committed to acoustic and folk music and to recording songs that have been described as "authentic," "raw," and "unpolished."[21] As we will see, these adjectives are important to Logan, the thirty-something worship director who chooses repertoire for the Collective.

After the song, children are dismissed to another section of the warehouse for Sunday school. Brett comes to the front of the room to introduce Jaxon, the morning speaker. "For the next six weeks, we're doing a summer series where we'll hear a variety of biblical passages, from a variety of genres of scripture, from a variety of preachers. Some of those folks, including Jaxon, have never preached before." Brett explains that this group of lay preachers has been regularly looking at each other's manuscripts and offering critique and encouragement. Preaching at the Collective is always a collaborative enterprise.

"When are times where you feel like you've been encouraged to use your imagination?" Jaxon asks the congregation. "Playing with toddlers!" one voice shouts out. "Reading fantasy novels," offers another. A few more individuals shared responses. "Let me ask another question," Jaxon continued. "Do you have any stories about being in a situation where your imagination was stifled?" "Being at work," groaned a loud voice from the back. The group chuckled empathetically. A goateed man in his thirties spoke up. "You know, sadly, I think the place where my imagination was stifled the most was probably at seminary. It seemed like the imagination—especially when you're talking about theology and the church– isn't really all that welcome." Jaxon nodded. "I share that experience. There's nothing like being critiqued because of a word you use when you're trying to say something about God. People would say, 'Well, you can't say that word because it leads to all these heresies.'"

Jaxon turns the congregation's attention to this morning's scripture passage in Genesis 28, which he reads aloud. In the passage, the main character, Jacob, is on the run. "He's leaving behind everything he knows and is heading to a new place," Jaxon explains. "He's entering into a space of unknowing." When Jacob stops for the night, he falls asleep and has a vivid dream of a ladder that connected heaven and earth, where angels ascended and descended. God, who was standing above the ladder, repeated the blessing he had made to Jacob and his family. When Jacob awakens from the dream, he is astonished: "Surely the LORD is in this place, and I was not aware of it."

Jaxon suggests that although most people in the congregation haven't been on the run for their lives, many of them have probably had the experience of "God was here and I didn't know it," a moment when "all of a sudden, we're aware of God's presence, or at least aware that there's something bigger than ourselves." Jaxon offers an example that connects to Portlanders: "Maybe you're going on a hike, and as you crush [conquer] the hill, you're struck with the beautiful view. You have to stop and go, 'Whoa. This is beautiful.'" Maybe it's the energy a person experiences in a conversation with a friend: "You're talking, and things are clicking, and you stop and go, 'Wow. This is a sacred space we're in right now. I feel like I sense the presence of God as we're having this conversation.'" Jaxon stresses that there are "millions of different ways" a person can be surprised by the sudden awareness of God's presence.

Jaxon notes a corollary. People can also experience the absence of God's presence, an experience commonly known as "the dark night of the soul." Jaxon suggests that this phrase, which comes from sixteenth-century poet and mystic St. John of the Cross, is better translated as "the obscure night of the soul." Furthermore, this phenomenon is a grace:

> We go to the well that we know to connect with God, and we try to get a drink, but our bucket comes up empty. Why? It's not because God isn't there. It's because God wants us to grow beyond the built-in expectations and ideas that we have of how he works. . . . God obscures himself from us so that we can be delivered from these expectations, so our imagination can be stretched. John [of the Cross] says this is a gift, because if we knew what God was doing, we would hate it.

Jaxon illustrates this point with a personal experience. Jaxon, who grew up in the Pentecostal church, summarizes his formative spirituality to the group with two words: "Big Things." "My faith was about big emotions," he reflects. "Feeling a certain way while I was singing. Being at an altar call and praying as fervently as possible. Getting slain in the spirit—like when the televangelists put their hands on somebody and they fall over. This was the image that I grew up with of what it means to connect with God." But at some point, all these things stopped working for Jaxon. He entered into what he calls "the dark night of the soul."

In an attempt to cure his spiritual malaise, Jaxon enrolled in a local seminary. There he discovered that the class discussions he most enjoyed were those that focused on social action. Jaxon also discovered contemplative worship practices. Jaxon learned that "the less I tried to make any 'God experience' happen, the more I would have moments where God would make his presence known to me. But if I tried to hold onto it in the moment, it would evaporate. It wouldn't stay." Jaxon reflected that something inside was beginning to shift.

Jaxon became part of a church that was active in its local neighborhood. Several congregants decided to de-pave an unsafe stretch of asphalt and plant a community garden. Jaxon found the work "really, really fulfilling, even though a lot of it was swinging a pickax and digging out big chunks of rock. Something about it felt right. As a community, we had a sense that God loved this project and was really happy it was happening. That's what we'd say to people when they asked us why we were doing it." Jaxon came across a quotation by Rabbi Abraham Joshua Heschel, who reportedly described his experience of being part of a civil rights march with the following words: "Even without words our march was worship. I felt like my legs were praying." Jaxon felt the same way about his physical labor in the church's community garden.

A few days later, Jaxon—who, by this point, had severed his ties with Pentecostalism—found himself walking down the street, praying aloud in tongues. "I thought I was over it," he confesses, "that there was no meaning behind it. And then this just happened, without me trying." Jaxon had an epiphany: he could experience God through contemplative worship and social justice *and* through the gift of tongues. "The temptation of religion is to put God in a box, to create a system of 'If you do this, then God does that.' But that's not how God works," Jaxon concludes. "God is bigger than any idea we have about him."

Jaxon assures the congregation that it's OK "to experience the dark night of the soul, to be in a space where maybe you're looking for God and God isn't showing up." He recommends the Ignatian spiritual practice of Examen, which he describes as "kind of like journaling," to the congregation:

Look back at your day, or week, or month, and ask, "What did I experience? What was good and life-fulfilling? What was hard and frustrating?" But don't stop there. It's just the first step. Once you ask those questions, say, "Where did I see God in this?" Then pray. Pretty soon, you'll begin to pray things like, "OK, God, help me to see where maybe you were present and I didn't even think to look." When we look at our moments of frustration and we go, "God, can you help me to see how you were present here in these moments when I had a hard time sensing that you were around?"—that's Examen.

Members of the congregation spend a few minutes reflecting aloud on moments when they have been surprised to discover the presence of God. One person volunteered that reading science fiction challenged and expanded the "box" into which he had put God. A visitor prefaced her remarks by noting that she was "a little insecure because I don't actually go here," then talked about God's nearness during a medical emergency. A third member shared how God had spoken to him through the lyrics of a song that came on the radio at precisely the right time.

As the conversation winds down, Jaxon reminds the congregation that one of the ways God reveals himself is through the Lord's Supper. After a short prayer, the congregation is then invited to come to the front to receive the elements while a small team of musicians leads the assembly in song. After communion, Brett dismisses the assembly with a prayer: "God, we ask that you would grow within us love for you, the world, and our community. In Jesus name we pray. Amen."

Homiletic Analysis

To understand Jaxon's hermeneutic, it is helpful to survey the work by Dallas Willard and N. T. Wright—two scholars who have influenced the leadership at Wayfarers Collective.

Willard (1935–2013) is an American philosopher who is also widely known for his writings on Christian spiritual formation. Willard's concern is that in recent decades, the fullness of the Christian message has been squeezed and pared down in order to fit one of two molds: the "gospel on the left" and the "gospel on the right." Christians in the first group don't talk about sin or heaven. Instead, they emphasize that Jesus came to teach us how to end human evil and overhaul social systems—what Willard calls "a mild little version" of discipleship, not something for which one would be willing to put their life on the line.[22] Christians in the second group define salvation as strictly a matter of having one's sins forgiven and the assurance of heaven "nailed down."[23] In both cases, the Christian message is truncated: the gospel becomes either the story of "exciting social work with an unhappy conclusion" or the story of "an atoning death with an extended introduction."[24]

In *A New Kind of Christian*, the book that helped spark the vision for Wayfarers Collective, Brian McLaren similarly argues that conservative Christians have focused too much on "the getting of individual butts into heaven." Christian identity is not rooted in the idea that a group of elites has been saved for privilege, but rather that ordinary people have been saved to lead lives of responsible service. McLaren defines salvation as "joining God's mission," arguing that "the real enemy isn't hell" but "living out of harmony with God."[25] While many traditional Christians reject McLaren's reinterpretation of heaven and hell, his words signal a rejection of dispensational theology and a shift in the way that younger evangelicals approach the task of evangelism. Josh Chen, director of the Portland branch of Cru, an interdenominational parachurch organization for college and university students, explains:

Older generations were asking: "How do I get to heaven?" and "What do I do with my guilt?" Millennials are asking, "What does it mean to thrive?" If we approach millennials with a pitch for Christianity that was designed to resonate with their parents, it isn't going to sound like good news to them. The way Jesus explained the kingdom of God was different from person to person. To one person it was that they can be healed in this life. To another person it was that they belonged, even if they were marginalized. He told them how the kingdom was good news to them, in their unique situation. We have to do that kind of customization.[26]

The founders of Wayfarers Collective concur. "More often than not, we need to be about *could* rather than *should*," one piece of church literature suggested. "Let's pull people, with love and hope, toward a picture of who they could be in Christ, rather than pushing them there out of guilt or obligation."

I saw examples of this ethos at work on both of the Sundays I attended the Collective. The first week, Brent concluded his message by stressing that the sum total of God's mission was more than "asking people if they died tonight would they go to heaven or hell." Brent admitted to the congregation, "We've never asked anybody to close their eyes and raise their hand if they accept Jesus as their Lord and Savior because that's not the kind of community that we are." Nevertheless, he stressed that the gospel demands a response: "Will we receive the gift of new life that Jesus offers? Will we accept God's invitation to participate in the mission of the rescue and renewal of all things?" Brent's words are an excellent illustration of the "pull" approach to evangelism. Strikingly absent are any "push" references to sin, guilt, or repentance. Instead, the emphasis is on joining God's mission to restore all of creation. Indeed, earlier in the sermon, Brent defined a *missionary* as one who "joins with God's mission to rescue and redeem all of creation through the work of Jesus on our behalf." A week later, Jaxon reiterated this theological perspective in his account of replacing asphalt with a community garden: "God loved this project, and was really happy it was happening." The Collective's emphasis on God's restorative justice strives to avoid what homiletics scholar Thomas Long calls "a gospel that is intellectually implausible, stuck in the clouds of a pious and irrelevant heaven that never touches earth."[27] Instead, it is focused on the inbreaking of the Kingdom of God.

N. T. Wright, a British New Testament scholar, Pauline theologian, and retired Anglican bishop, argues that life in the Kingdom of God is not an after-death experience only but is accessible now, in this life. Wright is careful to distinguish between the final Kingdom of God—God's supreme act of new creation—and present anticipations of it. "God alone will sum up all things in Christ, things in heaven and things on earth. . . . It would be the height of folly to think that we could assist in that great work."[28] Christians who are following Christ and indwelt by the Spirit can, however, build *for* the kingdom. In stark opposition to dispensational theology, Wright offers this encouragement:

> You are not oiling the wheels of a machine that's about to roll over a cliff. You are not restoring a great painting that's shortly going to be thrown on the fire. You are not planting roses in a garden that's about to be dug up for a building site. You are—strange though it may seem, almost as hard to believe as the resurrection itself—accomplishing something that will become in due course part of God's new world.[29]

Willard's theology similarly emphasizes the Kingdom of God. Willard explains that every person has a "kingdom"—a realm over which he or she has the deciding voice. In Willard's definition, a person's kingdom is "that tiny part of visible reality where the human will, for a time, has some degree of sway, even contrary to God's will."[30] Individuals have larger or smaller kingdoms, depending on their spheres of influence. A college student's kingdom may be half of a dorm room. A parent, self-employed professional, or prime minister's kingdom expands even further. God's kingdom is the largest kingdom of all.

Successful living depends not only on taking responsibility for our own realm, but also on meshing our kingdom with the kingdoms of others—learning to share space, or take part in teamwork. Most importantly, we must learn to fit our individual kingdoms inside God's big kingdom: we retain sovereignty, but our desires align with those of God. Willard understands Jesus's statement, "The kingdom of God is within you" to mean human will is the deciding factor as to whether or not the Kingdom of God will be manifest in an individual's life. In other words, the kingdom is as close (or as far away) from each of us as our individual choices allow.[31]

Of course, kingdoms clash when the will of one individual bumps up against the will of another. However, God's intent is for humans to learn to mesh their kingdoms together on the basis of relationship, rather than by brute force: "Love of neighbor, rightly understood, will make this happen."[32] The same principle holds true when an individual's kingdom clashes with God's kingdom. God will not coerce us or force our submission. According to Willard, God is sovereign over, but not necessarily in active control of, every aspect of reality. In Willard's words, "God does not like to be present where he is not wanted. And he knows when he is wanted and when he is not. . . . He does not intrude—generally speaking."[33] Instead, God works with humans through relationship, inviting them to be his disciples and apprentices in the art of kingdom living.

For example, consider the caveat that North Point pastor Andy Stanley offers to other pastors when he explains North Point's "Be Rich" campaign: "While I care about the poor, the issue of local or global poverty doesn't keep me up at night. . . . [My passion] is my concern for the reputation and cultural positioning of the local church."[34] Christians at Wayfarers Collective would argue that Stanley's rationale for acts of justice and mercy—namely, to bolster the church's reputation in society—is theologically thin. According to Wayfarers Collective, the work of eradicating poverty is not the means to an evangelistic end: it is an announcement that the Kingdom of God is here. Wayfarers Collective believes that evangelism and discipleship cannot be separated, since the ultimate apologetic "is the believer acting in faith in an interactive life with God."[35] A robust understanding of salvation involves finding where God is working, and partnering with him in the work of healing and restoration, according to our God-given skills and abilities.

Read through the lens of Willard's and Wright's "kingdom theology," Jaxon's homiletical decisions become more clear. A paraphrase of Jaxon's sermon might read as follows: "Sometimes God intentionally obscures himself from his followers to subvert the false expectations and constraints they have placed upon him. If Christians continue to work toward justice and accomplishing God's will on earth, God will reveal himself to them in new and surprising ways." One of the most striking features of this message is how firmly it is rooted in the present, with no references to the past or the future. For example, Jaxon does not draw on God's mighty deeds in the past to reassure his listeners of God's work in the present. There is no reference to biblical salvation history: specifically, to Jesus's own "dark night of the soul" when he used the words of Psalm 22 in the Garden of Gethsemane to plead, "My God, why hast thou forsaken me?" (Jaxon singles out Mother Teresa as his historical exemplar instead.) Perhaps this is because focusing on Jesus's agony in Gethsemane skirts too close to the "gospel on the right" and its perceived overemphasis on atonement. Furthermore, Jaxon is silent on the subject of traditional Christian eschatology, which asserts that the God of all history will return in unobscured glory at the end of time to set all things right. Emphasizing God's triumphal reign at the end of time has two potential dangers: it obscures the fact that God invites rather than coerces, and it reiterates the idea that the Kingdom of God is off in the distance, rather than being built in the here and now.

Music Analysis

Logan, the worship director at the Collective, has a parallel set of challenges to navigate. Both the "gospel on the left" (mainline liberalism) and the "gospel on the right" (conservative evangelicalism) have an identifiable soundtrack. Logan describes the former as a "noses-in-hymnals, no emotional investment" kind of singing, and the latter as a "happy-clappy, hands-in-the-air" style of worship.

Logan wants the equivalent of a "gospel of the kingdom" in its singing: full-throated engagement in the present moment, as described in Jaxon's sermon. But this turns out to be a difficult task for several reasons.

Consider the 2014 blog post of Portland-based writer Donald Miller, whose bestselling book *Blue Like Jazz* was especially popular among disenfranchised evangelicals like those at Wayfarers Collective. The post began with an intentionally provocative title: "I Don't Worship God by Singing: I Connect with Him Elsewhere." Miller explained that after attending a church service that had "perhaps the most talented worship team I've ever heard," he finally allowed himself to admit he felt no connection to God during the act of singing. Instead, Miller reported:

> I connect with God by working. I literally feel an intimacy with God when I build my company. I know it sounds crazy, but I believe God gave me my mission and my team and I feel closest to him when I've got my hand on the plow. It's thrilling and I couldn't be more grateful he's given me an outlet through which I can both serve and connect with him.[36]

Miller posits a dichotomy between worshipping God through a "traditional church service" and "worship[ing] God every day through my work."[37] The same dichotomy is reiterated in Jaxon's sermon: like Miller, Jaxon felt unable to worship God through traditional means in his Pentecostal church, but rediscovered God in the surprising work of "swinging a pickax and digging out big chunks of rock." Both stories emphasize nontraditional ways of encountering the holy outside of church, while minimalizing the importance of traditionally "churchy" activities like corporate singing.

The next factor that makes singing at Wayfarers Collective difficult is the question of repertoire. The stories of Alec and Phoebe are illustrative. Alec—one of the most passionate and outspoken members of the Collective—is in his mid-forties, and joined the congregation about five years ago. Alec has vociferous objections to the way he was taught to understand the gospel: "God seemed very distant and needed to be appeased. There was a price to be paid, and God got his vengeance by taking Jesus down on the cross. Sorry for my language, but that bullshit doesn't jive with me at all." One of the main reasons Alec left his former congregation was because of its music: "So much of my [previous church] experience was about this solitary, angry God that we need to appease. The hymns we sang really reflected that."

For Alec, God's immanence is more important than his transcendence: "I like to think of [Jesus] right beside me. He wants me as I am, in my ugly muck." Subsequently, Alec strongly objects to what he calls "the whole 'high and lifted up' notion that seems to dominate worship music today." In Alec's words, "The 'high and lifted up' thing makes humans into puppets, like we're impotent to do much of the kingdom work of helping." Alec's opinions echo those of Dan Kimball, one of the leading voices in the early years of the emerging church movement in the United States:

> [I] wish that worship songwriters would choose to write more songs that focus on the character of God and teachings of Jesus and what we should be like in this life, in addition to the thousands and thousands of songs about the cross and the substitutionary atonement. If we only view worship through the atonement, we don't focus Jesus' teaching on this life and on being a kingdom-minded disciple.[38]

Phoebe, a twenty-something member of the Collective, also wanted more emphasis on human agency in the congregation's worship. In his role as worship director, Logan often composes original songs for the Collective. Generally, his music is very well received by the community. However, Phoebe recounts a time when she was bothered by one of Logan's lyrics:

> I have nothing good to give;
> I have nothing good to say
> Loving you just seems so hard;
> I'm so quick to turn away.

Phoebe was concerned that the line "I have nothing good to give" overemphasized human depravity. As she explained, "I feel like I have something to offer, something I can bring to God, even when I'm at a spiritual low point." Logan considered Phoebe's point, then tweaked the lyric by adding a qualifying word:

> *When* there's nothing good to give;
> *When* there's nothing good to say
> *When* loving you just seems so hard;
> *When* we're quick to turn away . . .

The meaning of the song shifted subtly but noticeably: having "nothing good to give" is now a temporary condition, not an ontological state of being. Phoebe described Logan's willingness to change the lyric in response to her concerns as "a healing moment for me. A worship leader who'd actually listen to somebody? Wow! That was amazing."

Alec's and Phoebe's comments indicate that the congregation must negotiate two kinds of authority. The first kind of authority—raised by Alec's story—is between God and humanity: namely, how much sovereignty does God have over human affairs? The second kind of authority—raised by Phoebe's story—is between the leaders of Wayfarers Collective and the congregation. Brett acknowledges that Portland "is a context that's very suspicious and skeptical of authority—things like the message coming from the top down, or someone preaching *at* you." During the first week of my study, Brett announced to the congregation: "Some of you are new to this [idea of church], and you're not really sure what you think exactly. That's totally cool. We are glad you're here. You're invited to ask hard questions and to disagree with us. We love to wrestle with those things." This invitation to questioning comes as a breath of fresh air, not only to unchurched individuals exploring Christianity for the first time, but also to "de-churched" individuals who have had negative experiences with strong authority figures.

Peter, a middle-aged father of two, is a good example. Peter recalls that during his seminary years, "a lot of the books I would read in my program were [business] management, which we would then apply to the church." Peter recalls his professors stressing that since "All truth is God's truth," secular writers had important wisdom to offer churches. However, the "pastor as CEO" model of ecclesial authority made Peter uneasy. Many at the Collective would empathize with Peter's frustrations. Recall the group conversation immediately prior to the sermon: "The place where my imagination was stifled the most was probably seminary" and "There's nothing like being critiqued because of one word you chose to use while saying something about God." As a corrective, Brett has developed a new approach to preaching that allows the congregation to ask questions and share their own stories, ideas, and insights during the sermon time. "Opening up the conversation goes a long way in a culture that is suspicious of authority," Brett acknowledges. "Allowing a variety of voices is huge for us."

Brett's approach has been strongly influenced by the book *As One without Authority*, written by homiletics scholar Fred Craddock. In this 1971 work, Craddock reflected on what he perceived as a crisis in American preaching. The war in Vietnam, the civil rights movement, feminism, and the rise of the US counterculture had eroded the public's trust in external authorities. Attendance in mainline churches was declining, in part because congregations were unwilling to accept preaching from a minister who mounted a high pulpit and talked down to them. Instead of a "top-down, deductive, 'my thesis for this morning'" approach to sermons, Craddock called for preachers to "lure people along on a journey of exploration and surprise with real-life stories and questions," ultimately bringing them to a place where they can exclaim, "Aha! I get it!"[39] Inductive preaching allows all members of the church to be on equal ground. In the service I have described, anyone was welcome to participate: even a first-time visitor to the Collective felt comfortable volunteering her personal story.

The Collective's dialogue approach to preaching and songwriting upends the hierarchical model of pastoral authority: what homileticians David Schlafer and Timothy Sedgwick describe as "essentially a 'command and obey' model" in which the preacher presented the truth of the gospel and offered a clear pastoral direction to the congregation.[40] In the twenty-first century, the preacher's authority is not assumed: it must be earned and granted by the congregation over the course of time.

However, the tension between leader and congregants is more acute when it comes to the question of congregational singing. Logan, the congregation's primary music leader, is quick to admit that the Collective "is the hardest place I've ever led [worship]." Many Sundays when Logan looks out from the front of the room, it seems like no one in the congregation is singing. Logan ventures an explanatory theory: "It's not because we're singing something that's musically difficult. It's because many people in the congregation come from negative church experiences, and music can be an unwelcome trigger." It doesn't matter that the repertoire is different: "When someone upfront says, 'Now we're going to stand and sing,' there's still a reaction to that," he explains. "It feels like there's almost a defiant opposition to it: 'You can't *make* me sing.' There's something performative about these practices that feel like they rub people the wrong way. That causes us tension."

Logan believes that the act of singing is nonnegotiable. He is discouraged by the fact that few Collective attendees actively participate in musical worship:

As a worship leader, I struggle with finding the barometer of "success." If no one is singing, am I still leading people in worship? Sometimes you can tell there's engagement there—not singing necessarily, but people are still engaged in worship. I wonder if people in the community are growing in the way that I feel they should [from my pastoral perspective]. If no one's singing, are people connecting? Maybe so; maybe not. I don't know. I can't read their thoughts or hearts, and there's not a lot of feedback.

On one hand, Logan is sympathetic to the congregation's concerns and reluctance. He recalls that when he started leading worship at the Collective, he struggled to find the right repertoire: "Commercial [worship] stuff didn't resonate with me . . . where everything's happy, clichéd, easy answers." Logan cast his net wider, searching for songs that were "much more contemplative, much more— this is not the right word—but like a downer, depressed a little bit": songs that better reflected the struggle of faith during the "dark night of the soul."

The three songs Logan selected for communion all address the question of doubt. The first, "Beloved," asks God a series of questions that echo the theme of the sermon:

How can I call out Your name
When You're so far away
And You're right by my side?
How can I speak of Your love
When You're so far above
But You hear when I cry?[41]

The second song, "To Hear Your Voice," asks God to take away the singer's "fears and reservations" and to replace them with a "holy desperation" for God.[42] The song was written by Eric Marshall of the group Young Oceans, and Marshall recorded it shortly after the suicidal death of his mother-in-law. Marshall reflects on how this experience shaped his musical outlook: "What is all this pain, death, trial? How do we form doxologies with this taste in our mouth? . . . [My] songs are about the struggle, the search, the brokenness and the ultimate Hope."[43] The final song, "Living Water," was written by the Portland-based band Five O'clock People. It too references the silence of God by referencing Psalm 88 (NIV): "Day and night I cry out before you . . . turn your ear to my cry." The thematic connections between the music and the sermon are intentional. Logan reports that "a lot of times the music I pick for the congregation to sing is really meaningful in the same way that the sermon is. A lot of times Brett preaches a sermon because everybody needs to hear it. I feel like the music I pick is the same thing."

Ultimately, Logan moved on from the spiritual malaise of his college years, and he wishes the same for the Collective. Logan acknowledges that singing may feel like a "weird thing to do," especially when a person "has a ton of reasons to be quiet, to not want to sing because it doesn't fit where they're at. A lot of us come here feeling dead, or maybe like God's far away, but he's not," Logan stresses. "Part of [spiritual maturity] is just exercising the discipline of singing and lift up your voice—even when you don't feel like it." One of the difficulties specific to this congregation is the fact that the Collective attracts people who are wrestling with their faith. "I would never *not* want that to be the case," Logan emphasizes, "but it does mean that things are constantly rotating." He explains:

You build a group of people that have matured musically: they've moved from not singing because of their past baggage to starting to sing. Eventually, they become rooted and part of the community voice. Then they leave, and a new down-and-out, frustrated-with-faith type of person who doesn't want to sing takes their spot. So it's a constant cycle. There are songs that we sang a while ago that were really down and in the mire of faith that we don't sing as much anymore because, as a community, we're no longer in that place. But we still have new people arriving who *are* in that place, so it's tricky balancing the songs with congregational needs.

When asked about his musical hopes for the future, Logan stops and starts as he thinks aloud. "I would love . . . I don't know what course this would take, but I think . . . an ongoing journey toward being able to sing loudly and joyfully." Logan recognizes that many people come to the Collective with "baggage" around worship music. Nevertheless, he would love to experience a Sunday morning where the singing is loud and full-throated. "That might seem like a surface-level thing," he reflects, "but it would mean something to me about the maturity of our church and the place where people are at."

7

"Not to Sing Is to Disobey"

Submitting to Paradox in Nashville

Within the world of American evangelicalism, it would be hard to find two more contrasting spiritual environments than Portland, Oregon, and Nashville, Tennessee. Oregon is consistently ranked as one of the nation's least religious states, and the city of Portland has more strip clubs per capita than any other municipality in America. Tennessee, on the other hand, ranks as the third most religious state in the nation—and the most evangelical state in the country.[1] The city of Nashville, nicknamed the "Buckle of the Bible Belt" and the "Protestant Vatican," houses the headquarters of the Southern Baptist Convention, the United Methodist Church's Publishing House, and religious publisher Thomas Nelson. It is reported to have more churches per capita than any other US city.[2]

Nashville is also the heart of the Christian music industry in America. As noted previously, Christian Contemporary Music (CCM) was originally a small, subcultural phenomenon, with roots in Southern California and the Jesus People of the 1970s. Churches and independent companies began producing recordings in the late 1970s and early 1980s, attracting the attention of large, "secular" labels in the mid-1980s. Over the course of the next decade, small Christian recording labels including Word, Sparrow, and Reunion were bought out by major corporations, including Warner Music Group, EMI, and Sony BMG. In the words of former Reunion president Terry Hemmings, in the late 1980s and early 1990s, "The Christian music market changed from an entrepreneurial environment to a corporate environment . . . almost overnight."[3] The consolidations, buyouts, and mergers necessitated a major geographic shift. Artists and executives associated with the Christian music business moved to Nashville and its suburbs of Franklin, Brentwood, and Hendersonville. John Lindenbaum noted in his 2016 history of the production of Christian music that "the Nashville area boasts at least 42 CCM record labels, five CCM distributors, three CCM music publishers, two CCM radio networks, *CCM Magazine*, the Gospel Music Association, and Christian Copyright Licensing International."[4]

Evangelical Worship. Melanie C. Ross, Oxford University Press. © Oxford University Press 2021.
DOI: 10.1093/oso/9780197530757.003.0008

Church History

Despite their geographic polarities and theological distinctions, Wayfarers Collective in Portland, and The Village Chapel (known colloquially as TVC) in Nashville—the church we meet in this chapter—share a striking point in common: both attract individuals who have grown disillusioned with Christian faith.

For many Christians in Portland, Wayfarers Collective was their last stop on the way out the door. These individuals were frustrated by the conservative theology, epistemic certainty, and dispensational theology of the previous evangelical churches they had attended. Wayfarers Collective offered them a place to express their dissatisfaction, heal from it, and make strides toward what they saw as a healthier spirituality. Particularly in its early years, TVC was also a church that attracted people with a troubled relationship to Christianity. Village Chapel cofounders Jim and Kim Thomas note that many talented individuals moved to Music City with dreams of becoming the next big name in Christian music. "The city is littered with the bodies of celebrity wannabes who didn't make it," Kim observes. Those who do achieve commercial success face a different, but equally difficult, struggle. Jim explains that to remain viable, an artist "always has to be thinking of ways to 'manipulate' [air quotes] somebody to buy their 'God product' [air quotes]. When God is your product, it's really hard for him to remain your object of worship," Jim reflects.

Jim and Kim Thomas understand the pressures of the Christian music industry firsthand. The two met as teenagers at summer camp and began writing music together. Romance and marriage eventually followed, and the couple settled into jobs in Philadelphia: Kim as a graphic arts designer at a publishing company and Jim as the manager of a Christian radio station. In 1986, they left their nine-to-five jobs to pursue music full time. For more than a decade, they traveled as an alternative pop duo, Say-So. One reviewer offered a description of their collaboration:

> He's the theologian; she's the poet. He is a teacher/philosopher who enjoys wrestling things down to their very essence; she uses paint and canvas to consider a thought, an idea, a morsel of truth. She sings and writes lyrics; he plays guitar and writes music. Call them a creative dichotomy, a marital paradox, a dissonant yet harmonious melody. Individually, they are Jim and Kim Thomas. Together, just call them Say-So.[5]

Say-So found a fan base among the college and adult alternative crowd and toured for more than a decade without a label contract, playing in hundreds of college campuses, coffeehouses, and clubs. In 1997, they recorded their first major label release (*Say-So*, Organic), followed by a second in 1999 (*Still Waters*, Organic). Their music was featured on the hit television shows *Dawson's Creek* and *Party of Five*.

One of the downsides to Say-So's heavy touring schedule was that the Thomases, like many other musicians who traveled on weekends, were rarely able to be in church on Sunday morning. Jim and Kim started a midweek Bible study for professional musicians in Nashville, which eventually turned into a church in 2001.

Shortly after their new church was started, the Thomases took a stroll through their neighborhood and passed by the historic St. Bernard Building. The four-story, Victorian-Gothic-style building was more than a century old, and until 1989 had been home to the Catholic Sisters of Mercy as a convent and academy. It housed twenty-eight dorm rooms and a large chapel—a total of sixty-four thousand square feet. After lying dormant for several years, the building had been redeveloped as office space. The Thomases began to research the former convent, eventually becoming friends with the owner of the property. In 2003, TVC began renting the three-hundred-person-capacity, thirty-foot-high chapel, which was showing signs of its age. Pleased that the congregation wanted to take care of the chapel, the property owner allowed the fledgling church to grow into the costs of the building. TVC worked slowly and steadily. They replaced the thin Plexiglas windows with real glass. They upgraded the old lighting system. The congregation grew. In 2015, after twelve years as St. Bernard's largest tenant, TVC purchased the former Catholic school-turned-office building. Today, TVC has thirteen core staff and a congregation of roughly twelve hundred people who attend services either at the St. Bernard Building, located in the Hillsboro Village neighborhood of Nashville, or at the church's newer campus, located in the Five Points section of East Nashville.

After two decades on the road as musicians, Jim and Kim Thomas had visited countless churches and Christian colleges. Jim recalls, "We saw the brightest and best, but we also saw the darkest and ugliest. We came back asking, 'In whatever becomes the worship service in our [new] church, how do we keep from adding to the cynicism?'" Both Thomases remember that, at least initially, TVC attracted a lot of jaded industry insiders. Jim reflects, "At one point, one of our council members said, 'You know folks, we can't really build a church on cynical people. We are going to need some [spiritually] healthy people at some point!' We all laughed, but we started thinking about it." Kim has a similar recollection. She was leading a women's Bible study on the book of Nehemiah, a book that tells the story of the Israelites returning home to rebuild the walls of the city, which had been decimated by war. Specifically, Kim remembers Nehemiah 3:8, which states that each priest was responsible for repairing the section of the wall that stood in front of his own house. Kim recounts, "It then hit me: 'We have people [at TVC] who cannot rebuild their own walls. Everybody needs help with their wall.'" She started to pray: "Lord, you may have called us to the cynics and the outcasts of the church, but we have to get some healthy people in here to help rebuild. *Then* we can have more of the walking wounded among us."

Kim, a visual artist whose art has been described as "Dave Barry with a dash of Rilke" believes that the identity of the chosen people of God is always tied to place. "The restoration of all things goes from a place (the garden) to a place (the heavenly fasting table). Place matters," she insists. In contrast to evangelical churches that feel pressured to purchase ever-higher-tech sound systems, sophisticated multimedia packages, and screens for projecting lyrics, or churches like Wayfarers Collective that have intentionally eschewed "churchy"-looking buildings, the Thomases work to retain the historicity of the one-hundred-year-old monastery that is now TVC's home. For the youngest members of the church, the warm patina of the building offers a sense of security and connection: "It makes them feel like mom and dad are here," Kim suggests.

Authenticity is an important word at TVC. In his study of authenticity and culture, Charles Lindholm suggests that there are two factors at play when characterizing an entity as authentic: genealogy (origin) and correspondence (content). "Authentic objects, persons and collectives are original, real, and pure," he explains. "They are what they purport to be, their roots are known and verified, their essence and appearance are one."[6] Similarly, Kim stresses that the patina of the old St. Bernard Building is something that cannot be reproduced:

Authenticity is a silent word to people when they come into your space. They may not look around [TVC] and go, "Oh, there's an authenticity to this space. This looks appropriate to today *and* referential to then. There's no fake wood on the floor." But those things are subtle statements that set the mood, and we find them to be important.

The church's furnishings reflect this understanding of authenticity. The Thomases replaced the shiny, plain, flat cross that had once hung in front of the sanctuary with one made out of two pieces of termite-ravished driftwood. This rustic cross serves as a reflection on the reality of the scars and imperfections that mark the body of Christ. "It serves as a shock to some people," Kim notes, "but we believe that the cross was not beautiful at first."[7]

Underneath the cross is a one-hundred-year-old carpenter's workbench, of the same vintage as the building (Figure 7.1). Kim explains that it too has meaning: as "a symbol that we are all on the carpenter's workbench, in process, at the foot of the cross." Kim acknowledges that people will not make these connections at first glance. "But they might think, 'That cross is different,' and 'I

Figure 7.1 A carpenter's bench stands under the foot of the cross
Nashville, Tennessee: March 2015. Photo by author.

wonder what that table is?' It begins a different conversation than one we might have if we used a gold metallic cross and a folding table with a tablecloth." The room is uncarpeted, which enhances the acoustics for congregational singing. There are no curtains on the windows. Kim explains, "For us, that says, 'This is all open. There's nothing to hide.' It's very vulnerable."

The podium from which Jim preaches every week was Kim's drafting table in art school (Figure 7.2). It was passed on to her by her father, and his father before that, and it bears the scars of generations of use. For Kim, this art-table-cum-pulpit is deeply significant: a physical representation of the coming together of art and theology. Kim points out that artists make thousands of decisions with every work: "We navigate the razor's edge of thoughtful or overthoughtful, self-aware or self-conscious . . . [deciding], How big? How small? How dark? How light? How much detail? How much to withhold, or disguise, or hide, or reveal?" Pastors and theologians work with different media—creeds, covenants, and confessions instead of paint, brushes, and canvas—but they too wrestle with paradox and tension, figuring out how to balance God's sovereignty with human responsibility, grace with works, and the Trinitarian mystery of a God who is Three-in-One. Both art and theology "wrestle with how to express the whole in the fragment, the aspects of an infinite God revealed in the finite creation."[8]

Figure 7.2 Drafting table used as a pulpit
Nashville, Tennessee: March 2015. Photo by author.

In some congregations, theology and the arts are at odds: the latter represents an "escape" from didactic sermons and systematic theologies. For example, musician and theologian Jeremy Begbie points out that "in the midst of what feels like an overly secure, oversystematized, word-imprisoned Protestantism," many people "run to the arts for refuge, [since] they appear to promise a semantic freedom, and allusiveness and openness that the discourses of doctrinal orthodoxy seem to disallow."[9] Recall the individual at Wayfarers Collective who declared that his imagination was stifled at seminary: "There's nothing like being critiqued because of the word you use when you're trying to say something about God."[10] This individual—and countless others like him—worry about what Nicholas Lash calls a "cataphatic cockiness": namely, "a breezy assurance that our speech and writing can name and grasp the things of God with relative ease."[11]

However, Begbie cautions against downplaying the importance of language, which is an intrinsic component of God's self-communication to humanity: "The Word becomes flesh, and our fallen language is integral to that flesh so assumed."[12] While arts are more than an emotional warm-up for the sermon, they must also be "responsible and faithful to the normative texts of the faith."[13] In Begbie's words, the arts "do their own kind of work in their own kind of way, articulating the depths of the Word of the gospel and our experience of it that are otherwise unheard or unfelt."[14] Or as Kim Thomas vividly puts it, "Apologetics takes us to the foot of the mountain; imagination gives us wings for the ascent." There is one more significant intersection point between arts and theology at TVC, and that is the friendship between Jim and Kim Thomas and another husband-wife team, Keith and Kristyn Getty. The Gettys are highly successful worship songwriters and touring musicians. Like the Thomases, they understand the inherent tension between ministry and commerce. Keith Getty explains,

> Music and business have always been uncomfortable companions. Business and religion have been uncomfortable companions. And religion and music have been, at times, uncomfortable companions. So trying to put the three together and expecting a happy result is not very realistic. But I've never tried to write a worship song as a commodity. I try to write a great song for a congregation and not what the industry wants. I've tried to write, asking, "How can I make everyone in this room stand taller, breathe deeper, and be excited to sing, and clench their fists, and raise their hands, and sing louder?" And that's what we're trying to achieve in our songs.[15]

The Gettys started writing music in their native Northern Ireland and moved to Nashville in 2011. They put down roots at TVC and quickly established a friendship with Jim and Kim Thomas. Although the Gettys are not in charge of leading weekly worship at TVC—that distinction belongs to Director of Worship Tommy Bailey—the congregation sings their music on a regular basis. Conversely, the Thomases are often speakers at the conferences the Gettys host, and the Gettys have featured Kim's artwork in their national tours.

The Thomases and the Gettys believe that pastors and musicians are an important partnership in the life of a church: one has a bent toward theology, the other a bent toward the arts. When the two work well together, "like the Wesley brothers or Cliff Barrows and Billy Graham, it's a one plus one equals three."[16] The Gettys talk to the Thomases and other pastoral advisers to find ideas about what songs to write. They also think about how their songs might help at particular moments in a service (evidenced, for example, in "The Communion Hymn," which is about the Lord's Supper, and "Speak, O Lord," a musical prayer for illumination that could be used immediately before or after a sermon).

Keith Getty (a composer) and Kristyn Getty (a lyricist) try to write poetry that "lifts our eyes" to God, "arrests our emotions, fascinates our minds, and sticks in our memories." This poetry must then "be married to melodies that are so sing-able . . . that we want to sing them over and over and pass them on to our children."[17] The Gettys' worship songs—commonly known as "modern hymns"—express musically what the Thomases' art-table-cum-pulpit symbolizes physically: the synthesis of art intellect and imagination.

Service Description

"Good morning, Village Chapel! Let's stand together as we sing to our Lord."
The morning service at TVC has begun. Sunshine streams through the large
windows lining both walls of the sanctuary. Tucked into a corner at the front
of the church, underneath a drop-down screen for projecting lyrics, are eight
musicians: two vocalists, two guitarists, two bassists, and a keyboardist and a per-
cussionist (Figure 7.3). TVC's music team is built differently every week, owing
to its deep bench of talented musicians. Jim and Kim require anyone who wants
to lead music to spend a minimum of six months in the community first. There is
also an expectation of a quality that the Thomases call "understated excellence."
Understated excellence means that a musician must be able to accompany the
congregation with a professional level of proficiency, without drawing attention
to him- or herself. Understated excellence also means that the band and the lead
vocalists are not focal points during worship: they remain seated and visually
obscured when the congregation stands to sing.

The principle of understated excellence came up repeatedly in my interviews at
TVC. Everyone stresses that TVC musicians were world-class performers: during
the week, they play in bands or headline in solo acts that audiences gladly pay
large sums of money to hear. As Director of Welcome Emily Bailey puts it, "TVC

Figure 7.3 Worship at TVC. Musicians are seated inconspicuously under the
projection screen
Nashville, Tennessee: March 2015. Photo by author.

could easily become a very 'show-driven' church because of all the talented people. But on Sunday morning, you don't think, 'Wow—check out that bass line!' Nothing about it says, 'Look at me because I can play this instrument so well.'" Another church member, Steve Guthrie, who is professor of theology and religion and the arts at Belmont University, helpfully suggests that TVC reflects "the sanctified wisdom of a session musician." He elaborates,

> A lot of the folks who play in the TVC band are A-list studio people who do recording sessions every day. But if you're playing on a Tide detergent commercial, or if you're playing behind Reba McEntire, nobody wants your five-minute guitar solo. Nobody wants you sticking out. You're there to hit the notes and support the featured artist. It's that kind of ethos among TVC musicians. We all recognize that we're here to support the congregation. We're supposed to provide a foundation that's solid enough that everybody can sing on top of it.

For TVC musicians, accompanying the congregation is as much about the notes they *don't* play as the ones they do. (Indeed, the congregation often sings verses in a cappella harmony.) If the congregation cannot hear itself sing over the sound of the band, people will not participate. This defeats the purpose of congregational singing, which Kim Thomas defines as an intrinsically corporate act: "There's a subtle text being spoken: 'We are together. We are not alone. Our praises are multiplied because there is more than one of us.'"

This morning, the congregation begins by singing three songs: two classic hymns ("All Hail the Power of Jesus' Name" and "How Great Thou Art"), and a modern worship song ("O Praise the Name," a 2015 piece by the band Hillsong). As director of worship at TVC, Tommy Bailey has the task of overseeing the church's rotation of music leaders, who change every Sunday. Each week, the leader submits their song selections to Bailey. "Rarely do I ever have to change them," Bailey reports, "but every once in a while, a leader will want to introduce a song that just doesn't fit TVC culture very well. For example, I have a thing against songs that use [the word] "oh" as a placeholder, with the congregation singing it over and over. Something like that, I might push back on." TVC congregation sings popular modern worship songs, although not as frequently as many other evangelical churches. "I don't have any particular problem with [modern worship songs]," Bailey reflects, "but I think they tend to lean toward the thinner side of theological sturdiness. That's just my judgment—they don't necessarily fit with what we do at TVC."

Traditional hymns are a better fit, and TVC sings them often. The sound is less "organ and church choir" and more "folk" or "Americana." "We're in Nashville," Bailey points out, "so sometimes there's a country bent to it. A lot of times our southern roots shine through." Steve Guthrie suggests that TVC's sound is influenced in part by the Nashville hipster demographic. "Younger people are growing handlebar mustaches, moving into old neighborhoods with old houses, and looking to decorate them with pieces from the 1930s. It's a very 'Mumford and Sons' kind of musical thing." However, TVC's theology of hymnody goes deeper than cultural trendiness. Bailey prefers to err on the side of theological longevity. "What are the songs that will last?" he asks. "What are the songs that today's children will sing around their parents' deathbeds?"

After the final song, K–5 children are dismissed for their own time of worship and teaching while members of the congregation greet one another. Kim Thomas offers a few administrative announcements, then settles in on a stool to lead the congregation in a time of intercessory prayer. Kim's prayer is notable for its length: a full ten minutes. Jim notes, "A lot of times when new people come to our church, one of the first things we hear from them is 'They pray pretty long in that worship service! What's that all about?' But after a few visits, it dawns on them: 'Of course! This is church—where else would you pray?' " Jim believes that visitors' surprise over the length of corporate prayer at TVC may be an indication that evangelicals have forgotten that the purpose of worship—what North Point's Andy Stanley calls "the win"—is not, in Jim's words, to "keep the entertainment level up," but rather to pray, feed the flock, and glorify God. The prayer ends with a hymn of thanksgiving ("Great Is Thy Faithfulness"), and Jim Thomas steps forward to preach the morning message.

Thomas begins by explaining that TVC studies through books of the Bible, and that this morning's focus is on Psalm 13—the first of twelve psalms the church would study in a row. Psalm 13, Thomas explains, is a lament. "But don't get all bummed out thinking, 'That's the last thing I want to do: sit around and talk about how horrible life is." Thomas stresses that the psalm ends in confidence, as so many laments do. He reads the psalm aloud to the congregation:

> How long, O Lord? Will you forget me forever? How long will you hide your face from me? How long will I take counsel in my soul, this sorrow in my heart all the day? How long will my enemy be exalted over me? Answer, O Lord my God. Light up my eyes, lest I sleep the sleep of death, lest my enemy say "I've overcome him," lest my adversaries rejoice when I'm shaken. I have trusted in your lovingkindness. My heart will rejoice in your salvation. I will sing to the Lord because he's dealt bountifully with me.

Thomas connects the words of the psalm with a story about a man named Carl who had a cycling accident. His injuries were severe, including damage to his spinal column that left him in a wheelchair, paralyzed from the chest down. "Carl said he had come to the place where he felt the absence of God. His physical suffering was terrible, but the spiritual suffering in his soul—his experience with the

hiddenness or the absence of God—was worse. Maybe your story isn't Carl's,"
Thomas continues. "Maybe your story isn't even David's. But this is what I like
about Psalm 13: we don't know with any specificity what the problem is. All we
know is the psalmist tells us he senses the absence of God."

"In 1985, one of the biggest songs of the year was by a band called 'Tears for
Fears.' Say it with me if you know it." Thomas begins to chant the refrain, and
many voices in the congregation join him in immediate recognition. Thomas
laughs at the memory of the times. "You got in your car, turned the radio on,
and pounded on the dashboard, didn't you?" He then turns serious. "But is
that it? Is that all we get? A primal scream to let some steam off? A little eu-
phoria, but then it stops?" Thomas clarifies that this is not the message of
Psalm 13: "You can shout, shout, and let it all out, but that's not where it stops.
There's a God who hears you, and welcomes you into his presence because he
loves you, and because he intends to do something about what is broken in
this world."

Thomas suggests that if Psalm 13 were set to a musical soundtrack, verses
1–4 would be in a minor key. But then there's a sharp turn to major in verse
5: "I have trusted in your lovingkindness." Thomas becomes animated as he
stresses the main point of the sermon. "Why does the psalm look forward
to God's lovingkindness and salvation. Because of what God has done in
the past." Thomas draws the congregation's attention to the past-tense verb
structure of verse 6: "I will sing to the Lord because he has *dealt* bountifully
with me. He's been good to me in the past," Thomas reiterates. "We do well
to recall God's faithfulness as we gather together." This is one of the most
important functions of the church: "I need you to remind me that God is
faithful. I know some of your stories and the severity of some of your pain.
And I know how faithful God was to you. Every time I see you, I'm reminded
of God's faithfulness."

Furthermore, Thomas points out that although there is a sharp emotional turn
between verses 1–4 (God's hiddenness and the experience of feeling forgotten by
God) and verses 5 and 6 (which express confidence in the steadfast love of God),
there is no indication that the psalmist's circumstances have actually changed.
"Nothing happened between verses 4 and 5. What happens is David volitionally
engages his will, saying to God, 'I'm down here asking how long, but I'm going to
trust in you.'"

Thomas stresses that the psalmist tells us to rejoice in *God's* salvation. "It's
not some kind of self-salvation. Not pulling yourself up by your bootstraps. The
world around us tells us we can save ourselves by looking inside ourselves, all
that sort of thing. The Bible says no." Thomas reminds the congregation that all of
us need outside help: "Here's what happens to me when I look inside myself. I see
a fool and a failure. I see a guy that is inconsistent." In contrast,

The Bible says that you're going to have to look outside yourself for help, to the one who made you, the one you belong to ultimately. Look to the one in Psalm 13, who invites you to come with your "how longs," who has set his love on you, and is still offering you his salvation that you can rejoice in, who will be dealing with you bountifully.

Thomas concludes the sermon with three highlights. First is the reality of pain: "The anguish of the soul is part of every life. There's a reality to our anguish. What are your 'how longs,' and how might God be using them as an invitation for you to turn to him, for the first time, or maybe the tenth time?" Second, Thomas stresses the opportunity for prayer, which is "how we deploy the cry of the soul in pain." Communing with God in prayer helps us "not only to 'shout, shout, let it all out,' but to be heard by a loving God who one day intends to set things right."

Finally, Thomas emphasizes the importance of singing. "At the end of the psalm, nothing has changed circumstantially. But *David* is changed. He fixes his trust and hope on God, and he employs his will to sing to the Lord. Somehow, in a way that I can't explain, it makes a difference to sing to the Lord because he's dealt bountifully with us." Thomas observes that when David sings, "it's not just singing anything. It's not, 'Row, Row, Row Your Boat.' It's not 'Shout, shout, let it all out.' It's 'I will sing of the mercies of the Lord forever. I will sing of his faithfulness to all generations.'"

Thomas notes that there might be those in the congregation who struggle to see how God has been faithful. He reminds the congregation that even when we have the sense that God has forgotten or abandoned us, God is closer than your breath and heartbeat. "Once you come to faith in Christ, and trust him with your life and your soul, you're never alone for all of eternity," Thomas concludes.

The congregation sings one final song together: the classic hymn "It Is Well with My Soul." As the last notes of the chorus die away, Thomas reminds the congregation that Horatio Spafford wrote the lyrics to this hymn not long after his four daughters were lost at sea. Before that, Spafford's son had died and his business had burned to the ground. "I have a feeling that Horatio Spafford knew a little bit about Psalm 13 as well: 'How long? How long? How long? Yet will I praise him.'" After a brief pause, Thomas lightens the mood with an announcement of the upcoming church picnic. He reminds the congregation that there is a prayer team available at the back of the sanctuary and that offering boxes are located near the exits. He closes the service with a final benediction: "May Almighty God make you faithful to his calling, cheerful in his service, and fruitful in his kingdom. May the blessing of God the Father, God the Son, and God the Holy Spirit rest upon you, and may that blessing flow through you like a mighty river to all of those to whom he will send you this afternoon, this evening, and the rest of this week." The congregation is dismissed to go in peace.

Homiletical Analysis

Both Jaxon (Wayfarers Collective) and Jim Thomas (TVC) dealt with the difficulty of the "dark night of the soul"—a spiritual struggle in which it feels like God is not present. Both pastors emphasized that the experience of God's silence is not necessarily a cause for alarm, nor an indication that a person has sinned. Both pastors also stressed the importance of continuing to participate in the life of the church during these spiritual dry spells. However, at several places their messages diverge in significant ways. To understand how, I turn to the work of philosopher Charles Taylor.

The ideas of Charles Taylor (b. 1931), from Montreal, Quebec, have been highly influential in the humanities, social sciences, and public affairs. His honors include the 2007 Templeton Prize for achievement in the advancement in spiritual matters, the 2008 Kyoto Prize, regarded as Japan's highest private honor, the 2015 John W. Kluge Prize for Achievement in the Study of Humanity (shared with Jürgen Habermas), and the inaugural 2016 Berggruen Prize awarded to a thinker "whose ideas are of broad significance for shaping human self-understanding and the advancement of humanity."

Taylor's thought is difficult to characterize. He is a progressive Catholic who denies hell and substitutionary atonement and is a strong supporter of secularism (in the sense of state neutrality toward religion, not hostility to it).[18] For Taylor, the advantage of Christianity has to do with what he calls the "Best Account principle."[19] Taylor argues that the first-person vernacular language we use to express our experiences can be tentative and uncertain. But in the process of groping for answers, we find words that are adequate enough—and we use them until we find something else that feels more adequate. At the end of the day, the apologetic debate between Christianity and atheism comes down to the question of which can offer the best account: "Who can respond most profoundly and convincingly to what are ultimately commonly felt dilemmas?"[20] Taylor's wager is on the Christian story. "How can one demonstrate this?" Taylor wonders aloud at the end of one of his books. Logical arguments and academic discourse fall short: the "better-ness" of the Christian account is something that has to be *felt*.[21] "There is a large element of hope," Taylor acknowledges. "It is a hope that I see implicit in Judeo-Christian theism."[22]

Over the past decade, Taylor's work—specifically, his nine-hundred-page book *A Secular Age*—has captured the attention of evangelical thought leaders who influence TVC, including pastor and apologist Tim Keller of Redeemer Presbyterian Church in New York City. Collin Hansen, journalist and editorial director for the Gospel Coalition, suggests that the book's popularity among evangelicals has to do with the way that Taylor unpacks and clarifies the cultural changes North Americans are experiencing in the twenty-first century.

Taylor will "take something that is rather obvious, but that no one has named before or that nobody has described," Hansen explains. "It's almost like somebody who gives you language to describe the air that you breathe."[23] Philosopher James K. A. Smith concurs. "If you've grown up in post-1960s North America, *A Secular Age*, which was published in 2006, is like an episode of 'This Is Your Life' or 'Finding Your Roots': It's the backstory to the fractured world in which we find ourselves."[24] Smith urges pastors and church planters to read *A Secular Age*, suggesting that the book "amounts to a cultural anthropology for urban mission" and helps Christians better understand the context in which they proclaim the gospel.[25] In what follows, I argue that Taylor's analysis also sheds new interpretive light on several of the congregations we have examined thus far.

Charles Taylor's Secular Age

Taylor's history starts in premodernity, where people lived in an "enchanted" cosmos full of spirits and forces, some evil and others benevolent. Rewards and punishments worked themselves out in "cures or their failure, the bumper harvest or famine, plagues or storms, rescue at sea or founder."[26] Water, wood, earth, sky, sun, and fire all carried energetic forces. There were places, people, and objects that channeled spiritual powers: relics, sacred trees, sacraments, saints, witches, and ghosts. People understood themselves to be organically and hierarchically connected to the spiritual world: part of what medieval theologians called the "great chain of being."[27] Everyone and everything had a predetermined place in this cosmos. The world was charged with transcendence, meaning, and power. There was an infinite mystery to the universe, of which destruction and violence were an ineradicable part. However, suffering had a purpose—either as a punishment or as a trial meant to teach something—and the knowledge that God was working out his plan made the experience both necessary and meaningful.

But Taylor argues that humans' understanding of God's design for the world underwent a "striking anthropocentric shift" around the turn from the seventeenth to the eighteenth century.[28] The ground for this shift had been prepared by philosophers like Hugo Grotius and John Locke, who believed that God created humans rational and sociable, each with an instinct to his or her own conservation. Subsequently, God's binding norms for his creation were clear: humans must "respect each other's life, liberty and estate."[29] Consider the opening words of the American Declaration of Independence: "We hold these truths to be self-evident, that all men are created equal, that they are endowed by their creator with certain unalienable rights, that among these are life, liberty and the pursuit of happiness." Since there is nothing foundational to life that our intellect cannot grasp, mystery and miracles amount to a defect in God's design for creation.

Because God expects humans to use their powers of reason to grasp the laws of the universe and carry out the divine plan, "It would be irresponsible of him and defeat his purposes to be intervening miraculously."[30]

As a result of the anthropomorphic shift, people came to understand God's will differently. In premodernity, God was first and foremost concerned with human beings' ultimate, transcendent good. This good was always defined in direct relationship to God: in humanity's loving and serving God, being in God's presence, or contemplating God in the beatific vision. After death, humans became partakers in the life of God through "theosis," a "becoming divine" that was part of human destiny. After providential deism, humanity's understanding of life and death changed. People believed God's will was for them to be happy in the here and now, with "happiness" defined as the attainment of things they desired and the absence of pain. The afterlife was no longer a place for any further spiritual transformation; at best, it was a longer-lasting version of the pleasures of earthly life and a place for reunification with loved ones. In time, many people dismissed the idea of an afterlife as a delusional wish of the weak who could not bear to face the harsh truth of death's finality.

Taylor notes that as humans moved away from the idea of "external props" (rewards and punishments beyond the grave) that kept them on the path toward their own good, the last reasons for justifying divine violence (as either punishment or pedagogy) disappeared. The anthropocentric turn has resulted in what Taylor calls "a strikingly modern phenomenon": namely, "the decline of Hell."[31] "The wrath of God disappears," concludes Taylor, "leaving only His love."[32] At Moody Church, this was precisely the concern of senior pastor Erwin Lutzer: "When I look at even my friends in evangelicalism, very few of them preach on the judgment of God. I wonder how many evangelical pastors have ever preached a full sermon on hell?"[33] Lutzer suggested that "Jonathan Edwards would not recognize the church of today. If somebody were to stand up and quote 'Sinners in the Hands of an Angry God' [in contemporary worship] the service would end in a riot."[34] Similarly, leaders at Wayfarers Collective in Portland aim to "pull people, with love and hope, toward a picture of who they could be in Christ, rather than pushing them there out of guilt or obligation"—or, one might also add, fear of hell.[35]

James K. A. Smith, a philosopher at Calvin University who has popularized Taylor's work for a general audience, notes that contemporary evangelicals deemphasize not only hell, but also heaven. Many twenty-first-century evangelicals reject a dispensational version of the Christian faith, which they regard as too heavenly minded for earthly good. Their rejection of dispensationalism has found expression in "a new emphasis on 'the goodness of creation' and the importance of social justice."[36] The themes of creation care and social justice were prominent in Jaxon's sermon at the Wayfarers Collective in Portland: when recounting his experience of planning a community garden in an under-resourced neighbor-hood, Jaxon explained that he "had a sense that God loved this project and was really happy it was happening."[37] Jaxon's comments reflect his community's belief that the Kingdom of God is not an after-death experience only, but is accessible in the here and now. Smith wonders whether this line of thinking is "a delayed replay" of the anthropocentric shifts in early modernity, where this-worldly ex-istence became an end in itself, and people began to believe that one could have a life of meaning without reference to transcendence or eternity.[38] If so, Taylor's account might serve as a cautionary tale.

For the purposes of our discussion, the most important result of the anthro-pomorphic shift is a new interpretation of Jesus's crucifixion. Once people came to believe (1) that God's ultimate goal is for us to be happy and (2) that God has endowed us with all the reason and moral sense necessary to understand the cosmos he designed, the idea that God would use something as violent as the crucifixion to fulfill his divine plan became taboo. Taylor notes that today the tra-ditional center of Christian piety—love and gratitude at the suffering of Christ—sounds frightening, even pathological, to many: "To celebrate such a terrible act of violence as a crucifixion, to make this the centre of your religion, you have to be sick; you have to be perversely attached to self-mutilation."[39] For an illustra-tion of this perspective, recall Alec's words at Wayfarers Collective: "God seemed very distant and needed to be appeased. There was a price to be paid, and God got his vengeance by taking Jesus down on the cross. Sorry for my language, but that bullshit doesn't jive with me at all."[40]

Taylor allows that the crucifixion is so much a part of Christian theology that it "can't be read out of the story at this late date": in other words, twenty-first-century Christians are not free to rewrite the plot line established in the gospels. They are, however, free to reinterpret the narrative, and Taylor suggests they have done so by making the crucifixion "an *accident de parcours*; not the main point." In late modernity, the important thing "is not what [Christ] *does* (atone, con-quer death, take captivity captive), but rather what he *says* or *teaches*."[41] However, Taylor sees this as a loss. While no fan of the doctrine of penal substitutionary atonement—the belief that Christ, by his own sacrificial choice, was punished in the place of sinners to satisfy the demands of God's justice—Taylor worries that by focusing myopically on Jesus's love and wise teachings, Christians in late mo-dernity have lost something important:

> A too benign picture of the human condition leaves something crucial out, something that matters to us. There is a dark side to creation, to use this (Barthian) expression; along with joy, there is massive innocent suffering; and then on top of this, the suffering is denied, the story of the victims is distorted, eventually forgotten, never rectified or compensated. Along with communion,

there is division, alienation, spite, mutual forgetfulness, never reconciled and brought together again. Even where a voice of faith wants to deny that this is the last word, as with Christianity, we cannot set aside the fact that this is what we live, that we regularly experience this as ultimate.[42]

Taylor concludes that "for all its faults," penal substitutionary atonement offers "an articulation of the dark side of creation." Simply negating the idea of atonement, "as many of us modern Christianity are tempted to do, leaves a vacuum."[43]

However, at TVC the crucifixion is a centerpiece of Jim Thomas's sermon. Thomas reminds the congregation that even Jesus experienced separation from God. In Gethsemane, Jesus goes through anguish, praying, "If it's possible, let this cup pass from me." While hanging on the cross, Jesus exclaims, "My God, my God, why have you forsaken me?" In the same way, Thomas acknowledges there are many times when "we may not understand what God is up to in his silence, or allowing this or that instance of suffering or personal pain, or permitting chaos to go on longer than we think it ought to." Indeed, the Bible's frank, unvarnished acknowledgment of the difficulty of the human condition is something Thomas especially appreciates: "The anguish of the soul is part of every life. Psalm 13 is honest, and I want truth that corresponds to reality, not some kind of falsehood that sounds like romanticism or a syrupy Hallmark card." Thomas does not offer answers for God's silence, but he does remind the congregation that "for whatever reason God allows all the pain and evil in the world, at least he was willing to take some of his own medicine. Christ took my sin on himself, your sin on himself, he died, and three days later he burst from the tomb. Christianity is a forward-looking faith. We have a hope in a God who can turn crucifixions into resurrections, and that's why we trust in him and in no other."

Taylor believes that is not possible to go back and time to "undo" the anthropocentric turn, which is "in the water [and] increasingly in the air we breathe. Not even orthodox Christians might realize the extent to which we've absorbed this by osmosis." [44] Taylor coins the adjective "fragilized" to describe religious belief in the twenty-first century. By this he means that "we live in a condition where we cannot help but be aware that there are a number of different construals, views which intelligent, reasonably undeluded people, of good will, can and do disagree on. We cannot help looking over our shoulder from time to time, looking sideways, living our faith also in a condition of doubt and uncertainty."[45] As Calvin University philosopher Smith puts it, "We don't believe instead of doubting; we believe while doubting. We're all Thomas now."[46] Even for Christians, believing doesn't come easy in a secular age.

Ironically, however, neither does doubt. Taylor notes that "there is a generalized sense in our culture that with the eclipse of the transcendent, something may have been lost"—a phenomenological insight that Smith describes as "cracks in the secular."[47] (Smith offers the example of the novelist Julian Barnes, who plaintively quipped in the opening line of his memoir, "I don't believe in God, but I miss Him.")[48] The so-called unbeliever can be "caught short by an epiphany of fullness that transcends her categories" or "confronted by a stubborn sense of something-more-ness that can't be squelched."[49]

Herein lies a unique opportunity for Christian apologetics. Taylor points out that there are some aesthetic experiences "whose power seems inseparable from their epiphanic, transcendent reference": for example, the literature of Dante, the music of Bach, and the artistry of Chartres Cathedral.[50] In Taylor's words, the challenge for the unbeliever is "to find a non-theistic register in which to respond to them, without impoverishment."[51] Smith offers a similar insight in the form of a rhetorical question: "What would it be like," he asks unbelievers, "to listen to Mozart's *Requiem* and take it as nonfiction?"[52] Often, Christian apologists assume that people change their lives by changing their ideas. However, Smith argues that human beings are less like containers waiting to be filled with ideas than like "desiring 'arrows'" aimed at something ultimate.[53] We are shaped by imagination as much as intellect, through stories and songs as much as by proofs and proposition.

Jim Thomas understands the importance of music in shaping faith, which is why he closes his sermon by reminding the congregation to sing about God's faithfulness to all generations. TVC's musical theology is also deeply shaped by the work of Keith and Kristyn Getty, who sponsor an annual conference on precisely this subject.

"Sing!"

The auditorium at Brentwood Baptist Church is filled to capacity. So too is the overflow room. Over four thousand pastors, church leaders, and musicians from more than forty states and twenty countries have come to Nashville for a conference with a one-word title that doubles as a command: "Sing!"

Keith and Kristyn Getty, the organizers of this conference, are well known in the evangelical music world. Keith, in his early forties, is an animated pianist, stomping the floor with his foot while his fingers fly across the keys, and using broad, full-armed gestures to encourage the congregation to sing with gusto. When Keith is excited, as he is today, he speaks with the tongue-twisting speed of an auctioneer. Kristyn, an alto vocalist, is quieter and more even-keeled. She has a calming presence; her gentle humor pairs well with her husband's dry wit. At one point in the session, Keith deviates from his prepared remarks and rattles off a stream of song lyrics, thoroughly confusing the tech crew running his slides. Kristyn shakes her head knowingly and calls out what the audience is thinking: "They probably can't understand a word you're saying, Keith. I certainly can't!" The room bursts into laughter. Keith flashes a chastened grin.

This Northern Irish duo—best friends since 2001 and married since 2004—have performed in such prestigious venues as Carnegie Hall in New York, the Kennedy Center in Washington, DC, and Royal Albert Hall in London. However, they recount, their favorite site for music-making has always been the local church. The Gettys are passionate about congregational song and have been credited with reinventing the traditional hymn genre. But their performing and publishing successes have not tempted the couple to lose sight of the goal they name as their highest calling. "The holy privilege is not writing songs, or playing them, or being the person at the front of the church," Keith stresses. "The holy privilege is God's people singing."

On this late September afternoon, Keith stands behind a podium and explains how the "Sing!" conference came to be. As they toured around the country, the Gettys asked hundreds of church leaders a simple question: "When you finish church on a Sunday, how do you assess the music?" The responses included everything from musical style and song choice to production values and personality. Keith looks intently around the auditorium. "But rarely, if ever, did anyone ask the question 'How did the congregation sing?' as a measure of how well the music in a worship service had gone." In other words, the primary value—singing—has become subordinated to stylistic and logistical concerns that are, at best, only secondary.

The Gettys point out that scripture contains more than four hundred references to singing, and at least fifty direct commands to do so. The Bible leaves no wiggle room: "We are not to disregard the command because we don't like the music or the personnel or are not in the mood." Corporate singing "is not a metaphorical or optional or seasonal suggestion, but a clear directive from our Lord and Savior"; therefore, it should "go without saying that the leadership of a church should be facilitating congregational [song]."[54]

The importance of corporate song does not "go without saying" in the twenty-first century. When asked about his hopes for music at North Point Community Church, Andy Stanley responded, "The 'win' for me is when someone can hear a song . . . and there's something in [it] that grabs them emotionally"—even if the person doesn't know the song, agree with the lyrics, or like the musical style.[55] There is no pastoral emphasis on active participation, and Stanley is unapologetic about its omission. "We give people permission not to sing at all if they prefer. . . . Some people just don't like to sing. And that's ok."[56] Stanley, and the evangelical pastors influenced by him, believe that music leaders ought not "guilt people into singing" because "an individual's willingness or unwillingness to participate in corporate singing is not a reflection of his or her . . . spiritual maturity."[57] For the Gettys, however, singing is directly tied to obedience and spiritual maturity. The matter is unequivocal: "We are commanded by God to sing—so we must do it. . . . Not to sing is to disobey."[58]

The challenges facing twenty-first-century congregational song are immense. At the "Sing!" conference, Kristyn acknowledges that we live in a time where people are more inclined to listen than they are to take part. But she reminds the leaders assembled in the auditorium this need not be an obstacle: "You need to educate a congregation more richly on singing, give them opportunities to sing, and build their confidence. Say to them 'You are, in fact, singers. We all are. This is not a professional or a specialist category. This is a gift given to the whole congregation.'" At the end of the day, "We are commanded to sing with the saints because we *need* to sing. Our spiritual health depends on it."[59]

Keith Getty, like Andy Stanley, is worried about the "nones" who have left the Christian church, in part because of Getty's own experience with intellectual doubts in his twenties. Getty grew up in a conservative church where he was sheltered from many cultural influences of the day. Getty reports that his family listened only to Christian and classical music: as a teenager, he knew more about the writings of the Puritan John Owen than he did about the music of Jon Bon Jovi.[60] Getty left Ireland to attend university in England, where he plunged into academic debates with atheists, Muslims, and students from other non-Christian faith traditions. These new encounters with religious pluralism shook Keith's understanding of Christianity: "Suddenly my faith in everything began to be tested. I got questions that I had no answers for, and I was confused."[61] He turned to a number of resources for help, including the writings of the scholar and novelist C. S. Lewis, and John Lennox, the Northern Ireland–born mathematician and philosopher of science who is famous for his debates with Richard Dawkins. Getty struggled with various intellectual aspects of Christianity during his late teens and early twenties, but believes his intellectual wrestling strengthened his faith.

As we saw in Chapter 4, at North Point Andy Stanley responds to intellectual challenges by offering university students an apologetic script. When skeptics challenge the veracity of the Christian faith on the basis of the violence, misogyny, and scientifically unverifiable claims of the Old Testament, Christians should change the sequence of the conversation: the resurrection is the best apologetic for the reliability of Christian scripture. Stanley suggests a script that high school and college students at North Point might use when engaging in debates with skeptics: "If somebody predicts their own death and resurrection and pulls it off, you should pay attention to what that person says."[62]

The Gettys would concur that verbal apologetic strategies are essential to effective evangelism. However, the Christian faith is affective as well as cognitive. The Gettys have four daughters, and Kristyn advises Christian parents to think especially carefully about the music they teach their young children, knowing that they might later become "nones":

> If a child is to [later] wander away or go through a period of rebellion, be thinking in your mind about some of the things that you would want to sing to them even when they're far away, knowing that music has this tremendous power that we can't even fathom. . . . What are the essential ideas of the gospel? What does the Christian faith actually mean? Let's find songs that explain that, so even if they wander away, these are the things that will continue to be in their mind.[63]

Herein lies an important contrast between Stanley and the Gettys. Recall that Stanley's musical "win" in worship is when there's something about the song that immediately captures the listener's attention and emotions. For the Gettys, such a vision is too shortsighted: they consider the shelf life of a song, its longevity after a person has been "grabbed" by it. Keith points out that when a committee chooses selections for a hymnal, they ask whether a congregation could sing the proposed song for the next thirty or so years (or beyond). "That's our approach," Keith explains. "When Kristyn and I write our songs, we try to evaluate them on 'Is this something I could potentially grow old with?' Of course, we get it wrong a lot of the time. But that's what we're trying to do."[64]

The Gettys occupy a unique space in church music today as writers of "modern hymns"—a genre they helped pioneer. The Gettys' hymns are used increasingly in both contemporary and traditional circles, being included in most modern hymnbooks (with a number of these now listing "Getty" as the most-featured composers). More than sixty of their songs are featured on CCLI's "Top 2000" list.[65] In 2017 Keith Getty was made an Officer of the Order of the British Empire (OBE) by Queen Elizabeth II. The event, which commemorates Getty's contribution to "Music and Modern Hymn Writing," marked the first occasion that the order has been bestowed on an individual involved in the world of contemporary church music.

When asked what makes a composition a hymn (as opposed to a contemporary worship song), the Gettys' answer has less to do with a musical style or structure than with intention. Can all generations sing the melody? Do the lyrics help the word of God to dwell richly in the believer's heart (Colossians 3:16) and build up the church?[66] If the answer to both questions is yes, the piece can be classified as a modern hymn.

A comparison to Park Street Church and Moody Church helps clarify the Gettys' modern hymn project. Park Street's official statement on corporate worship notes that the church feels "no insistence or compulsion to mirror the music or aesthetics of the popular culture" in its worship music. Park Street uses the three adjectives *didactic, exhortative,* and *inspiring* to describe its music. Music minister Nathan Skinner suggests that "Western sacred music has developed over time to intrinsically facilitate these [three] goals, while commercial/pop music develops in a way that is just as well suited to its own quite different goals."[67] The Gettys, however, might respond that this dichotomy is a false one. The commercially successful worship music they write appeals to a twenty-first-century audience; at the same time, it is also intended to be educational, exhortative, and inspirational. "We're trying to preserve hymnody—not for the sake of conservation, but to reinvent it so it can live and breathe for a new generation," Keith explains. Kristyn suggests that composing modern hymns is like watching a tree grow: "You add rings to your understanding without leaving the old behind."[68]

In many ways, the Gettys have more in common with Moody Church's philosophy of worshipping across the continuums of ancient/modern, simple/eloquent, and familiar/new. The difference is simply that the Gettys attempt to do in a single song what Moody music minister Tim Stafford hopes to accomplish across the entirety of a worship service. Kristyn explains:

> We hear the word "blended" an awful lot—people trying to do the best of the old with the best of the new. Everybody sings the songs they like. And that's a practical effort at trying to do your best in a complicated situation. But there have to be occasions when the whole body is singing the same song together.[69]

Kristyn believes that singing is an act of unity: "You join the same melody line, the same words. Music, like air, connects us. We're all breathing the same melody."[70]

"In Christ Alone"

One of the best examples of the Gettys' philosophy of congregational song is their most famous modern hymn, "In Christ Alone," which was penned in 2001 by Keith and his longtime writing partner, Stuart Townend. The Gettys explain that this hymn developed, in part, "out of a frustration with the lack of depth in the songs that were being sung in many churches (in this sense it was a kind of 'protest' music)."[71] Churches around the world embraced the new composition, as the Gettys' website reports:

> ["In Christ Alone"] holds the #1 position of most-frequently-sung in UK churches for the past 9 consecutive years. It was voted the #2 best-loved hymn of all time in the UK according to a BBC Songs of Praise national survey and among the top 5 hymns of all time by the UK Hymns Society. According to CCLI, it is estimated that 40 to 50 million people sing "In Christ Alone" in

church services each year—which does not include the unique reach the cat- alog has into traditional and classical contexts, as well as the popularity of the song throughout Asia.[72]

"In Christ Alone" was sung at the 2013 enthronement of the archbishop of Canterbury, and church historian Timothy George suggests that the song is "well on its way to becoming the 'Amazing Grace' of this generation."[73] Astute readers will notice that "In Christ Alone" was sung during two earlier congregational visits: at Moody Church and North Point.

In this piece—and all of their music—the Gettys strive to accomplish musically what North Point pastor Andy Stanley strives to accomplish homiletically. In his book *Communicating for a Change*, Stanley suggests that preachers have wrongly embraced the idea that theologically sound doctrine is all that is required to en- gage a congregation. Stanley, whose bachelor's degree is in journalism, reminds his colleagues in ministry, "It's not enough to say [to the congregation], 'I have the truth of God's Word up here and it's your job to listen.'" Instead, the pastor must "raise in them an awareness of a past, present, or future need in their lives that makes them want to listen to you and follow you to the answer."[74] Presentation matters just as much as content: or, in Stanley's words, "*How* you say what you say is as important as *what* you say."[75]

Presentation matters for songwriters as well and has two crucial components. The first is melody. Like Stanley, Getty recognizes that sound doctrine is not enough: "If you have the best lyric in the entire world, it's not leaving the gates without a melody." Conversely, "If you have a great tune, people will sing it."[76] A great melody will make a congregation *want* to sing, just as a great pastoral communicator will make a congregation *want* to listen.

Keith Getty works hard at crafting melodies. Before turning his attention to hymn-writing, Keith produced and/or orchestrated music for more than two hundred projects, including recordings, concerts, television, and film.[77] However, when writing melodies for congregational singing, Getty employs his skills and training to craft tunes that are deceptively simple. One of Getty's com- positional inspirations is Irish folk music, which he describes as "singable," "so- cial," and "almost tailor-made for congregational singing," due to its naturally rising and falling contours.[78] (For example, think of LONDONDERRY AIR, the tune to which the lyrics of the song "Danny Boy" are set.)

One of the contrasts between much contemporary worship music and Irish folk melodies is that in the former, the congregation must rely on the lead singer, the song's syncopation, and the groove in order to follow along. "If you take out the drum [in contemporary worship], the song doesn't work," Kristyn observes. Irish folk music is much more versatile. Kristyn cites "Be Thou My Vision" as an example: "You've heard it with a big rock band, and you've heard it with just voices and nothing else. . . . It's not bound by any generation or style."[79] In the same way, Keith aims to write melodies that can be passed on and sung without written music. The songs he writes are "not supposed to sound like 'now,'" he explains.[80]

The second critical component of songwriting presentation is the lyrics. Keith explains from a songwriter's perspective, "If I've got non-Christian friends coming to church, I'd far rather give them four verses of comparatively heavy theology . . . which explains the gospel, than give them twenty repeated words that could be said about your pet horse or your girlfriend."[81] Subsequently, the Gettys face a challenge that Keith summarizes in the form of a question: "How do you take people who want four-line worship songs and get them to sing thirty-two-line [hymns]?"[82] Paraphrasing Stanley's observation, it is not enough for the musician to say, "I have set the truth of God's Word to music and it's your job to sing." The songwriter must "woo" the people into *wanting* to sing. For the Gettys, this means structuring their hymns as stories. As Keith puts it, "People will sing doxological truth and theology within a story [until] they're blue in the face." He continues, using the example of "In Christ Alone":

> A lot of people are moved by the fact that through the verses, Jesus takes on flesh as a helpless babe and ends up on the cross. *They've sung through half of Romans by the end of the song, but because you've taken them through a story rather than just giving them didactic truth, it really communicates to them.*[83]

Here again, the notion of "story" is deceptively simple. Talented lyricists consider a variety of factors in determining how best to tell a song's story, and one of the most important is meter: the recurring pattern of stresses or accents that provides the pulse of music. Songwriter Bobby Gilles points out that song meters "transmit meaning regardless of the words used." He offers the following example, which demonstrates why a limerick is a poor metrical choice for a song about the cross:

> There once was a man on a cross,
> He paid such a horrible cost
> Was battered and bruised
> Mistreated, abused,
> He died there to save all the lost.[84]

Despite the fact that the words *bruised, battered, abused,* and *mistreated* appear, the meter is too light and frivolous to convey the gravity of the message.

Table 7.1 Trochees and iambs in lines 1–4 of the second verse of "In Christ Alone" (eight syllables per line)

	1	2	3	4	5	6	7	8
L1	In	CHRIST	a-	LONE	who	TOOK	on	FLESH
L2	FULL-	ness	of	GOD	in	HELP-	less	BABE
L3	This	GIFT	of	LOVE	and	RIGH-	teous-	NESS
L4	SCORNED	by	the	ONES	he	CAME	to	SAVE

Conversely, Gilles points out that one reason why "In Christ Alone" evokes powerful feelings is lyricist Stuart Townend's masterful use of meter. To understand this point, two technical terms will be helpful. The first, a *trochee*, is a two-syllable metrical pattern in poetry in which a stressed syllable is followed by an unstressed syllable: for example, the words *poet* (PO-et) and *glory* (GLO-ry). The opposite of a trochee is an *iamb*, which consists of an unstressed syllable followed by a stressed syllable, as in the word *define* (de-FINE) or *alone* (a-LONE).

"In Christ Alone" is written in Long Double Meter, which means that every verse has eight lines, and every line has eight syllables. Odd-numbered lines (L1, L3) establish the stately, prevailing iambic pattern. Even-numbered lines (L2, L4) start with a strong trochee before returning to iambic meter (Table 7.1).

This pattern of trochaic substitution in iambic lines "produce[s] the effect of sudden movement or emphasis."[85] Furthermore, the pattern Townend employs in his lyric is the most common metrical variation in all of English poetry: one that has been used by Milton, Pope, Yeats, Auden, Wordsworth, Keats, and Frost. Whereas too much metrical precision can produce a "'greeting-card' sing-song effect,"[86] well-placed variations create powerful emotional impact. The popular appeal of "In Christ Alone" belies the hymn's underlying musical artistry and lyrical sophistication.

"The Wrath of God Was Satisfied"

In 2013, the Presbyterian Committee on Congregational Song voted to exclude "In Christ Alone" from the hymnal it was about to publish, *Glory to God: The Presbyterian Hymnal*, after Stuart Townend and Keith Getty refused to change a lyric in the hymn's second stanza. The roots of the controversy began in 2010, when the Baptists published a hymnal, *Celebrating Grace*, that included an unauthorized lyrical modification to the second stanza of "In Christ Alone":

Till on that cross as Jesus died
the wrath of God was satisfied (Getty/Townend)
Till on that cross as Jesus died
the love of God was magnified (*Celebrating Grace*)

Three years later, when the Presbyterian committee began making song selections for their new hymnal, they voted to include the Baptist version of "In Christ Alone." However, in the process of clearing copyrights, it came to light that Getty and Townend had never approved the Baptist "modification" of their text. Furthermore, the authors informed the Presbyterian Publishing Company that since the lyrical change in question was too great a departure from the theological meaning they had intended, they would not allow it to be reprinted. The hymnal committee was faced with a choice: to print "In Christ Alone" with its original wording ("the wrath of God was satisfied") or to remove it from the list. After much debate, the final vote was six in favor of inclusion and nine against. In May 2013, Presbyterian hymnal committee chair Mary Louise Bringle reported to *Christian Century* that "the song has been removed from our contents list, with deep regret over losing its otherwise poignant and powerful witness."[87]

The hymnal committee's decision captured national headlines. Media outlets such as the *Huffington Post*, the *Nashville Tennessean* (whose story was picked up by Religion News Service), and conservative radio talk show host Glenn Beck all published stories about the absence of "In Christ Alone" from *Glory to God*. "Why do so many Christians shrink from any thought of the wrath of God?" Keith Getty posted on the Getty Music website on July 30, 2013. Getty praised as "spot on" a *First Things* article by theologian Timothy George that characterized God's love as "tender, but not squishy," because it includes "not only compassion, kindness, and mercy beyond measure (what the New Testament calls grace) but also indignation against injustice and unremitting opposition to all that is evil."[88] In another outlet, George commented that the Presbyterians' decision to drop "In Christ Alone" from its hymnal "fits into a wider pattern of downplaying parts of Christian doctrine that are offensive."[89] Speaking for the Presbyterians, hymnal committee chair Mary Louise Bringle pushed back: "People think that we've taken the wrath of God out of the hymnal," she commented a few days later. "That's not the case. It's all over the hymnal. The issue was the word *satisfied*."[90]

In one sense, this controversy is nothing new. For centuries, theologians have debated what exactly it means to say, in the words of the Nicene Creed, that Jesus's death was "for our sake." The notion of penal substitutionary atonement was in the background of many of the early church fathers, including Justin Martyr, Gregory of Nyssa, Athanasius, and Augustine. It came to full expression in the theology of the medieval theologian Anselm of Canterbury, whose ideas sixteenth-century reformer John Calvin, trained as a lawyer, later transformed into legal terminology. Some of the greatest theological minds of the twentieth century, including Karl Barth and Wolfhart Pannenberg, gave substitutionary atonement pride of place in their work. British historian David Bebbington identifies belief in substitutionary atonement as one of the four defining marks of evangelicalism.[91] Former *Christianity Today* editor Mark Galli suggests this is because substitutionary atonement emphasizes the fact that in the crucifixion, "God was enduring in his own self the divine wrath that we deserved—that I deserved. . . . It doesn't get any more personal than that. And evangelical religion is nothing if not personal."[92]

However, other twenty-first-century Christians have distanced themselves from substitutionary atonement for ethical reasons. Bob Terry, longtime editor of the *Alabama Baptist*, echoed the Presbyterians' angst when he argued, "Sometimes Christians carelessly make God out to be some kind of ogre whose angry wrath overflowed until the innocent Jesus suffered enough to calm Him down. It is the ultimate 'good cop/bad cop' routine where God is against us but Jesus is for us."[93] In his book *The Lost Message of Jesus*, British Baptist Steve Chalke made waves when he described the doctrine of penal substitutionary atonement as "a form of cosmic child abuse," then argued:

> If the cross is a personal act of violence perpetrated by God towards mankind but borne by His Son, then it makes a mockery of Jesus' own teaching to love your enemies and to refuse to repay evil with evil. The Truth is, the cross is a symbol of love. It is a demonstration of just how far God as Father and Jesus as His Son are prepared to go to prove that love.[94]

Chalke's work is an excellent summation of the "moral exemplar" model of the atonement, in which Jesus lives the perfect example of a moral life and dies as a martyr to demonstrate the depth of his love for us. Other historical interpretations of the atonement include the ransom model (we are held in the power of the devil until Christ dies and frees us from his grasp), and the *Christus Victor* model (Christ's work on the cross was a nonviolent protest that defeated the powers of evil).

It is worth noting that the moral exemplar, *Christus Victor*, and ransom theories of the atonement are in keeping with twenty-first-century spiritual sensibilities. As Charles Taylor notes, when earlier thinkers tried to make sense of God's response to the human condition, "Wrath had to be part of the package." Salvation was inseparable humanity's sinful, fallen state, which in turn was inseparable from the need for punishment. Before modernity, people saw "destruction and violence as an ineradicable part of our world and condition. The fact that the divine plane gave some meaning to it, and some ultimate path beyond it, was sufficient grounds for gratitude."[95] Conversely, in today's anthropocentric climate, any idea of the spiritual "must be totally constructive, positive . . . [We are] less and less able to allow for a God who punishes."[96] As we saw earlier, Taylor argues that "simply negating" the notion of penal substitutionary atonement leaves us with a picture of reality that is too benign to be believable. "Christianity is inconceivable without sacrifice, without the possibility of some positive meaning to suffering," he warns. "The Crucifixion cannot be sidelined as merely a regrettable by-product of a valuable career of teaching."[97]

An example from North Point confirms Taylor's observation that twenty-first-century spirituality tends toward the constructive and positive. In Atlanta, Executive Creative Director Evan McLaughlin praised the lyrics of a popular worship song written by North Point recording artist Hawk Nelson:

Cause I [God] am for you
I'm not against you
If you want to know
How far My love can go
Just how deep, just how wide
If you want to see
How much you mean to Me
Look at My hands, look at My side
If you could count the times I say you are forgiven
It's more than the drops in the ocean.[98]

There is no hint of God's anger against sin in these lyrics: an omission McLaughlin appreciates. "When I walked through these [church] doors fourteen years ago, I was pretty sure I wasn't 'for' God and I didn't know where I stood with him. Today, to understand that there is a God who is actually *for* me, who actually *likes* me, and that's why we sing." McLaughlin trails off. "That's what we what a visitor to North Point to know: 'We believe in a God who loves us so much—irrespective of our past and our future—that he is *for* us.'"

As McLaughlin's story illustrates, not everyone at every point in life is moved by the penal substitutionary atonement model. For example, an individual caught in the chains of addiction might better grasp the miracle of the crucifixion through the ransom model. At the same time, however, evangelicals have historically given priority to substitutionary atonement, seeing it as the one model that holds all the others together.[99] This is why Keith Getty insists that songwriters "need to demonstrate a grasp of the whole biblical context" and not be afraid to write about "hard things" or the "mysterious sections of Scripture."[100]

Jeremy Begbie offers helpful insight on this point by noting that twenty-first-century congregations are often cajoled into "compulsory joy": an emotion that is "perhaps authentic for some on certain occasions but often disturbingly out of touch with what others have to endure in a world so obviously far from its final joy, the very world Christ came to redeem."[101] Begbie's words echo Charles Taylor's earlier warning: "A too benign picture of the human condition leaves something crucial out, something that matters to us."[102] At North Point, Wayfarers Collective, and TVC, we have observed three strikingly different responses to the idea of "compulsory joy." North Point gives people permission to "opt out," and those who lead music are instructed not to "guilt" people into participating. At Wayfarers Collective, worship leader Logan reacted so strongly against commercial worship music and its "happy, clichéd, easy answers" that he searched out worship music that resonated with the experience of the dark night of the soul. Especially in its early years, according to Logan, music at Wayfarers Collective was "like a downer, depressed a little bit." His hope for the Collective is that the congregation will eventually learn how to sing loudly and joyfully.

TVC resists both these extremes by firmly insisting on the "both-and" paradox of joy and lament. Begbie illustrates this principle by contrasting visual and musical arts. In visual art, "Objects occupy bounded locations and cannot overlap without their integrity being threatened."[103] For example, we cannot see red and yellow in the same place at the same time. We see either one color or the other or—if the two are allowed to merge—orange, a mixture of the two. The situation is different in music, where notes of the scale do not occupy a bounded location in our aural field. If a pianist plays the two notes of a major third, we can hear both tones simultaneously: as Begbie explains, "The sounds neither merge nor exclude each other but interpenetrate" even as they remain irreducibly different.[104] In the same way, the stories of Good Friday and Easter can be

> told and heard, believed and interpreted, two different ways at once—as a story whose ending is known, and as one whose ending is discovered only as it happens. The truth is victim when either reading is allowed to drown out the other; the truth emerges only when both readings are audible, *the separate sound in each ear creating, as it were, a stereophonic unity.*[105]

Ultimately, the relationship between Christian hope and lament is less like the visual field of colors than the aural field of music. A healthy spirituality must be able to perceive both simultaneously and without reduction: "Beauty without horror is kitsch; horror without beauty is absurdity."[106]

Jim Thomas agrees. "That driftwood cross up front?" He nods slowly at the front of the TVC sanctuary. "It's brutal but beautiful at the same time."

PART III
SAMENESS VERSUS DIFFERENCE

8

"One Voice in Many Languages"

Pentecostal Praises in the American Southwest

In March 2018, the *New York Times* reported on a steady departure of African Americans from predominately white evangelical churches—a decline the headline characterized as a "quiet exodus":

> White evangelicals voted for Mr. Trump by a larger margin than they had voted for any presidential candidate. They cheered the outcome, reassuring uneasy fellow worshipers with talk of abortion and religious liberty, about how politics is the art of compromise rather than the ideal. Christians of color, even those who shared these policy preferences, looked at Mr. Trump's comments about Mexican immigrants, his open hostility to N.F.L. players protesting police brutality and his earlier "birther" crusade against President Obama, claiming falsely he was not a United States citizen. In this political deal, many concluded, they were the compromised.[1]

The article quoted Michael Emerson, the author of *Divided by Faith*, a seminal work on race relations within the evangelical church: "The election itself was the single most harmful event to the whole movement of reconciliation in at least the past thirty years. It's about to break apart."[2]

Every evangelical congregation I studied struggled with how to address race in their worship. In fact, *Divided by Faith* was inspired in part by Emerson's experiences at Moody Church. Emerson and his wife attended Moody while he was undergraduate student at Loyola University Chicago, and every week their route took them directly past an African American church on the same block. "I was naive about most things then," Emerson recalls. "New to Christianity, I thought it odd that we should walk by one body of believers to worship with another congregation but a block away. I found it even odder that one body of believers was all black and the other, all white. . . . I simply had an uneasy feeling that something seemed far from right."[3] Especially striking to Emerson was the fact that both churches preached the same message: God loves all people, who are equal in the Creator's eyes. Decades later, as Emerson went around the country interviewing mostly black and white Christians for *Divided by Faith*, he reported feeling "catapulted back to that block in Chicago—the black church at one end,

Evangelical Worship. Melanie C. Ross, Oxford University Press. © Oxford University Press 2021.
DOI: 10.1093/oso/9780197530757.003.0009

the white church at the other."[4] In the years between his undergraduate and professional experience, Emerson had come to learn that a "color-blind" approach to race severely limits whites' understanding of the causes of racial injustice and their ability to combat them.

Evan McLaughlin, executive creative director at North Point Community Church in Atlanta, grew up in the South. Like Emerson, he reports that "I have always felt something around this idea of reconciliation." But whereas Emerson argued that institutional changes were needed to end racialization, the "something" McLaughlin feels is emphatically interpersonal. When talking about his decades-long friendship with an African American family, he reflects, "It's our faith, our belief in the Spirit of God that really binds us together. We've never talked politics. We've never talked black and white." McLaughlin suggests that the North Point congregation takes a similar approach:

> When I look around at the faces of North Point—and none of this is empirical—we are just still really white and still, by and large, really affluent. But we're not trying to say that we want everyone to be white and conservative. No! Set your politics aside. We're always going to disagree about how to vote, but I think we need to make decisions that first and foremost keep it about Jesus. There are more things we can agree on than we could ever disagree on. Can't we agree that Jesus doesn't just offer a better solution to the end of life: he offers a better solution to life *now*?

McLaughlin is not naive: he knows that reconciliation, even among Christians who share a common faith, is a difficult task. "How do you tap into [discussions of race] in a way where whites don't feel like they have to right the wrongs of centuries and blacks don't feel like they have to 'sell out'?" he mused. "I don't know. It's very complicated."

Many evangelical churches are primarily Caucasian and content with their status as monoracial congregations (defined by the fact that at least 90 percent of attendees are from one ethnic group). During the time of my travels, LifeWay Research published a 2015 poll revealing that 80 percent of American congregations (a sampling that included Catholic, Protestant, nondenominational, and Orthodox churches) are made up of one predominant racial group. Evangelicals were most likely to say their church was diverse enough (71 percent), while whites were most likely to say that their church should become more diverse (37 percent).[5] In Nashville, pastor Jim Thomas explained it this way:

> On the one hand, it's true that Sunday morning is the most segregated hour of the church of the week. But on the other hand, I argue that that's by choice for a lot of people—and not just the white people. The folks who are African

American actually choose to do that. They don't want to come to The Village Chapel's kind of church service. They don't like Irish music. They don't like acoustic music. They want much more physical expression in the worship—frankly, I do too! The body of Christ is diverse by design, so that's OK. But I also think we [black churches and white churches] need to be able to come out of our cocoons once in a while.

At the Wayfarers Collective in Portland, an elder named Esther debated questions of racial diversity:

Should Wayfarers Collective try to reach people of different cultures and ethnicities? That's one way to come to racial reconciliation: through personal relationships in a faith community. But I also think, "Wow. That would take a long time. The culture that we have at the Collective has been going on for more than twelve years, and it would be hard to change. It would take a commitment from everyone, and I'm not sure . . . I don't get a sense or feeling that we'd change easily. We have a really contemplative, ancient-future worship culture. The black community is just not that way.

Esther summed up her internal debate this way: "Is it important for the congregation itself to be diverse? Maybe. But I also want to preserve churches where people feel safer within their own ethnic community. There's value to that. What is the right thing to do?"

Esther poses a salient question. At "Holy Inheritance," pseudonym for a medium-sized, multiethnic, Pentecostal church in the American Southwest, a pastor named Enrique looks to the book of Acts for guidance on how to answer it.[6] "God used languages to confuse people at the tower of Babel," Enrique stresses, referencing the story told in Genesis 11:1–9 in which a common language becomes many languages, and people are scattered across the face of the earth. But in the story of Pentecost, told in Acts 2, tongues descend and all the people miraculously hear the gospel in their own language. "The church was confused through language [in Genesis], but at Pentecost, God used languages to bring them back together again," Enrique points out. "Even today, I know that the Lord is using languages to regain the voice that we have lost: not to confuse us and separate us, but to give us back our one voice in many languages again."

Church History

The church I am calling "Holy Inheritance" takes its name from Psalm 2:8: "Ask me, and I will make the nations your inheritance, the ends of the earth your possession." It was started by Frank and Gigi (both Caucasian), an American couple who met in South America and served as missionaries there for several years. In the late 1960s, the couple decided to move back to the United States, where they raised their children in a midsized city in a state that borders Mexico. In 1969, they began a Bible study for college students in their home. When the study grew too large to meet in a private home, they relocated to a city park that could accommodate the crowds of two hundred who were regularly attending. Frank and Gigi offered a warm welcome to the long-haired, blue-jeaned, and beaded Jesus People that traditional congregations in the area had scorned.

Frank and Gigi purchased a small church building to house their growing ministry. Parents of the youth joined their children, and the church quickly grew. Frank quit his part-time jobs and became a full-time pastor. He soon joined forces with another man who had a ministry to "street people," and the church began attracting hippies from all over the county. In a matter of months, the small church building was filled to overflowing with Jesus People and newly saved hippies, and the leadership banded together to begin construction on a new facility that could hold a thousand people. The church thrived for thirty years, until Frank and Gigi retired.

Shortly after the couple's retirement, a scandal split the church, which led to a leadership restructuring.[7] Enrique, who had been serving as head of the church's Spanish-language ministries, was promoted to the senior pastorate. Born in the United States and raised in Mexico, Enrique was at first uncomfortable with the promotion: "I was very happy pastoring Latinos. I thought I'd do that until I die." Furthermore, he questioned whether the primarily white congregation would accept a Latino senior pastor.

However, Enrique explains that his heart was stirred by professional conference. "It was a Latino conference led by an English pastor. He said, 'I challenge every one of you to pastor your city. You are not to limit yourself anymore. Whoever is in your city, you are called to pastor.'" Enrique recalls hearing God speak to him during the conference:

> The Lord told me, "Listen, it's very easy to build with bricks because every brick looks the same: same texture, same length, etc." But scripture says that we are living stones. Stones have different shapes and sizes and colors and textures. When you build with stones, you have to look for just the right place to put each one. The Lord is building his church with stones, not bricks. We are not going to all look the same.

At the time of the conference, Holy Inheritance was primarily an Anglo congregation. However, the demographics of the neighborhood had changed significantly over the church's thirty-plus years of existence. When Holy Inheritance had opened its building thirty years earlier, the congregation was entirely Anglo. Over time, apartment complexes sprung up around the neighborhood, and were filled by predominately African American renters. Enrique explained that the church's home city is also within easy driving distance of the Mexican border: "We have noticed that many Mexicans who may be on their way to their cousin in Boston, or San Francisco, or Denver—whatever the case may be—decide to stay in our city and rest for a while first." The city has also attracted many immigrants from Africa.

Enrique wanted his congregation to reflect the diversity of this landscape, and set out to form a more intentionally multiethnic congregation. The structure Holy Inheritance eventually developed was that of one church with three distinct communities.

Defining "Multiethnic"

An often-cited definition of a multiethnic church comes from sociologist Michael Emerson, who asserts that congregations can be classified as multiethnic when "no one racial group comprises 80 percent or more of the people."[8] In other words, the church must have a minority population of over 20 percent. (That 20 percent could represent white people in an African American church, or a congregation that is 10 percent African American, 5 percent Latino, and 5 percent Asian but otherwise white.) The 80/20 ratio is grounded in research that shows that 20 percent "constitutes the point of critical mass. At this percentage, the proportion is high enough to have its presence felt and filtered throughout a system."[9] Holy Inheritance easily meets Emerson's definition of a multiethnic church. At the time of my study, Holy Inheritance attracted nearly one thousand worshippers to its three Sunday services: one for English-speakers (four hundred attendees, a mix of Caucasian and African American), one for Spanish-speakers (five hundred attendees, predominantly Hispanic), and a third for African immigrants (one hundred attendees). For the rest of the chapter, I will identify these as "Service 1," "Service 2," and "African Fellowship." (Service 1 and the African Fellowship meet concurrently, in separate rooms, during the first hour of worship.)

In her book *Crossing the Ethnic Divide*, Kathleen Garces-Foley points out that Emerson's 80/20 definition does not consider the dynamics of interaction within a congregation. As she points out, a church can be less of a single community than an aggregate of separate groups who share the same space but do not interact with each other. Garces-Foley identifies four ways congregations might approach integration and racial diversity. First, there is the space-sharing approach, which is particularly common in urban areas. Small immigrant congregations borrow or rent the facilities of established churches until they can afford their own buildings. Space-sharing congregations have separate finances and memberships; the two congregations may not interact apart from discussions of procedural or logistical issues.

The second model is that of the multilingual church. In contrast to the space-sharing church, the multilingual church is a single entity that conducts services in multiple languages. Garces-Foley cites the example of Catholic parishes in major urban centers where masses are said in multiple languages (Spanish, English, Tagalog, or Vietnamese), depending on the size and influence of the group and the availability of a priest or minister who speaks the language. The drawback to this model is that it has the potential of forming de facto parallel congregations when members of various language groups do not think of themselves as part of a single church community. To counter that tendency, many multilingual churches will hold occasional joint services for all congregants (for example, on Pentecost Sunday) or sponsor multicultural social events where members can taste each other's food and hear one another's music.

In the third category are pan-ethnic churches, comprising people who identify with distinct ethnic groups but share a common language and racialized status. For example, a church made up of members from various cultures in Latin America might think of itself as pan-Latino; a church with Lao, Cambodian, Chinese, Japanese, and Vietnamese members might consider itself pan-Asian. Garces-Foley notes that although the diversities within pan-ethnic congregations can be significant, they are also made easier by the fact that all members share an ascribed racial category.

Finally, there is the multiethnic church, a label Garces-Foley argues is as much qualitative as it is quantitative. Inclusion is what distinguishes multiethnic churches from space-sharing, multilingual, and pan-ethnic churches. Multiethnic congregations feel like a true community, not because "everyone is interacting with everyone else" but because "the *potential* exists to form a bond with any member."[10] The authors of *United by Faith: The Multiracial Congregation as an Answer to the Problem of Race* explain the "feel" of these congregational communities:

> The integrated multiracial congregation has developed a hybrid of the distinct cultures that have joined together in one church. Elements of different racial cultures are not incorporated to "appease" diverse constituencies; rather, the new hybrid culture is an expression of the congregation's unified collective identity. The relationships among members of different races in the congregation are strictly egalitarian. There is no sense of "us" and "them" according to race, but it is more "us" as a congregation and "them" outside our congregation.[11]

A multiethnic congregation is a theological ideal seldom found in practice. Garces-Foley reports that after speaking to evangelicals across the United States, "I was surprised how many of them doubted that there are any churches in the United States that are *truly* multiethnic." The two criticisms repeatedly encountered were that these churches were either "too internally fragmented by diversity to be considered a single community," or that they were "too homogeneous in terms of culture to be considered ethnically diverse."[12] The ideal multiethnic church lies somewhere between these two extremes.

Positioning Holy Inheritance

Holy Inheritance is a unique mixture of all four categories. The three communities comprise a single church. Nevertheless, there are internal tensions to be negotiated.

Pastor Obasi, the leader of the African Fellowship, was born in the Democratic Republic of Congo and first discerned a call to ministry at the age of fifteen while living in a refugee camp in Kampala, Uganda. Pastor Obasi confided that his group sometimes feels like a "space-sharing" congregation because it is significantly smaller than either the Service 1 or Service 2 communities. "Since we are using the same building, all of us, three services, it's a little bit hard. You have to be constantly on the schedule to know that today the English [Service 1] are using the building, so we [African Fellowship] have to be in at another time." Obasi explains that all-night prayer services, which run from 7:00 p.m. to 7:00 a.m., are an important part of the African Fellowship's worship. Pastor Obasi reminisces, "Back home in Africa, prayer warriors spend the night at church. They practically live there twenty-four hours, seven days a week. They have prayer rotations."

However, the Service 1 and Service 2 communities fill Holy Inheritance's weeknight calendar with evening activities for youth and adults. Since the African Fellowship is numerically the smallest group, "We are limited, space-wise, on what we can do." Obasi dreams of a day when his fellowship might be able to afford a separate facility. "I hope, in the next five years, God will open the way for us to be able to have our own . . ." He stops himself, then starts again. "It's still Holy Inheritance, but in our own building, where we will be more able to do all that we want to do."

Holy Inheritance also exemplifies elements of the pan-ethnic model, particularly in the Spanish-language and the African Fellowship services. Political science professors Zoltan L. Hajnal and Taeku Lee suggest that pan-ethnic groups are "characterized by the simultaneous coexistence of externally perceived homogeneity and internally lived heterogeneity."[13] This juxtaposition is true of both the Service 2 congregation and the African Fellowship: at first glance, both groups may appear to be homogeneous, but each must negotiate significant internal diversities. Service 2 attracts first-generation individuals from across Central and South America and the Caribbean, including Colombians, Hondurans, Mexicans, Puerto Ricans, Venezuelans, and Panamanians. One leader offered an example of how these differences can complicate corporate worship:

> There are different kinds of Spanish. For example, Cuban Spanish is different from Mexican Spanish. So, once in [Service 2], we were making a welcome video where someone read something aloud. Later, Pastor Enrique listened to it and was like, "Oh my gosh, no! We can't have him say that: the word he just used is totally 'gang.'" It was like a full-on cuss word. But in Cuban Spanish, it was totally non-offensive. We always have to go through and look at, "OK, what does that mean? Do you think it means the same?" We go back and forth.

In the African Fellowship, which includes people born in the United States and people from across the continent of Africa, language is not a divisive issue. A few participants—those from Cameroon, Burkina Faso, and Rwanda—speak French. However, Obasi explains that since the majority of the congregation is comfortable in English, that is the language that is used. The use of English is in fact one of the things that attracts participants to Holy Inheritance: "There are many African churches in [our city], but they are small and tribal. They say, for instance, 'I'm from Congo, so I speak only Congolese and want to go to a Congolese-speaking church.'" By contrast, the African Fellowship at Holy Inheritance is "trying to break that so that we can all be one and work together to make it a strong ministry."

But internal divisions are an ongoing challenge for the Fellowship. Obasi reports that in many of the African countries from which his congregants immigrate, pastors do not always work well together:

> They feel like, maybe, "You know more than me, so if you come work with me you will take over the ministry and I will lose. So, I'd rather just have my own ministry." They think, "Maybe having my own ministry will help me become financially prosperous since I've never been to school." The stealing of sheep [church members] is a problem.

The move to the United States can exacerbate jealousies, according to Obasi: "People are like, 'I was a pastor back home, and now I'm coming here and nobody recognizes me.' They feel like they're rejected." In response, he has created a policy that states that no more than two elders can come from the same African nation. "I'm trying to get all of our communities together so they don't feel like one country is overtaking church. That mixture of leadership [in the elder team] will help us make a good vote that is strong, not 'Oh, he is from my country, so I will just support him.'" Obasi explains that his own position as leader of the Fellowship will end after three years for the same reason: "It gives [others in the Fellowship] hope. They can think, 'Even if I'm not the pastor today, someday I can be because he is not keeping power. It is not his church.' They can feel like it is *our* church."

Perhaps the model with which Holy Inheritance best corresponds is the multilingual church. The benefit of this model is that all constituencies can worship in their own tongue. The challenge of this model is that members may not think of themselves as part of a single church community. Indeed, in practice, the multilingual church can look much like the space-sharing arrangement. At Holy Inheritance, there are subtle tensions among the three services. For instance, Pastor Obasi points to economic and educational disparities that separate the African Fellowship and the Service 1 congregation:

Sometimes they [Africans] withdraw or limit themselves. They don't want to be a part of [Service 1] because they feel like "These people are highly educated," or "They're more prosperous." It's a challenge to make them understand that they have the same value in the kingdom as those people that are highly educated. We are all equal. We are all the same. But it's hard for us [African Fellowship] to get there.

Mabel, an African American worship leader who attends Service 1, cites another source of intra-congregational tension: immigration issues. She points out that the African Fellowship and Service 2 have higher numbers of undocumented immigrants than does Service 1:

I'm just going to tell it like it is. A good quarter—maybe even half or more— of our Spanish-speakers in that sanctuary right now are undocumented. We also have some of our African Fellowship people that have come here on visas for education and just didn't leave. Unfortunately, we've not been able to hire people because of that. We believe in following the law, but it's also a challenge because you want to be able to say, "Oh, come on." This person's been here for fifteen, twenty, some of them thirty years, and they're afraid to go anywhere because they're scared they'll get deported.

For Mabel, the irony is that many of the people in Service 2 service *chose* to enter the United States illegally, while many of the African Americans in Service 1 are grappling with the legacy of slavery. "The black people are saying, 'Hey, we didn't have no choice. We just got brought.'"

Nevertheless, the leadership of Holy Inheritance would insist that "multi-ethnic"—not "space-sharing," "pan-ethnic," or "multilingual"—is the adjective that best describes their community. Members across the different services report forming significant bonds with one another. Inez, director of worship ministries, is Caucasian, and her husband was born and raised in Mexico. Inez believes that the dynamics of the church mirror those of her marriage:

> For many years it was us [English] versus them [Spanish], at least culturally. It was really divided in a lot of ways. People weren't interested in integrating or even having a conversation. Now it's different. We still have some people with prejudices, but there are many people, like me and my husband, who are bilingual and comfortable in both cultures. Children's ministry is a melting pot. Even if the parents only speak Spanish, their children speak English, and relationships form that way: "Your kids know my kids." Church becomes a coming-together place.

The worship ministry team is another place of intentional integration. Several years ago, the English- and Spanish-speaking congregations had separate teams to meet the needs of each service: two sound teams, two bands, two choirs, and so on. When Inez started in her position, she decided to try a different format: one worship ministry that ministered in both services. The English-speakers learned the Spanish lyrics and vice versa. As a general rule, the worship team stays within the language of the hour. On the five or six Sundays a year when the congregations meet together for a "Unity Sunday," the team sings alternate between Spanish and English verses within the same song.

Inez reports, "The joy for me is seeing an English-speaker and a Spanish-speaker side-by-side, worshipping, asking each other, 'How do you say this word?' or 'How do you pronounce that?' Really embracing the good in each culture." However, Mabel, the African American worship leader, stresses that the process of blending cultures to create a single worship team was initially fraught:

> I'm going to tell it straight up, OK? The white people aren't going to sit up here [on the platform] all day. OK? Then the black people going to be like, "Hey, the music better be good. It better be down. What is this Hillsong stuff?" Then you've got the Latinos going, "Where's the salsa?" [The Latinos] are good with forty-five minutes of announcements. I ain't sitting here through forty-five minutes of announcements! It's just totally different. Totally different. The challenge is to take all of those cultural senses of how you do church and what the service is and to meld them.

The next section examines how Holy Inheritance takes up the challenge of melding cultures in its Service 1 congregation.

Service Description

Holy Inheritance, which is located in a small city neighborhood, meets in a low, unassuming brick building that might be easily mistaken for an office complex. The sanctuary is dark and windowless; flags from around the world line three of the four walls (Figure 8.1). At the front of the sanctuary is a low, raised platform where the Service 1 worship team has assembled. A large screen with song lyrics is at the center of the platform. To the left of the screen are large block letters proclaiming, "Living the Life of a Disciple." To the right of the screen, the same message is spelled out in Spanish: "Viviendo la Vida de un Discípulo."

Keyboards, guitars, and percussion equipment litter the stage. A small worship choir is assembled on risers. There are twelve members: four groups of three, each clustered around a microphone stand. The band starts an instrumental introduction to the first worship song. Inez steps forward to open the service, and the band continues to play softly as she prays:

> God, we ask that you would have your way in this place, that you would have a word of encouragement for us, that you would bring healing to the broken places, that you would bring freedom to those places where we're bounded. Above all else, we want your presence and we want you to be praised this morning. And everyone in the house said . . ."

Figure 8.1 Flags from around the world line the sanctuary walls at Holy Inheritance
March 2017. Photo by author.

The congregation replies "Amen" in a loud unison.

The music grows louder and faster as Inez continues her introductory remarks. "Today we're singing about how God is great and good. Our greatest desire is to be in his presence and the wonders of his love. How many of you want the Lord to ignite a fire within you?" The energy builds as the congregation joins in the first song of the morning, "You Are Good," which was written by a Pentecostal band from Australia. The second worship song, "Derrama de tu Fuego," was made popular by Marcos Witt, widely considered to be the most influential and famous Spanish-speaking figure in Christian music. Although the song was originally composed in Spanish, Inez has translated the words so that the first service can participate in English. Inez notes that in the church's early years, "it used to be that all the really good [worship] songs were in English, and we would translate them into Spanish so that the second service could sing." Today, however, "The trend seems to be that there's so much good music on the Spanish side of things that when I hear the songs I think, 'I want that in English.'" Inez acknowledges that "some of the concepts aren't as meaningful when you start to translate, but we do our best." So, for example, first lines of the chorus, "Derrama de Tu fuego sobrenatural / Derrama de Tu gloria sobre este lugar," have become "Send me down your fire supernaturally / Send me down your glory / Ignite something in me."

After two more songs—"We Worship You," by gospel singer Israel Houghton (a former worship leader at Joel Osteen's Lakewood Church) and "Open Up the Heavens," a song that asks God to be revealed to worshippers—there is a brief time of announcements. A missionary couple is commissioned, an offering is collected, and Pastor Enrique slides in one final all-church programming reminder. Next week, the men of the church will come together for a carne asada (the Mexican equivalent of a barbeque) and an evening of sports competition. "The African Fellowship has an incredible team put together. So do the Latinos," Enrique enthuses. "We're also putting together a team from the first service. We're going to worship, hang out, and help the men of the three services get to know each other. Amen? Amen!"

Enrique shifts his attention to the biblical text and takes on a more serious tone. He begins by reading a well-known passage from Ecclesiastes 3: "There is a time for everything, and a season for every activity under the heavens." Enrique quickly runs through the list: a time to be born, a time to die, a time for war, a time for peace, a time for sowing, a time for reaping, a time to speak, a time to be quiet. Enrique then explains that there are two ways to talk about time. *Chronos* time happens as the clock passes from one minute to the next. We mark it with calendars and watches, through birthdays and anniversaries. *Kairos* time is God's time. It cannot be measured in minutes, hours, or years. Enrique stresses, "God is involved in our seasons. Your life is not an accident. Everything in your life that happens is because of God's *Kairos* time."

However, God's sovereignty does not spare humans from difficulties in life. Some of these difficulties are of our own making. For instance, some people fail to discern how God is working in their lives and react inappropriately. "They're rebuking the devil when it's not the devil. They're thinking it's God when it wasn't God: it was something they did because of disobedience." The sooner a Christian is able to discern the right season, the better able they are to cooperate with God and receive a blessing. Conversely, if Christians fail to discern the right season or go through it the "wrong way" by refusing to cooperate with God, they risk missing the blessing God has in store. "Can you say this with me,?" Enrique enjoins the congregation. "I'm going to know my season, and it's going to be my time." The sanctuary hums as individuals murmur the sentence to themselves and to their neighbors.

Next, Enrique offers a few points of comfort. God works in cycles and gives second chances. "Sometimes the Lord will give you a test, and if you don't pass it, it's not going to go away." If this happens, God will often graciously allow us a chance to "fight the battle and to win it the right way the next time around." Enrique finds biblical support for this idea in 2 Kings 20, where God set a sundial ten degrees back for the prophet Isaiah, and in Joshua 10:11–13, where God causes the sun to stand still and gives the Israelites an extra day to defeat their enemies. Enrique connects these biblical events to the present day:

> The Lord wants to give you a time again to do things right. Listen husbands, the Lord is going to give you the chance to win the love that you had before in your marriage, your children, your job—whatever it is, the Lord wants to give it back. That's what seasons are for sometimes, to go through them the right way or to correct something that you haven't been able to correct.

Once more, Enrique encourages the congregation to speak a sentence aloud: "Raise your hand and say, 'Lord, this time I'm going to get it right in the name of Jesus! Amen.'"

Enrique moves back to the book of Ecclesiastes and reads chapter 9, verse 1: "I have seen something else under the sun: The race is not to the swift or the battle to the strong, nor does food come to the wise or wealth to the brilliant or favor to the learned; but time and chance happen to them all." He tells the English-speaking congregation that the Spanish translation of the passage says that "time and *opportunity*—not chance—happen to them all. What Solomon is saying," Enrique continues, "is that because you took your time to prepare for the opportunity, you were ready to seize it when it came." Furthermore, the best way that

Christians can prepare for their opportunities is by giving their *chronos* time to God and living in *Kairos* time. "Nothing supernatural happens in *chronos* time," Enrique stresses. "It only happens when we allow him to invade our *chronos* with his *Kairos*." Enrique reminds the congregation that the best place to exchange *chronos* time for *Kairos* time is in church:

> Let me give you the news today. Whether you knew it or not when you came in, this morning you are in *Kairos* time. Stop looking at your watch. God says, "In my time, I can do in one hour of your life what you haven't been able to do in three months. What your psychologist hasn't been able to do in a year, I'm going to do in half an hour." Next time you want to stay home and sleep in on Sundays, remember: the Lord says, "Give me half an hour of worship and see what I can do. Get into your car, come to church, come into the presence of the Lord, and watch what I can do."

Specifically, Enrique suggests, "Your job can be transformed. Your business can be successful again. All because God's presence has the fullness of joy."

Another reason why it is important to come to church is because "there is power in unity." Enrique cites Ecclesiastes 4:9–10: "Two are better than one, because they have a good return for their labor. If either of them falls down, one can help the other up." He also reminds the congregation that Genesis 2:18—"It is not good for man to be alone"—applies to community life as well as marriage. "It is not good that you isolate yourself," he insists. "Within God's mathematics and economy, a lot of your breakthroughs and seasons endings are going to come by being among other people." Enrique encourages the congregation:

> You're only one person away from changing your season. You are not five years away. You are not ten years away. You are only one person away from God changing your season. You don't know how many times I've heard in all three services here at Holy Inheritance, "I didn't have a job, and the Wednesday that I came in and I wasn't going to come, I found a job because somebody was saying that they had need." Or they say, "You know, I wasn't going to come that Sunday, but when I was fellowshipping with others, I found out that that person had the key to change my season."

Enrique encourages everyone to come to church, take a class, attend a service, and grow in grace. "If you say no, you may be missing an opportunity for *Kairos* time. The Lord hides the blessings behind invitations and persons."

After a short prayer, Enrique invites anyone forward who wishes to receive prayer. Congregants stream to the front of the room, and a post-service time of informal ministry begins.

Enrique and other members of the staff lay hands on and pray over all who request intercession. Those who seek healing are anointed with oil. Some speak softly in tongues. Others step backward or even fall to the ground in an overwhelming experience of divine contact that Pentecostals call being "slain in the spirit." These acts of prayer and ministry continue long after the service has "officially" ended.

Service Analysis

Holy Inheritance is unique among the churches in this book, not only for its multiethnic composition, but also for its Pentecostal theology. When asked where his church would fit on a theological map of the United States, Pastor Enrique responded:

> We are evangelical. We are a Holy Spirit–filled church. We believe in speaking in tongues. We believe in the whole explosion of the Holy Spirit living in a human being. We give liberty to the Holy Spirit in our congregation. We pray and we sing. According to the Word of God, when the Holy Spirit came at Pentecost [the early Christians] were filled and speaking in tongues. We not only teach that; we also walk in it.

Pastor Enrique's description of Holy Inheritance highlights a dual phenomenon that scholars have described as the "evangelicalization of Pentecostalism" and the "pentecostalization of evangelicalism."[14]

Fuller Theological Seminary professor Russell Spittler suggests that the evangelicalization of Pentecostalism occurred between World War II and the Vietnam War. In the first decade of the twentieth century, Pentecostalism existed only on the fringes of society; by the 1930s and 1940s, these churches were growing exponentially. By the 1950s, the popularity of Pentecostalism drew the attention of the larger American public, evidenced in Henry P. Van Dusen's 1958 *Life* magazine article that included Pentecostals as part of the emerging "third force in Christendom."[15] Pentecostals recognized the need to define themselves in terms that would be understood by most Americans. However, the theological definitional options available to Pentecostals in the mid-twentieth century were limited. Americans generally thought of Protestantism as divided into two competitive parties: conservative versus liberal, fundamentalists versus modernist, or evangelical versus mainline. Douglas Jacobsen notes that given these simplistic choices, Pentecostals easily chose to identify with the emerging neo-evangelical movement. Evangelicals like Harold J. Ockenga concurred with this alignment, arguing—contra stiff resistance from fundamentalists—that Pentecostals were "evangelical, Bible-believing, Christ-honoring, Spirit-filled brethren, who manifest in character and life the truths expressed in the statement of faith of the NAE."[16]

On one hand, the evangelicalization of Pentecostalism brought charismatic Christians a new degree of social and ecclesial upward mobility. Conversely, since the 1970s, evangelicals have grown increasingly open to Pentecostal practices they once eschewed, including prayers for healing, anointing with oil, greater physical expression in worship, and the restoration of "charismatic gifts" like speaking in tongues, prophecy, and healing (1 Corinthians 12:7–11). One observer notes that whereas Pentecostals used to feel like the " 'weird uncle' of the Evangelical family; now, in some ways, they just might have become the favorite son."[17]

Today, the evangelical-Pentecostal relationship is complicated. Scholars who trace the roots of contemporary evangelicalism back to the Reformation churches of the sixteenth century may see Pentecostalism as a subset of the larger evangelical movement. Others argue that Pentecostalism originated before modern-day evangelicalism. (The three-year-long Azusa Street revival began in 1906, decades before the National Association of Evangelicals was founded in 1942.)[18] Holy Inheritance identifies as both Pentecostal *and* evangelical, and I will use both adjectives to describe the congregation in the discussion that follows.

Radical Openness to God

The church that holds the most theological common ground with Holy Inheritance is Koinonia Vineyard—the congregation introduced in Chapter 7. Both Koinonia Vineyard and Holy Inheritance are part of a tradition that Douglas Jacobsen calls "small-p" Pentecostalism: nomenclature that honors "the diversity of pentecostal/charismatic theologies while at the same time recognizing important family resemblances and shared sensibilities."[19] Pentecostalism is often traced back to the grassroots revival that broke out in Los Angeles, California, at the Azusa Street Mission under the leadership of African American Holiness preacher William J. Seymor.[20] The Azusa Street revival engendered what came to be described as "classical" Pentecostalism associated with denominations such as the Assemblies of God, the Church of God in Christ, and the Church of God (Cleveland, Tenn.) "Classical" Pentecostalism tended to emphasize an experience of grace and sanctification, subsequent to and distinct from salvation, that was evidenced by speaking in tongues. Holy Inheritance falls under the "classical" Pentecostal tradition.

Some fifty years after the Azusa Street revival, a new wave of Pentecostalism began in mainline Protestant churches. The second wave—which came to be known as the charismatic movement—began on a Sunday morning in 1959, when Reverend Dennis Bennett, pastor of an Episcopal church in Van Nuys, California, announced to his congregation that he had been baptized with the Holy Spirit and had spoken in tongues. Bennett's story hit the local media, then *Time* and *Newsweek*, then national television. Soon after, the movement spread to Baptist, Methodist, Presbyterian, Lutheran, and Roman Catholic churches. Like first-wave Pentecostals, charismatics emphasize the work of the Holy Spirit and the continued operation of "miraculous" gifts. In contrast to the first wave, however, charismatics did not separate into new denominations, but chose instead to remain within their existing liturgical and theological structures.

The "third wave" or "neo-charismatic" movement followed and gained momentum in the 1980s through the ministry of leaders such as Chuck Smith and John Wimber. Missiologist Peter Wagner explained the third wave as "a gradual opening of straightline evangelical churches to the supernatural ministry of the Holy Spirit without the participants becoming either Pentecostals or Charismatics."[21] The third wave stressed that after conversion, there was hope for more than one filling with the Holy Spirit, which could include events like receiving healing, casting out demons, or announcing prophecies. Those who were "Spirit-filled" adamantly shunned the idea that they were spiritually elite or better than other kinds of Christians.[22] Koinonia Vineyard is an example of a third-wave church.

Despite theological differences between the three waves of Pentecostalism, philosopher James K. A. Smith argues that all three share a worldview that is radically open to God's doing something *differently* or *new*.[23] Smith locates the origins of this worldview in the Acts 2 biblical account of the story of Pentecost:

This inbreaking of the Spirit was not something that was anticipated or expected . . . in fact, [the apostles] likely expected God to move quite differently, in ways that their past experience could imagine and anticipate. But despite all the strangeness and chaos; despite the fact that this is not what they had expected; despite the fact that God had never done this before, Peter stood up and boldly proclaimed: "*This is* God! *This is* what the prophets spoke about! *This is* what we've been waiting for! *This is* the Spirit!" Such a claim required a unique hermeneutic able to nimbly respond to the advent of surprise, as well as a kind of hermeneutical courage to make such a claim. In short, it required forsaking existing, status quo ideas and expectations of how God works.[24]

At their core, a Pentecostal church remains constantly open having its expectations changed by God. Pentecostal communities therefore emphasize the continued ministry of the Spirit, including revelation, prophecy, and the practice of charismatic gifts, in their ecclesial gatherings.

At Koinonia Vineyard, we discussed anthropologist Jon Bialecki's insight that Vineyard Christians look for a divine inbreaking that is so sharp and shockingly unexpected that it could only have been occasioned by a divine hand.[25] At Wayfarers Collective, Jaxon recounting the story of walking down the street and unexpectedly finding himself praying aloud in tongues, discovering in the process that "God is bigger than any idea we have about him."[26] Worship leaders at Holy Inheritance are similarly expectant that God will act in miraculous ways.

For example, the first song of the morning at Holy Inheritance beseeches God to re-enact the events of Pentecost: "Derrama de Tu fuego sobrenatural / Derrama de Tu gloria sobre este lugar" ("Send me down your fire supernaturally / Send me down your glory / Ignite something in me"). [27] The last two songs of the worship also recalled the Pentecost event. One song asked God to fill the worshipper "like a rushing wind"—an echo of the Acts 2:1 report that immediately prior to Pentecost "there came from heaven a sound like a mighty rushing wind, and it filled the entire house." The final song of the morning was a prayer for God to "open up the heavens" and to send "glory like a fire" to burn worshippers' hearts with truth.

Even as they pray for the miraculous, worship leaders are keenly aware that they cannot force God's hand. As Daniel Albrecht notes in his ethnographic study of charismatic churches, *Rites in the Spirit*, Pentecostal worship leaders believe God alone controls the experience for which congregants wait expectantly.[28] Mateo, who often leads worship in Service 2, corroborated this view with his own philosophy of worship:

> My view is that we [worship leaders] are not here to bring down the glory of God. We're here to help the congregation see the glory of God. I mean, if there was a magic wand we could wave and say, "God—come down!" and *poof*... that would be so awesome. But that's not how it is. God is so much greater than I am or whoever is up there [on stage], and it's not our place to say, "God, descend."

At the same time, Inez expressed confidence that God would indeed be present whenever the church sang praises:

> The Bible says that God inhabits the praises of his people, so his presence comes. And when his presence comes, he doesn't just hang around doing nothing. The work of the Holy Spirit begins to happen. I don't know if you've ever felt God's presence, but I believe it can happen in worship *because you're open*. You sing, "God, come touch my heart." Why wouldn't he? If you're singing a song about "I believe you are my Healer"—if you believe that and ask God for healing, it could happen in a worship setting. It could happen.

Pentecostals eschew traditional dichotomies between the spiritual and the material, heaven and earth, human and divine. As Pentecostal theologian Cheryl Bridges Johns writes, "The most ordinary of spaces can become sacred space. The most common people are potentially saints and the mundane can provide opportunity for the miraculous."[29] This realization is at the heart of Pastor Enrique's sermon: supernatural things can happen if believers will allow God to invade their *chronos* time with his *Kairos*.

"This Is That" Hermeneutic

Pentecostals' radical openness to God also shapes their distinctive approach to scripture. Like all the evangelical churches we have examined so far, Christians at Holy Inheritance would maintain that the record of scripture is historically accurate, including the accounts of Noah and the flood, the ten plagues of Egypt, the crossing of the Red Sea, the virgin birth of Jesus, and the resurrection.[30] Furthermore, Holy Inheritance affirms the inerrancy of scripture in its public doctrinal statements.

However, Pentecostals approach scripture from a different starting point. Pentecostal biblical interpretation is shaped by a "this is that" hermeneutic taken from the King James translation of Acts 2:16. In this passage, which recounts the story of Pentecost, Peter reads aloud from the Old Testament book of Joel and proclaims to his listeners, "*This* [what you see here today] *is that*." The *that* to which Peter refers is the prophecy recorded in Joel 2:17: "God declares . . . I will pour out my Spirit upon all flesh, and your sons and your daughters shall prophesy, and your young men shall see visions, and your old men shall dream dreams." Pentecostal scholar Nimi Wariboko offers a contemporary paraphrase of Peter's sermon:

> What you are seeing now is what was promised, prophesied, or done in the past. The miracles or the extraordinary events you are witnessing today are similar (if not identical) to what happened in the days of the Old Testament prophets, Jesus Christ, and his disciples. The *this is that* in a sense means there is virtually no distance between the past and now. . . . What is happening today, the current miracle (the *this*), speaks to and at the same time reenacts what transpired in the past, the *that*.[31]

In short, "what happened then" becomes a template for the possibilities of "what can happen today."[32]

It is impossible to overstate the role of the Holy Spirit in Pentecostal hermeneutics. Pentecostal readings of scripture are characterized by what biblical scholar French Arrington calls "pneumatic illumination," wherein the Holy Spirit creates a "spiritual kinship" between the authors of the ancient text and contemporary readers by bridging the cultural and historical gulf that divides them. Stephen Land explains pneumatic illumination with a helpful analogy: in theological interpretation, the Holy Spirit acts as a kind of time machine, tacking back and forth across the arc of salvation history, enabling believers to imaginatively participate in events that have been and are yet to be.[33]

The "this is that" hermeneutic distinguishes Holy Inheritance from other churches in this study. For example, consider the dispensational theology of Moody Church. On one hand, early Pentecostals were significantly influenced by dispensationalism: the Scofield Reference Bible was endorsed by official Assemblies of God publications, and the denomination's chief publication, *The Pentecostal Evangel*, similarly affirmed dispensationalism.[34] Like Moody Church, Holy Inheritance affirms dispensationalism in the doctrinal statement on its website. Many aspects of dispensationalism appealed to early Pentecostals, including its use of apocalyptic images to encourage revival.

At the same time, scholars have noted that the relationship between Pentecostalism and dispensationalism has always been strained.[35] For example, dispensationalists believe that the "sign gifts" of the Spirit—divine healing, the working of miracles, speaking in tongues—were confined to the apostolic age. Moody Church's theological statement reflects this interpretation:

> We do not believe that the gift of tongues is necessary as proof of salvation or of the filling of the Spirit; nor is it the result of being baptized by the Holy Spirit. We believe that the birth of the church at Pentecost cannot be repeated just as the birth of Christ cannot be repeated. . . . The gift of tongues, which marked a transition from Old Testament Jewish rituals to the New Testament Gentile/Jewish church, is a gift that is no longer necessary.[36]

However, dispensationalists' insistence on an absolute dichotomy between Israel and the church directly contradicts the way Pentecostals read scripture. Pentecostals reject the idea that God has withdrawn the "dispensations" (miracles, tongues) he once granted: the gifts of the Spirit are for all time and for all believers. Furthermore, they see direct continuity between Israel (the book of Joel), the early church (the book of Acts), and the church in the twenty-first century. Accordingly, in its doctrinal statement Holy Inheritance endorses "baptism of the Holy Spirit, with the evidence of speaking in tongues" and "divine healing and deliverance through the power and Name of Jesus Christ."

The "this is that" hermeneutic also distinguishes Holy Inheritance from an evangelical church like Park Street in Boston. Generally speaking, evangelical scholars have adopted a historical-grammatical approach to scripture that seeks to understand the world "behind" scripture and interpret biblical texts in their original context. Recall the process of interpretation detailed at Park Street Church in Chapter 2: by studying the grammar of a passage and its historical background, the preacher can discern the intentions of the biblical writer, which communicate God's own ideas.[37] Subsequently, Pastor Hugenberger's sermon reflected his confidence that Abraham was a historical person and that the historicity of his journey in Genesis could be corroborated by archaeological evidence. Hugenberger was trained in the "Old Princeton" tradition of theology, which sought to match liberal scholarship footnote for footnote by amassing evidence from paleography, archaeology, and other ancient sources to prove the veracity and historicity of scripture.

Some Pentecostals in the academy strongly endorse the historical-grammatical approach to hermeneutics.[38] However, for many Pentecostal preachers and laypersons, a hermeneutic that relies solely on philological nuances, historical context, and authorial intent is ultimately unsatisfying. In contrast to evangelical scholars who sought to develop an intellectually respectable apologetic for orthodox Christianity in response to the rise of liberalism, Pentecostals simply assume that the Bible gives its readers truthful factual knowledge about the past. As Pentecostal scholar Kenneth Archer explains:

> Early Pentecostals did not place a lot of emphasis on explaining the historical context of Scripture, nor were they concerned with the author's original intention. They used Scripture in such a way as to allow for slippage between what it meant and what it means. They read the Bible as the Word of God and attempted to understand it presently. The horizons of past and present were fused, or from a critical perspective, confused.[39]

We see evidence of this "slippage" between past and present in Enrique's sermon. Enrique matter-of-factly refers to miraculous events in the Old Testament—occasions where God turned the sun back in time for the prophet Isaiah and the Israelite leader Joshua—and then connects them to God's workings in the present day. Just as God gave his people "extra time" in biblical days, so too God at times grants spouses, parents, and employees an opportunity to go back and correct past mistakes.

To a casual observer, Pentecostal interpretations of scripture may seem to be driven by a straightforward, literal approach to the Bible. However, theologian Tony Richie argues that in spite of some tendency toward naivete, this way of reading scripture has served the movement well. Richie argues that, if under fire for a simplistic hermeneutic, a Pentecostal might well retort, "At least 'this is that' is better than 'that was then!'"[40] That is to say, interpreters in the Holiness-Pentecostal tradition tend to minimize concerns about the world *behind* the biblical text and prioritize the world of the reader in *front* of the text. In the words of Pentecostal theologian Amos Yong, the Word of God "tells us about what happened in the past not for its own sake but for the sake of God's ongoing and eschatological salvation plan."[41] Scripture is "living and active, sharper than any two-edged sword, piercing until it divides soul from spirit, joints from marrow; it is able to judge the thoughts and intentions of the heart" (Hebrews 4:12, NRSV). Although they share evangelicals' concern that the record of scripture be taken seriously, Pentecostals do not base their understanding of the Bible's authority on a doctrine of inerrancy. Doctrine rests on something more fundamental and dynamic: their personal experience of the living God. Pentecostal scholar Scott Ellington explains, " Doctrines may be challenged and even overturned without striking at the very heart of Pentecostal faith because the central emphasis of Pentecostalism is not a teaching which must be believed or a proof which can be deduced and defended against all challenges, but a God who must be reckoned with in direct encounter."[42] In many ways, Pentecostals' approach to scripture is closely aligned with that of North Point Community Church. Chapter 4 discussed founding pastor Andy Stanley's concern that evangelicals have focused too narrowly on the doctrine of inerrancy. While Stanley affirms traditional evangelical beliefs about the authority of scripture, he is concerned by New Atheists who argue that "as the Bible goes, so goes the Christian faith": if something in the Bible is not true—for instance, the flood narrative, Israel's exodus from Egypt, or God's destruction of the walls of Jericho—then all of Christianity is false. However, Stanley refuses to engage in academic debates about the historicity of scripture. He insists that credibility of Christian faith is not contingent upon the biblical text being infallible or inerrant. Instead, it rests securely on Jesus's resurrection: "We don't believe because of a book; we believe *because of the event that inspired the book*."[43]

Pentecostals worry that during the fundamentalist-modernist controversies of the first half of the twentieth century, their fellow evangelicals bought into a worldview that demanded that all experience be measured according to a set of objective and scientific measures. Indeed, evangelicals now defend their notion of biblical authority within the confines of rationalism. Pentecostals have taken a different approach, insisting that the Bible makes absolute and universal claims that cannot be adequately documented and verified within the limits of a scientific worldview.[44]

Central to Pentecostal belief is the confession that God speaks and acts today, a claim that values personal experience and nonrational forms of knowing.[45] As Ellington insists, "The Bible is not simply a text about whose propositions we can debate; it is the authoritative word of God because the same Holy Spirit who inspired its writers meets us today."[46] Thus for Pentecostals, the authority of scripture resides not in a text that can be objectively proven, but in the God that readers come to know in and through its pages.

Soteriology

A third Pentecostal distinctive evidenced in Pastor Enrique's sermon is an emphasis on holy living and sanctification. To understand this point, a comparison with The Village Chapel (TVC) in Nashville will be helpful. Chapter 7 discussed the work of philosopher Charles Taylor, and specifically his claim that Christ's crucifixion and the doctrine of penal substitutionary atonement are underemphasized in twenty-first-century Christianity. By focusing so strongly on Jesus's love, churches paint too benign a picture of the human condition, one that omits the suffering, division, violence, and alienation that so regularly experienced as ultimate. However, the pastors and musicians at TVC strive to keep crucifixion front and center in congregational worship. They do so through the visual aid of a driftwood cross that is "brutal and beautiful at the same time," through homiletical reminders that "for whatever reason God allows all the pain and evil in the world, at least he was willing to take some of his own medicine," and through hymn lyrics stressing that "on that cross as Jesus died / the wrath of God was satisfied."[47]

Like the evangelicals at TVC, Pentecostals agree that the life, death, and resurrection of Jesus have made possible reconciliation between God and humanity. As Pentecostal theologian Amos Yong puts it, "By repenting from their sin and placing faith in the person and work of Christ, human beings are regenerated by the power of the Holy Spirit, adopted as sons and daughters of God, and justified, sanctified, and, eschatologically, glorified. This, in gist, is what it means to confess Jesus as savior."[48] However, Yong notes an additional soteriological emphasis that is uniquely Pentecostal: from the beginning, Pentecostals have experienced Jesus as saving them not only from their sins, but also from their sicknesses and diseases:

> In the world pentecostal context, especially in the global south, this salvation includes a redemption from the powers of the devil and his demons since these are, ultimately, the causes of sickness (both physical and psychosomatic), poverty, and other material and socio-economic ills that keep human beings from experiencing the abundant life promised by God.[49]

One corollary of this emphasis on Jesus as healer is that Pentecostals take a different approach to what mystics have called the "dark night of the soul." At TVC, Pastor Thomas's sermon offered no reasons for why a person might experience the absence of God: "Anguish is not always connected to some sin we have committed. Even when we are most squarely in the center of God's will and purposes for our lives, we can experience the hiddenness of God." If they are feeling abandoned, Thomas encouraged the congregation to remember God's sovereignty and faithfulness in the past. Rather than "some kind of self-salvation" or "pulling yourself up by your bootstraps," Christians should "look outside yourself for help, to the one who made you, the one you belong to ultimately."[50] The problem of theodicy—the fact of evil in the world vis-à-vis the reality of a loving and sovereign God—remains a mystery.

However, Pentecostals worry that reducing the problem of evil to the mystery of God's dealings with the world neglects the role of agency, both demonic and human. As a corrective, Pentecostals "locate theodicy within a discussion of how creaturely freedom (angelic and human) and the way that freedom has created various forms of enslaved existence that only intensify over time."[51] Indeed, Pentecostal theologian Simon Chan even asserted that "Pentecostals have no place in their schema for the dark night [of the soul]. More often, they are likely to dismiss such an experience as due to a lack of faith or an attack from the devil."[52]

In Pentecostal spirituality, Satan and his legion of demons are real entities who actively attempt to undermine God's workings. Pastor Enrique reiterated this point throughout his sermon. "The enemy fights you coming together with other Christians," he reminded the congregation. "The enemy fights you signing up for Wednesday night [church activities]. The enemy fights you coming on Sunday." Later in the message, Pastor Enrique points out that even good things can be used as Satan's weapons: "The enemy is very astute. He's not stupid. He won't tempt you with obvious stuff. But he may try to bamboozle you with good things that are bad for you."

Finally, not all trials are sent from the devil. Sometimes they are of our own making. Pastor Enrique counsels the congregation not to "go through the season the wrong way," by which he means, "Don't rebuke the Devil when it's not the Devil" or "think [the struggle] is from God when it isn't God." Instead, "It might be something you did because of disobedience." Pastor Enrique explains that "the sooner you discern that, the better you can cooperate with God, who wants to take you through it and teach you something that is going to be a blessing at the end of it."

Conclusion

Pentecostals have taken pride in their historical emphasis on reconciliation: in the early twentieth century, the Pentecostal movement helped bring people of differing ethnicities together in integrated revival meetings and church services.

As historian Grant Wacker has observed, in early Pentecostalism, blacks and whites routinely came together for worship and fellowship and seemed genuinely fond of one another.[53] Furthermore, sociological research suggests that congregations with more upbeat, charismatic-like services—defined as saying "Amen," raising hands, jumping, shouting, or dancing spontaneously, and speaking in tongues—are more likely to be racially mixed.[54]

But multiethnicity, Pentecostal theology, and charismatic worship in and of themselves are not magic bullets capable of ending America's racial tensions. Sociologist Michael Emerson points out that decades ago, his colleagues predicted that multiethnic churches would help bring about "common understanding of issues across race, which [could] in turn lead to real change."[55] There were promising indications that this hypothesis might prove true: early research into multiethnic congregations suggested that white attitudes changed to resemble those of their African American or Latino co-worshippers.

More recent data shows that influence actually moves in the opposite direction. A sociological study published in 2015 examined what congregants thought explained socioeconomic differences between blacks and whites. Racial discrimination? Inadequate access to quality education? Blacks' lack of motivation or willpower? Seventy-two percent of African Americans in predominantly black churches believed that the reasons for racial inequality were structural, rather than an individual's lack of motivation. But only about half (53 percent) of African Americans in multiracial churches believed the same thing—a percentage that brings their views closely in line with white and Hispanic members in those same congregations.[56] In other words, African Americans in multiethnic congregations now tend to take on the racial attitudes of their white co-worshippers. "In the aggregate, multiracial congregations are doing exactly what pastors of color tell me they fear—that they will serve merely as a tool into white assimilation," reports Emerson. "Multiracial congregations are 'underachieving,' or to put it another way, not living up to their promise."[57]

I am reminded of the piercing questions Machelle raised at Koinonia Vineyard: "Can we talk about what's going on in our nation right now with all these black bodies dying? Where's the church in all that? How should we posture ourselves?" Machelle, one of the only African American members in her white-majority congregation, longed to hear her pastor say the phrase "Black lives matter" from the pulpit and was frustrated by sermons that waxed eloquent on "diversity" and the "beautiful variety in the Body of Christ" without addressing race in any specificity.

Would Machelle be any happier at Holy Inheritance? Some aspects of congregational life would perhaps be easier: for instance, in a multiethnic context, Machelle might worry less about church members touching her child's hair inappropriately. Many of her other deep concerns, however, would remain unaddressed. Like Casey, Machelle's pastor, who aims to minimize intra-congregational conflict by keeping "Jesus at the center, not focusing on political issues that are polarizing," Enrique ostensibly avoids politics from the pulpit. "God puts Trump [in power], or he puts Hillary, or he puts Obama—he puts in whoever he wants to put in," Enrique declared during my visit. "Our job is to recognize that the Lord is the one who changes times and seasons: not presidents, not parties, not Republicans, not Democrats. God alone has our lives in his hands." When political disagreements do arise, they are quickly squelched. Mabel, the African American worship leader, recounted a story that took place shortly after the 2016 election:

> It must have been Veterans Day or something right after the election, because one lady was like, "Dear God, thank you so much for my son, who is a veteran." Then she goes, "Lord, just please, in all this unrest we have—for those who are just so upset about Trump winning, help them get over it." Some of the African Americans are like, "What?! *Get over it?!*" And then the Latinos were like, "Excuse me?! Get over it?!" We had to kind of go back and say, "OK, let's leave the political out of it." It was a challenge though!

Holy Inheritance leaders try to remain similarly nonpartisan on the issue of immigration, which impacts a significant percentage of those in the congregation. Inez, director of worship ministries, reports that "the political comes up not necessarily face to face in church, but maybe on Facebook." Inez is privy to a variety of church members' opinions on social media: some champion more protection and support for undocumented immigrants, and others want stricter enforcement of deportation laws. "In my opinion, we have to be Christians first—to choose each other first and not let policy divide us," reflected Inez.

It is unlikely that Holy Inheritance will ever be on the forefront of political activism by taking a prophetic stance against structural injustices in American society, a reality that may come as a disappointment to evangelicals like Machelle. At the same time, multiethnic churches go about the work of reconciliation in other important ways. In *Public Religion and Urban Transformation*, Lowell Livezey, a leader in the field of congregational studies and urban ministry research, noted in his study of public religion in Chicago that although only a small percentage of the congregations he studied were engaged in political action on race issues, they frequently addressed questions of race or ethnicity nevertheless:

> Whether or not to conduct a worship service in an additional language, whether to add or change a picture or icon, how hard to try to evangelize a neighborhood or to recruit new members from a wider region—choices such

as these entail racial values and choices. And the decision of whether to articulate the racial dimension or to leave it latent beneath the surface is itself a moral choice.[58]

These negotiations are always fraught. Congregants who are committed to keeping their racially/ethnically centrist identification often leave multiethnic congregations in favor of worshipping communities that are more wholly committed to their particular racial-ethnic expressions of faith. However, successful multiracial churches accomplish what sociologist Gerardo Marti calls "ethnic transcendence." They are not "color-blind"—an approach to diversity that intentionally seeks to overlook differences. Instead, these churches leverage their theological resources to reorient their congregants around a shared ecclesial identity: one that supersedes their (acknowledged and celebrated) differences in ancestral history.[59] At Holy Inheritance, the process of identity reorientation takes place through Unity Sunday celebrations, worship choirs that sing in two languages, friendly church sporting competitions, and shared carne asada. While these gestures are too small, in and of themselves, to overthrow the entrenched racial divisions of American society, they represent preliminary attempts to speak the church's one voice in a multiplicity of languages.

9

"Navigating the Beautiful Tension"

Evangelical Worship as Eschatological Culture

Type the word *evangelical* into a Google image search and colorful images will flood your screen: church logos, headshots of individual leaders, maps of the United States, and more. But scroll down and one scene will seem to recur more than any of the others. This stock image is so recognizable that it has become a visual cliché: middle-class worshippers in large auditoriums, swaying to the music of praise bands with eyes closed, faces lifted heavenward, and hands raised to the sky.[1] As we have seen, this photograph is not representative of every evangelical congregation. There are complexities of evangelical faith and practice that the lens is cropping out. I know, for example, contrasts to the oft-photographed "fully abandoned" worshipper in the front of the room. His hands are stuffed deep into his pockets. The woman next to him shifts her weight from foot to foot. Neither is singing: the volume is too loud, the key too high, the stanzas too repetitive. Tired after twenty-five minutes of standing, both wish the band would stop playing unfamiliar songs and release the congregation to sit back down.

Even so, something about this photograph rings truer than any academic definition of the word *evangelical*. The outstretched hand, tightly closed eyes, and gently furrowed brow are examples of what French literary philosopher Roland Barthes calls the *punctum* of a photograph: that small detail—different for every viewer—"which triggers a succession of personal memories and unconscious associations, many of which are indescribable by the individual."[2] Perhaps the closest analogy is sonic memory:

> Sometimes we will hear a piece of music that . . . seems to elicit within us not so much a memory as an inner psychic constellation laden with images, feelings, and bodily acuities. However much we may try to tell someone about what is happening to us . . . we shall fail to convey the texture of our inner experience.[3]

Increasingly, even observers with no emotional or spiritual attachment to evangelicalism now equate the movement with its worship. For example, the following political articles all reference the word *evangelical* in their headlines: "Some Evangelicals Struggle with Black Lives Matter Movement,"[4] "Immigrant-Bashers Will Lose the Evangelical Vote,"[5] "Evangelicals Are Changing Their Minds on

Evangelical Worship. Melanie C. Ross, Oxford University Press. © Oxford University Press 2021.
DOI: 10.1093/oso/9780197530757.003.0010

Gay Marriage."[6] Although none of these stories treats worship at any length, each features a photo of congregants with eyes closed and hands raised aloft—evidence that its worship has become foundational to evangelicalism's public identity in the twenty-first century.

Despite the fact that worship has become symbolic of evangelicalism's identity, it remains a surprisingly understudied locus of academic inquiry. One reason for this lacuna is that evangelical worship falls between the cracks of two academic disciplines. Historians of American evangelicalism tend to define the movement by its political entanglements (the "rise of the religious Right") and intellectual trajectories (the formation of the "evangelical mind"), not its ecclesial practices. Conversely, liturgical scholars who focus on American worship traditions concentrate their attention on churches with established liturgies and a high view of the sacraments. In the absence of robust scholarly analysis, evangelical worship is frequently dismissed as a derivative imitation of secular entertainment (three Christian rock songs and a spiritual TED talk). But by failing to engage this worship seriously, we miss vital insights into a form of Protestantism that exerts widespread influence in the United States and around the world.

Evangelical worship, like the wider evangelical movement itself, is never static. I undertook the fieldwork for *Evangelical Worship: An American Mosaic* between the years 2014 and 2018, a uniquely fraught period in American evangelical history. Halfway through my research, in November 2016, Donald Trump was elected forty-fifth president of the United States. In 2018, the final year of my fieldwork, the nation mourned the death of evangelical statesman and "America's Pastor" Billy Graham. That same year saw Bill Hybels, founding pastor of Willow Creek, the nation's most famous megachurch, step down in disgrace amid allegations of sexual harassment and misconduct that an independent advisory council later deemed credible. As I write these words, the world is in the grips of a coronavirus pandemic that has claimed thousands of lives and forced congregations to find new ways of worshipping through virtual platforms.

The churches introduced in this book have changed as well. "People are the primary liturgical document," James F. White once claimed, and I believe he is right.[7] But in contrast to textual liturgical resources, congregations are in constant flux: like Heraclitus's river, the same one can never be "stepped into" twice. Since 2014, some of the congregations in this study have installed new senior pastors. Others have changed locations, started new worship ventures, or weathered internal crises. All have had to adapt to the changes wrought by Covid-19. None is immune to the effects of America's ever-increasing political polarizations, racial divisions, and economic disparities.

Given the ever-evolving nature of this mosaic, *Evangelical Worship* concludes with a redefinition of its titular phrase. Rather than a static *structure*, I contend that evangelical worship is best understood as a theological *culture* that must continually negotiate the paradoxes of continuity and change, consensus and contestation, and sameness and difference.

Liturgical Structure: James F. White

Historian James F. White (1932–2004) was the first liturgical scholar to suggest that evangelical worship had a distinctive structure.

White emerged as one of the leading scholars of the history of Protestant worship during his tenure at the Perkins School of Theology of Southern Methodist University, and later at the University of Notre Dame. During his lifetime, White served at the forefront of Methodist liturgical revision and became one of the leading advocates for the establishment and development of a North American guild of liturgical scholars.[8] In 1980, he was awarded a grant by the Association of Theological Schools "to do a study on the teaching of worship in North American seminaries."[9] The results of this study convinced White of the dearth of qualified worship professors in North American seminaries. In 1983, he was hired by the University of Notre Dame, an appointment that powerfully symbolized the ecumenical impact of the Second Vatican Council. Within a decade of his arrival, the majority of doctoral students in the Liturgical Studies program at Notre Dame would be Protestants.[10]

Before coming to Notre Dame, White had demonstrated a clear preference for ecumenical post–Vatican II liturgical reforms, writing in 1982 that "all of worship history belongs to all of us. . . . Because the post–Vatican II approach recognizes this catholicity, it constitutes the best option for the contemporary Christian worshiper."[11] Over time, however, White became increasingly concerned that Protestant denominations were losing their own sense of liturgical identity.[12] "If convergence becomes too prominent, we must ask whether some of the richness of the variety of Protestant worship will suffer," he cautioned. "The richness of Protestant worship consists in its diversity and its consequent ability to serve a wide variety of peoples." White continued to believe that liturgical "borrowing" from other traditions was important, even a "sign of health," but stressed that healthy borrowing was only possible when "a certain sense of knowing and respecting one's own tradition had been achieved." "Scholarship is necessary to this security," he concluded.[13]

White's own scholarly contribution was a thorough and thoughtful taxonomy of Protestant worship, a project he began in 1975 and concluded with the publication of *Protestant Worship* in 1989. White spoke of eight familiar traditions of Protestant worship: Lutheran, Reformed, Anglican, Quaker, Methodist, Separatist/Puritan, Anabaptist, and Pentecostal. White's book was a departure from previous liturgical scholarship in at least two ways. First, White chose to emphasize each tradition's ethos and enduring characteristics rather than its liturgical texts. Second, after observing that "the most prevalent worship tradition in American Protestantism (and maybe in American Christianity) lacks any recognized name" and "has been almost totally ignored in liturgical scholarship," White created a new, ninth category of Protestant worship called the "frontier tradition."

The frontier tradition had a threefold shape—preliminary songs that "soften up" an audience, a fervent sermon, and an altar call for new converts—that effectively marginalized the Lord's Supper. In White's reading, the trajectory of the frontier order (he used the Latin word *ordo*) could be traced from Charles Finney to the church growth movement. He believed the pattern suffered from a series of theological deficiencies: the audience's attention is drawn from the glory of the risen Christ to the magnetic personality of the speaker; there is too much emphasis on an individual's "decision for Christ"; and worship is made the means to an evangelistic end, rather than an end in and of itself.

White's frontier *ordo* offered a convenient handle for other liturgical scholars. Baffled and alarmed by new worship trends infiltrating mainline Protestant denominations, they accepted his analysis, almost without question.[14] Frank Senn (Lutheran), Thomas Schattauer (Lutheran), Rhoda Schuler (Lutheran), Gordon Lathrop (Lutheran), and Todd E. Johnson (Evangelical Covenant) all discussed contemporary worship as a phenomenon with origins in frontier camp meetings, standardization through Finney, resurgence in the Church Growth Movement, and new expression in megachurches.[15] Many complained that the "novelty" of this threefold pattern threatened the normativity of a fourfold transcultural, transdenominational pattern of Christian worship (Gathering, Word, Table, Sending) that had endured in Christian worship from the second century to the present day.

Little has changed in the guild of liturgical scholars over the last two decades. Recently, Methodist scholar Matthew Sigler pointed out that the "frontier worship" category has become the "dominant lens through which many evaluate worship within the American context."[16] Lester Ruth—White's former doctoral student, now research professor of worship at Duke University—makes a similar observation: "The histories of contemporary worship produced by liturgical scholars have stagnated on the whole. No one has questioned the basic Frontier framework although there has been some nuancing."[17]

Problematizing Liturgical Taxonomies

Taxonomies can be useful tools, especially for the work of classifying objects' typical properties and arranging this data on the basis of similarities and differences.

However, as Andrea Bieler, professor of practical theology at the University of Basel, points out, because they cannot account for internal diversities, deviations are likely to be seen as "annoying exceptions rather than central areas for inquiry."[18] The inability to accommodate exceptions is a significant limitation of White's frontier *ordo*.

In addition to their inability to account for internal differences, taxonomies suffer from a second limitation: they reinforce the idea of a detached observer with a bird's-eye view. Critical hermeneutics scholar Hans-Herbert Kogler explains the problem this way: structuralism accords "a privileged position to the theorist over and above the situated agent. Whereas agents are viewed as acting and thinking *within* specific symbolic frameworks . . . [only] the theorist is granted epistemically privileged, objective, and undistorted insight into the hidden and underlying mechanisms through which these symbolic frameworks are reproduced."[19] White's "objective" vantage point as an outside observer of evangelical worship thus carries more authoritative weight than the interpretive perspectives of practitioners themselves.[20]

When grammarians attempt to describe a language they do not speak, they are "prone to impose categories from their own internalized linguistic system" while remaining "blind to categories and distinctions that their own system lacks."[21] In the same way, White sought to impose liturgical structure—a category familiar to his own experience—over a movement that does not think primarily in those terms. As Baptist liturgical scholar Christopher Ellis points out, "Tradition does not carry for the Free Churches the burden of authority which it would carry in Roman Catholic or Orthodox churches. Authority is found elsewhere— in Scripture, the missionary imperative, pastoral need and common-sense rationalism."[22]

Consequentially, I do not intend to propose a new taxonomy to replace White's frontier *ordo*. Instead, I set aside the notion of structure, concurring with Bieler that taxonomic frameworks need to be put in tension with "more open approaches to the description and interpretation of ritual practices."[23] As a corrective, I conclude by forging a new understanding of evangelical worship as a culture in conversation with theologians Kathryn Tanner and John Webster.

Kathryn Tanner's *Theories of Culture*

Kathryn Tanner's 1997 book *Theories of Culture* has been widely influential in the fields of practical and systematic theology. Initially, Tanner may seem like the ideal conversation partner in a discussion of evangelical worship that moves beyond structures and taxonomies: her work eschews the notion of theological "essence" by foregrounding churches as communities of struggle as well as faith.

Although this is not the direction I ultimately choose, Tanner's proposal is worth considering at length, particularly for the ways it has influenced the study of American evangelicalism (a point to which I will return).

Tanner's starting point is "the anthropological notion of culture," which she argues "can be profitably employed in theology."[24] Tanner begins by tracing the evolution of the term *culture* through three historical eras. In the seventeenth through nineteenth centuries, the term was used to denote a sense of sophistication: persons and societies could become more "cultured" through education and self-discipline. In the early twentieth century, the definition of *culture* began to take on anthropological overtones: people groups formed self-contained units with clear boundaries that separated one culture from another. *Culture* became a "group-differentiating, holistic, nonevaluative, and context-relative notion."[25]

Post-1920s anthropologists emphasized that there was no universal culture applicable to all people and places. Instead, there were a diversity of local cultures, each one an autonomous, self-contained, internally consistent entity. Clifford Geertz (1926–2006) and other anthropologists sought to study cultures from a supposedly objectivist stance, setting aside their own value-laden notions of truth, beauty, and goodness to better attend to the particularities of the people groups they observed and described. This anthropological understanding of culture had a ripple effect in theological studies as scholars began to query in what sense Christianity could be seen as its own distinct culture, asking, in Tanner's words, "What do Christians say and do that others do not? How is Christian identity established with reference to, specifically in contradistinction from, other ways of life?"[26]

The notion of *culture* further evolved under the influences of poststructuralism and postmodernity in the late twentieth century. It is this shift—and the possibilities it invites for constructive theology—that is at the heart of Tanner's work. In contrast to modern anthropology, which emphasized culture as a consensus-building social phenomenon that resisted change, postmodern cultural theory attends to hybridity and interactive boundaries. Cultures are not homogeneous. They are "contradictory and internally fissured wholes," writes Tanner, where members vie for power as they struggle to make sense of the current moment. Nor are cultures self-contained. They are always interacting by mixing, intersecting, overlapping, or resisting one another. From a postmodern anthropological perspective, culture "forms the basis for conflict as much as it forms the basis for shared beliefs and sentiments. Whether or not culture is a common focus of *agreement*, culture binds people together as a common focus for *engagement*."[27]

Tanner queries how a postmodern understanding of culture that prioritizes differences, equality, tolerance, and freedom might inform Christian theology. (She is particularly concerned about the conservative methodological tendency to "insulate a Christian perspective from external criticism, and to ignore serious diversity, contest and change within Christianity.")[28] Tanner's pressing question is how to do theology positively, in a way that respects diversity without eliminating it through division.

Her solution begins with the assertion that there is no such thing as a singular "Christian community." It is true that Christians are agreed that their beliefs and practices witness to God; however, these beliefs and practices look different across time and space. Scripture, creeds, liturgies, and discipleship practices are, by their nature, time-bound and contextualized for a specific group of people and often generated in response to particular opponents and problems. Consequentially, they can never serve as that to which Christians must attest everywhere and always. Tanner elaborates,

> Christians may all be revolving around much the same materials—say, a simple rule of faith to be found in the Apostle's Creed. But if they always affirm it only under very different, often opposed, formulations (since no one holds the worldview or precise theology of bygone times that inform that creed), one would be hard pressed to say they are of a common mind about it.[29]

This is not to suggest that the whole set of Christian beliefs and practices must be completely dismantled and constructed anew in each generation. Instead, theology emerges out of culture, as Christians employ whatever tools are on hand to make the case that God is revealed in Christ. Changes in the shape of "true discipleship" come from the rearrangement of practices and ideas, a mode of theological construction Tanner describes as bricolage.

If Christian identity is in flux, constantly intermingling with the contents of surrounding culture and without a "transcendent standard of correctness," then what distinctive content does it contain? Tanner responds that the desire for firm content runs counter to God's freedom. She contends that "what holds all these different practices together as a unity is nothing internal to the practices themselves; the center that holds them all together should remain, as Barth says, empty."[30] In other words, no liturgy, confessional document, doctrinal statement, or theological essence can take the place of God in God's self. To suggest otherwise would be to worship creation rather than the Creator.

Ultimately then, Tanner proposes, Christians share a set of biblical claims, some basic ritual forms, and "a strong enough belief in the significance of Jesus and of initiation into the community of his followers to put [their lives] in motion around the question of what exactly this person and that initiation means for it."[31] But in the absence of universally agreed-upon propositions of belief, Christian unity rests upon participation in what Tanner calls a "community of argument" that shares a sense "of the importance of figuring it out."[32] In the end,

Christianity "is true to the extent that it inspires attractive communities of faith," and its identity can only be "in the form of a task of looking for one."[33]

John Webster's "Theological Theology"

Tanner's account emphasizes the ways that Christians construct and reconstruct their faith (and, we might add, worship) from the cultural materials that are at hand. However, Michael Aune, professor of worship at the Pacific Lutheran Theological Seminary, raised objections to this approach in a two-part essay published in 2007 in the journal *Worship*.[34] Aune worried that liturgical scholars were placing too much emphasis on "what the assembly does" during worship without acknowledging that "all we do in liturgy is but a response to the over-arching, grace-filled initiative of God."[35] Surveying recent liturgical scholarship, Aune feared that attention to *God's* action in liturgy "has been all but lost or certainly overshadowed in the nearly endless emphasis on church, assembly, etc." In light of Aune's critique, I examine an alternative proposal by theologian John Webster, who roots his discussion of culture in the doctrine of God.

In 1997, John Webster (d. 2016), then newly minted Lady Margaret Professor of Divinity in the University of Oxford, devoted his inaugural lecture to the subject of "theological theology," a phrase that has become central to his legacy.[36] Webster's argument was that much of modern theology had surrendered that which makes it a unique discipline:

> The theological disciplines have, in effect, been "de-regionalized," that is, they have been pressed to give an account of themselves in terms drawn largely from fields of enquiry other than theology, fields which, according to prevailing criteria of academic propriety more nearly approximate to ideals of rational activity. . . . For example, the study of Scripture, or doctrine, or the history of the church draw their [sic] modes of enquiry from Semitics, or the history of religions, or social anthropology, from philosophy, or from general historical studies.[37]

Already we note a clear difference from Tanner, who takes an anthropological notion of culture as her methodological starting point. Webster believes that theology should be characterized by a "focused intensity" on God: a single-minded focus that necessitates "declining pressing invitations to involve itself in all sorts of intramural work" in fields like sociology, anthropology, or ritual theory.[38]

Webster is concerned that Tanner's arguments in *Theories of Culture* are "underpinned by a (rather severely) apophatic doctrine of God."[39] By this, Webster means that Tanner confines herself to remarks about who God is *not*, rather than setting forth claims about who God *is*. Tanner's account of the culture of faith is indeed devoid of doctrinal specifics, and intentionally so: she wants readers to acutely feel this lack. Christian identity is elusive because God is utterly free. By withholding something firm to hold onto—a doctrine, a liturgy, a prayer book—Tanner presses Christians to examine places where the Spirit may be at work unexpectedly.

By contrast, Webster cautions that "a doctrine of the church is only as good as the doctrine of God which underlies it."[40] Subsequently, Webster's discussion of the church starts with God's perfection, which forms the foundation of his ecclesiology. Briefly sketched: God exists in self-contained and self-originating perfection. Out of that perfection, he extends grace and salvation to humanity, inviting us into relationship with him and each other in the image of the loving relations of the Trinity. This invitation is made possible only through the life, death, resurrection, and glorification of Jesus, through the power of the Holy Spirit. Since the person is the recipient of God's grace, the fundamental dynamic of the church is that of the person's *being chosen* and the fundamental action of the church is to testify. Drawing on the biblical book of Revelation, Webster explains:

> The church is . . . not first and foremost a speaking but a hearing community. John the seer says that he turned to the voice that was speaking to him (Rev 1:12); and there are few more succinct statements of the primary dynamic of the Christian assembly. The church *is* that turning. And, further, in making that movement, in fear and trembling, falling at the feet of the Son of Man, the church receives its appointment to a specific task: it is summoned to speech.[41]

Perhaps hinting at Tanner's work, Webster worries that "some recent ecclesiology has been (alarmingly) relaxed" about God's sovereignty and election, "making free use of social or ethical or cultural theory to frame an account of the church to which talk of divine action is then rather loosely attached."[42] This approach is problematic because it puts the cart before the horse. God's gracious self-communication *precedes* and *defines* the church, which is why a robust ecclesiology must be more than "a rather indeterminate set of cultural negotiations in which the church figures out some kind of identity for itself."[43]

Tanner's approach starts "from below" by bringing insights from cultural anthropology to bear on the human institution of the church. She argues that ever since the earliest days of the church, Christian communities have borrowed from the worldview, structures, and practices of the culture around them. There is no distinctive "Christian culture," or any practices that could be considered "indigenous" to Christianity. Even something as "quintessentially Christian" as the Eucharist emerged out of Jewish ritual meals. In Tanner's estimation, a Christian way of life is "essentially parasitic; it has to establish relations with other ways of life, it has to take from them in order to be one itself."[44] In the end, "It is not so much what cultural materials you use as what you do with them that establishes identity."[45] Christian practices "are always the practices of others made odd."[46]

Webster would offer qualified agreement to Tanner's point that Christian culture is just like any other distinctive, large-scale pattern of human life. "In one sense, of course, [Christian culture] is made by us: to say anything less would be docetic."[47] But Webster stresses that because Christianity is more than a mere set of human undertakings and activities, the term *culture* also has serious limitations. The culture of Christianity is unique, so unlike all other human cultures, because it "both emerges from and is ceaselessly called into question by the resurrection of Jesus from the dead."[48] In Webster's words, the culture of Christian faith is most properly described as *eschatological*:

> Culture is not a steady, stable world which affords those who belong to it the security of being placed in some definitive way. It is, paradoxically, a place which is no place, a place made by the presence of God who invades and interrupts all places. Being located in that kind of culture is equally a matter of dislocation, of discovering how to be more theological by encountering once again the shock of the gospel.... It is a culture which is generated, sustained, and perfected, and also exposed to radical questioning, by the utterly gratuitous presence of God in the risen Jesus.[49]

Herein lies the most important difference between Webster and Tanner. While both agree that Christian tradition is not static, they offer different explanations about the nature of its fluidity. For Tanner, the Christian faith is always being negotiated. Christians may never reach consensus about the things that matter most; however, this is no problem because consensus is not the goal. Instead, Christians need to be able to agree about how to disagree. In Tanner's words, "Christian agreements . . . are agreements about how to have an argument, an argument that can, at any particular point, turn back against what was initially agreed upon, in an effort to rework it."[50] Thus the church is best understood as a "community of argument," united not by any specificity of belief, but by the common task of discerning together the content of true discipleship.

For Webster, the church's precarity has less to do with its ongoing internal negotiations than with the baptismal character of Christian faith. Disagreements between Christians across time and space pale in comparison the most fundamental of all fights: humanity's stubborn and sinful resistance to the gospel. Jesus Christ, "the comprehensive interruption of all things" and the "great catastrophe of human life and history," is the one who "absolutely dislocates and no less absolutely renders." Christian faith subsequently emerges "out of the shock of the gospel." At the heart of the church are "perplexity and delight—that sense of being at one and the same time overwhelmed and consumed yet remade and reestablished."[51]

This Pauline baptismal pattern of dying and rising in Christ (Romans 6, Colossians 2:8–15) is evident across the whole of Webster's theology. Reading the Bible "is an incident in the baptismal process of mortification and viv-ification, of overthrow and re-establishment," wherein God's revelation "comes to do battle with us: to overcome our refusal to confess the sheer over-whelming goodness, beauty, and truth of God."[52] So too the task of academic theology: "Good theologians are those whose life and thought are caught up in the process of being slain and made alive by the gospel and of acquiring and exercising habits of mind and heart which take very seriously the gospel's provocation."[53]

Gratitude, not discord, is the *cantus firmus* that sustains Webster's the-ology. He urges the church to remember "that there have been others who have loved, studied and contemplated divine instruction, and loved their fellows and successors sufficiently to pass on what they have learned."[54] These saints who strained to hear God's voice in the past can help the church learn to speak God's word in the present:

> The past of theology can never absolve us from present responsibility: we must use our words, not those of our forebears, and speak to our contemporaries, not an audience which left the room ages ago. But if we do not acquire the skills to listen to what the communion of saints says to us, what we have to say in our turn will be thin and unedifying, solemn at all the wrong places and lacking in joyful seriousness about the gospel.[55]

Certainly, Webster acknowledges, Christians must exercise discrimination and theological judgment when choosing which materials from its past to engage ("the church and its traditions are imperfect, sometimes wicked"). But he stresses that contemporary theologians should adopt a critical pos-ture toward tradition "only after patient, grateful attentiveness towards [their] benefactors, in full awareness of [their] debts and mindful of [their] own limitations and culpability."[56] By humbly displacing themselves to listen closely to voices from the past, today's Christians are invited to receive "the possibility of a more spacious domain, a greater store of intellectual goods."[57] In the end, he contends, the church needs more than agreements about how to disagree. It also requires "skills of theological judgement schooled by the Christian past, alert to present opportunity, and enacted with deference and hope."[58]

The Culture of Evangelicalism

At first glance, Tanner's proposal for how to construe culture theologically speaks more directly to evangelicalism. Craig Blaising, former executive vice president and provost of Southwestern Baptist Theological Seminary, acknowledged as much in the 2005 presidential address to his colleagues in the Evangelical Theological Society:

> In some respects, we [evangelicals] may look like Tanner's community of argument. A quick glance at our membership list quickly reveals that we are a "diverse" society. There are different ecclesiastical traditions represented here, and on top of that each of us, engaged in our various scholarly projects, bring[s] a diversity of views and interpretations into the presentations, discussions, and debates that make up our annual meetings. And it is a legitimate question to ask whether our work amounts to something more than the constant rearranging of theological material in response to a ceaseless flow of novel ideas and opinions.[59]

Molly Worthen: Evangelical Fractures

Duke historian Molly Worthen fleshes out the intra-evangelical conflicts to which Blaising alludes in her magisterial intellectual history *Apostles of Reason: The Crisis of Authority in American Evangelicalism*. According to Worthen, evangelicalism is a constellation of Protestant traditions that disagree about "frankly almost everything except the divinity of Christ."[60] Sounding much like Tanner, Worthen portrays evangelicals as Christians who "have been part of the same conversation over the centuries" and "have a stake in what one another gets up to—because they orbit around the same questions. If they don't share a single statement of faith, they do share a set of worries and concerns."[61] In Worthen's reading, these concerns are threefold: "how to reconcile faith and reason; how to know Jesus; and how to act publicly on faith after the rupture of Christendom."[62] Worthen acknowledges that hers is "a historian's definition meant to account for the patterns of history," rather than "a believer's self-description that tries to relay evangelicals' internal perspective in language that they might use themselves."[63]

Worthen believes that observers have fundamentally misunderstood evangelicals, labeling them as "anti-intellectual because their community is totally authoritarian and they unthinkingly obey their pastor."[64] She argues the opposite: evangelicals are torn by many conflicting authorities—the standards of secular reason, their own spiritual experiences, the dictates of scripture—but have no recognized magisterial authority like a pope to adjudicate their disagreements. This means that there is no such thing as an "evangelical mind," an image that conjures up one brain shared by many. Instead, Worthen proposes the metaphor of an "evangelical imagination," which is something a community can share, "no matter how furious its internal quarrels."[65] This imagination is a source of energy that propels institution-building, evangelism, care for the suffering, and intellectual inquiry, but offers no clear path through or beyond evangelicalism's vexing impasses.

For Worthen, evangelicals' commitment to continued discussion is more important than any consensus they might produce. Her argument parallels Tanner's assertion that cultures are inherently fluid: their unity proceeds from engagement more than agreement. Worthen's "evangelical imagination," much like Tanner's example of "the American Way," is a cultural reference point. Participants are bound together by their common attachment to the idea and by their shared sense of the importance of the idea, but not by any mutual consensus about what exactly the idea means.

But many evangelicals object to Tanner's and Worthen's construal of their identity. Blaising ultimately rejected Tanner's "community of argument" characterization in his remarks to the Evangelical Theological Society, insisting that evangelicals' agreements are stronger and more important than their disputes. "We disagree on some confessional points," Blaising acknowledged, but more importantly, "We work with a simple doctrinal basis concerning God and his Word. The various theological boundaries that divide evangelicals are not in that doctrinal basis. Rather, we have a common affirmation of the triune God and the authoritative, inerrant, written Word of God."[66]

In the same vein, Thomas Kidd, professor of history at Baylor University, raises the issue of doctrine in his review of Worthen's *Apostles of Reason*. Picking up on Worthen's assertion that "American evangelicalism owes more to its fractures and clashes, its anxieties and doubts, than to any . . . doctrine," Kidd wonders whether the "real target in the book is the concept of orthodoxy itself."[67] He presses Worthen:

> Can any movement like evangelicalism—or its affiliated institutions or denominations—really operate without any sense of orthodoxy? May we draw any lines between evangelicals and non-evangelicals? Or lines between helpful debate and rabble-rousing? Surely we can all agree, for example, that someone who denies the existence of God cannot be an evangelical. What about someone who denies the divinity of Jesus? . . . Where we should draw the lines, and what issues are non-negotiable, will remain points of contention. But an evangelicalism that is all rootless inquiry—one that regards no belief as beyond

the pale—is not likely to remain the potent force it has been in American and around the world.[68]

Although Kidd has strong praise for *Apostles of Reason*, he registers a caution: "Worthen's highly engaging book may not garner as much of an audience among American evangelicals as one might hope, because in the contest between evangelical conservatives and myriad evangelical dissenters, Worthen is not hesitant to take sides. Her preference is for the dissenters."[69]

Many reviewers observe that the gap between Worthen's "historian's definition" and evangelicals' self-understanding was not negligible: "Inasmuch as evangelicals struggle to reconcile their heartfelt faith with secular reason, *Apostles of Reason* is thoroughly convincing. Still, it is not clear that this dilemma is as central to the movement as Worthen claims."[70] "While I do believe that Worthen is correct in that evangelicals have sought for some sort of authoritative basis for knowledge, I do not believe she is correct in seeing this as unique or even central to the identity of being evangelical."[71] Worthen's "desired objectivity in her research keeps her from conveying the essence of evangelicalism to her readers. It is largely 'head' with very little 'heart,' and while this literary vantage point is admirable it does not allow for readers fully to understand the movements and nuances within evangelicalism."[72] "If Worthen offers a definitive account of the evangelical intellect, she has not captured the essence of evangelicalism itself. To get at the heart of religion, scholars need to go . . . to the habits of piety practiced by the rank-and-file."[73]

And yet every reviewer cited also praised the book as exhaustively researched, beautifully written, compelling argued, and a game changer in the field. Their critiques are a striking illustration of the difference between *looking at* and *living in*. As practical theologian John Swinton writes, these two modes of perception "may complement one another, but they are not the same, nor are they inevitably or necessarily equal," and a dialogue between the two requires hospitality.[74] Building on Swinton, I suggest that evangelicals (*living in*) might need to acknowledge that scholars from outside the tradition know much more about certain issues than they do. But it also might mean non-evangelical academics who study the tradition (*looking at*) might need to recognize that what evangelical insiders know is "more foundational and more important for [the] journey together toward proper understanding."[75]

Kevin Vanhoozer: Evangelical Unity

Kevin Vanhoozer, research professor of systematic theology at Trinity Evangelical Divinity School, is a theologian who "lives in" the evangelical tradition. (Vanhoozer affirms that he willingly uses the term *evangelical* as a qual-ifier to theology.)[76] After John Webster died unexpectedly in 2016, Vanhoozer continued the spirit of his work, acknowledging his debt in a testimonial to the late theologian: "For the past fifteen years, [Webster's] published essays and his informal tutorials (emails) have served me well as crucial guidelines and points of reference for my own research and writing. . . . Holding up and supporting a number of my own signature theological moves [is] John's strong Protestant arm."[77] Just as Kathryn Tanner's theological proposals are in the background of Molly Worthen's history of evangelical arguments, so too Webster laid the theo-logical groundwork for Vanhoozer's writings on evangelical unity.

When Vanhoozer looks at evangelicalism's internal diversity, he sees a boat that is securely tethered. Evangelical theology is "anchored" by its Trinitarian, crucicentric emphasis. Trinitarianism is the "structure, substance, and sum-mary of the gospel." The cross event (which includes the resurrection) is the "hinge of history, the decisive turning point in the God-world relationship."[78] Being anchored is not the same as being rigidly fixed. Instead, "An anchored set resembles an inverted cone, with its greatest latitude at the surface, at the mouth of the cone."[79] The church is the vessel that the anchor holds fast. The "rope" that establishes limits on the church's range of motion is catholic tradition. Thus, evangelicalism has both doctrinal fixation (the anchor) and delimited flexibility (the rope).

Vanhoozer offers a practical gauge for distinguishing between three levels of doctrine that allow evangelicals to maintain a healthy tension between unity (on essentials) and diversity (on nonessentials). First-level doctrines are the things on which the communion of saints has formed a consensus, the things that Christians at all times and places must confess to preserve the gospel's intelligi-bility. To deny them is tantamount to apostasy or heresy.[80] These doctrines, pre-served in the New Testament, put Jesus's death, burial, and resurrection at center stage and represent the agreed-upon universal judgements of the church.

Second-level doctrines are the doctrines on which evangelicals have not reached full agreement. They treat "events (e.g., atonement) and aspects of sal-vation history (e.g., the image of God, sin, justification) that must be affirmed, though there is some scope for different interpretations."[81] Many second-level doctrines are an answer to the question of *how* (e.g., different atonement theories). Debates about second-level doctrines represent points of significant "regional" difference between evangelicals—points important enough to be required for membership within a church or denomination—yet theological disagreement about them does not impede translocal cooperation between evangelicals of dif-ferent stripes. Finally, there are third-level doctrines. Differences over them are not damaging to the gospel or divisive to congregational life. Vanhoozer offers an example of his orders: "That Jesus will return to judge the living and the dead is *first order*; the nature of the millennium is *second order* and the exact sequence of events pertaining to the millennium is probably *third order*."[82] The evangelical challenge is "to know the difference between courageously preserving the truths of the gospel that cannot change and charitably acknowledging the interpretive diversity of nonessential truths."[83]

The evangelical congregations I analyzed in this book have several "second level" doctrinal disagreements. For example, if asked to explain how God works over the course of history, North Point would likely emphasize striking differences between Old and New Testament covenants, while Park Street would stress the continuity in God's unified plan across all of time. When asked to explain the nature of God's salvific work through Christ, the leaders of TVC would foreground Jesus's substitutionary death on the cross, while their colleagues at Wayfarers Collective would begin with Jesus's exemplary life and ministry. There are many "third level" areas of contrast as well. Koinonia Vineyard and Holy Inheritance are strongly influenced by Pentecostalism: their congregations would be the most open to miraculous healings and speaking in tongues during worship. North Point stresses that worship must change and adapt to the times; Park Street and Moody value a strong sense of connection to the past. At Moody, Park Street, and TVC, robust corporate singing is a marker of healthy worship. At North Point and Wayfarers Collective, musical participation is encouraged but not required.

While these debates are significant, they do not undermine the unity-in-plurality that is the evangelical movement. As Vanhoozer explains,

> Scripture is sufficient, yet it takes four Evangelists to tell the story of Jesus Christ. In similar fashion, could it not take a number of different voices (denominations, cultures, even eras) to articulate all the wisdom and blessings that are in Christ? Pentecostal plurality is the miracle of different voices speaking the same thing in different languages and the increase of understanding in which hearing this diversity results.[84]

Just as many members with different gifts make up the one body of Christ, so do many faithful readings make up the full catholicity of evangelical worship.

Evangelical Worship as Eschatological Culture

To summarize the argument, I have proposed the notion of evangelical worship as a culture rather than a structure. However, theologians define culture in conflicting ways. On one hand are scholars like Kathryn Tanner (and, by extension, Molly Worthen), who understand the culture of Christianity and/or evangelicalism as an essentially contested concept. Participants are bound to-gether by their shared sense of the importance of the idea, but not by any mu-tual consensus about what it means. On the other hand, theologians like John Webster (and, by extension, Kevin Vanhoozer) understand evangelicalism eschatologically, as a unified diversity. Thus Webster makes a helpful distinction between the phenomenon of the church (its historical and social aspects) and the being of the church (which can only be understood in relation to the doctrine of God). The former is accessible for empirical study; the latter is not.[85] To believe in that which all too often seems an impediment to faith requires that there be more to the church than meets the eye.[86]

A scholar like Molly Worthen, who writes about evangelicalism from a *looking at* perspective, might disagree with Webster's prioritization of the invisible na-ture of the church's reality. Worthen argues that history, not theology, is the most useful lens for understanding evangelicalism: despite the fact that they may "scoff at history's claims on them ... [evangelicals] are creatures of history like everyone else, whether they like it or not."[87] However, a scholar like Kevin Vanhoozer, who writes about evangelicalism from a *living in* perspective, will echo Webster's con-viction that there is more to the church—and to evangelicalism—than meets the eye. "I now own the term [*evangelical*] in its theological rather than sociological sense," Vanhoozer writes, explaining that the term refers to "a guiding hope and eschatological reality, not an already-accomplished historical achievement.[88]

The idea of evangelical worship as an eschatological culture may sound eso-teric and far removed from the concrete experience of life in a local congregation. Yet the paradoxes of eschatological culture that Webster identifies—of being slain and made alive, dislocated and re-established, grounded yet subverted by the shock of the gospel—are realties that all the churches in this study intuitively understand. At Park Street, pastors wrestle with how to be both grounded and subverted through worship that "connects [the congregation] with the history of the church" but also provides an entry point for seekers with little or no church background. At Moody, worship leaders live in the tension between music that is both ancient *and* modern, familiar *and* new. At North Point, staff are keenly aware of God's tendency to interrupt prevailing norms: "The day will come when our season of ministry will take a backseat to the next movement in the church. . . . [It] could be one hundred years from now. It could be next week. We just don't know."

In Portland, worshippers at Wayfarers Collective know firsthand the reality of existing in "a place which is no place." By continuing to rent warehouse space, the Collective risks losing its long-term members with young children; if it were to purchase its own building, it would risk alienating the single young adults that it originally set out to reach. At Koinonia Vineyard, Casey and Machelle agonize over the reality of their placement in a congregation that holds no political, legal, or military power and the gospel call to *displacement*, which requires "saying something" about the racial tensions that headline daily news. For Pentecostal Christians at Holy Inheritance, disruptions and surprises of the Spirit are expected norms since, at any given moment, God may choose "to invade our *chronos* with his *Kairos*."

Perhaps the most revealing reflection on evangelical worship as an eschatological culture comes from Kim Thomas at The Village Chapel in Nashville. She suggests:

> Worship is not either/or. It's not even the middle. It's all about navigating the beautiful tension—and it has to be tight; you have to be able to walk on it— between tradition and innovation, evangelism and social justice, even between the extremes that happened between Catholics and Protestants during the Reformation. If you are aware that the pendulum will never land on the perfect spot until Christ comes back, then you always hold the swinging loosely. You don't build your house on that pendulum because it's not going to be plumb.

Thomas's reflection is noteworthy for its mixed metaphors. Worship is both a tightrope and a pendulum, taut yet loose, stable yet swinging. Evangelical worship lives, moves, and has its being within such paradoxes.

Thomas's words illustrate that although theology is primarily *logoi* (words) about *theos* (divinity), human language inevitably breaks down in its attempts to express divine mysteries. God's love is beyond all formulas and calculations that would seek to control its limits. This awareness of the finitude of human speech and thought—what theologians call the apophatic dimension of Christian faith—is a guardrail that prevents worship from drifting into legalism and idolatry. It is also an invitation to awe: a recognition that no matter how many words we use to glorify God, there will always be more to say.

Because the gospel proclamation of the crucified and resurrected Christ forever runs ahead of all human attempts to contain or codify it, the glue is not yet dry on the work-in-progress that is the church. When congregations gather in the presence of the living God, they are dislocated and re-established, changed into something they were not before the event began. As the seven case studies in this volume have shown, corporate worship is not a peripheral "extra" tacked on to a fully formed spiritual/political/cultural movement, but rather the crucible in which congregations forge, debate over, and enact their unique contributions to the American mosaic known as evangelicalism.

Research Methods

My decision to study evangelical worship ethnographically is based on Mary McGann's observation that ethnography is "uniquely suited to probing the cultural particularity of specific communities, the deep structures of thought and feeling that shape their practice and by which they interpret their defining encounter with the living God in Jesus Christ."[1] McGann, adjunct associate professor of liturgical studies at the Jesuit School of Theology (Santa Clara University) and the Graduate Theological Union, Berkeley, California, was the first scholar to use the term "liturgical ethnography."[2] Liturgical ethnography, she explains, is a method of study that can be traced to the fourth-century pilgrim Egeria, who created a descriptive travel-diary of her pilgrimage to the Holy Land for the community from which she came.[3] Writing in 2004, McGann observed that "scholars have yet to formulate models for such liturgical ethnography—forms that remain faithful to the complex, ambiguous modes of a community's ritual action and true to the polyvocality of local interpretations."[4] McGann's award-winning book, *A Precious Fountain: Music in the Worship of an African American Catholic Community*, was a pioneer in the genre.[5]

More than fifteen years later, McGann's call for liturgical scholars to engage in ethnographic research has gone almost entirely unheeded.[6] *Evangelical Worship* takes it up, and does so from a unique reflexive location. Most contemporary ethnographers who set out to study evangelical culture enter the field from one of two perspectives. On one hand, the researcher may be someone like James White: an individual who is not familiar with, or even sympathetic to, evangelical worship. White celebrated communion every Sunday at a United Methodist service that he described as "little different from a lively Catholic Mass except that we use real bread and they use real wine." However, White worried that his chosen form of worship was being threatened: "The majority of American Protestant worship does not even use a service book and looks at liturgical law as an oxymoron with sinister connotations. I am not at all optimistic that the majority tradition in this country will ever find congenial what . . . I prefer."[7] To his credit, White's commitment to telling a robust liturgical history meant treating Protestant worship in *all* of its contemporary expressions, including the ones he found distasteful: "If the Willow Creek mega-church type of worship survives, one must concede it value, little though I appreciate it at present."[8] However, the tension between White's own liturgical preferences and his appreciation for the varieties of Protestantism was a perpetual one, and it shaped the way he wrote about the frontier tradition.[9]

On the other hand, the ethnographer may be an individual who grew up as an evangelical "insider" but now rejects (or feels strong equivocation about) claiming the label *evangelical* as an adult. The following statements by ethnographic researchers are representative: "A series of personal circumstances, including impatience with a political agenda that I found now, as then, reprehensible, prompted my withdrawal from the evangelical subculture in the late 1970s . . . the reader will early on detect my own ambivalence toward the subculture and all it represents."[10] "[I was a] self-identified former evangelical who couldn't quite shake all the ways that tradition's traces remain in [me]—both for ill and for good."[11] "When I first began explaining to friends why my research had come to focus on a fundamentalist Baptist church . . . I found myself adding wryly that it was . . . because it harbored 'ghosts of my past,' as I sometimes put it."[12]

As ecclesiologist and ecumenist Paul Avis rightly stresses, anyone is free to study Christianity ethnographically.[13] Scholarship written by those with little or no involvement in evangelicalism holds up a mirror to those closer to the movement, revealing warts that they might otherwise be unable (or unwilling) to see. We also need the perspective of those who have a love-hate relationship with evangelicalism. Avis notes that there many Christians, including theologians, who have been hurt or damaged by "the church." The temptation is "to hit back, to allow oneself to be driven by (understandable) negative impulses, so that destructive, hyper-critical elements creep in to the work." Instead, Avis encourages these scholars to contribute as "wounded healers," offering their contribution "in an irenic and constructive spirit as far as is humanly possible, but without being bland and the ecclesiastical equivalent of politically correct."[14]

Finally, Avis points out a third kind of ethnographer. Neither adversarial nor ambivalent, she is happily committed to her tradition and writes from within it:

> It does make a difference to our approach if we see ourselves as working within the church and for the church. Karl Rahner spoke of doing theology "in the bosom of the church," but that imagery sounds a little quaint today. However, it remains true that it makes a huge difference if one loves the church—and one's own particular branch of it too, though without arrogance, triumphalism, invidious comparisons, or even complacency. Christians sometimes need to be given permission to love the church in spite of all its deficiencies and therefore to serve it (or rather to serve God in and through it) willingly and gladly. Then the work of ecclesiology becomes not a chore, but a joy and privilege—we may say a calling, a vocation.[15]

I write from within this third category: as someone who loves (not uncritically) the Christian church, and my own particular evangelical branch of it. This commitment to studying evangelicalism from within affects my ethnography in at least four significant ways. *Evangelical Worship* is marked by a predisposition toward hope, an assumption of evangelicalism's underlying unity, a prioritization of the voices of pastors and worship leaders, and an emphasis on homiletics and music.

Predisposition toward Hope

Ecclesiological ethnographers have critiqued theologians who rely on a "Rolls-Royce conception of the church." Avis explains that, "cosseted by the luxury of dreams and fantasies about the church," these ecclesiologies "glide smoothly on, oblivious to the faults and failings that compromise its witness, and to the sins and crimes that are being committed in its name."[16] What is needed, ethnographers argue, is a bit of "*negative ecclesiology*, church theology in a minor key."[17] Avis refers to this as the challenge of "ecclesial theodicy," which he defines as "the problem of explaining (without excusing) evil in the Church, the problem of the Church gone wrong." The task of ecclesial theodicy is to attempt to defend or justify the Christian claim that God owns and uses the church—"a body for which the word 'imperfect' is seriously, even ludicrously, understating the matter."[18]

In response to this challenge, theologians now take the historical, social, cultural, economic, and political dimensions of the church seriously. Their accounts are informed by ideological critique: What about all those who have been tortured and killed in the name of the Christian faith? Or the relative silence of the European churches in the 1930s and 1940s—Protestant, Catholic, and Orthodox alike—concerning the evils of fascism? Or contemporary charges of pedophilia in the ranks of the clergy?[19] An ethnographic study written in the key of ecclesial theodicy might query how the rituals of Sunday morning contribute to evangelicals' captivity to a particular brand of politics, or to the idolatries of white supremacy and American free-market capitalism.

This study acknowledges the other side of the coin: that the ludicrously imperfect church belongs to the structure of faith itself. Before all else, the church is something biblical and credal—something that "we believe." John Webster makes a helpful distinction between the phenomenon of the church (its historical and social aspects) and the being of the church (which can only be understood in relation to the doctrine of God). The former is accessible for empirical study; the latter is not.[20] To believe in that which all too often seems an impediment to faith requires that there be more to the church than meets the eye.[21]

In saying this, I am going a step beyond James White's rather grudging admission that "if something survives in worship, presumably the Spirit uses it and it has value."[22] Instead, I write from the perspective of Christian hope, which dictates that "in all its dissipation, complexity and misery, human history is by the mercy of God on the way to perfection."[23] The observable phenomena of evangelical worship are signs of a joyous deeper reality that will, ultimately, always be a mystery beyond historical or social scientific inquiry.

Assumption of Underlying Unity

One of the persistent tensions within ecclesiological ethnography is the gap between the "the church" (universal) and "churches" (the particular).[24] As theologian Clare Watkins notes, "ethnographic studies of the church are, by their very nature, particular, detailed, contextual; doctrine is, of its nature, tending towards universal, abstract articulation."[25] Subsequently, scholars tend to fall into two camps. One side is committed to speaking doctrinally and normatively about the church, while the other is committed to studying the complex actualities of specific communities.

The dilemma comes when scholars try to move from granular description to universal principles. Systematic theologian Nicholas Healy stresses that ecclesial ethnographers should not expect coherency and consistence among the members of any particular congregation given that "most of us disagree with ourselves, holding beliefs or engaging in practices that are in tension or conflict with others we also believe and practice."[26] This inconsistency extends to the study of congregations: even if most members seem to hold certain beliefs in common, there will always be individuals who disagree with the majority, sometimes in surprising and counterintuitive ways. The problem is compounded exponentially when scholars try to construct a systematic framework of the global church's faith.

This book will not resolve the tension between "the church" and "churches." I do, however, propose a more nuanced way forward with a three-tiered conceptual schema. Here I follow John Keane, an influential political theorist, who writes about a "complex mosaic of differently sized, overlapping and interconnected public spheres." Keane divides "public life" into three categories: macro, meso, and micro public spheres, which intersect and permeate each other. *Macro public spheres* involve billions of people and have a global, supranational character (think of international media conglomerates and the internet). *Meso public spheres* involve millions of people who share a common language and who interact with the same media on a variety of topics of mutual concern (for example, American listeners of National Public Radio, or the audiences who tune into Fox News). Finally, *micro public spheres* are "bottom-up, small scale" public spheres that consist of "dozens, hundreds, or thousands of people" (such as a townhall meeting, Rotary club gathering, or political chat over a drink with a group of friends).

Generally speaking, ecclesiological ethnographers talk about *church* at the macro level (the universal church, with members across the world) and at the micro level (local, particular congregations). The meso level between these two extremes remains undertheorized. Church at the meso level might include denominational groupings: for instance, the United Methodist Church, the Evangelical Lutheran Church of America, or the Episcopal Church. A meso-level understanding of church also includes less formal, more loosely defined entities: for example, "the mainline church," "the African American church," or—most importantly for our purposes—"the evangelical church."

One advantage of distinguishing between macro, meso, and micro public spheres is that it allows for a nuanced discussion of the relationships between them. From the perspective of political theory, Keane points out that meso-publics produce and circulate media to millions of people through powerful, well-established distribution structures; they thrive by appealing to particular national or regional groupings. Meso-publics feed off of micro-publics, and vice versa: "Readers of national newspapers, for instance, may and do consult locally produced magazines or bulletins, precisely because of their different themes and emphases."[27] A similar dynamic is operative in the study of evangelical worship. Evangelicals produce meso-public resources like *Christianity Today*, *Leadership Journal*, and *Worship Leader Magazine*, which circulate to millions of theologically likeminded readers in print and online. A church leader might consult these resources when planning services, but he or she would also draw on micro-public sources of knowledge closer to home (i.e., the teaching pastor, the worship-planning committee, the talented songwriter in the congregation) for local ideas and perspectives. Micro public spheres (including congregations) are "local laboratories" where participants test, develop, mix, and remix a diversity of opinions and reactions.[28]

An ethnographer who focuses on Christian identity in a meso public sphere need not deny the rich diversity of individual (micro-public) congregations. As noted previously, churches within the same denomination—even the same town—often differ substantially. Healy points to a study by Jerome Baggett that describes differences among six Roman Catholic parishes in the San Francisco Bay region:

> One is a largely gay congregation, another is centered on the Latin Mass; one is oriented toward supporting suburban families, another is mostly Latino, and so on. Certainly all six share some characteristics, but each congregation's life, language, and what it does indicate *a substantially different understanding of Christianity* from the other five. The beliefs, practices, and attitudes of the six congregations are not sufficiently held in common or "shared" such that together they form a single community, as in, say, "the Bay Area Roman Catholic community."[29]

Similarly, the seven congregations featured in this book are recognizably distinct from one another. But to suggest that each congregation's understanding of Christianity is "substantially different" from the other six is going a step too far. To understand this point, consider a cartographic analogy. Theologian Kevin Vanhoozer notes that a plurality of maps—historical, topographical, geological, political—can describe the same reality without sharing a conceptual framework. To be reliable, these maps must "ultimately correspond with this or that aspect of what is really there" without contradicting one another. In the same way, each congregation in this study draws a "map" of evangelical faith that is strikingly different from the other six. While all seven congregations have unique theological frameworks, they are nevertheless compatible with one another. Local (micropublic) worship is both the site where these unifying theological truths are proclaimed and celebrated, and the place where individual congregations carve out their second- and third-level doctrinal positions in ongoing (meso-public) conversation with other evangelical churches across the United States.

Emphasis on Music and Homiletics

I have made the methodological decision to focus my analysis primarily on evangelical music and sermons. Liturgical scholars are rightly fascinated by the complex interplay of *all* the elements of a service: sound, movement, gesture, dress, gendered and racial dynamics, structures of authority, socioeconomic class, architectural space, and light and color, to cite just a few. In particular, my colleagues in liturgical studies may be startled to notice that sacraments are not among my analytic priorities. The reason for this intentional omission is twofold.

Scholars who undertake richly complex ethnographic projects tend to remain in a single community for a number of months, if not years. (Two examples are McGann's liturgical ethnography of the Our Lady of Lourdes community, which involved five years of focused research, and Mary McClintock Fulkerson's study of Good Samaritan United Methodist Church, which involved two and a half years of interviews and participant observation.)[30] The duration of my studies was considerably shorter—I spent two weeks at each site—which required limiting the scope of my investigation.

More importantly, however, this study is written in conversation with James F. White's work, and music and preaching were the two elements of corporate worship that White correctly identified as most important to evangelicals. In his lifetime, White was an anomaly in the liturgical studies guild for arguing that scholars who held to a "normative" *ordo* for all Christian traditions—one that included a weekly celebration of the Lord's Supper—were ignoring the worship practices of a significant number of churches. "We face a basic problem in ignoring the worship of most North American Christians. . . . In trying to marginalize the worship life of so many millions, we have violated one of the basic motifs of *lex orandi*." White believed that respecting the varieties of Protestant worship might "change significantly the way liturgical theology is done."[31]

White's point about studying evangelicalism on its own (non-Eucharistic) terms was a vital one. Unfortunately, scholars writing after White have not followed his recommendation, evidenced by Alan Rathe's observation of a "rift" between "rank-and-file evangelicals and their scholars." In his extensive survey of evangelical worship literature, Rathe discovered that scholars continue to be disproportionately interested in sacraments—even though contemporary evangelical worship is largely non-sacramental. While the sacramentally minded scholars may represent the cutting edge of evangelical thinking, Rathe believes the more likely possibility is that academics are "riding on a train of thought that runs on a perpetually parallel track—one that will not intersect with popular evangelical thought unless something unexpected happens."[32] *Evangelical Worship* is that "something unexpected." It takes popular faith seriously, acknowledging that "good music" and "good preaching" are the things that evangelicals value most in corporate worship.

Prioritization of Church Leaders

In his influential book *Church, World and the Christian Life*, Healy argues that researchers who undertake congregational ethnographies must be especially sensitive to those members of the church who are not theological specialists: people who do not have the theoretical apparatus to share their insights, but who may well "have clearer insights into [the church's] sinfulness and inadequacies, into the challenges it faces, and perhaps as to how it should be reformed."[33] Healy thus advocates for an emancipatory ecclesiology: one in which theologians actively give voices to marginalized groups in the church.[34] Following Healy, a scholar committed to the principles of postmodern ethnography might approach the study of evangelical worship by focusing on places where congregants' "everyday" theologies are in tension with the church's "official" theology, since ethnography benefits from as inclusive a theological assessment of the church body as possible.[35]

In *Evangelical Worship*, however, I have chosen to prioritize the voices of pastors and worship leaders. I do so because, ironically, it is their voices that have been marginalized in liturgical scholarship. For example, pastor Glenn Packiam speaks for many when he that argues that today's so-called liturgical experts are not listening to evangelical leaders well enough:

> If one wants to prove the shallowness of modern worship, examples abound; but if you want to really understand and assess the subject, you need a more careful eye. And you must account for an insider perspective. What matters is not simply what the outside observer/blogger/professor *thinks* is going on; what matters is also what the pastor or worship leader *says* is going on, and what the worshipper is *experiencing*. . . . If all we get are theoretical assessments from afar, we will evaluate modern worship without knowing if we are actually evaluating modern worship or our impression of it—which is almost always a caricature.[36]

Packiam's observations ring true: too many descriptions of evangelical worship are written by outsiders on the basis of isolated visits or secondhand reports. By contrast, I draw on the wisdom of the formal and informal leaders of the churches that I studied, who typically have long institutional memories and nuanced understandings of the communities in which they minister. Deep liturgical ethnography, like the kind undertaken in this book, contextualizes the community's worship within the larger rhythms of its life and faith, and within the historical, cultural, and social forces that have shaped its practice.

Demographic Information

With the exception of Moody Church (whose demographic information comes from a Lifeway Research Group survey undertaken in 2017), all racial composition statistics are rough estimates reported to the author by church leadership.

Park Street Church

Location: Boston, MA
Established: 1809
Average weekly attendance: approximately 900
Racial composition: approximately 5 percent African American, 5 percent Latino, 25 percent Asian, 65 percent Caucasian

Moody Church

Location: Chicago, IL
Established: 1864
Average weekly attendance: approximately 2,000
Racial composition: 57 percent European-American/white, 17 percent African American/black, 13 percent Asian, 7 percent Hispanic, and 6 percent other ethnic groups

North Point Community Church

Location: Alpharetta, GA
Established: 1995
Average weekly attendance: 40,455 across seven campuses
Racial composition: predominantly Caucasian

Koinonia Vineyard (pseudonym)

Location: Pacific Northwest
Established: 1987
Average weekly attendance: fewer than 100
Racial composition: predominantly Caucasian

Wayfarers Collective (pseudonym)

Location: near Portland, OR
Established: 2004
Average weekly attendance: approximately 250
Racial composition: predominantly Caucasian.

The Village Chapel

Location: Nashville, TN
Established: 2001
Average weekly attendance: approximately 1,100, across two campuses
Racial composition: predominantly Caucasian, with growing racial diversity that falls in
    line with the surrounding area

Holy Inheritance (pseudonym)

Location: Southwest
Established: 1970
Average weekly attendance: approximately 1,000
Racial composition: approximately 40 percent Caucasian (non-Hispanic), 30 percent
    Hispanic, 20 percent African American, 10 percent other

Notes

Introduction

1. Beth Moore, "Next Year in Church," Twitter, April 13, 2020, https://twitter.com/BethMooreLPM/status/1249521153833676800.
2. Kevin Breuninger, "Trump Wants 'Packed Churches' and Economy Open Again on Easter Despite the Deadly Threat of Coronavirus," CNBC, March 24, 2020, https://www.cnbc.com/2020/03/24/coronavirus-response-trump-wants-to-reopen-us-economy-by-easter.html.
3. Daniel Harrell, "An Easter without Going to Church," *Christianity Today*, March 25, 2020, https://www.christianitytoday.com/ct/2020/march-web-only/easter-without-church-covid-19-coronavirus.html.
4. Ruth Marcus, "Opinion: Next Year, May We Be Together," *Washington Post*, April 7, 2020, https://www.washingtonpost.com/opinions/2020/04/03/next-year-may-we-be-together/.
5. Donald S. Whitney, *Spiritual Disciplines for the Christian Life* (Colorado Springs, CO: NavPress, 1997), 92.
6. D. W. Beddington, *Evangelicalism in Modern Britain: A History from the 1730's to the 1980's* (London: Routledge, 1996), 1–19.
7. Michael S. Hamilton, "A Strange Love? Or: How White Evangelicals Learned to Stop Worrying and Love the Donald," in *Evangelicals: Who They Have Been, Are Now, and Could Be*, ed. Mark A. Noll, D. W. Bebbington, and G. M. Marsden (Grand Rapids, MI: Eerdmans, 2019), 218.
8. Molly Worthen, "How to Escape from Roy Moore's Evangelicalism," *New York Times*, November 17, 2017, https://www.nytimes.com/2017/11/17/opinion/sunday/escape-roy-moores-evangelicalism.html.
9. Kristin Kobes Du Mez, *Jesus and John Wayne: How White Evangelicals Corrupted a Faith and Fractured a Nation* (New York: Liveright, 2020), 8.
10. Kevin W. Irwin, *Context and Text: A Method for Liturgical Theology* (Collegeville, MN: Liturgical Press, 2018), 558.
11. Park Street Church, Moody Church, and North Point Community Church are flagship congregations in evangelical history. The Village Chapel is less well known, but the internationally recognized musicians I discuss in this chapter have publicly named it as their home church.
12. Wayfarers Collective, Koinonia Vineyard, and Holy Inheritance are pseudonyms.
13. "About the Institute," Rural Matters Institute, May 10, 2019, www.bgcruralmatters.com/home/.
14. Wayfarers Collective, as I explain in Chapter 5, is a little more complicated.

15. See Bahar Rumelili and Jennifer Todd, "Paradoxes of Identity Change: Integrating Macro, Meso, and Micro Research on Identity in Conflict Processes," *Politics 38*, no. 1 (2018), 3–18.

Chapter 1

1. The names of "Warren" and "Pastor Timothy" have been changed to protect anonymity. Some quotations have been lightly edited for clarity and/or to obscure identifying details.
2. Christopher Ellis, Tony E. Adams, and Arthur P. Bochner, "Autoethnography: An Overview," *Historical Social Research / Historische Sozialforschung* 36, no. 4 (2011), 273.
3. Christopher Ellis, Tony E. Adams, and Arthur P. Bochner, "Autoethnography: An Overview," *Historical Social Research / Historische Sozialforschung* 36, no. 4 (2011), 274.
4. Natalie Wigg-Stevenson, "You Don't Look Like a Baptist Minister: An Autoethnographic Retrieval of 'Women's Experience' as an Analytic Category for Feminist Theology," *Feminist Theology* 25, no. 2 (2017), 185.
5. Martin D. Stringer, *On the Perception of Worship* (Birmingham: University of Birmingham Press, 1999).
6. Carolyn Ellis and Arthur P. Bochner, "Autoethnography, Personal Narrative, Reflexivity," in *The Handbook of Qualitative Research*, ed. Norman K. Denzin and Yvonna S. Lincoln (Thousand Oaks, CA: Sage Publications, 2000), 739.
7. Ellis and Bochner, "Autoethnography, Personal Narrative," 744.
8. Bob Gersztyn, *Jesus Rocks the World* (Santa Barbara, CA: Praeger, 2012), 49.
9. Gersztyn, *Jesus Rocks the World*, 52.
10. James I. Elliot, "Maranatha! Music," in *Encylopedia of American Gospel Music*, ed. W. K. McNeil (New York: Routledge, 2005), 240.
11. Paul Baker, *Why Should the Devil Have All the Good Music* (Waco, TX: Word Books, 1979), 35.
12. See Wen Reagan, "A Beautiful Noise: A History of Contemporary Worship Music in Modern America" (PhD diss., Duke University, 2015), 189.
13. Baker, *Why Should the Devil*, 40.
14. See Tom Wolfe, "The Me Decade and the Third Great Awakening," *New York Magazine* 23, no. 8 (1976), 26–40.
15. Anna Garvey, "The Oregon Trail Generation: Life before and after Mainstream Tech," *Social Media Week*, Crowdcentric Media, April 21, 2015, https://socialmediaweek. org/blog/2015/04/oregon-trail-generation/.
16. Garvey, "Oregon Trail Generation."
17. "Input, Output (The Computer Song)," by Kathie Hill and Gary McSpadden, copyright © 1996 Ariose Music (ASCAP) Universal Music—Brentwood Benson Publ. (ASCAP) (adm. at CapitolCMGPublishing.com). All rights reserved. Used by permission.

18. Tom Fettke, "Preface," *The Hymnal for Worship and Celebration* (Waco, TX: Word Music, 1986).

19. Gerard L. DeMatto, "The Hymnal for Worship and Celebration," *Journal of the Evangelical Theological Society* 32, no. 2 (June 1989), 248.

20. DeMatto, "Hymnal for Worship."

21. Bert Polman, "The Hymnal for Worship and Celebration," *The Hymn* 38, no. 3 (July 1987), 38.

22. Don Cusic, *The Sound of Light* (New York: Hal Leonard, 2002), 382.

23. Quoted in Andrew Mall, "The Stars Are Underground: Undergrounds, Mainstreams, and Christian Popular Music" (PhD diss., University of Chicago, 2012), 194.

24. Don Cason, interview by the author, March 12, 2015.

25. Quoted in Stan Moser, "'We Have Created a Monster,'" *Christianity Today*, May 20, 1996, 25.

26. Lyle Schaller, interview, "Lyle Schaller on the Contemporary Worship Movement," *Worship Leader* 4, no. 4 (July–August 1995), 34–35.

27. John Styll, "The Christian Music Industry: Under New Ownership," *Worship Leader* 4, no. 4 (July–August 1995), 29.

28. Styll, "Christian Music Industry," 30.

29. Styll, "Christian Music Industry," 30.

30. Styll, "Christian Music Industry," 30.

31. Styll, "Christian Music Industry," 30.

32. Deborah Evans Price, "Worship Music Targets Youth," *Billboard*, May 1, 1999.

33. Deborah Evans Price, "Start-Up Labels Respond," *Billboard*, May 1, 1999.

34. Price, "Start-Up Labels Respond."

35. Price, "Worship Music Targets Youth."

36. Monique Ingalls, "Transnational Connections, Musical Meaning, and the 1990s 'British Invasion' of North American Evangelical Worship Music," in *The Oxford Handbook of Music and World Christianities*, ed. Suzel Ana Reily and Jonathan Dueck (New York: Oxford University Press, 2016), 432.

37. Ingalls, "Translational Connections," 431.

38. Ingalls, "Transnational Connections."

39. Greg Scheer, unpublished manuscript, 2006, "Praise and Worship from Jesus People to Gen X," 16, 23. Cited in Robert Woods, *The Message in the Music: Studying Contemporary Praise and Worship* (Nashville, TN: Abingdon Press, 2007), 163.

40. See Scheer, "Praise and Worship," 189.

41. The phrase "personality-driven praise and worship" comes from Deborah Evans Price, "'Praise and Worship' Music Extending Its Retail, Radio Reach," *Billboard*, December 5, 1998, 118.

42. See Reagan, "A Beautiful Noise," 182.

43. Price, "Music Extending Its Reach," 118.

44. Price, "Music Extending Its Reach," 118.

45. Geoff Twigg was founding editor of *Guitarist* magazine, was a consultant at Music Maker Publications, and served as music adviser to the bishop of Ely, England. He

also worked as a freelance musician, worship leader, and adjunct professor. He was trained under and worked for renowned British composer John Tavener.

46. Monique M. Ingalls, *Singing the Congregation: How Contemporary Worship Music Forms Evangelical Community* (New York: Oxford University Press, 2018), 85.

47. Harold Best, *Music through the Eyes of Faith* (New York: Harper Collins, 1993), 1999.

48. Some writers who emphasize historic continuity, tradition, high culture, and theological exposition in worship are Marva Dawn, *Reaching Out without Dumbing Down* (Grand Rapids, MI: Eerdmans, 1995); and David Wells, "A Tale of Two Spiritualities," in *Losing Our Virtue* (Grand Rapids, MI: Eerdmans, 1998).

49. Ken Myers, *All God's Children and Blue Suede Shoes* (Wheaton, IL: Crossway Books, 2012), 77.

50. Myers, *All God's Children*, 98.

51. Myers, *All God's Children*, 77.

52. Myers, *All God's Children*, 99.

53. David Di Sabatino, "Boundary Crossing: How CCM Is Seeking to Find the Heart of Worship," *Worship Leader* 11, no. 8 (November–December 2002).

54. Sabatino, "Boundary Crossing," 12.

55. Davin Seay, "Worshipping in the Marketplace: What Is Worship Worth?," *Worship Leader* 12, no. 5 (July–August 2003), 17.

56. Anna E. Nekola, "Negotiating the Tensions of U.S. Worship Music in the Marketplace," in Reily and Dueck, *Oxford Handbook of Music*, 520.

57. Seay, "Worshipping in the Marketplace," 17.

58. Quoted in Bob Liparulo, "The United State of Worship," *Today's Christian*, July–August 2003, https://web.archive.org/web/20040222091623/http://www.christianitytoday.com/tc/2003/004/8.20.html.

59. Quoted in "The Call to Worship: The Movers and Shakers of the Contemporary Worship Movement Speak Out," *Worship Leader* 11, no. 8 (November–December 2002), 24.

60. Quoted in Seay, "Worshipping in the Marketplace," 17.

61. Robert H. Woods, "Praising God with Popular Worship Music," in *Understanding Evangelical Media: The Changing Face of Christian Communication*, ed. Quentin Schultze and Robert Woods (Downers Grove, IL: InterVarsity Press, 2008), 132.

62. Russ Breimeier, "Worship as an Afterthought?," *Christianity Today*, March 22, 2006, http://web.archive.org/web/20060322144421/https://www.christianitytoday.com/lyris/music/archives/.

63. Lillie Cottrell, "Worship Music Overkill?," *Christianity Today*, March 20, 2006, http://www.christianitytoday.com/ct/2006/marchweb-only/worshipmusicoverkill.html?paging=off.

64. Cottrell, "Worship Music Overkill."

65. Seay, "Worshipping in the Marketplace," 17.

66. Twila Paris, "Table Talk: Twila Paris," *Worship Leader* 11, no. 2 (March–April 2002), 14–15.

67. Cited in Anna E. Nekola, "'I'll Take You There': The Promise of Transformation in the Marketing of Worship Media in US Christian Music Magazines," in *Christian*

Congregational Music: Performance, Identity and Experience, ed. Monique Ingalls et al. (Farnham, UK: Ashgate, 2013), 127.

68. Nekola, "I'll Take You There," 127.

69. Nekola, "I'll Take You There," 127.

70. For more on "Becky," see Michael Gungor, *The Crowd, the Critic, and the Muse: A Book for Creators* (Denver, CO: Woodsley Press, 2012), Appendix 2.

71. Dave Perkins, "Music, Culture Industry, and the Shaping of Charismatic Worship: An Autobiographical/Conversational Engagement," in *The Spirit of Praise: Music and Worship in Global Pentecostal-Charismatic Christianity*, ed. Monique Ingalls and Amos Yong (University Park: Pennsylvania State University Press, 2015), 239.

72. Perkins, "Music, Culture Industry," 239.

73. Brant Hansen, "I'm a Christian Radio Host: Our Music Isn't High Art—but It's Just What People Want," *Washington Post*, July 14, 2016, https://www.washingtonpost.com/news/acts-of-faith/wp/2016/07/14/im-a-christian-radio-host-our-music-isnt-high-art-but-its-just-what-people-want/.

74. Donald P. Hustad, "George Beverly Shea, CCM, and the Church," *Worship Leader* 4, no. 4 (July–August 1995), 38.

75. Gungor, *The Crowd*, 204.

76. Carlton Young, "Church Music, American Style: What's Ahead?," *Christian Ministry*, March 1977, 8. Quoted in Larry Eskridge, *God's Forever Family: The Jesus People Movement in America* (New York: Oxford University Press, 2013), 268.

77. Stephen Miller, *Worship Leaders: We Are Not Rock Stars* (Chicago: Moody Press, 2013).

78. Zac M. Hicks, *The Worship Pastor: A Call to Ministry for Worship Leaders and Teams* (Grand Rapids, MI: Zondervan, 2016).

79. David Talley, "The Worship Pastor: An Interview with Zac Hicks," *Good Book Blog*, February 22, 2017, http://www.thegoodbookblog.com/2017/feb/22/the-worship-pastor/.

80. Sheila Wray Gregoire, "My 7 Pet Peeves about Worship Music in Church," *To Love, Honor, and Vacuum*, April 30, 2012, http://tolovehonorandvacuum.com/2012/04/my-7-pet-peeves-about-worship-music-in-church/.

81. Bob Kauflin, "Is It Biblical for a Woman to Lead Worship?," *Worship Matters*, March 2, 2007, https://worshipmatters.com/2007/03/02/is-it-biblical-for-a-woman-to-lead-in-worship-prayer/.

82. Kauflin, "Is It Biblical."

83. Zac Hicks, "Worship Leading, Ageism, and the Fear of Getting Old (Repost)," *Zac Hicks*, July 24, 2014, http://www.zachicks.com/worship-leading-ageism-and-the-fear-of-getting-old-repost/.

84. Manuel Luz, "The Issue of Age in Modern Worship," *Adventures in Faith & Art*, January 6, 2014, https://manuelluz.wordpress.com/2014/01/06/the-issue-of-age-in-modern-worship/.

85. Hicks, "Worship Leading, Ageism."

86. I thank our faithful Blue Russian, Shelby, for inspiring this analogy. In fairness to her memory, it should be noted that Shelby never bit in anger, but only gnawed gently on the humans she most loved.

87. Stephen Miller, "The Modern Worship Music Wars," *Relevant*, August 29, 2013, https://relevantmagazine.com/god/church/modern-worship-music-wars. Note that I am not taking aim at Miller in particular. Variations of this line of argument are commonly rehearsed in evangelical circles. I cite Miller's work because it is a particularly eloquent example.

88. "Modern Worship Music Wars."

89. "Modern Worship Music Wars."

90. "Modern Worship Music Wars."

91. Mark Chaves and Alison Eagle, *Religious Congregations in 21st Century America: National Congregations Study*, 2015, Durham: Duke University, http://www.soc.duke.edu/natcong/Docs/NCSIII_report_final.pdf.

92. "In 2006, 48% of congregations with more than one service reported important difference between those services, but only 30% reported such differences in 2012." Chaves and Eagle, *Religious Congregations*.

93. Chaves and Eagle, *Religious Congregations*.

94. Josh Kun, *Audiotopia: Music, Race, and America* (Berkeley: University of California Press, 2005), 3.

95. Kun, *Audiotopia*, 2.

96. Kun, *Audiotopia*, 3.

97. Kun, *Audiotopia*, 3.

98. Kun, *Audiotopia*, 13.

99. Mark A. Noll, "The Defining Role of Hymns in Early Evangelicalism," in *Wonderful Words of Life: Hymns in American Protestant History and Theology*, ed. Richard J. Mouw and Mark A. Noll (Grand Rapids, MI: Eerdmans, 2004), 4.

100. Vinita Hampton Wright, *Velma Still Cooks in Leeway* (Nashville, TN: Broadman & Holman, 2000), 81.

101. For more on the "modern hymns" of Keith and Kristyn Getty, see Chapter 7.

102. See Lester Ruth and Swee Hong Lim, *Lovin' on Jesus: A Concise History of Contemporary Worship* (Nashville, TN: Abingdon Press, 2017), 11–14.

Chapter 2

1. Henry James, *The American Scene* (New York: Harper & Bros., 1907), 231.

2. H. Crosby Englizian, *Brimstone Corner: Park Street Church, Boston* (Chicago: Moody Press, 1968), 55 n. 1.

3. Rich Barlow, "Park St. Church Taking a Year to Make the Most of Its 200th," *boston.com*, March 8, 2009, http://archive.boston.com/news/local/articles/2009/03/08/park_st_church_taking_a_year_to_make_the_most_of_its_200th/.

4. For more information, see Garth M. Rosell, *Boston's Historic Park Street Church: The Story of an Evangelical Landmark* (Grand Rapids, MI: Kregel Publications, 2009), 118–20.

5. Elizabeth Lohnes, "Park Street Church—a History," Park Street Church, October 2016, https://www.parkstreet.org/profile/history.pdf, 1.

6. Lohnes, "Park Street Church," 1.

7. Cited in Margaret Lamberts Bendroth, *Fundamentalists in the City: Conflict and Division in Boston's Churches, 1885–1950* (New York: Oxford University Press, 2005), 156.

8. Lohnes, "Park Street Church," 1.

9. "'The Unique and Unparalleled Position of Park Street Church in Boston's Religious History,' by Harold John Ockenga, Preached at Park Street Church, Boston, Mass.," (n.p., n.d.), 22. Cited in Lohnes, "Park Street Church," 174.

10. Rosell, *Boston's Historic Park Street Church*, 102.

11. Cited in Bendroth, *Fundamentalists in the City*, 163.

12. Cited in Owen Strachan, *Awakening the Evangelical Mind* (Grand Rapids, MI: Zondervan, 2015), 54.

13. Bendroth, *Fundamentalists in the City*, 164.

14. Curtis Lee Laws, "Convention Side Lights," *The Watchman-Examiner*, July 1, 1920, 834–35.

15. Bendroth, *Fundamentalists in the City*, 165.

16. Englizian, *Brimstone Corner*, 221.

17. Englizian, *Brimstone Corner*.

18. Bendroth, *Fundamentalists in the City*, 145.

19. Englizian, *Brimstone Corner*, 221.

20. A. Z. Conrad, *The Seven Finalities of Faith* (Philadelphia: Sunday School Times, 1926), 86.

21. A. Z. Conrad, *The Gospel for an Age of Thought* (Chicago: Fleming H. Revell, 1928), 26. See George W. Harper, "'It Is a Battle-Royal': A. Z. Conrad's Preaching at Boston's Park Street Church during the Fundamentalist-Modernist Controversy," *Fides et Historia* 45, no. 1 (2013), 40.

22. Harper, "Battle-Royal," 41.

23. Cited in Garth M. Rosell, *The Surprising Work of God: Harold John Ockenga, Billy Graham, and the Rebirth of Evangelicalism* (Grand Rapids, MI: Baker Academic, 2008), 54.

24. See Harper, "Battle-Royal," 31.

25. Cited in Rosell, *Surprising Work of God*, 56.

26. Cited in Rosell, *Surprising Work of God*, 58.

27. See Joel A. Carpenter, *Revive Us Again: The Reawakening of American Fundamentalism: The Reawakening of American Fundamentalism* (New York: Oxford University Press, 1997), 142–43.

28. This description comes from the only published account of Wright's work in the New England Fellowship: Muriel Wright Evans and Elizabeth M. Evans, *Incidents and Information of the First 48 Years: Rumney Conference's 75th Anniversary* (Rumney, NH: n.p., 1978). See also Carpenter, *Revive Us Again*, 143.

29. Elizabeth Evans, *The Wright Vision: The Story of the New England Fellowship* (Lanham, MD: University Press of America, 1991), 54.

30. See Bendroth, *Fundamentalists in the City*, 170.

31. Bendroth, *Fundamentalists in the City*, 172.

32. Cited in Arthur H. Matthews, *Standing Up, Standing Together: The Emergence of the National Association of Evangelicals* (Carol Stream, IL: National Association of Evangelicals, 1992), 28.

33. Cited in Donald Dayton, "The Pietist Theological Critique of Biblical Inerrancy," in *Evangelicals and Scripture: Tradition, Authority, and Hermeneutics*, ed. Vincent Bacote, Laura C. Miguelez, and Dennis L. Okholm (Downers Grove, IL: InterVarsity Press, 2004), 76.

34. See Rosell, *Boston's Historic Park Street Church*, 139.

35. Harold Ockenga, "Boston at the Crossroads," sermon preached on May 21, 1950, at Park Street Church, Park Street Church Papers, Congregational Library, Boston, Massachusetts. Cited in Strachan, *Awakening the Evangelical Mind*, 59.

36. Ockenga received his bachelor's degree from Taylor University in Indiana and his master's and doctorate degrees from the University of Pittsburgh. He also held a bachelor of divinity degree from Westminster Theological Seminary in Philadelphia, a school that he helped found.

37. E. Brooks Holifield, *God's Ambassadors: A History of the Christian Clergy in America* (Grand Rapids, MI: Eerdmans, 2007), 173.

38. Ockenga was appointed seminary president in 1947, but, reluctant to relinquish his pastoral post at Park Street, he served in absentia from 1947 to 1954.

39. Dayton, "Pietist Theological Critique," 86.

40. Park Street Church, *The Semi-centennial Celebration of the Park Street Church and Society: Held on the Lord's Day, February 27, 1859, with the Festival on the Following Day* (Boston: H. Hoyt, 1861), 149.

41. Thomas Farragher, "Park Street Church's Steeple Is Steeped in History," *Boston Globe*, August 31, 2017, https://www3.bostonglobe.com/metro/2017/08/31/park-street-church-steeple-steeped-history/ffDe8YCF6dQYTnLLIjUnMP/story.html?comments=all&sort=NEWEST_CREATE_DT&arc404=true.

42. Nathan Skinner, "Corporate Worship," Park Street Church, March 16, 2017, https://parkstreet.org/profile/worship.pdf.

43. Elizabeth Lohnes and Nathan Skinner, " Park Street Pulse: Episode 6: Nathan Skinner, Sacred Music on Apple Podcasts," Apple Podcasts, May 19, 2017, https://podcasts.apple.com/us/podcast/episode-6-nathan-skinner-sacred-music/id1227237793?i=1000385608297.

44. R. Scott Clark, "Covenant Theology Is Not Replacement Theology," August 21, 2013, https://heidelblog.net/2013/08/covenant-theology-is-not-replacement-theology/.

45. Robert Dick Wilson, *Scientific Investigation of the Old Testament* (Philadelphia: Sunday School Times, 1926), 8.

46. For more on Wilson's methods, see John J. Yeo, *Plundering the Egyptians: The Old Testament and Historical Criticism at Westminster Theological Seminary (1929–1998)* (Lanham, MD: University Press of America, 2010), 16; and Mark A. Noll, *Between Faith and Criticism: Evangelicals, Scholarship, and the Bible in America*, 2nd ed. (Vancouver: Regent College Publishing, 2004), 110.

47. James Maxwell Miller and John Haralson Hayes, *A History of Ancient Israel and Judah* (Louisville, KY: Westminster John Knox Press, 2006), 78.

48. Iain William Provan, V. Philips Long, and Tremper Longman, *A Biblical History of Israel* (Louisville, KY: Westminster John Knox Press, 2003), 111. Emphasis mine.

49. Provan, Long, and Longman, *Biblical History of Israel*, 170–71.

50. Englizian, *Brimstone Corner*, 114.

51. Gavin James Campbell, "Shape-Note Singing/Singing Schools," *Encyclopedia of Appalachia*, March 1, 2011, https://web.archive.org/web/20180810232600/http://encyclopediaofappalachia.com/entry.php?rec=189.

52. Will Robin, "Shape Notes, Billings, and American Modernisms," New Music USA, July 24, 2013, https://nmbx.newmusicusa.org/shape-notes-billings-and-american-modernisms/.

53. "The Music of William Billings," Amaranth Publishing, 2013, http://www.amaranthpublishing.com/billings.htm.

54. Melissa Block, "Preserving the Sacred Harp Singing Tradition: Tunebooks, Shaped Notes and Full-Body Harmonies in Alabama," *All Things Considered*, December 5, 2003, https://www.npr.org/templates/story/story.php?storyId=1534280.

55. Lowell Mason also served as choir master and organist at Park Street Church from 1829 to 1831.

56. Edward James Kilsdonk, "Scientific Church Music and the Making of the American Middle Class," in *The Middling Sorts: Explorations in the History of the American Middle Class*, ed. Burton J. Bledstein and Robert D. Johnston (New York: Routledge, 2001), 128.

57. William Billings, *The singing master's assistant, or key to practical music, being an abridgement from the New-England psalm-singer; together with several other tunes not before published* (Boston: Draper and Folsom, 1778).

58. Carol A. Pemberton, *Lowell Mason: His Life and Work* (Ann Arbor, MI: UMI Research Press, 1985), 40.

59. Pemberton, *Lowell Mason*, 40.

60. "Historical Report on Various Topics Made before the Annual Meeting, 1845, Park Street Church," unpublished paper, cited in Pemberton, *Lowell Mason*, 286.

61. "Historical Report," cited in Pemberton, *Lowell Mason*, 286.

62. Neil Swidey, "God on the Quad," November 30, 2003, boston.com, http://archive.boston.com/news/globe/magazine/articles/2003/11/30/god_on_the_quad/.

63. Rosell, *Boston's Historic Park Street Church*, 139.

64. 2015 Annual Report, https://webcache.googleusercontent.com/search?q=cache:cZuLgnVonmgJ:https://www.parkstreet.org/sites/default/files/ann_report_2015_web.pdf+&cd=1&hl=en&ct=clnk&gl=us, accessed March 22, 2021.

65. 2015 Annual Report.

66. Marilynn Johnson, "The Quiet Revival: New Immigrants and the Transformation of Christianity in Greater Boston," *Religion and American Culture* 24, no. 2 (2014), 243.

67. Johnson, "Quiet Revival," 244.

68. Johnson, "Quiet Revival," 242.

69. Matthews, *Standing Up, Standing Together*, 28.

70. Paul Strand, "New Kind of Evangelism Transforming Boston," *CBN News*, September 7, 2014, https://www1.cbn.com/cbnnews/us/2014/February/New-Kind-of-Evangelism-Transforming-Boston.

71. R. Albert Mohler Jr., *"The Eclipse of Christian Memory,"* March 27, 2009, https://albertmohler.com/2009/03/27/the-eclipse-of-christian-memory.

72. Johnson, "Quiet Revival," 250.

73. Harold John Ockenga, "The Unvoiced Multitudes," in *Evangelical Action! A Report of the Organization of the National Association of Evangelicals for United Action, Compiled and Edited by the Executive Committee* (Boston: United Action Press, 1942).

74. Bruce Ware, "Summaries of the *Egalitarian* and *Complementarian Positions,*" Council on Biblical Manhood and Womanhood, June 26, 2007, https://cbmw.org/2007/06/26/summaries-of-the-egalitarian-and-complementarian-positions/.

75. Skinner, "Corporate Worship."

76. One of the most popular worship songs from 1997 to 2003 was Rick Founds, "Lord I Lift Your Name on High," *Double Praise 12* (Maranatha! Music, 1989).

77. Ben Witherington III, *Is There a Doctor in the House? An Insider's Story and Advice on Becoming a Bible Scholar* (Grand Rapids, MI: Zondervan Academic, 2011).

Chapter 3

1. Harper, "Battle-Royal," 30.

2. Englizian, *Brimstone Corner*, 186.

3. Rosell, *Surprising Work of God*, 313 n. 34.

4. Moody Bible Institute was originally founded as the Chicago Evangelization Society.

5. *Christian Work*, February 1886, 5–6. see also *Chicago Tribune*, January 23, 1886, 3.

6. Michael Hamilton, "The Interdenominational Evangelicalism of D.L. Moody and the Problem of Fundamentalism," in *American Evangelicalism: George Marsden and the State of American Religious History*, ed. Thomas S. Kidd, Darren Dochuk, and Kurt W. Peterson (South Bend, IN: University of Notre Dame Press, 2016), 233.

7. James F. Findlay, *Dwight L. Moody: American Evangelist, 1837–1899* (Chicago: University of Chicago Press, 2007), 411.

8. Findlay, *Dwight L. Moody*, 411.

9. Hamilton, "Interdenominational Evangelicalism," 235.

10. H. E. Fosdick, *The Modern Use of the Bible* (New York: Macmillan, 1932), 231–32.

11. Quoted in Henry Drummond, *Dwight L. Moody: Impressions and Facts* (New York: McClure, Phillips, 1900), 25–30.

12. Timothy Gloege, *Guaranteed Pure: The Moody Bible Institute, Business, and the Making of Modern Evangelicalism* (Chapel Hill: University of North Carolina Press, 2015), 220.

13. *Christian Century*, July 12, 1932. Quoted in Gloege, *Guaranteed Pure*, 221.

14. Warren W. Wiersbe, *Be Myself: Memoirs of a Bridgebuilder* (Grand Rapids, MI: Baker Publishing Group, 1997), 321, 318.

15. Wiersbe, *Be Myself*, 318.

16. Wiersbe, *Be Myself*, 318.

17. Wiersbe, *Be Myself*, 321.

18. Wiersbe, *Be Myself*, 320. Graham's ecumenical willingness to work with Roman Catholics in his evangelistic campaigns made him anathema to strict fundamentalists.

19. Erwin W. Lutzer, *Is God on America's Side?* (Chicago: Moody Publishers, 2009), 77.

20. Erwin W. Lutzer, *The Church in Babylon* (Chicago: Moody Publishers, 2018), 239.

21. Lutzer, interview by the author [September 22, 2014]. This story is also recounted in Erwin W. Lutzer, *The Cross in the Shadow of the Crescent* (Chicago: Harvest House Publishers, 2013), 110.

22. Lutzer, *God on America's Side*, 83.

23. Lutzer, *Cross in the Shadow*, 110.

24. Lutzer, *God on America's Side*, 77.

25. Lutzer, *The Church in Babylon*, 83.

26. John R. Fugard, "How the Architects Conceived the Moody Memorial Church Building," Moody Church Media, 1925, https://www.moodymedia.org/articles/how-architects-conceived-moody-memorial-church-bui/.

27. Fugard, "How Architects Conceived Moody."

28. Cited in The Moody Church, *Celebrating the Joy of Changed Lives: The Moody Church, 1864–2014* (Chicago: Moody Church), 108.

29. Lutzer recounts this story in his autobiography. See Erwin W. Lutzer, *He Will Be the Preacher* (Chicago: Moody Publishers, 2015), 97–99.

30. Lutzer, "Preaching for a Change," https://www.google.com/url?sa=t&rct=j&q=&esrc=s&source=web&cd=11&cad=rja&uact=8&ved=2ahUKEwiUouOn3q3kAhURVN8KHe9KCT8QFjAKegQIARAC&url=http%3A%2F%2Fstorage.cloversites.com%2Fgreatlakesdistrictefca%2Fdocuments%2FPreaching%2520for%2520Change.pdf&usg=AOvVaw0EBeLWuy8xEQ7jiMj4gwHf.

31. William Shakespeare, *Macbeth*, Act 5, Scene 1, 2–3.

32. Erwin W. Lutzer, *The Power of a Clear Conscience: Let God Free You from Your Past* (Eugene, OR: Harvest House Publishers, 2016), 59.

33. Ed Stetzer, "The Christian Struggle with Mental Illness," *Christianity Today*, May 23, 2016, https://www.christianitytoday.com/edstetzer/2016/may/christian-struggle-with-mental-illness.html.

34. "Before the Throne of God Above," original words by Charitie Lees Bancroft (1841–1892). Public domain.

35. Erwin Lutzer, "Preaching and the City," in *Preaching with Power*, ed. Michael Duduit (Grand Rapids, MI: Baker Books, 2006), 95–106.

36. Lutzer, *Clear Conscience*.

37. For more on conversational Bible readings, see B. M. Pietsch, *Dispensational Modernism* (Oxford: Oxford University Press, 2015), 100–105; and Timothy P. Weber, *On the Road to Armageddon* (Grand Rapids, MI: Baker Publishing Group, 2004), 37–38.

38. James H. Brookes, *The Truth* 5 (1879), 314; James H. Brookes, *The Truth* 23 (1897), 80–82. Cited in Timothy P. Weber, "The Two-Edged Sword: The Fundamentalist Use

of the Bible," in *The Bible in America: Essays in Cultural History*, ed. Nathan O. Hatch and Mark A. Noll (New York: Oxford University Press, 1982), 110.

39. Francis Patton, "Preaching," *Presbyterian and Reformed Review* 1 (1890), 36–37. Quoted in Pietsch, *Dispensational Modernism*, 106.

40. Erwin Lutzer, "How I Preach," *Homiletix*, February 16, 2016, http://homiletix.com/erwin-lutzer-how-i-preach/.

41. See Weber, "Two-Edged Sword," 112.

42. See Weber, *Road to Armageddon*, 38.

43. See George Marsden, "Everyone One's Own Interpreter? The Bible, Science, and Authority in Mid-Nineteenth-Century America," in Hatch and Noll, *The Bible in America*, 91–92.

44. Hugenberger sermon.

45. Lewis Sperry Chafer and John F. Walvoord, *Major Bible Themes* (Grand Rapids, MI: Zondervan, 2010), 128.

46. Greg L. Bahnsen, "The Theonomic Reformed Approach to Law and Gospel," in *Five Views on Law and Gospel*, by Greg L. Bahnsen et al., Counterpoints (Grand Rapids, MI: Zondervan, 1999), 98.

47. John F. Walvoord, *Israel in Prophecy* (Grand Rapids, MI: Zondervan, 1982), 58.

48. Walter Kaiser, "Response to Douglas Moo," in Bahnsen et al., *Five Views*, 393.

49. Lutzer, *Clear Conscience*, 59. Emphasis mine.

50. This phrase was used in the live Sunday morning service, but does not appear in the published version of the sermon.

51. Emphasis mine. As before, this phrase was used in the live Sunday morning service, but does not appear in the published version of the sermon.

52. Timothy Weber, "How Evangelicals Became Israel's Best Friend," *Christianity Today*, October 5, 1998, 38–49.

53. Finney, *Lectures on Revival of Religion*, 305–6.

54. Dwight L. Moody, "The Return of Our Lord," in *American Evangelicals, 1800–1900*, ed. William G. McLaughlin (New York: Harper & Row, 1968), 184–85.

55. Quoted in Findlay, *Dwight L. Moody*, 253.

56. Weber, *Road to Armageddon*, 15.

57. Dennis L. Ockholm, "The Fundamental Dispensation of Evangelical Ecclesiology," in *The Community of the Word: Toward an Evangelical Ecclesiology*, ed. Mark Husbands and Daniel J. Trier (Downers Grove, IL: InterVarsity Press, 2005), 44.

58. W. D. Chamberlain, "Dispensationalism," in *The Church Faces the Isms*, ed. Arnold Black Rhodes (New York: Abingdon Press, 1958), 98.

59. Pietsch, *Dispensational Modernism*, 123.

60. Todd Mangum, "The Modernist-Fundamentalist Controversy, the Inerrancy of Scripture, and the Development of American Dispensationalism," in *Interdisciplinary Perspectives on the Authority of Scripture: Historical, Biblical, and Theoretical Perspectives*, ed. Carlos R. Bovell (Eugene, OR: Wipf and Stock Publishers, 2011), 68.

61. Harold M. Best, *Unceasing Worship: Biblical Perspectives on Worship and the Arts* (Downers Grove, IL: InterVarsity Press, 2003), 185–86.

62. Best, *Unceasing Worship*, 185–86.

63. Arthur Tappan Pierson, *Knowing the Scriptures* (New York: Gospel Publishing House, 1910), 50.

64. Pierson, *Knowing the Scriptures*, 50.

Chapter 4

1. Warren Bird, "World's First Megachurch?," *Leadership Network*, May 4, 2012, http://leadnet.org/worlds_first_megachurch/.

2. Bruce Shelley, "The Rise of Evangelical Youth Movements," *Fides et Historia* 18, no. 1 (1986), 49.

3. Thomas E. Bergler, *The Juvenilization of American Christianity* (Grand Rapids, MI: Eerdmans, 2012), 4.

4. Terry W. York, *America's Worship Wars* (Peabody, MA: Hendrickson, 2003), 24.

5. Bill Hybels and Lynne Hybels, *Rediscovering Church* (Grand Rapids, MI: Zondervan, 1995), 45.

6. Hybels and Hybels, *Rediscovering Church*, 55.

7. See interview by Carey Nieuwhof, "CNLP 154: Todd Fields on the Constant Change in Worship Music, What Makes a Great Worship Leader, Working with Andy Stanley and More," *CareyNieuwhof*, October 9, 2017, https://careynieuwhof.com/episode154/.

8. Andy Stanley, *Next Generation Leader* (Sisters, OR: Multnomah, 2011), 1.

9. Much of the following account is drawn from "History—North Point," https://web.archive.org/web/20150316102036/http://northpoint.org/about/history, accessed May 16, 2020.

10. Andy Stanley, *Deep and Wide: Creating Churches Unchurched People Love to Attend* (Grand Rapids, MI: Zondervan, 2012), 31.

11. Andy Stanley and Bill Willits, *Creating Community: Five Keys to Building a Small Group Culture* (Sisters, OR: Multnomah, 2004), 52.

12. Stanley, *Deep and Wide*, 51.

13. Stanley, *Deep and Wide: Creating Churches*, 269.

14. Ed Young, *Can We Do That? Innovative Practices That Will Change the Way You Do Church* (New York: Howard Books, 2010), 179.

15. "Spreading God's Word in the 21st Century: Video and Satellite Churches," Technologies for Worship, February 21, 2014, http://tfwm.com/spreading-gods-word-in-the-21st-century-video-and-satellite-churches/.

16. Stanley, *Deep and Wide: Creating Churches*, 285.

17. Stanley, *Deep and Wide: Creating Churches*, 285.

18. "2014 Outreach 100 Largest and Fastest-Growing Churches in America," 2014 Special Edition of *Outreach* magazine, http://www.outreachmagazine.com/2014-outreach-100/outreach-100-largest-churches-america.html.

19. See "Welcome," North Point Ministries, http://northpointministries.org/, accessed May 16, 2020.

20. Bill Kinnon, "Sure. It's Funny to Some, but . . . ," May 8, 2010, https://web.archive. org/web/20180903064604/http://kinnon.tv/2010/05/sure-its-funny-to-some-but. html.
21. Cathy Lynn Grossman, "Video Parody Riffs on Megachurch Modern Worship," *USA Today*, May 12, 2010, http://content.usatoday.com/communities/Religion/post/2010/05/christian-worship-parody-north-point-church/1#.V6iuPY56Rpk.
22. Bob Kauflin, "The Contemporvant Service—What Can We Learn?," *Worship Matters*, May 17, 2010, http://www.worshipmatters.com/2010/05/17/the-contemporvant-service-what-can-we-learn/.
23. Jon Reid, "'Contemporary Church' Video Makes Me Laugh, and Wonder," *Blogoneanother*, May 7, 2010, https://web.archive.org/web/20150219123424/http://blogoneanother.com/contemporary-church-video-makes-me-laugh-and-wonder/.
24. Kinnon, "Sure."
25. Taft borrows this distinction from Lévi-Strauss's structural analysis of myths. See Claude Lévi-Strauss, *Structural Anthropology*, trans. Claire Jacobson and Brooke Grundfest Schoepf (New York: Basic Books, 1963), chapters 11 and 12; and Robert Taft, "The Structural Analysis of Liturgical Units: An Essay in Methodology," in *Beyond East and West: Problems in Liturgical Understanding*, 2nd ed. (Rome: Edizioni Orientalia Christiana, 2001), 202.
26. Taft, "Structural Analysis," 200.
27. See Jeffrey Gros, Harding Meyer, and William G. Rusch, *Growth in Agreement II: Reports and Agreed Statements of Ecumenical Conversations on a World Level, 1982–1998* (Grand Rapids, MI: Eerdmans, 2000), 242.
28. Marva J. Dawn, *A Royal "Waste" of Time: The Splendor of Worshiping God and Being Church for the World* (Grand Rapids, MI: Eerdmans, 1999).
29. Stanley, *Deep and Wide: Creating Churches*, 273.
30. Stanley, *Deep and Wide: Creating Churches*, 96.
31. Stanley, *Deep and Wide: Creating Churches*, 81.
32. Stanley, *Deep and Wide: Creating Churches*, 222.
33. Stanley, *Deep and Wide: Creating Churches*, 240.
34. Stanley, *Deep and Wide: Creating Churches*, 203.
35. Stanley, *Deep and Wide: Creating Churches*, 215.
36. Stanley, *Deep and Wide: Creating Churches*, 114.
37. Andy Stanley and Lane Jones, *Communicating for a Change* (Sisters, OR: Multnomah, 2008), 96.
38. Stanley, *Deep and Wide: Creating Churches*, 236.
39. North Point Media, "*Be Rich Celebration 2014: North Point Community Church,*" https://vimeo.com/114256809, accessed March 22, 2021.
40. Andy Stanley, "Planning Your Service with Visitors in Mind," *Christianity Today*, January 1, 2000, http://www.christianitytoday.com/pastors/2000/winter/andy-stanley-planning-service-visitors.html.
41. Barry Kosmin and Ariela Keysar, *American Nones: The Profile of the No Religion Population, A Report Based on the American Religious Identification Survey 2008* (Hartford, CT: Program on Public Values, Trinity College, 2009), available at https://

commons.trincoll.edu/aris/publications/2008-2/american-nones-the-profile-of-the-no-religion-population/.

42. Kosmin and Keysar, *American Nones*.

43. See Drew Dyck, "The Leavers: Young Doubters Exit the Church," *Christianity Today*, November 19, 2010, https://www.christianitytoday.com/ct/2010/november/27.40.html.

44. Quoted in Dyck, "The Leavers."

45. Dyck, "The Leavers."

46. Andy Stanley, *Going Deep and Wide: A Companion Guide for Churches and Leaders* (Grand Rapids, MI: Zondervan, 2017), 16. Emphasis mine.

47. Barna Group, *The Bible in America: The Changing Landscape of Bible Perceptions and Engagement* (Ventura, CA: Barna Group, 2016), 8.

48. Andy Stanley, *Irresistible: Reclaiming the New That Jesus Unleashed for the World* (Grand Rapids, MI: Zondervan, 2018), 279–80.

49. Stanley, *Irresistible*, 209.

50. Lindsay Elizabeth, "Andy Stanley Tells Us about His Mission to Combat 'Misinformation about Faith, the Bible, and Christianity' and Reach an Unbelieving Generation," *Faithwire*, September 19, 2018, https://www.faithwire.com/2018/09/19/exclusive-andy-stanley-is-on-a-mission-to-combat-misinformation-about-faith-the-bible-and-christianity-and-reach-an-unbelieving-generation/.

51. Stanley, *Irresistible*, 305–6.

52. Andy Stanley, "*Your Assumption Is Showing*," presentation at Dallas Theological Seminary, Dallas, TX, February 13, 2009, https://voice.dts.edu/chapel/your-assumption-is-showing/.

53. Stanley, "Your Assumption Is Showing."

54. Stanley, *Irresistible*, 293.

55. Stanley, *Irresistible*, 299.

56. Stanley, *Irresistible*, 194–95. Emphasis mine.

57. Andy Stanley, "*Be Rich*," sermon, North Point Community Church, Alpharetta, GA, October 26, 2014.

58. Stanley, *Going Deep and Wide*, 115–16.

59. Stanley, "Be Rich."

60. John D. Hannah, *An Uncommon Union: Dallas Theological Seminary and American Evangelicalism* (Grand Rapids, MI: Zondervan, 2009), 19.

61. See Hannah, *Uncommon Union*, 17–18.

62. Stanley, "*Your Assumption Is Showing*."

63. Stanley, *Irresistible*, 102.

64. Stanley, *Irresistible*, 159.

65. Stanley, *Irresistible*, 154.

66. Stanley, *Irresistible*, 154.

67. The church offers a monthly "night of worship" for Christians who want more depth than Sunday morning allows.

68. C. I. Scofield, *Addresses on Prophecy* (Chicago: Bible Truth Depot, 1914), 13.

69. Stanley, *Deep and Wide: Creating Churches*, 278. Emphasis mine.

70. Dan Wilt, "*Is It Too Loud? Worship Accompaniment vs. Worship Immersion Culture,*" https://www.danwilt.com/is-it-too-loud-worship-accompaniment-vs-worship-immersion-culture/. Emphasis in original.

71. Interviewee's emphasis.

72. Stanley, *Deep and Wide: Creating Churches*, 217.

73. Stanley, *Deep and Wide: Creating Churches*, 217.

74. John Bell, *The Singing Thing: A Case for Congregational Song* (Chicago: GIA Publications, 2000), 95.

75. Wilt, *"Is It Too Loud?"*

Chapter 5

1. Stanley, *Deep and Wide: Creating Churches*, 199.

2. Stanley and Jones, *Communicating for a Change*, 47–48.

3. Jay Croft, "Philando Castile Shooting: Dashcam Video Shows Rapid Event," *CNN*, June 21, 2017, https://www.cnn.com/2017/06/20/us/philando-castile-shooting-dashcam/index.html.

4. Manny Fernandez et al., "Five Dallas Officers Were Killed as Payback, Police Chief Says," *New York Times*, July 8, 2016, https://www.nytimes.com/2016/07/09/us/dallas-police-shooting.html.

5. "With Everything" by Joel Houston. Copyright © 2008 Hillsong Music Publishing (APRA) (adm. in the US and Canada at CapitolCMGPublishing.com). All rights reserved. Used by permission.

6. Margaret A. Farley, "Beyond the Formal Principle: A Reply to Ramsey and Saliers," *Journal of Religious Ethics* 7, no. 2 (1979), 198.

7. Jemar Tisby, "Are Black Christians Evangelicals?," in Noll, Bebbington, and Marsden, *Evangelicals*, 272.

8. Richard A. Bustraan, *The Jesus People Movement: A Story of Spiritual Revolution among the Hippies* (Eugene, OR: Pickwick Publications, 2014), 37.

9. Eskridge, *God's Forever Family*, 4.

10. Gretchen Lemke-Santangelo, *Daughters of Aquarius: Women of the Sixties Counterculture* (Lawrence: University Press of Kansas, 2009), 35.

11. Bustraan, *Jesus People Movement*, 15–16.

12. Quoted in Lemke-Santangelo, *Daughters of Aquarius*, 35.

13. Eskridge, *God's Forever Family*, 54.

14. Eskridge, *God's Forever Family*, 55.

15. Bustraan, *Jesus People Movement*, 45.

16. Larry Eskridge, "Jesus People," in *The Encyclopedia of Christianity*, ed. Erwin Fahlbusch et al., vol. 3 (Grand Rapids, MI: Eerdmans, 1999), 30.

17. See Eskridge, *God's Forever Family*, 5.

18. Quoted in Findlay, *Dwight L. Moody*, 253.

19. Cited in Eskridge, *God's Forever Family*, 87.

20. See Eskridge, *God's Forever Family*, 1.
21. "Wimber's Wonders," *Christianity Today*, February 9, 1998, https://www.christianitytoday.com/ct/1998/february9/8t2015.html.
22. Bill Jackson, *Quest for the Radical Middle* (Cape Town: Vineyard International Publishing, 2006), 52.
23. Eskridge, *God's Forever Family*, 99.
24. Jon Bialecki, *A Diagram for Fire: Miracles and Variation in an American Charismatic Movement* (Oakland: University of California Press, 2017), 40–41.
25. George Eldon Ladd, *The Presence of the Future: The Eschatology of Biblical Realism* (Grand Rapids, MI: Eerdmans, 1974), 211.
26. Jackson, *Quest for the Radical Middle*, 52.
27. Carol Wimber, *John Wimber: The Way It Was* (London: Hodder & Stoughton, 1999), 120.
28. Tim Stafford, "Testing the Wine from John Wimber's Vineyard," *Christianity Today*, August 8, 1986, 19.
29. "The Vineyard: A Community of Churches," n.d., https://web.archive.org/web/20060715183628/http://www.vineyardusa.org/about/history.aspx, accessed March 22, 2021.
30. Wimber and Smith disagree on how many Calvary Chapels defected from the movement to join the Vineyard's more charismatic emphasis. Wimber estimated thirty; Smith said as many as a hundred. See Donald Miller, "Routinizing Charisma: The Vineyard Christian Fellowship in the Post-Wimber Era," *Pneuma* 25, no. 2 (Fall 2003), 224.
31. On July 3, 2016, ISIL militants carried out coordinated suicide bomb attacks in Baghdad that killed 340 civilians and injured hundreds more. On June 23, 2016, 51.9 percent of the British people voted to leave the European Union after a historic referendum. On June 28, 2016, a gun and bomb attack on Istanbul's Ataturk airport killed 41 people and injured more than 230. See Moni Basu, "Iraq's Unnamed Victims of Terror." *CNN*, January 12, 2017, https://edition.cnn.com/2017/01/12/world/iraq-terrorism-faceless-victims/index.html; Anushka Asthana et al., "UK Votes to Leave EU after Dramatic Night Divides Nation," *The Guardian*, June 24, 2016, https://www.theguardian.com/politics/2016/jun/24/britain-votes-for-brexit-eu-referendum-david-cameron; "Istanbul Ataturk Airport Attack: 41 Dead and More than 230 Hurt," *BBC News*, June 29, 2016, https://www.bbc.com/news/world-europe-36658187.
32. https://www.biblegateway.com/passage/?search=Proverbs%2029:17-19&version=MSG
33. On June 17, 2015, a twenty-one-year-old white supremacist murdered nine African Americans during a prayer service at the Emanuel African Methodist Episcopal Church in downtown Charleston, South Carolina. See Robert Costa et al., "Church Shooting Suspect Dylann Roof Captured amid Hate Crime Investigation," *Washington Post*, June 19, 2015, https://www.washingtonpost.com/news/morning-mix/wp/2015/06/17/white-gunman-sought-in-shooting-at-historic-charleston-african-ame-church/.

34. Tomeka Davis, "How Schools Fail Black Boys (and Girls Too): Race, Gender, and Academic Trajectories from Kindergarten through Eighth Grade," in *The Handbook of Research on Black Males: Quantitative, Qualitative, and Multidisciplinary*, ed. Theodore S. Ransaw et al. (East Lansing: Michigan State University Press, 2019), 173.

35. Eduardo Bautista Duran and Jonathan Simon, "Police Abolitionist Discourse? Why It Has Been Missing (and Why It Matters)," in *The Cambridge Handbook of Policing in the United States*, ed. Tamara Rice Lave and Eric J. Miller (New York: Cambridge University Press, 2019), 98.

36. Cited in Shari J. Stenberg and Charlotte Hogg, *Persuasive Acts: Women's Rhetorics in the Twenty-First Century* (Pittsburgh: University of Pittsburgh Press, 2020), 57.

37. I. Bennett Capers, "Citizenship Talk," in Lave and Miller, *Cambridge Handbook of Policing*, 476. For more on "the talk," see Tauhid Chappell, "Parents Are Having 'the Talk' with Their Children: What Did Yours Say?," *Washington Post*, July 11, 2016, https://www.washingtonpost.com/posteverything/wp/2016/07/11/parents-are-having-the-talk-with-their-children-about-police-what-did-yours-say/; Taylor Pittman, "Inside the Heartbreaking Talk Black Parents Must Have with Their Kids," *Huffington Post*, November 4, 2016, https://www.huffpost.com/entry/inside-the-heartbreaking-talk-black-parents-must-have-with-their-kids_n_581ca092e4b0d9ce6fbb465b; Geeta Ghandbhir and Blair Foster, "A Conversation with My Black Son," *New York Times*, March 17, 2015, https://www.nytimes.com/2015/03/17/opinion/a-conversation-with-my-black-son.html.

38. In Chicago, Trinity United Church of Christ—a large congregation on the city's South Side—dedicated a church bulletin to educating people about interacting with the police and held safety forums for youth and their parents. An infographic used during that training was developed into a short film in 2015 by the SALT Project, an Indianapolis-based nonprofit production company, in partnership with Trinity UCC and Christian Theological Seminary. The film, *Get Home Safely: 10 Rules of Survival*, outlines steps for navigating police encounters. It was nominated for an Emmy and has been featured by the *BBC, CNN, MSNBC, PBS*, and hundreds of other media outlets. See "10 Rules of Survival If Stopped by the Police," Public Broadcasting Service, n.d., https://www.pbs.org/black-culture/connect/talk-back/10_rules_of_survival_if_stopped_by_police/.

39. See Lisa Respers France, "'Can I Touch It?' The Fascination with Natural, African-American Hair," *CNN*, July 25, 2011, http://www.cnn.com/2011/LIVING/07/25/touching.natural.black.hair/index.html.

40. For liturgy as formation, see Don Saliers, *Worship as Theology: Foretaste of Glory Divine* (Nashville, TN: Abingdon Press, 1994); Irwin, *Context and Text*. For liturgy and politics, see William Cavanaugh, "Liturgy as Politics," *Christian Century*, https://www.religion-online.org/article/liturgy-as-politics-an-interview-with-william-cavanaugh/.

41. Cavanaugh, "Liturgy as Politics."

42. Saliers, *Worship as Theology*, 187.

43. Ross Douthat, "God and Politics," *New York Times*, April 17, 2009, https://www.nytimes.com/2009/04/19/books/review/Douthat-t.html.

44. Cited in William C. Martin, *A Prophet with Honor: The Billy Graham Story* (Grand Rapids, MI: Zondervan, 218) 170.

45. Douthat, "God and Politics."

46. James S. Bielo, *Emerging Evangelicals: Faith, Modernity, and the Desire for Authenticity* (New York: New York University Press, 2011), 143.

47. T. M. Luhrmann, *When God Talks Back: Understanding the American Evangelical Relationship with God* (New York: Alfred A. Knopf, 2012), 63–64.

48. Jon Bialecki, "Jon Bialecki: Winner of the Sharon Stephens Prize for His Book *A Diagram for Fire: Miracles and Variation in an American Charismatic Movement,*" interview by Bryan Dougan, American Ethnological Society, April 9, 2018, https://americanethnologist.org/features/interviews/aes-interviews-jon-bialecki.

49. Jon Bialecki, "Disjuncture, Continental Philosophy's New 'Political Paul,' and the Question of Progressive Christianity in a Southern California Third Wave Church," *American Ethnologist* 36, no. 1 (2009), 116.

50. James McWilliams, "The Miracle of Trump: Why Did Evangelicals Deliver the Votes for a Sinner?," *Pacific Standard*, February 13, 2017, https://psmag.com/news/the-miracle-of-trump-why-did-evangelicals-deliver-the-votes-for-a-sinner.

51. Margery Post Abbott, *To Be Broken and Tender: A Quaker Theology for Today* (Portland, OR: Friends Bulletin Corp., 2010).

52. Lloyd Lee Wilson, *Essays on the Quaker Vision of Gospel Order* (Wallingford, PA: Pendle Hill Publications, 1993), 4.

53. Wilson, *Quaker Vision*, 17.

54. Wilson, *Quaker Vision*, 3–4.

55. Wilson, *Quaker Vision*, 5.

56. Katherine Murray, "Social Justice and Sustainability," in *The Cambridge Companion to Quakerism*, ed. Stephen W. Angell and Pink Dandelion (Cambridge: Cambridge University Press, 2018), 88.

57. Susan Robson, "Conflict in the Peaceable Kingdom," *Journal of Religion, Conflict, and Peace* 4, no. 1 (Fall 2010), http://www.religionconflictpeace.org/volume-4-issue-1-fall-2010/conflict-peaceable-kingdom.

58. Jackie Leach Scully, "Virtuous Friends: Morality and Quaker Identity," *Quaker Studies* 14, no. 1 (2009), 114.

59. Scully, "Virtuous Friends," 114.

60. Nancy D. Wadsworth, *Ambivalent Miracles: Evangelicals and the Politics of Racial Healing* (Charlottesville: University of Virginia Press, 2014), 261.

Chapter 6

1. Quoted in Sarah Mirk, "Why Don't Portlanders Go to Church? A Young Sociologists Digs into Portlanders' Religious Apathy," *Portland Mercury*, August 9, 2012, https://www.portlandmercury.com/portland/why-dont-portlanders-go-to-church/Content?oid=6687243.

2. W. E. Whitelaw and E. G. Niemi, "Money: The Greening of the Economy," *Old Oregon* 68, no. 3 (1989), 26–27.

3. Mark A. Shibley, "Sacred Nature: Earth-Based Spirituality as Popular Religion in the Pacific Northwest," *Journal for the Study of Religion, Nature & Culture* 5, no. 2 (2011), 164–85.

4. Mark A. Shibley, "Secular but Spiritual in the Pacific Northwest: The None Zone," in *Religion and Public Life in the Pacific Northwest: The None Zone*, ed. Patricia O'Connell Killen and Mark Silk (Lanham, MD: Rowman Altamira, 2004), 165.

5. Dean Inserra, "The Bible Belt: Four Challenges to Ministry in the Land of the Over-Churched and Under-Reached," *Conventional Futures*, May 31, 2016, https://conventionalfutures.com/2016/05/20/the-bible-belt-four-challenges-to-ministry-in-the-land-of-the-over-churched-and-under-reached/.

6. Andy Stanley, Lane Jones, and Reggie Joiner, *Seven Practices of Effective Ministry* (Colorado Springs, CO: Multnomah, 2008), 142.

7. J. Shawn Landres and Ryan K. Bolger, "Emerging Patterns of Interreligious Conversation: A Christian-Jewish Experiment," *Annals of the American Academy of Political and Social Science* 612, no. 1 (2007), 229.

8. Eddie Gibbs and Ryan K. Bolger, *Emerging Churches* (Grand Rapids, MI: Baker Academic, 2005), 33.

9. For example, D. A. Carson, *Becoming Conversant with the Emerging Church: Understanding a Movement and Its Implications* (Grand Rapids, MI: Zondervan, 2005); Mark Driscoll et al., *Listening to the Beliefs of Emerging Churches: Five Perspectives*, ed. Robert Webber (Grand Rapids, MI: Zondervan, 2007); Doug Pagitt and Tony Jones, eds., *An Emergent Manifesto of Hope* (Grand Rapids, MI: Baker Books, 2007); William D. Henard and Adam W. Greenway, *Evangelicals Engaging Emergent: A Discussion of the Emergent Church Movement* (Nashville, TN: Broadman & Holman, 2009); Gibbs and Bolger, *Emerging Churches*; Dan Kimball, *The Emerging Church: Vintage Christianity for New Generations* (Grand Rapids, MI: Zondervan, 2003).

10. In 2004, D. A. Carson (a theologian critical of the movement) delivered a three-part Staley Lecture series on the emergent church at Cedarville University. On October 26–28, 2006, Westminster Theological Seminary held a conference on the emerging church entitled "An Eternal Word in an Emerging World." On May 30, 2006, Dallas Theological Seminary presented a learning dialogue entitled "The Emerging Church." This series offered a discussion between the school's president (Mark Bailey) and three other faculty members regarding "an introductory exploration into a movement hopeful of meeting the complexities of ministering to an emergent culture." Wheaton College offered a course on the emerging church (EVAN 694—The Emerging Church) as part of their MA program in evangelism and leadership. Fuller Theological Seminary listed specific courses related to topic: Leading an Emerging Church and The Emerging Church in the Twenty-First Century.

11. Ed Stetzer, "The Emergent/Emerging Church: A Missiological Perspective," *Journal for Baptist Theology and Ministry* 5, no. 2 (2008), 62.

12. Stanley J. Grenz, *Created for Community* (Grand Rapids, MI: Baker Academic, 1998).

13. "Wayfarers Collective" is a pseudonym I created that parallels the ethos and rationale of the congregation's actual name.

14. Scot McKnight, "Five Streams of the Emerging Church," *Christianity Today*, January 19, 2007, 38.

15. Mark Driscoll, the former pastor of the now-defunct Seattle megachurch Mars Hill, became famous for his evangelical brand of toxic masculinity and was forced to resign in 2014 following accusations of bullying, plagiarism, and misuse of church funds.

16. Carson, *Becoming Conversant*; Kevin DeYoung and Ted Kluck, *Why We're Not Emergent: By Two Guys Who Should Be* (Chicago: Moody, 2008).

17. Url Scaramanga, "R.I.P. Emerging Church," *Christianity Today Pastors* (*Leadership Journal*), October 16, 2017, https://www.christianitytoday.com/pastors/2008/september-online-only/rip-emerging-church.html.

18. C. Michael Patton, "Obituary: The Emerging Church (1994–2009)," *Credo House Ministries*, January 24, 2016, https://credohouse.org/blog/obituary-the-emerging-church-1994-2009.

19. Tony Jones, "Emerging Church Movement (1989–2009)?," December 30, 2009, http://tallskinnykiwi.typepad .com/tallskinnykiwi/2009/12/emergingchurch-movement-1989---2009.html; Tony Jones, "Lonnie Frisbee and the Non-Demise of the Emerging Church," *Theoblogy*, December 30, 2009, http://www.patheos.com/blogs/tonyjones/2009/12/30/lonnie-frisbee-and-the-non-demise-of-the-emerging-church/; Adam Smith, "The End of the Emergent Movement?," in *Relevant Magazine* (2010); https://web.archive.org/web/20150428085445/http://www.relevantmagazine.com/god/church/features/21181-the-end-of-emergent.

20. Ed Stetzer, "Thoughts on Recent Movements in Evangelicalism: Part 1, Post Emerging Church Clarification," *The Exchange: A Blog by Ed Stetzer*, May 21, 2019, https://www.christianitytoday.com/edstetzer/2019/may/some-thoughts-on-recent-movements-in-evangelicalism-part-1.html.

21. "All Sons & Daughters," *Wikipedia*, January 25, 2020, https://en.wikipedia.org/wiki/All_Sons_&_Daughters#cite_note-8.

22. Cited in Keith Giles, "The Gospel of the Kingdom: An Interview," August 2005, http://old.dwillard.org/articles/artview.asp?artID=150.

23. Dallas Willard, "Spiritual Formation as a Natural Part of Salvation," in *Life in the Spirit: Spiritual Formation in Theological Perspective*, ed. Jeffrey P. Greenman and George Kalantzis (Downers Grove, IL: InterVarsity Press, 2010), 47.

24. N. T. Wright, *Surprised by Hope: Rethinking Heaven, the Resurrection, and the Mission of the Church* (New York: HarperOne, 2008), 204.

25. Brian D. McLaren, *A New Kind of Christian* (San Francisco: Jossey-Bass, 2008), 188.

26. Quoted in Melissa Binder, "Evangelism Is Alive in Portland," *Christianity Today*, March 17, 2017, https://www.christianitytoday.com/ct/2017/april/evangelism-is-alive-in-portland.html.

27. Thomas G. Long, *Preaching from Memory to Hope* (Louisville, KY: Westminster John Knox Press, 2009), 123.

28. Wright, *Surprised by Hope*, 208.

29. Wright, *Surprised by Hope*, 208.

30. Dallas Willard, *The Divine Conspiracy* (New York: HarperCollins, 2009), 190.
31. Gary Black, *The Theology of Dallas Willard* (Eugene, OR: Wipf and Stock Publishers, 2013), 120.
32. Willard, *The Divine Conspiracy*, 26.
33. Willard, *The Divine Conspiracy*, 190.
34. Andy Stanley, *How to Be Rich: It's Not What You Have, It's What You Do with What You Have* (Grand Rapids, MI: Zondervan, 2014).
35. Dallas Willard, *The Allure of Gentleness* (New York: HarperOne, 2015), 168.
36. Donald Miller, "I Don't Worship God by Singing: I Connect with Him Elsewhere," February 3, 2014, http://storylineblog.com/2014/02/03/i-dont-worship-god-by-singing-i-connect-with-him-elsewhere/.
37. Miller, "*I Don't Worship God by Singing.*"
38. Dan Kimball, "The Emerging Church and Missional Theology," in Driscoll et al., *Listening to the Beliefs*, 100.
39. Long, *Preaching from Memory*, 3.
40. David Schlafer and Timothy F. Sedgwick, *Preaching What We Practice* (Harrisburg, PA: Morehouse Publishing), 151.
41. "Beloved" by Enter the Worship Circle. Copyright © 2001 Enter the Worship Circle. Used by permission.
42. "To Hear Your Voice" by Eric Marshall. Copyright © 2014 Street Talk Media. Used by permission.
43. "Young Oceans Biography," November 18, 2014, https://web.archive.org/web/20141231114011/https://www.last.fm/music/Young+Oceans/+wiki.

Chapter 7

1. Joseph Dedeon and Grant Suneson, "Tennessee Is the 3rd Most Religious State," *Nashville Stats*, October 26, 2017, http://nashvillestats.com/tennessee-is-the-3rd-most-religious-state/.
2. See John Lindenbaum, "The Production of Contemporary Christian Music: A Geographical Perspective," in *Sound, Society, and the Geography of Popular Music*, ed. Ola Johansson and Thomas L. Bell (New York: Routledge, 2016), 287.
3. Deborah Evans Price, "Shake-Ups Hit Christian Labels," *Billboard*, March 27, 1999, 98.
4. Lindenbaum, "Contemporary Christian Music," 286.
5. Laura Harris, "So Far, So Good," *CCM*, May 1999, 43.
6. Charles Lindholm, *Culture and Authenticity* (Malden, MA: Blackwell, 2008), 2.
7. Kim Thomas, "Encouraging Creative Congregations," Breakout Session, "Sing!," Nashville, TN, September 12, 2018.
8. Thomas, "Encouraging Creative Congregations."
9. Jeremy S. Begbie, *A Peculiar Orthodoxy: Reflections on Theology and the Arts* (Grand Rapids, MI: Baker Academic, 2018), 206.

10. Chapter 6.

11. Nicholas Lash, *The Beginning and the End of "Religion"* (Cambridge: Cambridge University Press, 1996), 170. See also Begbie, *Peculiar Orthodoxy*, 202.

12. Begbie, *Peculiar Orthodoxy*, 205.

13. Begbie, *Peculiar Orthodoxy*, 207.

14. Begbie, *Peculiar Orthodoxy*, 207.

15. Nicholas Zork, "Speaking beyond a Single Moment: An Interview with Keith Getty," *Curator Magazine*, March 5, 2014, http://www.curatormagazine.com/nicholas-zork/ speaking-beyond-a-single-moment-an-interview-with-keith-getty/.

16. Keith Getty and Kristyn Getty, "With One Voice: These Young Musicians Are Committed to Writing Modern Hymns with Timeless Truths Everyone Can Sing," interview by Brandon J. O'Brien, https://www.christianitytoday.com/pastors/2009/ winter/withonevoice.html.

17. John Greco, "The Song of the Redeemed: A Conversation with Keith Getty," *Facts & Trends*, December 11, 2014, https://factsandtrends.net/2014/12/11/the-song-of-the-redeemed-a-conversation-with-keith-getty/.

18. See Julian Baggini, "Charles Taylor: How to Win the Argument," *New Humanist*, April 3, 2017, https://newhumanist.org.uk/articles/5170/charles-taylor-how-to-win-the-argument.

19. Charles Taylor, *Sources of the Self: The Making of the Modern Identity* (Cambridge, MA: Harvard University Press, 1989), 58–59.

20. Charles Taylor, *A Secular Age* (Cambridge, MA: Harvard University Press, 2007), 675.

21. James K. A. Smith, *How (Not) to Be Secular: Reading Charles Taylor* (Grand Rapids, MI: Eerdmans, 2014), 138.

22. Taylor, *Sources of the Self*, 521.

23. CT Editors, "How Charles Taylor Helps Us Understand Our Secular Age," *Christianity Today*, June 27, 2018, https://www.christianitytoday.com/ct/2018/june-web-only/ charles-taylor-secular-age.html.

24. James K. A. Smith, "How My Millennial Students Found Their 'Hitchhiker's Guide' to a Secular Age," *HuffPost*, October 24, 2016, https://www.huffpost.com/entry/charles-taylor-philosopher_b_58067afde4b0180a36e700f3.

25. Smith, *How (Not) to Be Secular*, xi.

26. Taylor, *A Secular Age*, 40.

27. Robert Joustra, "Our Haunted Age," *Literary Review of Canada*, November 2014, https://reviewcanada.ca/magazine/2014/11/our-haunted-age/.

28. Taylor, *A Secular Age*, 222.

29. Taylor, *A Secular Age*, 126.

30. Taylor, *A Secular Age*, 224.

31. Taylor, *A Secular Age*, 650.

32. Taylor, *A Secular Age*, 649.

33. Erwin Lutzer, interview by the author, September 22, 2014.

34. Lutzer, interview by the author.

35. Church literature, quoted in Chapter 6.

36. Smith, *How (Not) to Be Secular*, 49.

37. See Chapter 6.
38. Smith, *How (Not) to Be Secular*, 49.
39. Taylor, *A Secular Age*, 650.
40. See Chapter 6.
41. Taylor, *A Secular Age*, 650.
42. Taylor, *A Secular Age*, 319.
43. Taylor, *A Secular Age*, 319.
44. Smith, *How (Not) to Be Secular*, 150–51.
45. Taylor, *A Secular Age*, 11.
46. Smith, *How (Not) to Be Secular*, 4.
47. James K. A. Smith, "Cracks in the Secular," *Comment Magazine*, September 1, 2014, https://www.cardus.ca/comment/article/cracks-in-the-secular/.
48. Julian Barnes, *Nothing to Be Frightened Of* (New York: Albert A. Knopf, 2008), 1.
49. Smith, "Cracks in the Secular."
50. Taylor, *A Secular Age*, 607.
51. Taylor, *A Secular Age*, 607.
52. Smith, *How (Not) to Be Secular*, 9.
53. James K. A. Smith, *Desiring the Kingdom: Worship, Worldview, and Cultural Formation* (Grand Rapids, MI: Baker Academic, 2009), 71.
54. Keith Getty and Kristyn Getty, *Sing! How Worship Transforms Your Life, Family, and Church* (Nashville, TN: B&H Publishing Group, 2017), 14–15.
55. Nieuwhof, "CNLP 154."
56. Stanley, *Deep and Wide: Creating Churches*, 217.
57. Stanley, *Deep and Wide: Creating Churches*, 217.
58. Getty and Getty, *Sing!*, 13.
59. Getty and Getty, *Sing!*, 14. Emphasis mine.
60. Getty and Getty, *Sing!*, 140–41.
61. Dan Wooding, "In Christ Alone: Keith and Kristyn Getty Bring the Beauty of Irish Music to American with Their Modern Hymns," *Assist News*, March 29, 2013, http://www.sloppynoodle.com/wp/in-christ-alone-2/.
62. Stanley, "Your Assumption Is Showing."
63. Quoted in Lindsay Williams, "Reason to Sing!," *Bible Studies for Life*, August 13, 2018, https://blog.lifeway.com/biblestudiesforlife/nehemiah-session-6-reason-to-sing/.
64. Keith Getty, "Opening Remarks," "Sing! 2017," Brentwood Baptist Church, Nashville, TN, September 18, 2017.
65. CCLI, short for Christian Copyright Licensing International, tracks the copyrights of Christian worship songs sung in churches around the world. See also "About Keith and Kristyn Getty," Getty Music, https://www.gettymusic.com/about-us, accessed March 23, 2021.
66. Kristyn Getty, "The Story of a Modern Hymn Writer," interview by Corrie Cutrer, *Today's Christian Woman*, May–June 2012, https://www.todayschristianwoman.com/articles/2013/may-june-issue/tcw-talks-to-kristyn-getty.html.
67. Skinner, "Corporate Worship."
68. Getty and Getty, "With One Voice."

69. Getty and Getty, "With One Voice."

70. Getty and Getty, "With One Voice."

71. Getty and Getty, *Sing!*, 14–15.

72. "About Keith and Kristyn Getty," Getty Music, https://www.gettymusic.com/about-us, accessed March 23, 2021.

73. Timothy George, "No Squishy Love (Part II)," *First Things*, August 26, 2013, https://www.firstthings.com/web-exclusives/2013/08/no-squishy-love-part-ii.

74. Stanley and Jones, *Communicating for a Change*, 59.

75. Stanley and Jones, *Communicating for a Change*, 146.

76. Keith Getty and Stuart Townend, "Songwriting, Collaboration and New Songs," Breakout Session, "Sing! 2017," Nashville, TN, September 20, 2017.

77. For a complete discography, see Marcy Donelson, "Keith Getty: Credits," AllMusic, https://www.allmusic.com/artist/keith-getty-mn0000765928/credits, accessed March 23, 2021.

78. Getty and Getty, "With One Voice."

79. Getty and Getty, "With One Voice."

80. Rich Burrough, "Towards a Deeper Song: Why Keith and Kristyn Getty Are Helping the Church to Sing [Again]," *Worship Fuel*, September 5, 2018, https://web.archive.org/web/20190401102449/https://worshipfuel.ccli.com/towards-deeper-song/.

81. Getty and Getty, "With One Voice."

82. Justin Taylor, "Keith Getty on Writing Hymns," *Gospel Coalition*, August 1, 2010, https://www.thegospelcoalition.org/blogs/justin-taylor/keith-getty-on-writing-hymns/.

83. Getty and Getty, "With One Voice." Emphasis mine.

84. Bobby Gilles, "3 Ways Hymn Meters Provide Meaning," *Church Leaders*, March 2, 2017, https://churchleaders.com/worship/worship-articles/299819-hymn-meters-provide-meaning-bobby-gilles.html.

85. Bobby Gilles and Kristen Gilles, "Modern Hymns," *My Song in the Night*, https://mysonginthenight.com/songwriting/modern-hymns/, accessed March 23, 2021.

86. Gilles, "3 Ways Hymn Meters Provide Meaning."

87. Mary Louise Bringle, "Debating Hymns," *Christian Century*, May 15, 2013, https://www.christiancentury.org/article/2013-04/debating-hymns.

88. Timothy George, "No Squishy Love," *First Things*, July 29, 2013, https://www.firstthings.com/web-exclusives/2013/07/no-squishy-love.

89. Bob Smietana, "Presbyterians Stir Debate by Rejecting Popular New Hymn," *Washington Post*, August 6, 2013, https://www.washingtonpost.com/national/on-faith/presbyterians-stir-debate-by-rejecting-popular-new-hymn/2013/08/06/7c5cda30-fed4-11e2-8294-0ee5075b840d_story.html.

90. Smietana, "Presbyterians Stir Debate."

91. The other three marks include biblicism (the adequacy and sufficiency of the Bible for revealing the gospel and what is to be believed), conversionism (the necessity for each person to have a personal experience of conversion in order to be finally acceptable to God), and activism (the expectation of a life shaped by active participation in church, evangelism, and social justice). See David W. Bebbington, *The Dominance of Evangelicalism* (Downers Grove, IL: InterVarsity Press, 2005), 21–40.

92. Mark Galli, "It Doesn't Get Any More Personal: Why Evangelicals Give Pride of Place to Penal Substitutionary Atonement," *Christianity Today*, January 11, 2018, https://www.christianitytoday.com/ct/2018/january-web-only/penal-substitutionary-atonement-it-doesnt-get-more-personal.html.

93. Bob Terry, "Why Disagree about the Words of a Hymn?," *Alabama Baptist*, August 8, 2013, https://web.archive.org/web/20130816235441/https://www.thealabamabaptist.org/print-edition-article-detail.php?id_art=28401&pricat_art=10.

94. Steve Chalke and Alan Mann, *The Lost Message of Jesus* (New York: HarperCollins, 2004), 183.

95. Taylor, *A Secular Age*, 650.

96. Taylor, *A Secular Age*, 650, 651.

97. Taylor, *A Secular Age*, 651.

98. "Drops in the Ocean Lyrics," Lyrics.com, https://www.lyrics.com/lyric/31774733/Hawk+Nelson, accessed September 11, 2020. Emphasis mine.

99. Galli, "It Doesn't Get Any More Personal."

100. Quoted in Collin Hansen, "Keith Getty on What Makes 'In Christ Alone' Accepted and Contested," *Gospel Coalition*, December 9, 2013, https://www.thegospelcoalition.org/article/keith-getty-on-what-makes-in-christ-alone-beloved-and-contested/.

101. Begbie, *Peculiar Orthodoxy*, 37.

102. Taylor, *A Secular Age*, 319.

103. Begbie, *Peculiar Orthodoxy*, 143.

104. Begbie, *Peculiar Orthodoxy*, 144.

105. Alan E. Lewis, *Between Cross and Resurrection: A Theology of Holy Saturday* (Grand Rapids, MI: Eerdmans, 2001), 33. Emphasis mine. Quoted in Begbie, *Peculiar Orthodoxy*, 41.

106. Brandon Ambrosino, "No Beauty without Ashes," *Peter Enns*, February 27, 2013, https://www.patheos.com/blogs/peterenns/2013/02/no-beauty-without-ash-the-paradox-of-true-christian-art-or-getting-ready-for-easter/.

Chapter 8

1. Campbell Robertson, "A Quiet Exodus: Why Black Worshipers are Leaving White Evangelical Churches," *New York Times*, March 9, 2018, https://www.nytimes.com/2018/03/09/us/blacks-evangelical-churches.html.

2. Quoted in Robertson, "A Quiet Exodus."

3. Michael O. Emerson, "Foreword," in *Christians and the Color Line: Race and Religion after Divided by Faith*, ed. J. Russell Hawkins and Philip Luke Sinitiere (New York: Oxford University Press, 2014), xi.

4. Emerson, "Foreword," xi.

5. Bob Smietana, "Sunday Morning in America Still Segregated—and That's OK with Worshipers." *LifeWay Research*, January 15, 2015, https://lifewayresearch.com/2015/01/15/sunday-morning-in-america-still-segregated-and-thats-ok-with-worshipers/.

6. The names of people in this chapter have all been changed, as has the identity of the church.

7. I am leaving the details of the scandal intentionally vague to protect the confidentiality of the congregation. They have no bearing on any of the issues discussed in this chapter.

8. Michael O. Emerson, *People of the Dream: Multiracial Congregations in the United States* (Princeton, NJ: Princeton University Press, 2008), 35.

9. Emerson, *People of the Dream*, 35.

10. Emerson, *People of the Dream*, 87.

11. Curtiss Paul DeYoung, Michael O. Emerson, and George Yancey, *United by Faith: The Multiracial Congregation as an Answer to the Problem of Race* (New York: Oxford University Press, 2004), 168.

12. Kathleen Garces-Foley, *Crossing the Ethnic Divide: The Multiethnic Church on a Mission* (New York: Oxford University Press, 2007), 83.

13. Zoltan L. Hajnal and Taeku Lee, *Why Americans Don't Join the Party: Race, Immigration, and the Failure (of Political Parties) to Engage the Electorate* (Princeton, NJ: Princeton University Press, 2011), 24.

14. See Russell P. Spittler, "Are Pentecostals and Charismatics Fundamentalists? A Review of American Uses of these Categories," in *Charismatic Christianity as a Global Culture*, ed. Karla Poewe (Columbia: University of South Carolina Press, 1994), 103–16.

15. H. P. Van Dusen, "The Third Force in Christendom," *Life*, June 9, 1958, 13.

16. Harold Ockenga, "The 'Pentecostal' Bogey," *United Evangelical Action* 6, no. 1 (February 15, 1947), 12–13.

17. Samuel Rodriguez and Robert C. Crosby, *When Faith Catches Fire* (Colorado Springs, CO: WaterBrook, 2017), 62.

18. For a nuanced discussion of the debate, see Amos Yong, "Evangelicals, Pentecostals, and Charismatics: A Difficult Relationship or Promising Convergence?," May 1, 2017, https://fullerstudio.fuller.edu/evangelicals-pentecostals-and-charismatics/.

19. James K. A. Smith, "Pentecostalism," in *The Oxford Handbook of the Epistemology of Theology*, ed. William J. Abraham and Frederick D. Aquino (New York: Oxford University Press, 2017), 606.

20. See Cecil M. Robeck, *The Azusa Street Mission and Revival: The Birth of the Global Pentecostal Movement* (Nashville, TN: Thomas Nelson, 2006). American Pentecostal scholarship revolves around whether the ministries of Charles F. Parham (Topeka, 1901) or William H. Seymour (Azusa, 1906) constitute the origins of Pentecostalism.

21. C. Peter Wagner, "Healing without Hassle," *Leadership* 6 (Spring 1985), 114.

22. Athony C. Thiselton, *The Holy Spirit—in Biblical Teaching, through the Centuries, and Today* (Grand Rapids, MI: Eerdmans, 2013), 422.

23. James K. A. Smith, *Thinking in Tongues: Pentecostal Contributions to Christian Philosophy* (Grand Rapids, MI: Eerdmans, 2010), 33.

24. Smith, *Thinking in Tongues*, 34.
25. Bialecki, "Jon Bialecki."
26. See Chapter 6.
27. "Derrama de tu Fuego," words and music by Josué Del Cid; interpreter Marcos Witt. Copyright ©2008 Admin. CanZion Editora. Used by permission.
28. Daniel E. Albrecht, *Rites in the Spirit: A Ritual Approach to Pentecostal/Charismatic Spirituality* (Sheffield: Sheffield Academic Press, 1999), 226–27.
29. Cheryl Bridges Johns, "What Makes a Good Sermon: A Pentecostal Perspective," *Journal for Preachers* 26 (2003), 46.
30. See Matthew Spencer Clark, "An Investigation into the Nature of a Viable Pentecostal Hermeneutic" (PhD diss., University of South Africa, 1997), 55.
31. Nimi Wariboko, *Nigerian Pentecostalism* (Rochester, NY: University of Rochester Press, 2014), 101.
32. Amos Yong, "Evangelicalism—and the Renewal of Christianity," http://www.respectfulconversation.net/ae-conversation/2013/4/30/evangelicalism-and-the-renewal-of-christianity.html.
33. Steven Jack Land, *Pentecostal Spirituality: A Passion for the Kingdom* (Sheffield: Sheffield Academic Press, 1993), 98.
34. Douglas A. Oss, "The Hermeneutics of Dispensationalism with the Pentecostal Tradition," paper presented at the Annual Meeting of the Dispensational Study Group of the Evangelical Theological Society, November 21, 1991, 2.
35. See Gerald T. Sheppard, "Pentecostals and the Hermeneutics of Dispensationalism: The Anatomy of an Uneasy Relationship," *Pneuma* 6, no. 1 (1984), 5–33.
36. See Erwin Lutzer, "Speaking in Tongues," *Moody Church Media*, https://www.moodymedia.org/articles/speaking-tongues/, accessed March 23, 2021. Lutzer writes, "God may grant the gift of tongues as He wills for His own specific purposes. For example, we've heard reports of an English preacher who miraculously was able to speak in Chinese for the benefit of some in his audience. If such reports can be verified, this would indicate a gracious work of God to get the Gospel to those who desperately wish to hear it."
37. See Chapter 2.
38. See L. William Oliverio Jr., *Theological Hermeneutics in the Classical Pentecostal Tradition* (Leiden: Brill, 2012), 16; cf. Veli-Matti Karkkainen, "Pentecostal Hermeneutics in the Making: On the Way From Fundamentalism to Postmodernism," *Journal of the European Pentecostal Theological Association* 18, no. 1 (1998), 76–115. See also Gordon D. Fee, *Listening to the Spirit in the Text* (Grand Rapids, MI: Eerdmans, 2000), 7–8.
39. Kenneth Archer, *A Pentecostal Hermeneutic for the Twenty First Century: Spirit, Scripture, and Community* (London: T&T Clark, 2004), 122.
40. Tony Richie, *Essentials of Pentecostal Theology* (Eugene, OR: Wipf and Stock Publishers, 2020), 3.
41. Amos Yong, "Living and Active: Renewing Evangelical Theologies of Scripture in the 21st Century," http://www.respectfulconversation.net/ae-conversation/2013/7/1/living-and-active-renewing-evangelical-theologies-of-scriptu.html.

42. Scott Ellington, "Pentecostalism and the Authority of Scripture," *Journal of Pentecostal Theology* 4, no. 9 (1996), 16–38.

43. Andy Stanley, *Irresistible: Reclaiming the New That Jesus Unleashed for the World* (Grand Rapids, MI: Zondervan, 2018), 294. Emphasis mine.

44. Ellington, "Pentecostalism," 22–23.

45. Marius Nel, "Attempting to Define a Pentecostal Hermeneutics," *Scriptura* 114 (2015), 8.

46. Ellington, "Pentecostalism," 24.

47. See Chapter 7.

48. Amos Yong, *In the Days of Caesar: Pentecostalism and Political Theology* (Grand Rapids, MI: Eerdmans, 2010), 123.

49. Yong, *Days of Caesar*, 123.

50. See Chapter 7.

51. Dale Coulter, "'Delivered by the Power of God': Toward a Pentecostal Understanding of Salvation," *International Journal of Systematic Theology* 10, no. 4 (2008), 463.

52. Simon Chan, *Pentecostal Theology and the Christian Spiritual Tradition* (Sheffield: Sheffield Academic Press, 2000), 75–76.

53. Grant Walker, *Heaven Below: Early Pentecostals and American Culture* (Cambridge, MA: Harvard University Press, 2003), 227.

54. Emerson, *People of the Dream*, 48.

55. Quoted in Sarah Eekhoff Zylstra, "Surprise Change in How Multiethnic Churches Affect Race Views," *Christianity Today*, December 2, 2015, https://www.christianitytoday.com/ct/2015/december-web-only/surprise-shift-in-how-multiethnic-churches-affect-race-view.html.

56. R. J. Cobb, S. L. Perry, and K. D. Dougherty, "United by Faith? Race/Ethnicity, Congregational Diversity, and Explanations of Racial Inequality," *Sociology of Religion* 76, no. 2 (2015), 177–98.

57. Quoted in Zylstra, "Surprise Change."

58. Lowell Livezey, *Public Religion and Urban Transformation: Faith in the City* (New York: New York University Press, 2000), 23.

59. Gerardo Marti, "Fluid Ethnicity and Ethnic Transcendence in Multiracial Churches," *Journal for the Scientific Study of Religion* 47, no. 1 (2008), 13–15.

Chapter 9

1. See Larry Eskridge, "Slain by the Music," *Christian Century*, March 7, 2006, 18–20.

2. Orla Cronin, "Psychology and Photographic Theory," in *Image-Based Research: A Sourcebook for Qualitative Researchers*, ed. John Prosser (London: Falmer Press, 1998), 63.

3. Christopher Bollas, *Being a Character: Psychoanalysis and Self Experience* (London: Routledge, 1992), 3.

4. Mark Oppenheimer, "Some Evangelicals Struggle with Black Lives Matter Movement," *New York Times*, January 22, 2016, www.nytimes.com/2016/01/23/us/some-evangelicals-struggle-with-black-lives-matter-movement.html.

5. Russell Moore and Samuel Rodriguez, "Immigrant-Bashers Will Lose the Evangelical Vote," *Wall Street Journal*, July 16, 2015, www.wsj.com/articles/immigrant-bashers-will-lose-the-evangelical-vote-1437088338.

6. Jim Hinch et al., "Evangelicals Are Changing Their Minds on Gay Marriage," *Politico*, July 7, 2014, www.politico.com/magazine/story/2014/07/evangelicals-gay-marriage-108608.

7. James F. White, *Protestant Worship: Traditions in Transition* (Louisville, KY: Westminster John Knox Press, 1989), 16.

8. From 1976 to 1980 White served as chairman of the Editorial Committee of the United Methodist "Section on Worship," recently structured under the General Board of Discipleship.

9. James F. White, "The Seminary Chapel Building as Spiritual Formation," *Theological Education* 38 (2001), 107.

10. R. Matthew Sigler, *Methodist Worship: Mediating the Wesleyan Liturgical Heritage* (New York: Routledge, 2019), 161. My account of White's life and impact is indebted to Sigler, 139–73.

11. James F. White, "Where the Reformation Was Wrong on Worship," *Christian Century* 99 (1982), 1077.

12. White, *Protestant Worship*, 212.

13. White, *Protestant Worship*, 212–13.

14. A striking exception is Lester Ruth, "Reconsidering the Emergence of the Second Great Awakening and Camp Meetings among Early Methodists," *Worship* 75, no. 4 (2001), 334–55.

15. Lester Ruth, "Divine, Human, or Devilish? The State of the Question on the Writing of the History of Contemporary Worship," *Worship* 88, no. 4 (2014), 298.

16. Sigler, *Methodist Worship*, 178.

17. Ruth, "Divine, Human, or Devilish," 299.

18. Renato Rosaldo, *Culture and Truth: The Remaking of Social Analysis* (London: Routledge, 1993), 27–28, quoted in Andrea Bieler, "Embodied Knowing: Understanding Religious Experience in Ritual," in *Religion: Immediate Experience and the Mediacy of Research. Interdisciplinary Studies, Concepts and Methodology of Empirical Research in Religion*, ed. Hans-Günter Heimbrock and Christopher P. Scholtz (Göttingen: Vandenhoeck & Ruprecht, 2007), 44.

19. Hans-Herbert Kögler, *The Power of Dialogue: Critical Hermeneutics after Gadamer* (Cambridge, MA: MIT Press, 1999), 4.

20. For more on the importance of "insider" theological perspectives, see Richard Osmer, *Practical Theology: An Introduction* (Grand Rapids, MI: Eerdmans, 2011). This issue is also well discussed by Tone Strangeland Kaufman, "From the Outside, within, or in between? Normativity at Work in Empirical Practical Theological Research," and Katherine Turpin, "The Complexity of Local Knowledge," both in *Conundrums in*

Practical Theology, ed. Joyce Ann Mercer and Bonnie Miller-McLemore (Leiden: Brill, 2016), 134–62 and 250–75.

21. Thomas Payne, "A Grammar as a Communicative Act; or What Does a Grammatical Description Really Describe," *Studies in Language* 30, no. 2 (2006), 380.

22. Christopher Ellis, *Gathering: A Spirituality and Theology of Worship in Free Church Tradition* (London: SCM Press, 2004), 67.

23. Bieler, "Embodied Knowing," 43–44.

24. Kathryn Tanner, *Theories of Culture: A New Agenda for Theology* (Minneapolis: Fortress Press, 1997), x.

25. Tanner, *Theories of Culture*, 24.

26. Tanner, *Theories of Culture*, 94.

27. Tanner, *Theories of Culture*, 57.

28. Gary Dorrien, "Truth Claims: The Future of Postliberal Theology," *Christian Century*, July 18–25, 2001, 534.

29. Tanner, *Theories of Culture*, 173.

30. Tanner, *Theories of Culture*, 135–36.

31. Tanner, *Theories of Culture*, 153.

32. Tanner, *Theories of Culture*, 153.

33. Dorrien, "Truth Claims," 28; and Tanner, *Theories of Culture*, 155.

34. Michael B. Aune, "Liturgy and Theology: Rethinking the Relationship, Part I," *Worship* 81, no. 1 (2007), 46–68; Michael B. Aune, "Liturgy and Theology: Rethinking the Relationship, Part II," *Worship* 81, no. 1 (2007), 141–69.

35. Aune, "Liturgy and Theology," Part I, 47. Quoting Kevin Irwin, "A Spirited Community Encounters Christ: Liturgical and Sacramental Theology and Practice," in *Catholic Theology Facing the Future: Historical Perspectives*, ed. Dermot A. Lane (Mahwah, NJ: Paulist Press 2003), 119–20.

36. See, e.g., the Festschrift that was published in honor of Webster's sixtieth birthday: R. David Nelson, Darren Sarisky, and Justin Stratis, eds., *Theological Theology* (London: T&T Clark, 2015).

37. John Webster, "Theological Theology," in *Confessing God: Essays in Christian Dogmatics II* (Edinburgh: T&T Clark, 2005), 22.

38. John Webster, *Holiness* (Grand Rapids, MI: Eerdmans, 2003), 21.

39. John B. Webster, *The Culture of Theology* (Grand Rapids, MI: Baker Academic, 2019), 86.

40. John Webster, "The Church and the Perfection of God," in Husbands and Treier, *Community of the Word*, 78.

41. Webster, "Church and Perfection of God," 11.

42. Webster, "Church and Perfection of God," 105.

43. John Webster, "'In the Society of God': Some Principles of Ecclesiology," in *God without Measure: Working Papers in Christian Theology*, vol. 1, *God and the Works of God* (London: Bloomsbury T&T Clark, 2016), 190–91.

44. Tanner, *Theories of Culture*, 113.

45. Tanner, *Theories of Culture*, 112.

46. Tanner, *Theories of Culture*, 113.

47. Webster, *The Culture of Theology*, 86.

48. Webster, *The Culture of Theology*, 53.

49. Webster, *The Culture of Theology*, 44, 53.

50. Tanner, *Theories of Culture*, 174.

51. Webster, *The Culture of Theology*, 43.

52. Webster, *The Culture of Theology*, 74, 123.

53. Webster, *The Culture of Theology*, 133.

54. John Webster, "Theology and the Order of Love," in *Rationalität im Gespräch— Rationality in Conversation*, ed. Markus Mühling (Leipzig: Evangelische Verlagsanstalt, 2016), 182.

55. John Webster, *Barth's Earlier Theology: Scripture, Confession and Church* (New York: T&T Clark, 2005), 65.

56. Webster, "Theology and the Order of Love," 183.

57. Webster, "Theology and the Order of Love," 182.

58. John Webster, "Theologies of Retrieval," in *The Oxford Handbook of Systematic Theology*, ed. Kathryn Tanner, John Webster, and Iain R. Torrance (New York: Oxford University Press, 2007), 596.

59. Craig A. Blaising, "Faithfulness: A Prescription for Theology," *Journal of the Evangelical Theological Society* 49, no. 1 (2006), 12.

60. Molly Worthen, "Defining Evangelicalism: Questions That Complement the Quadrilateral," *Fides et Historia* 47, no. 1 (2015), 83.

61. Worthen, "Defining Evangelism," 83–84.

62. Molly Worthen, *Apostles of Reason: The Crisis of Authority in American Evangelicalism* (New York: Oxford University Press, 2014), 6.

63. Worthen, *Apostles of Reason*, 4.

64. Molly Worthen, "The Intellectual Civil War within Evangelicalism: An Interview with Molly Worthen," *Religion & Politics*, December 20, 2013, https://religionandpolitics. org/2013/12/03/the-intellectual-civil-war-within-evangelicalism-an-interview-with-molly-worthen/.

65. Worthen, *Apostles of Reason*, 265.

66. Blaising, "Faithfulness," 13.

67. Thomas S. Kidd, "Review: *Apostles of Reason: The Crisis of Authority in American Evangelicalism*," *Church History* 84, no. 1 (2015), 276–77, citing Worthen, *Apostles of Reason*, 264.

68. Kidd, "Review," 277–78.

69. Kidd, "Review," 276.

70. Timothy E. W. Gloege, "Review: *Apostles of Reason: The Crisis of Authority in American Evangelicalism*," *Fides et Historia* 46, no. 2 (2014), 144.

71. Ronald Burwell, "Review: *Apostles of Reason: The Crisis of Authority in American Evangelicalism*," *Brethren in Christ History and Life* 40, no. 2 (2017), 286.

72. J. Tirrell, "Review: *Apostles of Reason*," *Journal of Religious History* 40, no. 1 (2016), 152.

73. David R. Swartz, "Review: *Apostles of Reason: The Crisis of Authority in American Evangelicalism*," *Mennonite Quarterly Review* 88, no. 4 (2014), 540.

74. John Swinton, "'Where Is Your Church?': Moving towards a Hospitable and Sanctified Ethnography," in *Perspectives on Ecclesiology and Ethnography*, ed. Pete Ward (Grand Rapids, MI: Eerdmans, 2012), 91.
75. Swinton, "Where Is Your Church," 92.
76. For more on Vanhoozer's theological background, see Kevin J. Vanhoozer and Daniel J. Treier, *Theology and the Mirror of Scripture: A Mere Evangelical Account* (Downers Grove, IL: InterVarsity Press, 2015), 10.
77. Kevin Vanhoozer, "John Webster: A Testimonial," Henry Center for Theological Understanding, April 4, 2017, https://henrycenter.tiu.edu/2016/06/john-webster-a-testimonial/.
78. Vanhoozer and Treier, *Theology and the Mirror of Scripture*, 78–79.
79. Vanhoozer and Treier, *Theology and the Mirror of Scripture*, 117.
80. See Vanhoozer and Treier, *Theology and the Mirror of Scripture*, 125, 198.
81. Vanhoozer and Treier, *Theology and the Mirror of Scripture*, 125–26.
82. Vanhoozer and Treier, *Theology and the Mirror of Scripture*, 126. Emphasis mine.
83. Vanhoozer and Treier, *Theology and the Mirror of Scripture*, 123.
84. Vanhoozer and Treier, *Theology and the Mirror of Scripture*, 121–22.
85. John Bainbridge Webster, "'In the Society of God': Some Principles of Ecclesiology," in *Perspectives on Ecclesiology and Ethnography: Studies in Ecclesiology and Ethnography*, ed. Pete Ward (Grand Rapids, MI: Eerdmans, 2012).
86. For more on the invisible nature of the church, see Gary Badcock, *The House Where God Lives: Renewing the Doctrine of the Church for Today* (Grand Rapids, MI: Eerdmans, 2009), x.
87. Worthen, *Apostles of Reason*, 4.
88. Vanhoozer and Treier, *Theology and the Mirror of Scripture*, 10.

Appendix A

1. Mary E. McGann, *A Precious Fountain: Music in the Worship of an African American Catholic Community* (Collegeville, MN: Liturgical Press, 2004).
2. McGann first used the term in 2002 ("Explorations"), but explores it more fully in *Exploring Music as Worship and Theology: an Interdisciplinary Method for Studying Liturgical Practice*. Collegeville, MN: Liturgical Press, 2002. .
3. For more on Egeria, see Anne McGowan and Paul F. Bradshaw, *The Pilgrimage of Egeria* (Collegeville, MN: Liturgical Press, 2018).
4. McGann, *Precious Fountain*, xix.
5. Winner of the Catholic Press Associations 2005 Book Award, First Place in Liturgy. For more on ethnography as a theological practice, see also Mary Moschella, "Ethnography," in *A Companion to Practical Theology*, ed. Bonnie Miller-McLemore (Oxford: Wiley-Blackwell, 2011), 224–33.
6. Ricky Manalo's *The Liturgy of Life: The Interrelationship of Sunday Eucharist and Everyday Worship Practices* (Collegeville, MN: Liturgical Press, 2014), is the only other book-length liturgical ethnography of which I am aware.

7. James F. White, "Review: *The Future of Protestant Worship* (Ronald P. Byars)," *Worship* 77, no. 4 (July 2003), 370–371. White pursues a similar line of argument in "How Do We Know It Is Us," in *Liturgy and the Moral Self: Humanity at Full Stretch before God. Essays in Honor of Don E. Saliers*, ed. E. Byron Anderson and Bruce T. Morrill (Collegeville, MN: Liturgical Press, 1998), 55–65.

8. James F. White, "Forum: Some Lessons in Liturgical Pedagogy," *Worship* 68 (1994), 447.

9. Sigler, *Methodist Worship*, 164.

10. Randall Balmer, *Mine Eyes Have Seen the Glory: A Journey into the Evangelical Subculture* (New York: Oxford University Press, 2014), 5–6.

11. Natalie Wigg-Stevenson, *Ethnographic Theology: An Inquiry into the Production of Theological Knowledge* (New York: Palgrave Macmillan, 2014), 67.

12. James M. Ault, *Spirit and Flesh: Life in a Fundamentalist Baptist Church* (New York: A.A. Knopf, 2004), 13.

13. Paul Avis, "Introduction to Ecclesiology," in *The Oxford Handbook of Ecclesiology*, ed. Paul Avis (New York: Oxford University Press, 2019), 26.

14. Avis, "Introduction to Ecclesiology," 26.

15. Avis, "Introduction to Ecclesiology," 26.

16. Avis, "Introduction to Ecclesiology," 17.

17. Edward Schillebeeckx, *The Church: The Human Story of God* (New York: Crossroad, 1990), xix. Quoted in Nicholas M. Healy, "Ecclesiology, Ethnography, and God: An Interplay of Reality Descriptions," in *Perspectives on Ecclesiology and Ethnography*, ed. Pete Ward (Grand Rapids, MI: Eerdmans, 2012), 183.

18. Avis, "Introduction to Ecclesiology," 21.

19. Badcock, *House Where God Lives*, 3–4.

20. Webster, "Society of God," in *Perspectives on Ecclesiology*.

21. For more on the invisible nature of the Church, see Badcock, *House Where God Lives*, x.

22. White, "Forum: Some Lessons in Liturgical Pedagogy," 447.

23. John Webster, "Hope," in *Confessing God*, 196.

24. Christian B. Scharen and Aana Marie Vigen, *Ethnography as Christian Theology and Ethics* (London: Continuum International Publishing Group, 2011), 35.

25. Clare Watkins, *Disclosing Church: An Ecclesiology Learned from Conversations in Practice* (New York: Routledge, 2020).

26. Healy, "Ecclesiology, Ethnography, and God," 187–88.

27. John Keane, "Structural Transformations of the Public Sphere," *Communication Review* 1 (1995), 11.

28. Keane, "Structural Transformations," 9–10.

29. Healy, "Ecclesiology, Ethnography, and God," 186, referencing Jerome P. Baggett, *Sense of the Faithful: How American Catholics Live Their Faith* (Oxford: Oxford University Press, 2009). Emphasis mine.

30. McGann, *Precious Fountain*; and Mary McClintock Fulkerson, *Places of Redemption: Theology for a Worldly Church* (New York: Oxford University Press, 2007).

31. White, "How Do We Know It Is Us," 58.

32. Alan Rathe, *Evangelicals, Worship and Participation: Taking a Twenty-First Century Reading* (London: Routledge, 2016), 235.

33. Nicholas M. Healy, *Church, World, and the Christian Life: Practical-Prophetic Ecclesiology* (Cambridge: Cambridge University Press, 2000), 178.

34. For more on Healy's approach, see Sjoerd Mulder, "Practical Ecclesiology for a Pilgrim Church," *Ecclesiology* 14, no. 2 (2018), 176.

35. See Tanner, *Theories of Culture*, 71.

36. Glenn Packiam, "What You (Probably) Don't Know about Modern Worship," mysteryoffaithblog.com, January 16, 2016, https://mysteryoffaithblog.com/2016/01/15/what-you-probably-dont-know-about-modern-worship/.

Selected Bibliography

Abbott, Margery Post. *To Be Broken and Tender: A Quaker Theology for Today*. Portland, OR: Friends Bulletin Corp., 2010.

Aune, Michael B. "Liturgy and Theology: Rethinking the Relationship, Part I." *Worship* 81, no. 1 (2007), 46–68.

Aune, Michael B. "Liturgy and Theology: Rethinking the Relationship, Part II." *Worship* 81, no. 2 (2007), 114–69.

Avis, Paul. "Introduction to Ecclesiology." In *The Oxford Handbook of Ecclesiology*, edited by Paul Avis, 1–31. New York: Oxford University Press, 2019.

Bahnsen, Greg L. "The Theonomic Reformed Approach to Law and Gospel." In *Five Views on Law and Gospel*, edited by Stanley N. Gundry, 93–143. Grand Rapids, MI: Zondervan, 1999.

Baker, Paul. *Why Should the Devil Have All the Good Music*. Waco, TX: Word Books, 1979.

Balfour, Glenn. "Pentecostal Eschatology Revisited." *Journal of the European Theological Association* 31, no. 2 (2011), 127–40.

Bebbington, David W. *The Dominance of Evangelicalism*. Grand Rapids, MI: InterVarsity Press, 2005.

Begbie, Jeremy S. *A Peculiar Orthodoxy: Reflections on Theology and the Arts*. Grand Rapids, MI: Baker Academic, 2018.

Bell, John. *The Singing Thing: A Case for Congregational Song*. Chicago: GIA Publications, 2000.

Bendroth, Margaret L. *Fundamentalists in the City: Conflict and Division in Boston's Churches, 1885–1950*. New York: Oxford University Press, 2005.

Bergler, Thomas E. *The Juvenilization of American Christianity*. Grand Rapids, MI: Eerdmans, 2012.

Best, Harold M. *Music through the Eyes of Faith*. New York: HarperCollins, 1993.

Best, Harold M. *Unceasing Worship: Biblical Perspectives on Worship and the Arts*. Downers Grove, IL: InterVarsity Press, 2003.

Bialecki, Jon. *A Diagram for Fire: Miracles and Variation in an American Charismatic Movement*. Oakland: University of California Press, 2017.

Bialecki, Jon. "Disjuncture, Continental Philosophy's New 'Political Paul,' and the Question of Progressive Christianity in a Southern California Third Wave Church." *American Ethnologist* 36, no. 1 (2009), 110–23.

Bieler, Andrea. "Embodied Knowing: Understanding Religious Experience in Ritual." In *Religion: Immediate Experience and the Mediacy of Research. Interdisciplinary Studies, Concepts and Methodology of Empirical Research in Religion*, edited by Hans-Günter Heimbrock and Christopher P. Scholtz, 39–59. Göttingen: Vandenhoeck & Ruprecht, 2007.

Bielo, James S. *Emerging Evangelicals: Faith, Modernity, and the Desire for Authenticity*. New York: New York University Press, 2011.

Bollas, Christopher. *Being a Character: Psychoanalysis and Self Experience*. London: Routledge, 1992.

Bringle, Mary Louise. "Debating Hymns." *Christian Century*, May 1, 2013, 24–25.

Bustraan, Richard A. *The Jesus People Movement: A Story of Spiritual Revolution among the Hippies*. Eugene, OR: Pickwick Publications, 2014.

Capers, Bennett I. "Citizenship Talk." In *The Cambridge Handbook of Policing in the United States*, edited by Tamara Rice Lave and Eric J. Miller, 473–90. New York: Cambridge University Press, 2019.

Carpenter, Joel A. *Revive Us Again: The Reawakening of American Fundamentalism*. New York: Oxford University Press, 1997.

Conrad, A. Z. *The Gospel for an Age of Thought*. Chicago: Fleming H. Revell, 1928.

Conrad, A. Z. *The Seven Finalities of Faith*. Philadelphia: Sunday School Times, 1926.

Cusic, Don. *The Sound of Light*. New York: Hal Leonard, 2002.

Davis, T. M. "How Schools Fail Black Boys (and Girls Too): Race, Gender, and Academic Trajectories from Kindergarten through Eighth Grade." In *The Handbook of Research on Black Males: Quantitative, Qualitative, and Multidisciplinary*, edited by Theodore S. Ransaw, C. P. Gause, and Richard Majors, 169–88. East Lansing: Michigan State University Press, 2019.

Dayton, Donald. "The Pietist Theological Critique of Biblical Inerrancy." In *Evangelicals and Scripture: Tradition, Authority, and Hermeneutics*, edited by Vincent Bacote, Laura C. Miguelez, and Dennis L. Okholm, 76–92. Downers Grove, IL: InterVarsity Press, 2004.

Duran, Eduardo Bautista, and Jonathan Simon. "Police Abolitionist Discourse? Why It Has Been Missing (and Why It Matters)." In *The Cambridge Handbook of Policing in the United States*, edited by Tamara Rice Lave and Eric J. Miller, 85–103. New York: Cambridge University Press, 2019.

Ellis, Christopher. *Gathering: A Spirituality and Theology of Worship in Free Church Tradition*. London: SCM Press, 2004.

Englizian, H. Crosby. *Brimstone Corner: Park Street Church, Boston*. Chicago: Moody Press, 1968.

Eskridge, Larry. *God's Forever Family: The Jesus People Movement in America*. New York: Oxford University Press, 2013.

Eskridge, Larry. "Jesus People." In *The Encyclopedia of Christianity*, vol. 3, edited by Erwin Fahlbusch, Jan Lochman, John Mbiti, Jaroslav Pelikan, and Lukas Vischer. Grand Rapids, MI: Eerdmans, 1999.

Evans, Elizabeth. *The Wright Vision: The Story of the New England Fellowship*. Lanham, MD: University Press of America, 1991.

Evans, Muriel Wright, and Elizabeth M. Evans. *Incidents and Information of the First 48 Years: Rumney Conference's 75th Anniversary*. Rumney, NH: n.p., 1978.

Farley, Margaret A. "Beyond the Formal Principle: A Reply to Ramsey and Saliers." *Journal of Religious Ethics* 7, no. 2 (1979), 191–202.

Findlay, James F. *Dwight L. Moody: American Evangelist, 1837–1899*. Chicago: University of Chicago Press, 2007.

Finney, Charles G. *Lectures on Revival of Religion*. Edited by William G. McLaughlin. Cambridge, MA: Belknap Press of Harvard University Press, 1960.

Fosdick, H. E. *The Modern Use of the Bible*. New York: Macmillan, 1932.

Gersztyn, Bob. *Jesus Rocks the World*. Santa Barbara: Praeger, 2012.

Getty, Keith, and Kristyn Getty. *Sing! How Worship Transforms Your Life, Family, and Church*. Nashville, TN: B&H Publishing Group, 2017.

Gloege, Timothy. *Guaranteed Pure: The Moody Bible Institute, Business, and the Making of Modern Evangelicalism*. Chapel Hill: University of North Carolina Press, 2015.

Gros, Jeffrey, Harding Meyer, and William G. Rusch. *Growth in Agreement II: Reports and Agreed Statements of Ecumenical Conversations on a World Level, 1982–1998.* Grand Rapids, MI: Eerdmans, 2000.

Gungor, Michael. *The Crowd, the Critic, and the Muse: A Book for Creators.* Denver: Woodsley Press, 2012.

Hamilton, Michael. "The Interdenominational Evangelicalism of D.L. Moody and the Problem of Fundamentalism." In *American Evangelicalism: George Marsden and the State of American Religious History,* edited by Thomas S. Kidd, Darren Dochuk, and Kurt W. Peterson, 230–80. South Bend, IN: University of Notre Dame Press, 2016.

Hannah, John D. *An Uncommon Union: Dallas Theological Seminary and American Evangelicalism.* Grand Rapids, MI: Zondervan, 2009.

Harper, George W. "'It Is a Battle-Royale': A. Z. Conrad's Preaching at Boston's Park Street Church during the Fundamentalist-Modernist Controversy." *Fides et Historia* 45, no. 1 (2013), 30–47.

Healy, Nicholas M. *Church, World, and the Christian Life: Practical-Prophetic Ecclesiology.* New York: Cambridge University Press, 2000.

Healy, Nicholas M. "Ecclesiology, Ethnography, and God: An Interplay of Reality Descriptions." In *Perspectives on Ecclesiology and Ethnography.* Grand Rapids, MI: Eerdmans, 2012.

Hicks, Zac M. *The Worship Pastor: A Call to Ministry for Worship Leaders and Teams.* Grand Rapids, MI: Zondervan, 2016.

Hindmarsh, Bruce. *The Spirit of Early Evangelicalism.* New York: Oxford University Press, 2018.

Holifield, E. Brooks. *God's Ambassadors: A History of the Christian Clergy in America.* Grand Rapids, MI: Eerdmans, 2007.

Ingalls, Monique M. "Awesome in This Place: Sound, Space, and Identity in Contemporary North American Evangelical Worship." PhD diss., University of Pennsylvania, 2008.

Ingalls, Monique M. *Singing the Congregation: How Contemporary Worship Music Forms Evangelical Community.* New York: Oxford University Press, 2018.

Ingalls, Monique M. "Transnational Connections, Musical Meaning, and the 1990s 'British Invasion' of North American Evangelical Worship Music." In *The Oxford Handbook of Music and World Christianities,* edited by Suzel Ana Reily and Jonathan Dueck, 425–48. New York: Oxford University Press, 2016.

Jackson, Bill. *Quest for the Radical Middle.* Cape Town: Vineyard International Publishing, 2006.

Johnson, Marilynn. "The Quiet Revival: New Immigrants and the Transformation of Christianity in Greater Boston." *Religion and American Culture* 24, no. 2 (2014), 231–58.

Kaiser, Walter. "Response to Douglas Moo." In *Five Views on Law and Gospel,* edited by Stanley N. Gundry, 377–407. Grand Rapids, MI: Zondervan, 1999.

Kilsdonk, Edward James. "Scientific Church Music and the Making of the American Middle Class." In *The Middling Sorts: Explorations in the History of the American Middle Class,* edited by Burton J. Bledstein and Robert D. Johnston, 125–36. New York: Routledge, 2001.

Kun, Josh. *Audiotopia: Music, Race, and America.* Berkeley: University of California Press, 2005.

Ladd, George Eldon. *The Presence of the Future: The Eschatology of Biblical Realism.* Grand Rapids, MI: Eerdmans, 1974.

Lash, Nicolas. *The Beginning and the End of "Religion."* Cambridge: Cambridge University Press, 1996.

Laws, Curtis Lee. "Convention Side Lights." *The Watchman-Examiner,* July 1, 1920.

Lemke-Santangelo, Gretchen. *Daughters of Aquarius: Women of the Sixties Counterculture.* Lawrence: University Press of Kansas, 2009.

Lévi-Strauss, Claude. *Structural Anthropology.* Translated by Claire Jacobson and Brooke Grundfest Schoepf. New York, 1958.

Lewis, Alan E. *Between Cross and Resurrection: A Theology of Holy Saturday.* Grand Rapids, MI: Eerdmans, 2001.

Lindenbaum, John. "The Production of Contemporary Christian Music: A Geographical Perspective." In *Sound, Society, and the Geography of Popular Music,* edited by Ola Johansson and Thomas L. Bell, 281–94. New York: Routledge, 2016.

Lindholm, Charles. *Culture and Authenticity.* Malden, MA: Blackwell Publishing, 2008.

Luhrmann, T. M. *When God Talks Back: Understanding the American Evangelical Relationship with God.* New York: Alfred A. Knopf, 2012.

Lutzer, Erwin W. *The Church in Babylon.* Chicago: Moody Publishers, 2018.

Lutzer, Erwin W. *The Cross in the Shadow of the Crescent.* Chicago: Harvest House Publishers, 2013.

Lutzer, Erwin W. *He Will Be the Preacher.* Chicago: Moody Publishers, 2015.

Lutzer, Erwin W. *Is God on America's Side?* Chicago: Moody Publishers, 2009.

Lutzer, Erwin W. *The Power of a Clear Conscience.* Eugene, OR: Harvest House Publishers, 2016.

Mall, Andrew. "The Stars Are Underground: Undergrounds, Mainstreams, and Christian Popular Music." PhD diss., University of Chicago, 2012.

Mangum, Todd. "The Modernist-Fundamentalist Controversy, the Inerrancy of Scripture, and the Development of American Dispensationalism." In *Interdisciplinary Perspectives on the Authority of Scripture: Historical, Biblical, and Theoretical Perspectives,* edited by Carlos R. Bovell, 46–70. Eugene, OR: Wipf and Stock Publishers, 2011.

Marsden, George. "Everyone One's Own Interpreter? The Bible, Science, and Authority in Mid-Nineteenth-Century America." In *The Bible in America,* edited by Nathan O. Hatch and Mark A. Noll, 79–100. New York: Oxford University Press, 1982.

Martin, William C. *A Prophet with Honor: The Billy Graham Story.* Grand Rapids, MI: Zondervan, 2018.

Matthews, Arthur H. *Standing Up, Standing Together: The Emergence of the National Association of Evangelicals.* Carol Stream, IL: National Association of Evangelicals, 1992.

Miller, Donald. "Routinizing Charisma: The Vineyard Christian Fellowship in the Post-Wimber Era." *Pneuma* 25, no. 2 (Fall 2003), 141–62.

Miller, Stephen. *Worship Leaders: We Are Not Rock Stars.* Chicago: Moody Press, 2013.

Murray, Katherine. "Social Justice and Sustainability." In *The Cambridge Companion to Quakerism,* edited by Stephen W. Angell and Pink Dandelion, 88–105. Cambridge: Cambridge University Press, 2018.

Myers, Ken. *All God's Children and Blue Suede Shoes.* Wheaton, IL: Crossway Books, 2012.

Nekola, Anna E. "Between This World and the Next: The Musical 'Worship Wars' and Evangelical Ideology in the United States, 1960–2005." PhD diss., University of Wisconsin–Madison, 2009.

Nekola, Anna E. "'I'll Take You There': The Promise of Transformation in the Marketing of Worship Media in Us Christian Music Magazines." In *Christian Congregational*

Music: Performance, Identity and Experience, edited by Monique M. Ingalls, Carolyn Landau, and Tom Wagner, 117–36. Farnham, UK: Ashgate, 2013.

Nekola, Anna E. "Negotiating the Tensions of U.S. Worship Music in the Marketplace." In *The Oxford Handbook of Music and World Christianities*, edited by Suzel Ana Reily and Jonathan M. Dueck, 513–32. New York: Oxford University Press, 2016.

Noll, Mark A. *Between Faith and Criticism: Evangelicals, Scholarship, and the Bible in America*. 2nd ed. Vancouver: Regent College Publishing, 2004.

Noll, Mark A. "The Defining Role of Hymns in Early Evangelicalism." In *Wonderful Words of Life: Hymns in American Protestant History and Theology*, edited by Richard J. Mouw and Mark A. Noll, 3–16. Grand Rapids, MI: Eerdmans, 2004.

Noll, Mark A. "Noun or Adjective? The Ravings of a Fanatical Nominalist." *Fides et Historia* 47 (Winter 2015), 73–82.

Ockenga, Harold John. "The Unvoiced Multitudes." In *Evangelical Action! A Report of the Organization of the National Association of Evangelicals for United Action, Compiled and Edited by the Executive Committee*. Boston: United Action Press, 1942.

Ockholm, Dennis L. "The Fundamental Dispensation of Evangelical Ecclesiology." In *The Community of the Word: Toward and Evangelical Ecclesiology*, edited by Mark Husbands and Daniel J. Treier, 41–62. Downers Grove, IL: InterVarsity Press, 2005.

Pemberton, Carol A. *Lowell Mason: His Life and Work*. Ann Arbor, MI: UMI Research Press, 1985.

Perkins, Dave. "Music, Culture Industry, and the Shaping of Charismatic Worship: An Autobiographical/Conversational Engagement." In *The Spirit of Praise: Music and Worship in Global Pentecostal-Charismatic Christianity*, edited by Monique Ingalls and Amos Yong, 230–46. University Park: Pennsylvania State University Press, 2015.

Pietsch, B. M. *Dispensational Modernism*. Oxford: Oxford University Press, 2015.

Provan, Iain William, V. Philips Long, and Tremper Longman. *A Biblical History of Israel*. Louisville, KY: Westminster John Knox Press, 2003.

Rathe, Alan. *Evangelicals, Worship and Participation: Taking a Twenty-First Century Reading*. London: Routledge, 2016.

Reagan, Wen. "A Beautiful Noise: A History of Contemporary Worship Music in Modern America." PhD diss., Duke University, 2015.

Rosell, Garth M. *Boston's Historic Park Street Church: The Story of an Evangelical Landmark*. Grand Rapids, MI: Kregel Publications, 2009.

Rosell, Garth M. *The Surprising Work of God: Harold John Ockenga, Billy Graham, and the Rebirth of Evangelicalism*. Grand Rapids, MI: Baker Academic, 2008.

Ruth, Lester. "Divine, Human, or Devilish? The State of the Question on the Writing of the History of Contemporary Worship." *Worship* 88, no. 4 (2014), 290–310.

Ruth, Lester. "The Eruption of Worship Wars: The Coming of Conflict." *Liturgy* 32, no. 1 (2017), 3–6.

Ruth, Lester, ed. *Essays on the History of Contemporary Praise and Worship*. Eugene, OR: Pickwick Publications, 2020.

Ruth, Lester. "A Rose by Any Other Name: Attempts at Classifying North American Protestant Worship." In *Conviction of Things Not Seen: Worship and Ministry in the 21st Century*, edited by Todd Johnson, 33–51. Grand Rapids, MI: Brazos Press, 2002.

Ruth, Lester, and Swee Hong Lim. *Lovin' on Jesus: A Concise History of Contemporary Worship*. Nashville, TX: Abingdon Press, 2017.

Saliers, Don. *Worship as Theology: Foretaste of Glory Divine*. Nashville, TX: Abingdon Press, 1994.

Scharen, Christian, and Aana Marie Vigen. *Ethnography as Christian Theology and Ethics.* London: Continuum International Publishing Group, 2011.

Scofield, C. I. *Addresses on a Prophecy.* Chicago: Bible Truth Depot, 1914.

Scully, Jackie Leach. "Virtuous Friends: Morality and Quaker Identity." *Quaker Studies* 14, no. 1 (2009), 108–22.

Shelley, Bruce. "The Rise of Evangelical Youth Movements." *Fides et Historia* 18, no. 1 (1986), 47–63.

Sigler, R. Matthew. *Methodist Worship: Mediating the Wesleyan Liturgical Heritage.* New York: Routledge, 2019.

Smith, James K. A. *Desiring the Kingdom: Worship, Worldview, and Cultural Formation.* Grand Rapids, MI: Baker Academic, 2009.

Smith, James K. A. *How (Not) to Be Secular: Reading Charles Taylor.* Grand Rapids, MI: Eerdmans, 2014.

Stafford, Tim. "Testing the Wine from John Wimber's Vineyard." *Christianity Today,* August 8, 1986.

Stanley, Andy. *Deep and Wide: Creating Churches Unchurched People Love to Attend.* Grand Rapids, MI: Zondervan, 2012.

Stanley, Andy. *Going Deep and Wide: A Companion Guide for Churches and Leaders.* Grand Rapids, MI: Zondervan, 2017.

Stanley, Andy. *Irresistible: Reclaiming the New That Jesus Unleashed for the World.* Grand Rapids, MI: Zondervan, 2018.

Stanley, Andy. *Next Generation Leader.* Sisters, OR: Multnomah, 2011.

Stanley, Andy, and Lane Jones. *Communicating for a Change.* Sisters, OR: Multnomah, 2008.

Stanley, Andy, and Bill Willits. *Creating Community: Five Keys to Building a Small Group Culture.* Sisters, OR: Multnomah, 2004.

Stenberg, Shari J., and Charlotte Hogg. *Persuasive Acts: Women's Rhetorics in the Twenty-First Century.* Pittsburgh: University of Pittsburgh Press, 2020.

Strachan, Owen. *Awakening the Evangelical Mind.* Grand Rapids, MI: Zondervan, 2015.

Stringer, Martin D. *On the Perception of Worship* (Birmingham: University of Birmingham Press, 1999).

Swinton, John. "'Where Is Your Church?': Moving towards a Hospitable and Sanctified Ethnography." In *Perspectives on Ecclesiology and Ethnography,* edited by Pete Ward, 71–94. Grand Rapids, MI: Eerdmans, 2012.

Taft, Robert. "The Structural Analysis of Liturgical Units: An Essay in Methodology." In *Beyond East and West: Problems in Liturgical Understanding,* 2nd ed., 187–202. Rome: Pontifical Oriental Institute, 2001.

Tanner, Kathryn. *Theories of Culture: A New Agenda for Theology.* Minneapolis: Fortress Press, 1997.

Taylor, Charles. *A Secular Age.* Cambridge, MA: Harvard University Press, 2007.

Taylor, Charles. *Sources of the Self: The Making of the Modern Identity.* Cambridge, MA: Harvard University Press, 1989.

Vanhoozer, Kevin J., and Daniel J. Treier. *Theology and the Mirror of Scripture: A Mere Evangelical Account.* Downers Grove, IL: InterVarsity Press.

Walvoord, John F. *Israel in Prophecy.* Grand Rapids, MI: Zondervan, 1982.

Weber, Timothy P. "How Evangelicals Became Israel's Best Friend." *Christianity Today,* October 5, 1998.

Weber, Timothy P. *On the Road to Armageddon.* Grand Rapids, MI: Baker Publishing Group, 2004.

Webster, John B. *Barth's Earlier Theology: Scripture, Confession and Church.* New York: T&T Clark, 2005.

Webster, John B. "The Church and the Perfection of God." In *The Community of the Word: Toward an Evangelical Ecclesiology,* edited by Mark Husbands and Daniel J. Treier, 75–95. Downers Grove, IL: InterVarsity Press, 2005.

Webster, John B. *The Culture of Theology.* Grand Rapids, MI: Baker Academic, 2019.

Webster, John B. *Holiness.* Grand Rapids, MI: Eerdmans, 2003.

Webster, John B. "Hope." In *Confessing God: Essays in Christian Dogmatics II,* 195–214. London: T&T Clark, 2005.

Webster, John B. "Theological Theology." In *Confessing God: Essays in Christian Dogmatics II,* 11–32. London: T&T Clark, 2005.

Webster, John B. "Theologies of Retrieval." In *The Oxford Handbook of Systematic Theology,* edited by John B. Webster, Kathryn Tanner, and Iain R. Torrance, 583–599. Oxford: Oxford University Press, 2007.

Webster, John B. "Theology and the Order of Love." In *Rationalität im Gespräch— Rationality in Conversation,* edited by Markus Mühling, 175–85. Leipzig: Evangelische Verlagsanstalt, 2016.

Wells, David. "A Tale of Two Spiritualities." In *Losing Our Virtue,* 21–52. Grand Rapids, MI: Eerdmans, 1998.

White, James F. "Evangelism and Worship from New Lebanon to Nashville." In *Christian Worship in North America: A Retrospective, 1955–1995,* ed. James F. White, 163.

White, James F. "Forum: Some Lessons in Liturgical Pedagogy." *Worship* 68 (1994), 438–50.

White, James F. "How Do We Know It Is Us." In *Liturgy and the Moral Self: Humanity at Full Stretch before God. Essays in Honor of Don E. Saliers,* edited by E. Byron Anderson and Bruce T. Morrill, 55–65. Collegeville, MN: Liturgical Press, 1998.

White, James F. *Protestant Worship: Traditions in Transition.* Louisville, KY: Westminster John Knox Press, 1989.

White, James F. "The Seminary Chapel Building as Spiritual Formation." *Theological Education* 38, no. 1 (2001), 101–10.

White, James F. "Where the Reformation Was Wrong on Worship." *Christian Century,* October 27, 1982, 1074–77.

Wiersbe, Warren W. *Be Myself: Memoirs of a Bridgebuilder.* Grand Rapids, MI: Baker Publishing Group, 1997.

Wigg-Stevenson, Natalie. *Ethnographic Theology: An Inquiry into the Production of Theological Knowledge.* New York: Palgrave Macmillan, 2014.

Wigg-Stevenson, Natalie. "You Don't Look Like a Baptist Minister: An Autoethnographic Retrieval of 'Women's Experience' as an Analytic Category for Feminist Theology." *Feminist Theology* 25, no. 2 (2017), 182–97.

Wilson, Lloyd Lee. *Essays on the Quaker Vision of Gospel Order.* Wallingford, PA: Pendle Hill Publications, 1993.

Wimber, Carol, and John Wimber. *The Way it Was.* London: Hodder & Stoughton, 1999.

Witvliet, John D. "The Blessing and Bane of the North American Mega-Church: Implications for Twenty-First Century Congregational Song." *Jahrbuch für Liturgik und Hymnologie* 37 (1998), 196–213.

Woods, Robert. *The Message in the Music: Studying Contemporary Praise and Worship.* Nashville, TX: Abingdon Press, 2007.

Woods, Robert H. "Praising God with Popular Worship Music." In *Understanding Evangelical Media: The Changing Face of Christian Communication*, edited by Quentin Schultze and Robert Woods, 124–36. Downers Grove, IL: InterVarsity Press, 2008.

Worthen, Molly. *Apostles of Reason: The Crisis of Authority in American Evangelicalism.* New York: Oxford University Press, 2014.

Yeo, John J. *Plundering the Egyptians: The Old Testament and Historical Criticism at Westminster Theological Seminary (1929–1998).* Lanham, MD: University Press of America, 2010.

York, Terry W. *America's Worship Wars.* Peabody, MA: Hendrickson, 2003.

Index